Windows System Policy Editor

Windows System Policy Editor

Stacey Anderson-Redick

O'REILLY®

Beijing · Cambridge · Farnham · Köln · Paris · Sebastopol · Taipei · Tokyo

Windows System Policy Editor
by Stacey Anderson-Redick

Published by O'Reilly & Associates, Inc., 101 Morris Street, Sebastopol, CA 95472.

Editor: Robert Denn

Production Editor: Maureen Dempsey

Cover Designer: Ellie Volckhausen

Printing History:

June 2000: First Edition.

Library of Congress Cataloging-in-Publication Data

Anderson-Redick, Stacey.
Windows system policy editor : managing workstation farms/Stacey Anderson-Redick
p. cm.
ISBN 1-56592-649-8
1. Microsoft Windows (Computers) 2. Microcomputer workstations—Management. I. Title.

QA76.76.O63 A532 2000
005.4'47682—dc21 00-042788

ISBN: 1-56592-649-8
[M]

Table of Contents

Preface

As a network administration tool, the System Policy Editor (SPE) is usually overlooked and frequently underrated. At first glance it often appears difficult and unwieldy, and on second glance, disappointingly full of elusive problems.

However, the SPE is an extremely adaptable tool, and its benefits far outweigh any initial technical difficulties. It provides an administrator with the means to centrally manage Windows 9x and Windows NT4 desktop environments, and is a flexible alternative to mandatory user profiles. The ability to create custom templates allows the SPE to provide almost unlimited software customization, and it provides a cheap, intermediate level of desktop security that is generally free of software conflicts. Knowing the SPE's strengths, weaknesses and idiosyncrasies is the key to successfully using it in any network environment.

Who Is This Book for?

This book is written primarily for network administrators, but it would be useful to anyone in charge of workstation setup and security. It assumes that you have a moderate to advanced level of knowledge about the Windows operating system in general, and about your own networking software in particular. Even though the book includes information on using the SPE with Windows NT4 workstations, a greater emphasis is given to the Windows 9x environment. Windows 9x lacks the filesystem security of NT, and so in my opinion benefits the most from the desktop control offered by the SPE.

Although those administrators who have not yet begun to use system policies would derive the greatest benefits from this book, the details provided on the available policy templates should appeal to even the most knowledgeable gurus.

How This Book Is Organized

This book is divided into nine chapters and two appendixes.

- Chapter 1, *The Hidden Cost of Computers,* introduces the System Policy Editor, the problem of shared workstations and situations where the SPE is useful.
- Chapter 2, *A System Policies Primer,* discusses user profiles and their relationship to system policies, then focuses on the individual components of the SPE.
- Chapter 3, *Preparation and Planning,* reviews considerations when planning and deploying system policies, including worksheets for your own network. Detailed system requirements for user, group and computer policies are covered, policy conflict resolution is discussed, and case studies are reviewed.
- Chapter 4, *Building the Policy File,* guides you through the creation of a sample Windows 9x policy file, and the preparation of a client workstation.
- Chapter 5, *It's Not Perfect,* exposes the security holes found specifically in the SPE and generally in Windows 9x, including methods to plug these holes.
- Chapter 6, *Troubleshooting,* is all about troubleshooting—error messages, problems and solutions.
- Chapter 7, *Standalone Windows 9x Workstations,* explains how to use the SPE on a standalone (non-networked) Windows 9x workstation.
- Chapter 8, *Creating a Custom Template,* describes how to create a custom policy template, and guides you through the creation of a sample template.
- Chapter 9, *The Policy Templates,* covers all of the most commonly used policy templates, including where they can be downloaded, comments on each policy, and the relevant registry keys and valuenames.
- Appendix A, *Sample Acceptable-Use Policy,* is a sample acceptable use policy for a school, which can be customized for your own organization.
- Appendix B, *Third-Party Security Programs,* lists many of the third-party security programs available for those who need more security than just the SPE.

Conventions in This Book

The following typographical conventions are used in this book:

`Constant width`
: is used to indicate command-line computer output, code examples, and keyboard accelerators.

`Constant width italic`
: is used to indicate placeholders for which a user would substitute a name or value in examples.

Italic
: is used to introduce new terms and to indicate URLs, variables or user-defined files and directories, commands, file extensions, filenames, directory or folder names and UNC pathnames.

This symbol indicates a tip.

This symbol indicates a warning.

How to Contact Us

We have tested and verified the information in this book to the best of our ability, but you may find that features have changed (or even that we have made mistakes!). Please let us know about any errors you find, as well as your suggestions for future editions, by writing to:

O'Reilly & Associates, Inc.
101 Morris Street
Sebastopol, CA 95472
(800) 998-9938 (in the U.S. or Canada)
(707) 829-0515 (international/local)
(707) 829-0104 (fax)

You can also send us messages electronically. To be put on the mailing list or request a catalog, send email to:

info@oreilly.com

To ask technical questions or comment on the book, send email to:

bookquestions@oreilly.com

We have a web site for the book, where we'll list examples, errata and any plans for future editions. You can access this page at:

http://www.oreilly.com/catalog/syspe

For more information about this book and others, see the O'Reilly web site:

http://www.oreilly.com

Acknowledgments

I would like to thank the people at O'Reilly. First I thank my editor, Robert Denn, for taking a chance on a new author, and for not being dismayed when he saw my first chapters. Steven Abrams kept me and the multiple versions of each chapter organized, and he even forgave me when Chapter 3 crashed his computer. Rob Romano, the technical illustrator, kindly answered all of my formatting questions. Finally, I want to thank Frank Willison, the Editor-in-Chief at O'Reilly, for his support.

A number of other people helped me along the way. I would have suffered acute anxiety and irrecoverable carpal tunnel syndrome if not for the help of Rose Campo-Anderson, who typed up the voluminous Chapter 9. The Perl script in Chapter 4 was kindly written for me by Coral Burns of Critical Mass. I cannot forget to thank all the network administrators who emailed me to discuss the finer points of system policies, including their own personal experiences. I owe thanks to Alan Bowen, Bill Moseley, Jonathan Cook and Paul Taylor, in particular. These discussions we had contributed to many aspects of this book. Finally, I want to thank Jeannine Fraser, wherever she is. Jeannine was my computer mentor many years ago, and without her support I would not be in the field I am today.

I had some exceptional technical reviewers; they picked out my errors and omissions and provided me with some valuable insights. The reviewer group for this book included Matt Beland, Jane Lybecker and Glenn Fincher. Glenn was particularly thorough, to my consternation, but in the end a far better book was produced. I'd particularly like to thank Jane who went above and beyond the call of technical reviewer by considerately giving up some of her time to provide me with email tutoring. Thanks, Jane.

When I began this book, I had no idea of the amount of work it would entail, nor how much of my life it would consume. I would not have been able to survive it without the support of my family, particularly my husband Les. He did far more than his share of child wrangling and household duties over this past year, and in my absorption I failed to say "Thank you" often enough. I am thankful to my children for remembering that their mother was once not attached to a keyboard, and I thank God for giving me this unique opportunity to potentially embarrass myself in front of thousands of readers.

1

The Hidden Cost of Computers

Your organization has just installed a number of new computers. This will be the largest outlay of money required to computerize your department, right? Well, not exactly. Although it may be the largest single expenditure, over time the total cost of ownership will far outweigh the initial expense. Over 10 years ago, the Gartner Group (an IT-specific research and analysis company) inaugurated the now common, and perhaps overused term, *Total Cost of Ownership* (TCO). TCO attempts to quantify all costs associated with owning and operating computers and networks. It is often used as a method to budget yearly Local Area Network (LAN) costs, or as a benchmark comparison of your PC-based client/server systems against other organizations.

So, just how much *does* it cost to own and operate a single computer on a LAN? Here are some of the TCO numbers published based on a single-networked PC per year:

Organization	TCO
Gartner Group	$9,000–$12,000
Forrester Research	$8,200
Fortune Magazine	$7,200
Interpose Inc.	$6,515

Although estimates of TCO vary widely (due to a lack of a consistent cost method), even the lower values are astounding.

TCO is actually the overall cost from a number of diverse areas, and for the original Gartner TCO model, was broken down in the manner shown in Table 1-1.

Table 1-1. Gartner TCO Cost Breakdown

End-User Operations, 46%	Technical Support, 21%	Capital, 20%	Administration, 13%
Applications development	Application consulting	Desktop	Add/move/change
Casual learning	Configuration review	Hardware	Asset management
Client-peer support	Disk management	IS allocated	Capacity planning
Data management	Documentation	Network	Client purchasing
Formal learning	End-user training	Server	Formal audit
"Futz" factor *(using computers for personal use, i.e., games)*	Install/move/upgrade	Software	Informal audit
Misdiagnosis	IS learning		Installation
Network costs	NOS configuration		Legal
Network-peer support	NOS maintenance		NOS administration
Peer training	Planning		P&P enforcement
Supplies	Product introduction		Security
	Product review		Security administration
	Security/virus		Server purchasing
	Software distribution		Upgrades
	Standards development		
	Technical training		
	Tier 1 help desk		
	Tier 2 or 3 support		
	Vendor liaison		

Gartner Group TCO Analyst White Paper, Nov. 18, 1997

The conclusion of TCO analysts is that even if these amounts seem exaggerated, PC TCO for most organizations is still excessively high.

A quick evaluation of the numbers shows that a large component of the TCO money spent is in the areas of technical support and administration. For those of us on the front lines of IT support, TCO represents frustration and stress. The consensus among IT support personnel is that too much time is wasted on a user's self-induced system problems and too little time is spent developing the system or learning new programs. To understand this stress, just spend a few hours with a technician trying to determine just what a particular user deleted/modified/added to her system before it crashed.

Communal Workstations

If a single person's workstation can stress, communal workstations are a helpdesk nightmare. For the purposes of this book, the definition of a *communal workstation* is a single computer with more than one user. This user may be transient or may be one of a group of permanent users. The user(s) may be assigned one particular workstation, or they may roam among several available workstations.

Communal workstations can be found in the following locations:

- Libraries
- Schools, colleges, universities

- Software training centers
- Retail stores (demo computers)
- Internet cafes
- Realty offices
- Offices with shift workers (banks, hospitals)

These users will have widely differing levels of computer expertise. Some will be comfortable using Explorer to find the necessary EXE file to run a required program, while others will have difficulty finding the Start button. Many of the users will want to reconfigure the desktop to suit their personal preferences, but not all of the users will appreciate the computer burping at them when they minimize a window.

The network administrator for these organizations runs into problems such as:

- Added/removed/renamed icons
- Settings changed through the use of Regedit
- Devices removed or altered from the Control Panel
- Wallpaper removed/changed
- Unapproved software or hardware installations

The challenge faced by these network administrators is to discourage natural curiosity and unnatural tampering, while providing all users with a stable and comfortable computing environment. The problem is, how can an administrator achieve this state of computing nirvana in a Windows environment?

To be useful in different working environments, any mode of desktop management must be adaptable and customizable. The system administrator should be able to control the computer configuration of individuals (or groups of users) based on work duties, computer literacy or the need for security.

In an effort to restrain TCO and make the working lives of countless technical support people more pleasant, Microsoft established the Zero Administration Initiative for Windows (ZAW). It refers to a set of management procedures that gives IT professionals a greater degree of control and manageability over their Windows-based environments. Microsoft pledges that the fully realized ZAW will provide tools for central administration as well as desktop system lockdown. There is no specific completion date for ZAW, although it has its highest expression in the Windows 2000's IntelliMirror concept. For Windows 9x and Windows NT4, a significant component of the ZAW initiative is the Zero Administration Kit (ZAK)—a tool intended to simplify the use of system policies and user profiles. However, for these workstations it is not the ZAK but specifically the use of *system policies* that will rescue your helpdesk support personnel.

System Policies

The attainment of your computing nirvana could be launched with policy-based administration. Particularly for communal environments, zero administration really comes down to whether or not your workstations are uniform and stable. It was system policies, using the System Policy Editor (SPE), which saved my sanity while working at a private school. I had heard about the SPE, but after days of searching the Internet, I could find only the most bare-bones description for how to use it. What I was searching for, but never really found, was a step-by-step method for implementing workstation security. I ultimately worked out most of the details in a trial by fire using our own students. Knowing that there were likely other desperate administrators looking for the same information, I posted my guidelines on the Internet. The response amazed me; within 11 months I had received hundreds of emails. The questions and problems I received through those emails helped me to improve my own network security and the information on my web page. As a result of this whole process, I discovered that the implementation of system policies significantly reduced not only my workload, but that of many other network administrators—and it may be just what you are seeking for your own network.

The Objective of System Policies

System policies, or simply *policies*, are a powerful tool that substantially adds to the level of control and manageability that administrators have over desktops on a network. Once configured, logging into the network permits the policy file to alter the workstation's user and computer registry settings. This registry change determines the customizations or restrictions on the resources available according to the particular user, group or computer. The alternative would be to individually edit the registry on each computer through the use of Control Panel applets or by direct registry manipulation.

More specifically, policies can define the particular aspects of the PC environment that a system administrator needs to control, such as:

- Restricting access to the Control Panel
- Defining desktop icons
- Removing taskbar options such as Run or Find
- Establishing default software options
- Determining which programs appear on the user's Start menu
- Restricting which software packages are permitted to be used
- Specifying which users have rights to change desktop attributes

Through the control and maintenance of the desktop's configuration, users will no longer be able to inadvertently delete or change system settings. This will reduce costly user downtime due to self-induced system problems (such as deleting hardware devices using the Control Panel). The ability to establish group policies, in addition to individual user policies, makes managing users' desktops that much more efficient.

Policies offer you a powerful mechanism for centrally managing Windows workstations, and for establishing a uniform set of rules to preserve computer and user environments across a network.

System Requirements

Unfortunately, policies cannot be used on every version of the Microsoft desktop OS, or with every network OS and client. However, a large percentage of systems in use today are compatible with policy-based administration.

Workstation

The System Policy Editor can create policy files for Windows 95, Windows 98 and Windows NT4 workstations. A separate policy file must be created for the Windows 9x and NT workstations due to the differences in the two registries. System policies cannot be used on workstations using Windows 3.1, DOS, Windows NT workstations below Version 4 or Windows 2000. Windows 2000 workstations use a different scheme called group policies, which are incompatible with other Windows versions.

Server

The policy file was specifically designed for Windows NT, Windows 2000 or Novell NetWare servers. However, I have also heard from network administrators who successfully load system policies from Unix and Linux servers through manual downloading of the policy file.

Where System Policies May Be Useful

By now you may be intrigued by the promise of lowered TCO and minimized helpdesk woes through the use of system policies. A review of the following scenarios may help you determine if policies would be useful in your particular networking environment.

Administration is unwilling to spend any capital on a software security system

It's a fact of life that a company will pay thousands of dollars for a PC, but then be reluctant to pay thousands of dollars more for desktop security programs. It's hard to get the budget makers to see the long-term picture: paying to secure your workstations now means less money spent later in technical support, particularly if the technical support people are on a yearly salary that is automatically included in each year's budget. It may even make financial sense for a company to take that extra $4,000 at year-end and spend it on increased advertising—to the dismay of the overworked technical support staff. However since the System Policy Editor comes bundled on your Windows CD-ROM, if you own a copy of Windows 9x or NT4 server, the policy editor is a free bonus.

Software and hardware conflicts are a concern

Combine a variety of chip sets, the chaos of dog-eat-dog code and one of the Windows operating systems, and you have conflicts. The more complex the system (such as a PC on a LAN), the more likely you are to have conflicts, not only between hardware but also between software packages. Conflicts can be caused by such things as competing DLLs or by so-called management software, often leading to the infamous "blue screen of death" (sometimes mispronounced as blue scream of death), the Windows STOP message screen.

If you find yourself holding your breath every time you install a new software package due to a system so delicately balanced that it tends to self-destruct with each new addition, then you should consider using policies. Since Microsoft system policies are a standard option of the Windows operating system, they are inclined to integrate seamlessly into your software environment. That is not true of other third-party security programs.

Administrators are weary of users changing system settings or using unproductive programs

You can nag them to death on avoiding the Windows administrative areas, or write a hundred "acceptable use" memos, but sometimes simply locking users out is the easiest solution. System policies that will allow only certain programs to be used (such as WordPerfect or MS Word) can be created and in addition lock out system areas such as the Control Panel.

Technicians are spending too much time fixing user-created problems

Even if you are only subjectively spending too much time with particular users who inadvertently change settings, you may still find system policies useful. Even a subjective waste of time can lead to short tempers and foot-in-the-mouth syndrome. The use of system policies can help calm the emotions of an overworked IT staff.

Summary

If you are reading this book, it is probably because you are desperate for some form of inexpensive desktop security. You are most likely in charge of a number of shared workstations, and the victim of repeated hacking attacks. Your communal workstations may be in a public library, school or hospital. For these workstations, system policies can offer consistent desktops, unavailable Control Panel applets, restricted software packages, and networkwide application settings. The resulting desktop control will lessen the user's need for support and consequently reduce your TCO. Although you are experienced enough (or jaded enough) to know that perfect security is unattainable, you will settle for enough of a reduced workload to be able to drink a cup of coffee while reading your favorite computing magazine. Policies can offer an intermediate degree of security, which is usually just enough to keep all but the more experienced hackers at bay.

System policies provide a powerful, though infrequently used, tool. As with any powerful tool, the key to successful use is a solid grasp of the basic concepts. Chapter 2, *A System Policies Primer*, will examine the capabilities of system policies, and give an overview of how these parts integrate together to created desktop security.

2

A System Policies Primer

Incomplete information on system policies is the primary cause of significant (but avoidable) errors in policy implementation. Likewise, sound knowledge of the basic concepts and components is the key to successful policy application. The purpose of this chapter is to present a concise overview of system policy concepts. Each successive chapter of this book will build upon this fundamental knowledge.

User Profiles

Every user is aware of the fact that certain system settings can be customized, settings such as desktop icons, colors, screensavers, application options, and so forth. In Windows 9x it is a lone default profile that changes whenever the desktop is customized. However, enabling *user profiles* (using the Passwords applet in the Control Panel; see Figure 2-1) allows customizable settings for every individual workstation user.

User profiles are essential since it is only after they are enabled that it becomes possible for system policies to be applied to the users of a Windows 9x workstation. Windows NT workstations have user profiles, and thus the capability of user policies, enabled by default.

If a workstation did not have user profiles enabled, only computer-based policies could be used and any existing user policies would be completely ignored. Considering that user profiles are essential to the function of system policies, let me take a moment to review their capabilities.

A complete user profile is composed of two parts, a user file and system folders. The user file is the user-specific information contained in the *user.dat* (Windows 9x) or the *ntuser.dat* (Windows NT) files. The system folders, if each user profile

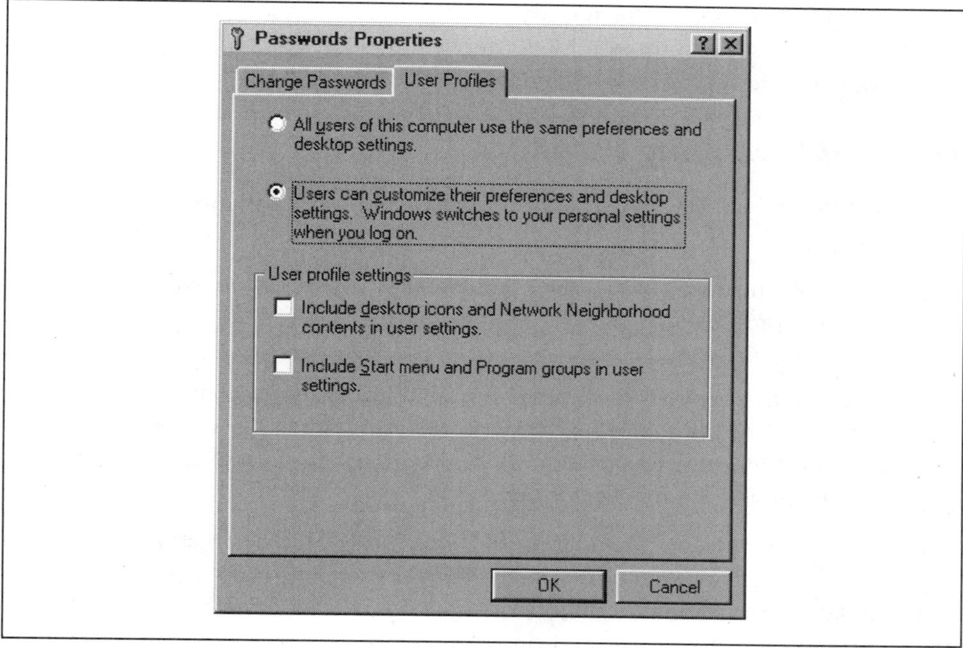

Figure 2-1. Enabling user profiles

setting is enabled in the Passwords applet (Figure 2-1), include the following directories:

Application Data
: Application-specific data, such as MS Outlook mail settings.

Cookies, Favorites, History
: Folders containing user-specific Internet Explorer data.

Desktop
: The icons (shortcuts, folders or programs) added by the user to the desktop.

My Documents (Personal in WinNT)
: The default document folder for Microsoft products, such as Office 97.

NetHood
: Shortcuts to network resources (such as mapped drives) found in Network Neighborhood.

Recent
: The recently opened files listed under Documents in the Start menu.

Start Menu
: The customizable Programs list in the Start menu. This includes the *Startup* folder, which contains the applications automatically loaded every time the user logs onto the workstation.

Thus a profile consists of the registry settings stored in the *user.dat* (*ntuser.dat*) file, as well as a set of profile folders. Between these two components, all of the user's configurable settings are documented and saved.

Local and Roaming Profiles

The manner in which Windows handles profiles allows for two main profile types:

Local profile
: Resides on the local hard drive. A standalone workstation will have one or more local profiles.

Roaming profile
: Resides on the network hard drive, typically in the user's home network directory (Win9x) or on a specified user profile path (WinNT). A user's profile can roam with him from workstation to workstation, due to the network availability of this profile to any client workstation.

Window's management of roaming profiles depends upon the location and modification date of the *user.dat* (*ntuser.dat*). When a user logs onto a preferred server or is validated by a domain controller, Windows checks for a copy of the user's profile on the local hard drive and on the network. If a profile is present only on the network server, then that copy is used. If a profile is present only on the local drive, then that copy is used. If profiles exist in both locations, the newest version is used and merged with the workstation's local registry. Finally, if both local and network versions of the profile have the same modification date, then the local version is used.

However, if a user profile cannot be found on either the local drive or network directory, then a new user subdirectory is created and a copy of the workstation's local default profile is used as the user's profile. This default workstation profile is located in *C:\Windows* on Windows 9x and in *\%systemroot%\Profiles\Default User* on Windows NT workstations. When the user logs off, any changes she made are typically written to this new user profile.

To fully support user profiles, NetWare servers require long filename support to be enabled on 4.1 servers, or the OS2 namespace for 3.x and 4.0x servers. If LFN support is not enabled, only the *user.dat* (*ntuser.dat*) portion of a roaming profile will be saved for each user. The profile folders, such as *Start Menu*, will not be saved.

Mandatory Profiles Versus Policies

Typically, changes to a user's profile are saved when she logs off. In certain cases, for reasons that were touched upon in Chapter 1, *The Hidden Cost of Computers*, it may be preferable *not* to allow a user the freedom to make changes to her profile. If it were desirable to prevent configuration changes, consequently guaranteeing that her desktop appeared exactly the same every time she logged on, then the administrator would use a *mandatory profile*. A mandatory profile is a roaming profile that has been altered by the network administrator to be read-only, thus preventing the user from customizing her settings. Although the user may be able to make temporary changes to her profile, the changes would not be saved when she logged off. A typical customizable roaming profile is changed to an unalterable mandatory profile simply by renaming the file extension from *.DAT* to *.MAN* (e.g., *user.dat* to *user.man* or *ntuser.man* for Windows NT).

This single required file extension change is what allows mandatory profiles to be easier to implement than system policies, and more commonly used. Mandatory profiles provide less flexibility and desktop control than system policies. Table 2-1 shows these differences, as well as the benefits of policy-based control.

Table 2-1. Comparing Mandatory Profiles and System Policies

Mandatory Profiles	System Policies
Changes must be made for every user individually, and as a result some users may be overlooked.	Changes made to the single policy file can affect all users or members of a group.
All aspects of the user's desktop are strictly controlled.	Control can be selectively applied, leaving other environment settings under the control of the user.
Areas such as the Control Panel cannot be locked out (Windows 9x).	User access can be restricted from the entire Control Panel or from just a few of the Control Panel applets.
Specific software programs cannot be restricted (Windows 9x).	Access can be permitted to only selected programs.
Restrictions can be applied only in a per-user manner, since common groups are not supported (Windows 9x).	Restrictions can be applied to a single user or to an entire group.
Aspects of the computer cannot be controlled, such as file and print sharing (Windows 9x).	Various aspects of the computer can be controlled and customized.
The *ntuser.man* or *user.man* file must be kept up to date for every user.	Only the single policy file must be updated for all users and groups.
Network-based Default User profiles are not supported (Windows 9x).	Policies allow a Default User profile to be defined for Windows 9x or Windows NT.
Using the local All Users profile, shortcuts and directories can be specified only for users of a single Windows NT workstation.	Common shortcuts and directories can be specified for groups and users across a domain.

Although a network administrator may use mandatory profiles in an attempt to gain some measure of control over a user's desktop, mandatory profiles have limitations—limitations that can be overcome through the use of system policies. Policies give control over single or multiple aspects of the desktop. They allow computer-specific settings rather than just the user settings allowed by mandatory profiles. Policies give the administrator additional flexibility through the use of profile folder sharing and by the addition of group as well as user restrictions.

Unlike mandatory profiles, with system policies it is possible to allow the user a degree of freedom in customizing her desktop. Customizable roaming profiles and system policy restrictions can be simultaneously active on a network. In this case, the user profile would detail the desktop configuration within the boundaries established by the system policy. In other words, the user profile could not grant access to areas that the system policies have restricted.

System Policies

System policies are the resource limits or customizations imposed on computers, individuals or groups of users. They allow the creation of an unchanging desktop and user environment. The following section describes the four components of system policies, namely:

- The software application (*poledit.exe*)
- The policy file it creates (*config.pol* in Windows 9x or *ntconfig.pol* in Windows NT)
- The three types of policies (user, group and computer)
- The policy templates used by the program (**.adm*)

Poledit

poledit.exe is the System Policy Editor; it is the utility used to create and edit the policy file. Poledit can be used not only to create a policy file, but also to directly edit the Windows registry (see "Poledit Versus Regedit" later in this chapter). Although Poledit is compatible with both Windows 9x and Windows NT, the file it creates is platform-specific (see the next section, "The Policy File").

The Policy File

The policy file is the collection of registry settings created and saved using Poledit. These settings can be visualized as a registry hive, a portion of the registry tailored to a specific user or computer and saved as a file. This registry hive is stored on the server as the policy file—*config.pol* for Windows 9x workstations and *ntconfig.pol* for Windows NT4 workstations. This file is a binary file and consequently cannot be edited with Notepad or any other existing Microsoft utility except Poledit. Unfortunately, there is no utility at all to print out the settings contained within the policy file.

The policy file is platform-specific. Reflecting basic differences in the organization of the registry, Windows NT policies are incompatible with Windows 9x policies and vise versa. To create a *config.pol* file, Poledit must be used on a Windows 9x workstation, and the resulting policy file will be compatible only with other Windows 9x workstations. For a policy file to be compatible with a Windows NT workstation, *ntconfig.pol* must be created and saved by using Poledit on either a Windows NT4 workstation or server. Therefore, if both types of workstations exist on your network, you will need two separate policy files, one created on a Windows 9x workstation and the other created on a Windows NT4 workstation or server.

By default, when a user logs onto a workstation with user profiles enabled, the Windows operating system attempts to locate a policy file. If found, the policy file is searched for the user's name, a group to which the user may belong, and the local computer name. If any of these labels is found, the appropriate policy settings are downloaded and merged with the registry.

The Policy Types

There are three policy types: computer, user and group (see Figure 2-2). It is important to note that Poledit cannot be used to create new network users or groups, but simply to define policies for those that already exist on the system.

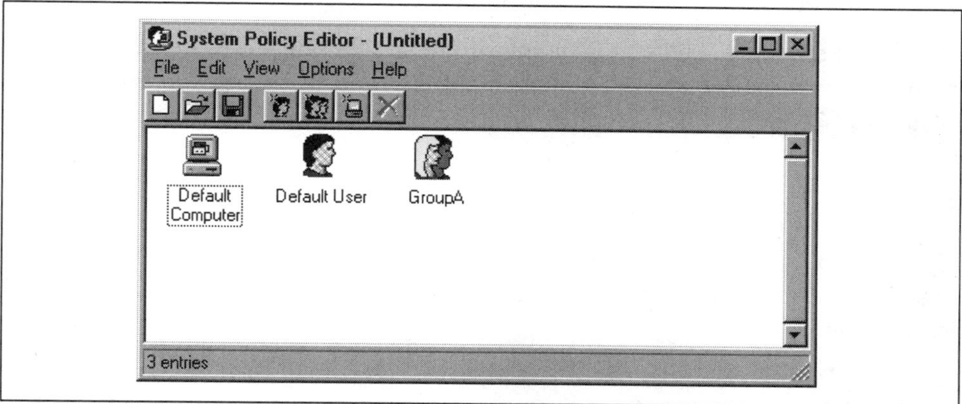

Figure 2-2. Policy types

Computer or workstation policies

The computer policy's counterpart in the registry is the `HKEY_LOCAL_MACHINE` (HKLM) registry key. This registry key contains the following default subkeys and information:

HKLM\Config
: Information about alternate hardware configurations.

HKLM\Enum
: Device information for hardware such as monitors, disks or PnP devices. Most values in this subkey are binary and so *cannot* be changed using policies.

HKLM\Hardware
: Serial communication port (including modems) information and settings. Since this key is recreated during each boot-up, values in this subkey *cannot* be changed using policies.

HKLM\Network
: Network information created when the user logs on. This key contains data such as user name, logon validation, and primary network server name.

HKLM\Security
: Information regarding network security settings.

HKLM\Software
: Computer-specific information for software, such as filename extensions and software version number. It is added by the application during installation.

HKLM\System
: Information regarding device drivers and startup services such as computer name, network providers, current printers and language preferences.

Other subkeys are possible, depending on the utilities and software installed on a particular workstation. Since data for HKLM is stored in the *system.dat* (*system* in Windows NT) system file, computer policies directly relate to settings saved in this file.

User policies

The user policy's counterpart in the registry is the HKEY_CURRENT_USER (HKCU) registry key. This registry key contains the following default subkeys and information:

HKCU\AppEvents
: The label name and directory location for WAV files played during system sound events.

HKCU\Control Panel

Control Panel settings including subkeys for the following: Accessibility settings for persons with disabilities; Appearance settings for desktop color schemes; Colors for specific aspects of the desktop such as window frame color; Cursors or mouse pointer schemes; Desktop wallpaper, background and screensaver settings; and International for local settings.

HKCU\Display

Display settings such as resolution.

HKCU\InstallLocationsMRU

Most recently used directory locations for software installations.

HKCU\Keyboard layout

The current keyboard layout.

HKCU\Network

Network connection information such as drive mappings.

HKCU\RemoteAccess

Information on current dial-up network settings.

HKCU\Software

User-specific software settings for the currently logged on user.

Other subkeys are possible, depending on the utilities and software installed on a particular workstation. Since data for HKCU is stored in the *user.dat* (*ntuser.dat*) system file, user policies directly relate to settings saved in this file.

Group policies

Like the user policy, the group policy's counterpart in the registry is the HKCU registry key. The same template-specific options that exist for the user will also exist for the group.

For Windows NT domains, policy labels will only refer to the group security identifiers from the Primary Domain Controller (DC). For this reason group membership, and so group policy labels, must be based on global rather than local groups.

Local groups

These groups are created using User Manager. These groups are local, in terms of the local computer (workstation or server) on which they are created. The function of local groups is to control or assign access to local resources such as printer and file sharing. Members of a local group may be user accounts from the local computer, user accounts from any trusted domain, or global groups. A local group cannot have as a member another local group from a different computer. During installation of an NT workstation or standalone server, the default local groups are:

- Administrators
- Users
- Guests
- Power users
- Server operators
- Print operators
- Backup operators
- Account operators
- Replicator

Global groups

These groups are created on a DC using User Manager for Domains. Only domain users can be members of a global group. However, since a global group can be a member of any local group, members of a global group can potentially have access to all network resources. During installation of an NT domain controller, the default global groups created are:

- Domain admins
- Domain users
- Domain guests

See the Windows NT Resource Kit for more information on creating local and global groups.

For NetWare servers, users can be members of NDS groups, although bindery emulation must be enabled on the server. See Chapter 4, *Building the Policy File*, for more information on group policies within a NetWare environment.

Note that group policies can potentially conflict with user policies. This potential problem is discussed in detail in Chapter 3, *Preparation and Planning*, but it's worth mentioning here as well.

All forms of policies—user, group and computer—will override any corresponding user profile settings, since the policies are downloaded and merged with the registry *after* the profile data is read.

The Policy Templates

Through the use of policy templates, Poledit allows for a graphical and easy-to-understand representation of registry keys and values. These templates (also referred to as administrative or ADM files) create the registry settings that are saved in the policy file. Templates allow for a predetermined range of values specifically for the local computer (HKLM) and current user (HKCU) portions of the registry. Unfortunately, templates cannot be created for the other dynamic registry keys, specifically:

- HKEY_CLASSES_ROOT
- HKEY_USERS
- HKEY_CURRENT_CONFIG
- HKEY_DYN_DATA (Windows 95)

Policy templates are simply ASCII files. Because of this, they can be added to and changed (unlike the policy file) using text editors such as Notepad. Figure 2-3 shows a portion of the *common.adm* template as it is viewed using Notepad.

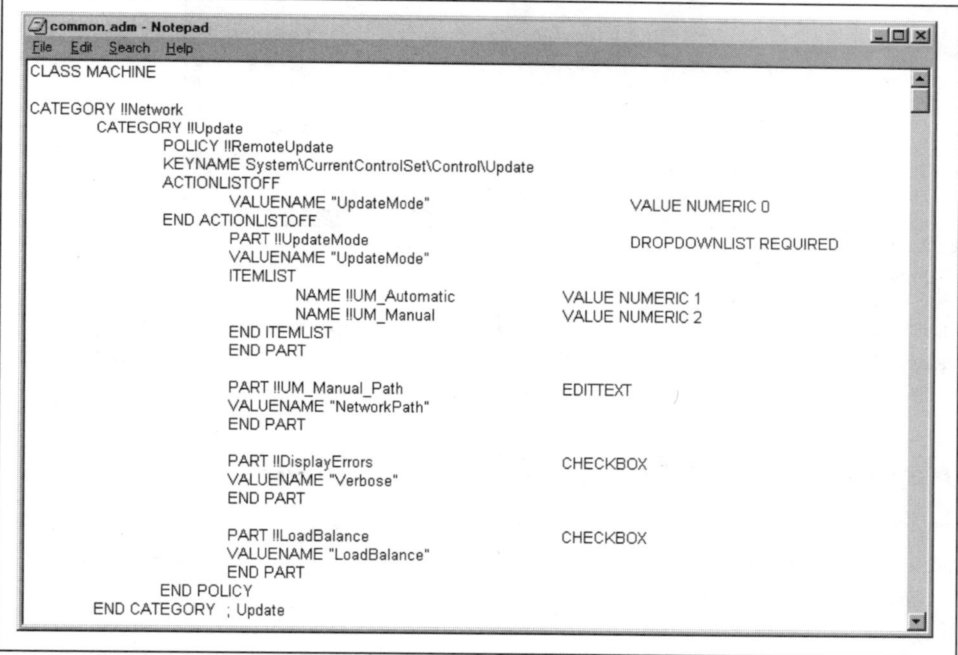

```
CLASS MACHINE

CATEGORY !!Network
        CATEGORY !!Update
                POLICY !!RemoteUpdate
                KEYNAME System\CurrentControlSet\Control\Update
                ACTIONLISTOFF
                        VALUENAME "UpdateMode"                  VALUE NUMERIC 0
                END ACTIONLISTOFF
                        PART !!UpdateMode                       DROPDOWNLIST REQUIRED
                        VALUENAME "UpdateMode"
                        ITEMLIST
                                NAME !!UM_Automatic     VALUE NUMERIC 1
                                NAME !!UM_Manual        VALUE NUMERIC 2
                        END ITEMLIST
                        END PART

                        PART !!UM_Manual_Path           EDITTEXT
                        VALUENAME "NetworkPath"
                        END PART

                        PART !!DisplayErrors            CHECKBOX
                        VALUENAME "Verbose"
                        END PART

                        PART !!LoadBalance              CHECKBOX
                        VALUENAME "LoadBalance"
                        END PART
                END POLICY
        END CATEGORY ; Update
```

Figure 2-3. common.adm template viewed using Notepad

Once this ASCII template is loaded into the Poledit program, these keys and values are displayed in a more user-friendly graphical fashion. Compare Figure 2-3 with Figure 2-4; both figures display the same section of the *common.adm* template.

Like the Windows registry, the template consists of keys, subkeys and values. Templates define the configuration choices that can be applied to specific users,

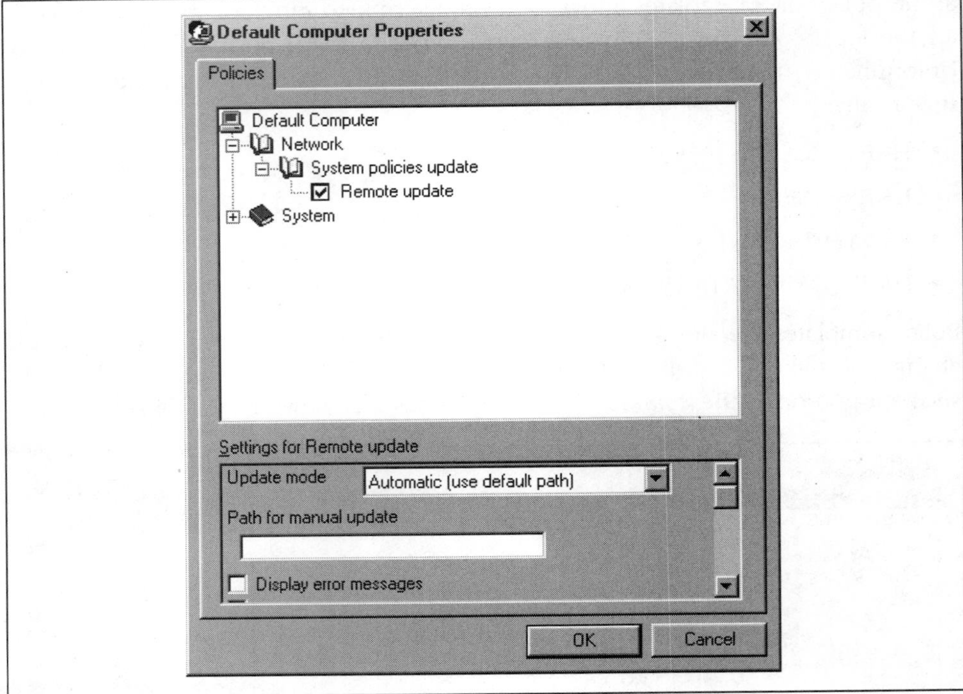

Figure 2-4. common.adm template viewed using Poledit

groups or computers and can be created for any application that uses the Windows registry to store settings. See Chapter 8, *Creating a Custom Template*, for more information on custom policy template creation.

Registry and Policy File Edit Modes

The System Policy Editor is a versatile program. Poledit can be used not only to create and edit the policy file but also for direct registry editing—either locally or remotely across the network.

Registry Mode

By selecting File → Open Registry, you can edit the local workstation's registry. In this case, the Poledit window will display the icons as in Figure 2-5 with the title bar at the top showing System Policy Editor—Local Registry. The Local Computer icon refers to the workstation you are currently using, while the Local User icon refers to the currently logged on user. On a workstation without user profiles enabled, editing Local User will in effect edit the default user profile on the local drive. Note that if you have an active policy file, changes made to the Local User or Local Computer will be temporary only. Upon the next logon, the policy file restrictions will be used overwriting the local settings. Despite being temporary, this method of editing the registry can be useful if you are disconnected from the network and unable to get the administrator's less restrictive settings. You could comfortably make changes to the local profile and gain temporary unrestricted access knowing that the policy file restrictions will be back in place the next time the user logs on.

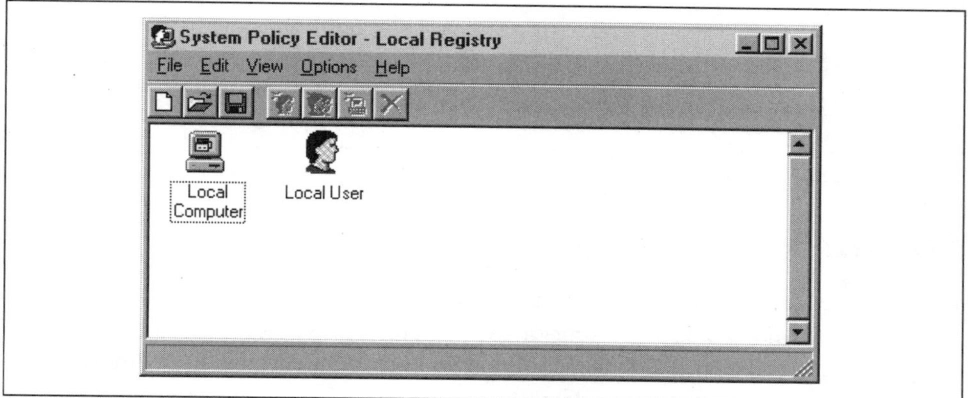

Figure 2-5. Poledit's local registry mode

It is also possible to directly edit a *remote* registry using Poledit. You can load the remote registry from across the network, make changes, and save it back to the remote computer. This is accomplished by selecting File → Connect and then typing the computer name. See Chapter 4 for information concerning the setup required to enable remote administration on a Windows 9x workstation.

Policy File Mode

By selecting File → New Policy (or Open Policy), you can create or edit a policy file. In this case, the Poledit window will show the same icons as in Figure 2-6. Default Computer refers to any workstation on the network that does not have a specific computer policy. Default User refers to any user on the network that does not have a specific user or group policy.

You can identify which of these two modes (registry or policy file) is active by the computer and user icon labels. When editing a local or remote registry, the icons are labeled Local Computer and Local User. When editing a policy file, the icons are labeled Default Computer and Default User. Since it is possible to unwittingly edit the local registry, take note of the differences in the icon names between Figures 2-5 and 2-6. Otherwise, you may find yourself locked out of a workstation, faced with the possibility of reinstalling the operating system.

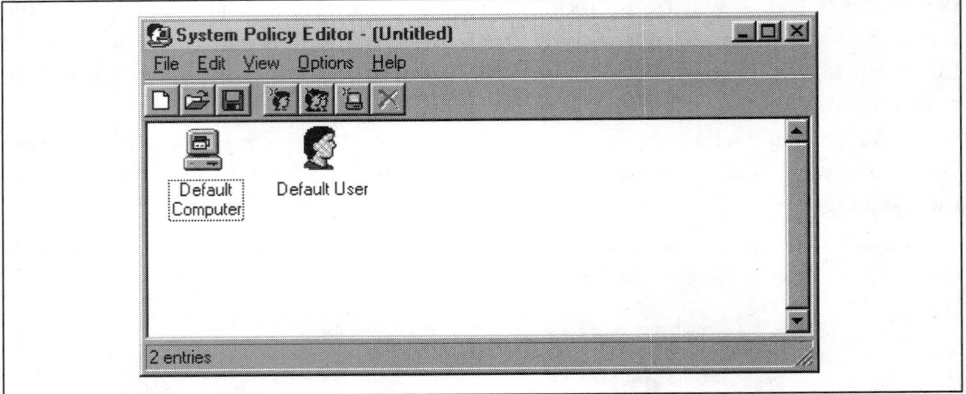

Figure 2-6. Poledit's policy file mode

Poledit Versus Regedit

regedit.exe is one of the utilities bundled with the Windows operating system that allows direct editing and browsing of the system registry. Regedit can be used to edit the three registry value types common to both Windows 9x and Windows NT: binary, DWORD, and string (or character).

The data revealed by Regedit could best be described as cryptic. Figure 2-7 shows a section of the HKCU displaying the current user's desktop settings. As you can see, without a manual detailing specific registry settings, it is often impossible to intuitively deduce which subkeys and values require editing. It also can be dangerous to use Regedit, as a single incorrect setting can cause Windows to fail to load properly. In contrast, Poledit uses clearly understood headings and will even warn the user if they have entered invalid characters (such as letters instead of numbers) for a particular field.

Poledit can be used to edit either a local registry or remote registry through the use of a policy file or via remote administration. Poledit is far more restrictive than Regedit in that editing can be performed only on the HKLM and HKCU sections of the registry and even then only the subkeys that have been defined by the template files.

Since Poledit cannot delete subkeys and values, however, it tends to be safer to use than Regedit. Poledit's use of natural language rather than cryptic key and value names also makes it more user-friendly. Compare Figures 2-7 and 2-8; both show the same wallpaper registry values. Using Poledit it is obvious where you enable tiled wallpaper, which is not the case using Regedit.

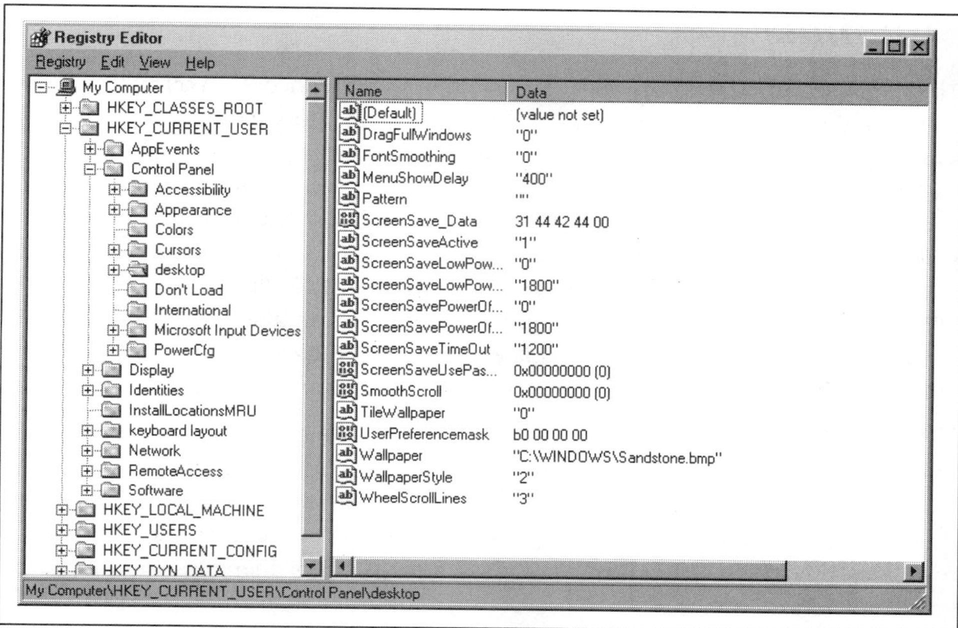

Figure 2-7. Editing the registry using Regedit

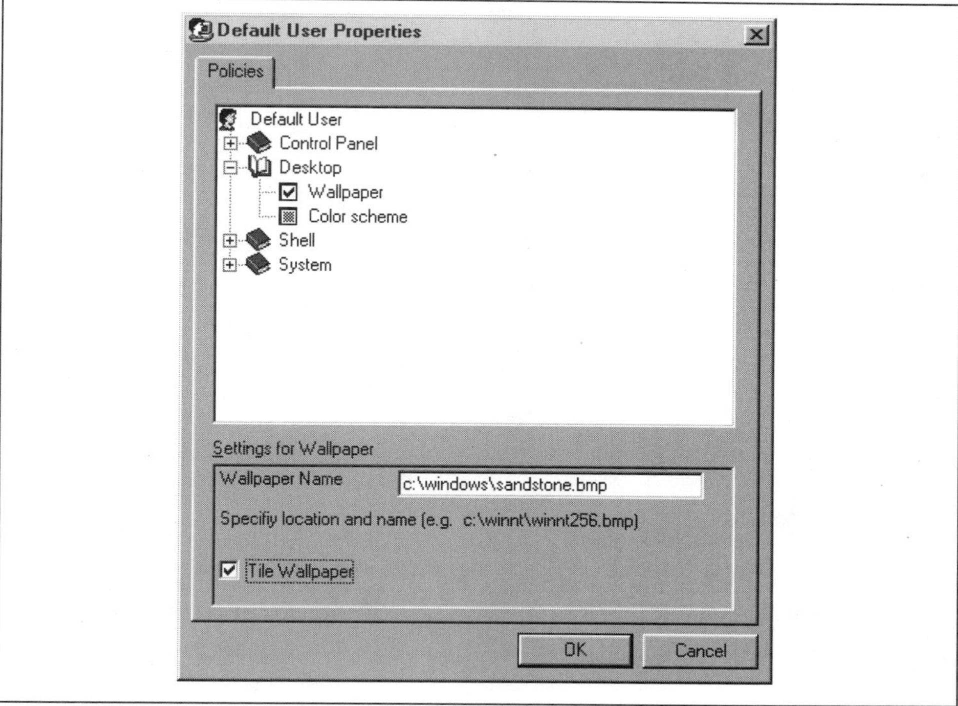

Figure 2-8. Changing the registry using Poledit

Summary

This overview should clarify the basic system policy concepts. You will now see that although many network administrators use mandatory profiles to keep desktop and computing environments consistent for their roaming users, the use of system policies can provide greater and more flexible control. This is because system policies can be created for users, groups or computers, and policy templates can provide almost unlimited software application control since they can be custom-built or existing templates can be edited as required. Poledit's registry mode even allows the program to be used in a limited manner as an alternative to Regedit for local registry editing. Although templates can only be used to edit the HKLM and HKCU sections of the Windows registry, they are safer and more user-friendly than Regedit.

The next step is to consider your own need for user, group or computer policies, and to identify any potential problems. Chapter 3 will help you to do this by going through an evaluation process using four different network examples, as well as reviewing other necessary considerations before you implement system policies on your network.

3

Preparation and Planning

Using the basic concepts from Chapter 2, *A System Policies Primer*, the next step is to prepare a specific plan for your own network. There are several issues you need to consider before beginning any system policy implementation. Do you want to use computer, user or group policies? In its present condition, does your network platform support all policy types? What kinds of basic limits and customizations would you like to establish and administer centrally? What possible policy conflicts are you likely to encounter?

To help you resolve these issues, I've prepared a system requirement checklist, identified possible conflicts though conflict resolution flowcharts and finally scrutinized four different case studies. Each case study begins with several questions about the users and network and then uses those answers to decide which policy types may be recommended.

This book makes numerous references to the file used to store the HKCU registry settings. In Windows 9x this file is called *user.dat,* and in Windows NT4 workstations, *ntuser.dat.* For brevity's sake, from now on both files will be simply referred to as *user.dat.*

You can ease your administrative burden by completing a well-thought-out plan before creating your policy file. A good strategy is to minimize the number of user or computer policies while identifying and preventing possible conflicts. The worksheets provided in this chapter will help you organize your own strategy. Finally, there is always the matter of preparing your users before any major change to their computing environment. Some suggestions on how to do this are offered at the end of the chapter.

System Requirements

Unfortunately, not all system policy types are available to all workstation and server environments, or they may be available only after completing specific software modifications. So before getting your heart set on using a particular policy type, and groups in particular, review the system requirements in this section. Learning the policy types supported by your particular network environment will enable you to determine if there are any limits on the restrictions and customized settings you can establish in a policy file. Tables 3-1 through 3-4 later in this chapter summarize all of these system requirements.

Remote Update

The remote update option (see Figure 2-4) on a Windows workstation allows for two methods of downloading the system policy file from the server. Automatic update downloads the file from the default network path:

NetWare network
: This is the *Public* directory of the preferred server (*\\Preferredserver\sys\Public*).

Windows NT4 network
: The default path is the *Netlogon* directory of the validating domain controller (*%systemroot%\winnt\system32\repl\import\scripts*).

Windows 2000 network
: The default path is the *Netlogon* directory of the domain controller (*%systemroot%\sysvol\DomainName\scripts*).

: To use the automatic remote update function, the client software must be either a Microsoft client or a 32-bit protected mode client that supports system policies.

Manual update downloads the file from any valid network server directory. This directory should allow unvalidated connections and have read/execute permissions for all users. Real-mode network clients (such as Novell NETX, VLM or some older Unix and Linux clients) may permit the use of user and computer system policies if remote update is set to Manual.

The remote update registry key is found in HKLM/System/CurrentControlSet/control/Update. The DWORD value UpdateMode should have a hex value of 1 for automatic remote update, and a hex value of 2 to enable manual remote update.

Computer Policies

A workstation can be forced to completely ignore any existing policy file by setting this hex value to 0 (or by unchecking the remote update option using Poledit and the *common.adm* template). See Chapter 4, *Building the Policy File*, for more information on using Poledit to set the remote update value.

A computer policy is the most basic system policy. If your network environment will not support its use, it will not support the use of user or group policies either.

Workstation

To enable computer policies, remote update must be enabled on the workstation. Although remote update is enabled by default on most workstations, some OEMs will have disabled this option. The workstation OS can be Windows NT4 or Windows 9x. A Windows NT4 workstation must minimally have Service Pack 3 installed. This service pack fixes many policy bugs such as the bug that required all users to have read/write access to the *Netlogon* subdirectory before the policy file could be accessed—essentially allowing users to modify or delete the policy file.

The network client should be either a Microsoft client or a protected mode 32-bit client if you want to use automatic remote update. For NetWare networks, the IntraNetWare clients were the first to support user and computer system policies, as did all subsequent Client32 versions. Other real-mode clients may work only if remote update is set to manual.

If the workstation is pulling the policy file from a NetWare server, it needs to have a preferred server defined and Client for NetWare networks must be the primary network logon. If a Windows 9x workstation is pulling the policy file from a Windows NT4 or Windows 2000 domain controller, it needs to have a domain name defined, Client for Microsoft Networks must be the primary network logon, and load balancing must be enabled.

If a Windows 9x workstation (using automatic remote update) does *not* have load balancing enabled, only the Primary Domain Controller (DC) will be checked for the policy file. With load balancing enabled, the policy file will be downloaded from any validating domain controller.

See Chapter 4, *Building the Policy File*, for information on using Poledit to set these options.

Server

The network server OS can be Novell NetWare, Windows NT4 or Windows 2000. Other server operating systems, such as Unix or Linux, may provide computer policy support either using manual remote update or, if their 32-bit client software supports policies, using automatic remote update. The policy file cannot be downloaded from a computer running File and Printer Sharing for NetWare networks.

With NetWare servers, the policy file must be saved in the *Public* directory of the preferred server. The NetWare server must have bindery emulation enabled for full compatibility.

With Windows NT4 servers, since the policy file will be downloaded from whichever domain controller answers the workstation's broadcast, the policy file should be saved in the *Netlogon* directory of all domain controllers that participate in user authentication. On Windows 2000 networks, the policy file can be saved in the *Netlogon* directory of any domain controller, and subsequently replicated to all other domain controllers. As well, the Windows NT4 or Windows 2000 server's filesystem must be NTFS. Only NTFS can allow, for example, the Everyone group just read and execute access to the policy file while simultaneously allowing the Administrator group full control.

User Policies

User policies have the following requirements in addition the workstation and server requirements for computer policies:

Workstation

A Windows 9x workstation *must* have user profiles enabled (user profiles are enabled by default on a Windows NT4 workstation). See Chapter 2 for information on how to enable user profiles on Windows 9x. Each Windows workstation should have at least 10 megabytes of free space on the local hard drive to temporarily or permanently store these profiles. To use roaming as well as local user profiles, the network client must be a Microsoft or other 32-bit client.

Server

If you use custom folders, it is a good idea to enable long filename (LFN) support on NetWare servers (long namespace on 4.1x and 5.x servers or the OS2 namespace for 3.x and 4.0x servers). If LFN support is not enabled, the custom folder name may not be read correctly. In addition, only the *user.dat* portion of a roaming profile will be saved for each user. The profile folders, such as *Start Menu*, will not be saved.

Novell's ZENworks

ZENworks (Zero Effort Networking) provides software distribution, desktop management, and maintenance capabilities. It is a combination of two previously separate Novell products: Novell Application Launcher (NAL) and the Novell Workstation Manager. These two products are available in the ZENworks Starter Pack (free for download from *http://www.novell.com*) while the ZENworks full package contains additional remote software management utilities.

Like the System Policy Editor, ZENworks allows policy packages to be created based on user, group or workstation. Policies can be created and administered, using the NetWare Administrator, for Windows NT4 and Windows 9x workstations. Unlike Microsoft policies, however, ZEN policies are actually NDS objects. Since it is dependent upon the NDS, ZENworks will work with NetWare 4.11 and up (Version 4.11 requires SP6 for full functionality), NDS for Windows NT and NDS for Unix. ZEN requires that Client32 be installed on all workstations.

ZEN policies and MS policies can co-exist on the same network, however, this creates a new level of conflict possibilities. For further information on ZENworks, link to *http://www.novell.com/coolsolutions/zenworks/index.html.*

User policies will not work on a peer-to-peer network but only on network servers that support a user database such as Unix, Linux, NetWare, Windows NT4 or Windows 2000 servers.

Group Policies

Group policies are more difficult to enable, as they are not as widely supported by the client software as computer and user policies are. In addition to the requirements listed previously for both computer and user policies, there are added requirements for group policies.

Workstation

For Windows 9x workstations on a NetWare network using NDS, the workstations must be using NetWare's *nwgroup.dll* in addition to the Microsoft *grouppol.dll,* as the two files work together to communicate group information. Microsoft's *grouppol.dll* asks for a list of all the NDS groups of which the user is a member, while *nwgroup.dll* makes the necessary requests to the Directory Services database and returns the list to *grouppol.dll.* The *nwgroup.dll* file was available first with the IntraNetWare Client for Windows 9x Version 2.11. All subsequent

NetWare Client32 versions contain this file. To avoid problems with some versions of the *nwgroup.dll* or *grouppol.dll* files, the policy group names should be less than 39 characters long. The names can become quite long as they are named according to the fully qualified NDS group name (see Chapter 4).

Note that groups are *not* supported with the real-mode MSNetWare client or for Windows NT4 workstations on a NetWare network. None of the available Novell NT or Microsoft NT clients for NetWare support group policies. To date, Novell has no plans to integrate the use of group policies into future client versions. So for now (unless you use Novell's ZENworks) if you have Windows NT4 workstations on a NetWare network, you will have to make do with only computer and user policies.

Server

Poledit does not create network groups; consequently, groups must already exist and be defined on the server. For Windows NT4 and Windows 2000 domains the group policy must refer to a global group rather than a local group (see Chapter 2). NetWare servers using NDS must have bindery emulation enabled and the group object and members of the group must be in the bindery context for the server.

System Requirement Checklists

Tables 3-1 through 3-4 can be used as checklists to determine if your network requires any adjustments to effectively use all three types of system policies. Note that the requirements are cumulative for the policy types. That is, the system requirements for user policies include the requirements for computer policies, while the requirements for group policies include those requirements for both user and computer.

Table 3-1. Workstation Checklist for Using Specific System Policies

Workstation	Computer policy	User policy	Group Policy
Windows 9x or later	Remote update is enabled. Policy file is called *Config.pol.* Primary network logon (Client for Microsoft Networks or NetWare networks) is defined. Domain name or preferred server is defined. Load balancing is enabled.	User profiles are enabled. Remote update is enabled. Windows 95 requires Service Pack 1. Policy file is called *Config.pol.* Primary network logon (Client for Microsoft Networks or NetWare networks) is defined. Domain name or preferred server is defined. Load balancing is enabled.	User profiles are enabled. Remote update is enabled. Windows 95 requires Service Pack 1. Policy file is called *Config.pol.* Primary network logon (Client for Microsoft Networks or NetWare networks) is defined. Domain name or preferred server is defined. Load balancing is enabled.
Windows NT4 or later	Workstation is member of domain. NT4 Service Pack 3 or later. Policy file is called *NTconfig.pol.*	Workstation is member of domain. NT4 Service Pack 3 or later. Policy file is called *NTconfig.pol.*	Workstation is member of domain. NT4 Service Pack 3 or later. Policy file is called *NTconfig.pol.*

Table 3-2. Server Checklist for Using Specific System Policies

Server	Computer Policy	User Policy	Group Policy
Novell NetWare	Bindery emulation is enabled. Policy file is in *Public* directory on preferred server.	Long filename support is enabled. Bindery emulation is enabled. Policy file is in *Public* directory on preferred server.	Groups must exist in a context with bindery emulation. Full NDS group names should be shorter than 39 characters. Long filename support is enabled. Bindery emulation is enabled. Policy file is in *Public* directory on preferred server.

Table 3-2. Server Checklist for Using Specific System Policies (continued)

Server	Computer Policy	User Policy	Group Policy
Windows NT4 and Windows 2000	Filesystem is NTFS. NT4 has Service Pack 3 or later. Policy file is in *Netlogon* directory of validating domain controller and replicated to other domain controllers.	Filesystem is NTFS. NT4 has Service Pack 3 or later. Policy file is in *Netlogon* directory of validating domain controller and replicated to other domain controllers.	Groups must exist as global groups on the domain controller. Filesystem is NTFS. NT4 has Service Pack 3 or later. Policy file is in *Netlogon* directory of validating domain controller and replicated to other domain controllers.
Other server OS	Support is dependent on client software.	Server must support user database—peer-to-peer networks do not. Full user policy support is dependent on client software.	Server must support user database—peer-to-peer networks do not. Full group policy support is dependent on client software.

Table 3-3. Platform Checklist for Using Specific System Policies

Workstation OS and Network Server OS Combination	Computer Policy	User Policy	Group Policy
Windows 9x and NetWare	First supported with original IntraNetWare Client for Windows 9x.	First supported with original IntraNetWare Client for Windows 9x.	Supported with IntraNetWare Client Version 2.11 and later client versions.
Windows 9x and NT4 server	Supported with NT4 server Service Pack 3.	Supported with NT4 server Service Pack 3.	Supported with NT4 server Service Pack 3.
Windows NT4 workstation and NetWare	Supported with IntraNetWare client for NT Version 4 and later.	Supported with IntraNetWare client for NT Version 4 and later.	Does *not* support group policies.
Windows NT4 workstation and NT server	Supported with NT4 server Service Pack 3.	Supported with NT4 server Service Pack 3.	Supported with NT4 server Service Pack 3.
Any Windows workstation and Windows 2000 server	Supported with Client for MS Networks.	Supported with Client for MS Networks.	Supported with Client for MS Networks.

Table 3-3. Platform Checklist for Using Specific System Policies (continued)

Workstation OS and Network Server OS Combination	Computer Policy	User Policy	Group Policy
Windows NT4 or Windows 9x workstations and other network server OS	Support is dependent upon client software and whether remote update mode is manual or automatic.	Support is dependent upon client software and whether remote update mode is manual or automatic.	Support is dependent upon client software and whether remote update mode is manual or automatic.

Table 3-4. Network Client Software Checklist for Using Specific System Policies

Computer and User Policy	Group Policy
Microsoft or 32-bit protected mode client which supports system policies.	Automatic or manual remote update can be used for all policy types. Roaming profiles can be used in addition to policies.
Real mode client, or 32-bit client which doesn't support system policies.	Only manual remote update may be used for all policy types. Roaming profiles are not supported by real mode clients.

Poledit Versions

There currently are three versions of *poledit.exe*. One is included with Windows 95 and the Windows 95 Resource Kit. This version (4.00.950) can be used to create policy files only for Windows 9x workstations; it is not recommended for use with the Office 97 or Office 2000 templates, and templates can be loaded only one at a time. According to Microsoft, the second version of Poledit included with the Microsoft Office 97 Resource Kit and Windows NT4 server will cause an access violation when large template files are used to create the policy file. The third version of Poledit is included with the Windows NT4 Service Pack 5, Windows 98, Windows 98SE and the Office 2000 Resource Kit. This version (4.00) can create policy files for both Windows 9x and Windows NT4 workstations, as well as allowing multiple templates to be loaded simultaneously.

Windows 9x policies must be created on a Windows 9x workstation; Windows NT policies must be created on either a Windows NT4 workstation or server.

You should use this third version to create your system policy file. To identify which version of Poledit you have, right-click on the file and choose Properties. In the Properties window, select the Version tab and verify that it is listed as Version 4.0. The General tab should show a modification date of May 1, 1997, or later.

Conflicts

Conflicts are the bane of any network administrator. You will find them in hardware, software, and yes—even in your policy file. If your policy file does not behave exactly as you expected, suspect policy conflicts. Each conflict can occur as the result of two conditions: conflicting template option states and/or the order of application of user or group policies. We will begin with the conflicting template option states and a review of the precise meaning of each state.

Template Option States

Each template option has three possible settings: grayed, checked or cleared (see Table 3-5). Selecting an option box will begin the cycle through the choices. The first mouse click changes the option from a grayed box to one with a check mark in it, the second mouse click changes it from a check mark to a clear white box, and the third mouse click changes it from a clear white box back to a grayed box.

Table 3-5. Template Option States

Option State	Meaning
▩	*Grayed* The registry key is ignored and the setting remains the same as the last time a user logged on. Grayed options are dealt with quickly at system startup since they require no processing.
☑	*Checked* The registry key will be set to the defined value. If the option was previously active the last time a user logged on, then Windows makes no changes.
☐	*Cleared* The registry key will be cleared of all values. Generally this indicates that the policy is not active, although it can also have the startling effect of eliminating all previous settings if the policy has an edit box.

Typically, setting the option to the checked state turns the option ON. Setting the option to the cleared state turns the option OFF. Setting the option to the grayed state allows the user to customize that setting, and save the new setting with their user profile.

However, if the option has an edit box, setting it to the cleared state may have unanticipated results. For example, you may decide to create a Default Computer policy and set the option that specifies a network path for Windows setup to the cleared state. Rather than the option simply being inactive, when the user logs on and the policy is downloaded a cleared state would completely erase the local configuration that specified the network path. See Chapter 9 for a detailed list of all the template options, and which options would be similarly affected by a cleared template option.

Template options for wallpaper: An example

As an example of the template option states, let's take a look at the portion of the *common.adm* template that allows the user's wallpaper to be specified.

The grayed state indicates the last wallpaper specified in the *user.dat* will not be altered. The user can choose a wallpaper image, and this wallpaper option will be written to their network profile or perhaps a local profile if they have no network directory to which a profile can be saved.

The checked state (Figure 3-1) indicates the wallpaper can only be the graphic image identified in the edit box, in this case *sandstone.bmp*. The last wallpaper specified in the *user.dat* will be altered. This wallpaper option will be written to the user's network profile or perhaps a local profile if they have no network directory to which a profile can be saved.

The cleared state removes any wallpaper setting. The last wallpaper specified in the *user.dat* will be deleted. The user will not have any wallpaper, nor be able to save a wallpaper choice from one logon to another. This wallpaper option will be written to the user's network profile or a local profile if they have no network directory to which a profile can be saved.

To avoid deleting settings, you could set the template option of a policy with an edit box to the grayed state when you no longer want to enforce the policy. However, this too could cause problems if you have the Default User policy active.

Policy Application Order

Policy application order can cause conflicts in two instances. First, a user can have more than one policy applied when they logon. Second, in certain circumstances one user's policy can affect another user simply because they share the same workstation. In each instance, since each policy option can have one of three states, overlapping user settings can create unpredictable results.

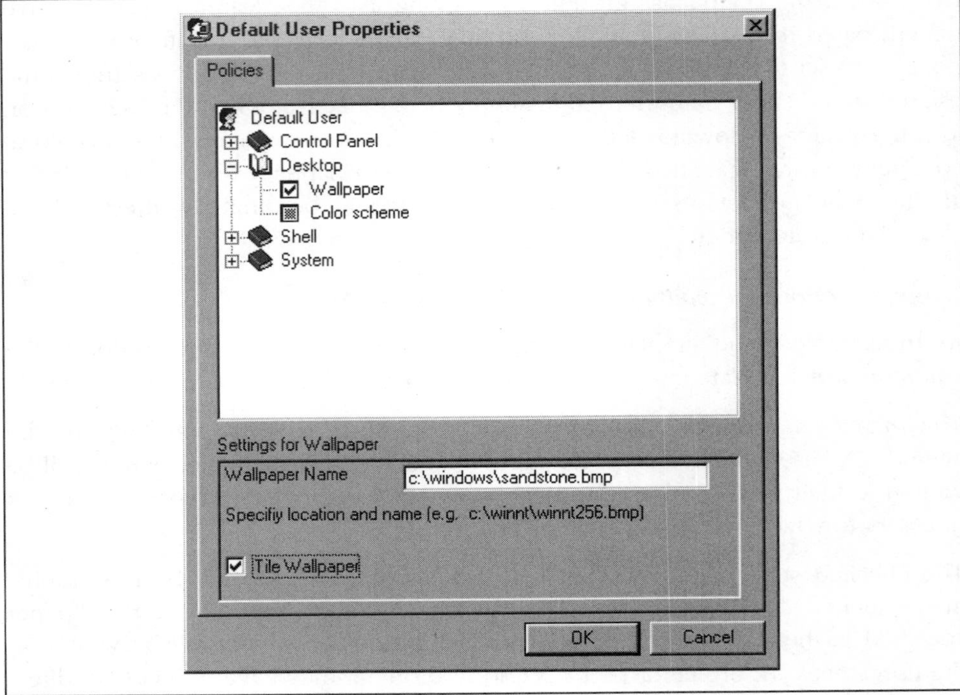

Figure 3-1. Wallpaper options with a checked setting

Let's begin with a few examples of how different option states for the same template setting can cause conflicts if a user is affected by more than one user or group policy.

Default User

If a Default User (DU) policy exists, it is applied to the registry first—even if the user has a specific user policy. If the DU has options that are either checked or cleared, and the matching option in a group or specific user policy is left grayed, unexpected results could occur. Figure 3-2, again using the *common.adm* template, illustrates the settings for two Shell options.

The Local User's profile (which can be the logged-on user's local or network *user.dat or ntuser.dat*) is first applied to the registry. Since all of the settings are cleared, no Shell restrictions are enforced. Next, the DU policy is applied to the registry. Two Shell restrictions are set to the checked position, enforcing the restriction. Specifically these are restrictions that remove the Run and Find commands from the Start menu. Finally, user Rachel's policy is applied to the registry. Since all of her settings are set to the grayed position, no changes are made to the registry. This leaves the DU's Shell restrictions active (see Figure 3-3).

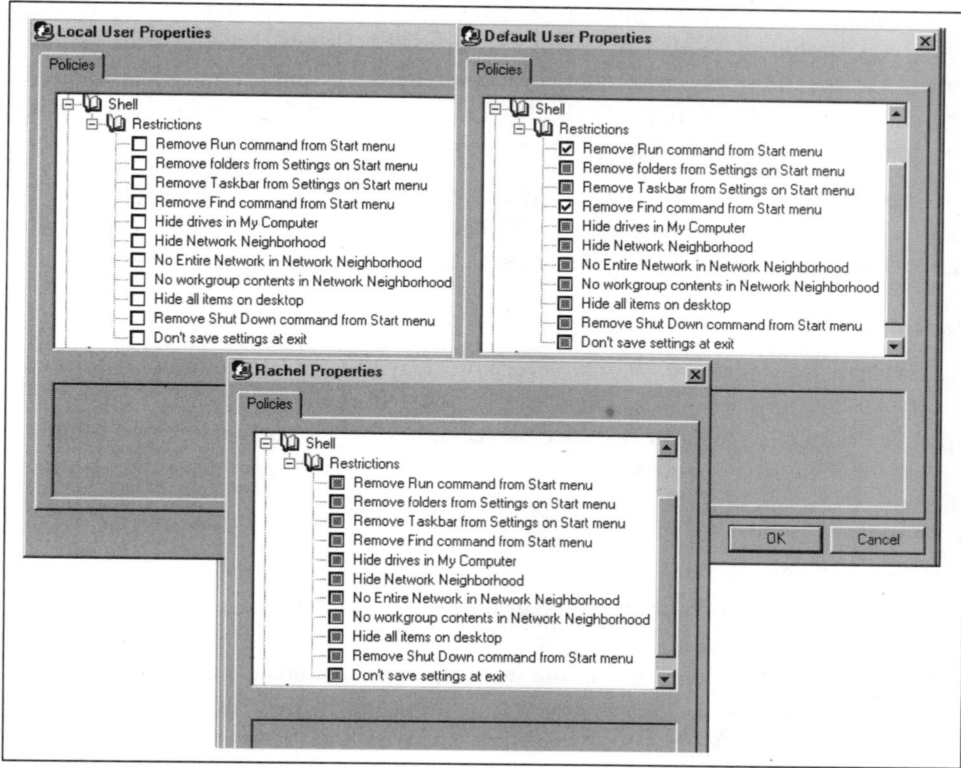

Figure 3-2. Conflicts and the Default User

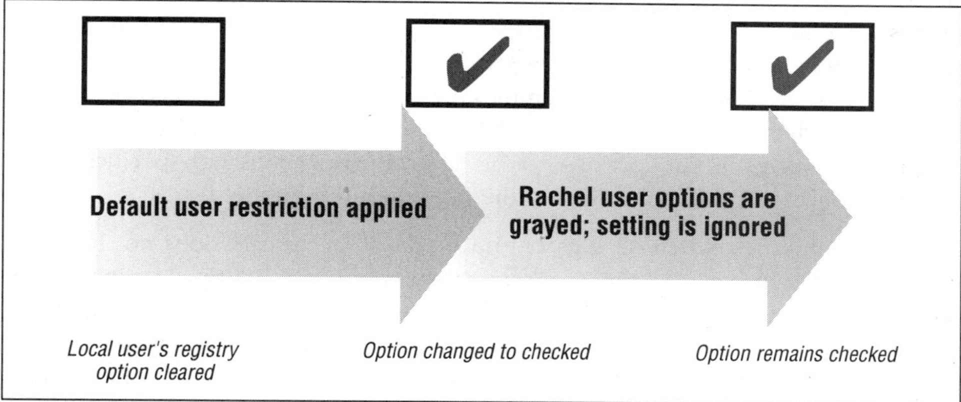

Figure 3-3. Default User and specific user-application order

The administrator, knowing that he had not made any restrictions active on the local workstation, may not be expecting this result.

If you have a DU policy, and desire a restriction to be inactive for a particular user, you should leave that template option in the cleared state. If user Rachel's policy had the "Remove run command" and "Remove find command" settings in the cleared position, then the DU's checked state would have been cleared when the specific user (Rachel) policy was applied.

The same problem would occur if a group rather then a user policy had matching settings in the grayed state and the DU had settings in the checked state. Again, the DU would be applied to the local user's registry before the group policy.

Default Computer

In the same way that the DU can overwrite grayed template options, so too can the Default Computer (DC). The DC policies are applied first, followed by any specific computer policy. If the specific computer policy contains grayed template options and the DC contains checked template options for corresponding settings, then the DC restrictions become active.

Multiple groups

If a user is a member of multiple groups, unexpected results can occur. Let's assume that Zachary is originally a member of the group Teachers. At a later date, some of the teachers need to be able to install applications on their workstations. A new group called Manager is created, with access to the Run command. If the DU had all restrictions in the checked position, the Shell restrictions for these two groups and the DU would appear as in Figure 3-4.

Group policies are applied in ascending order according to their priority. If the user is a member of multiple groups then the group allocated lowest priority will be applied first, followed by the other groups in ascending order. Group priority is established using Poledit. In the example in Figure 3-5, policies would be applied for GroupB, then, GroupA and finally for GroupC. GroupC would overwrite any conflicting policies in GroupA or GroupB. If group priority is not specifically set, as each group is created it is added to the bottom of the priority list.

Zachary reports that when he logs onto a workstation, he still does not have the Run command. In this case the Teachers group was created during the initial production of the policy file. Then at a later date the Managers group was created and added to the policy file. By default, the Managers group was saved to the bottom of the group priority list. The Teachers policy, with its higher group priority, took precedence over the Manager policy settings (Figure 3-6).

If your policy file contains a DU, a DC or multiple group policies, you must be aware of the potential for policy conflicts.

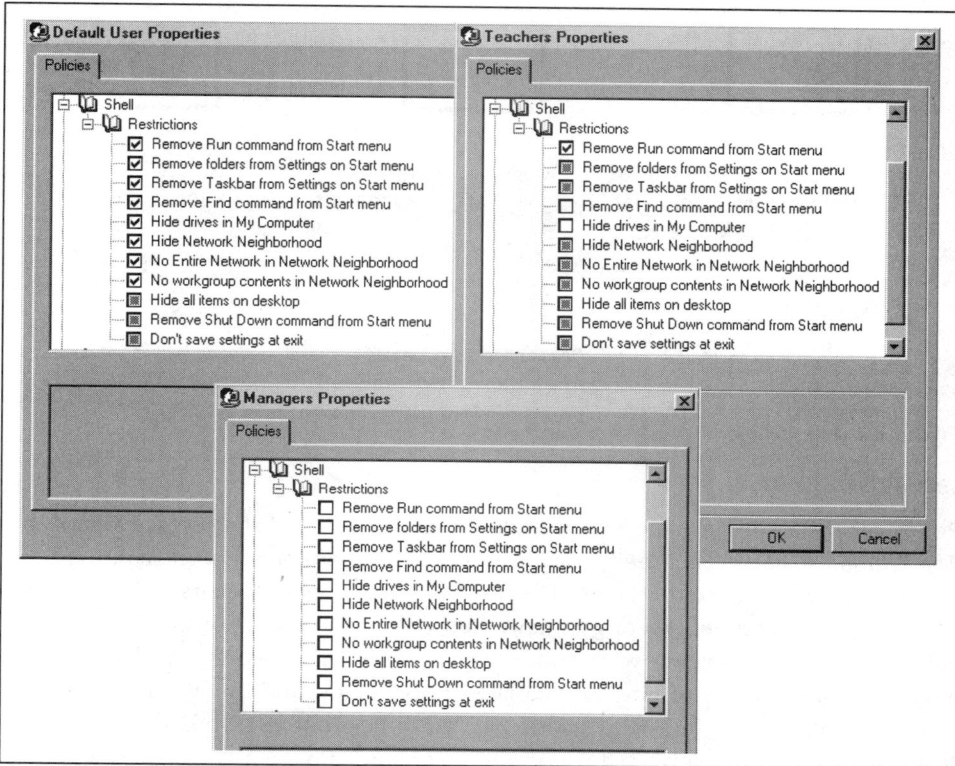

Figure 3-4. Conflicts and multiple groups

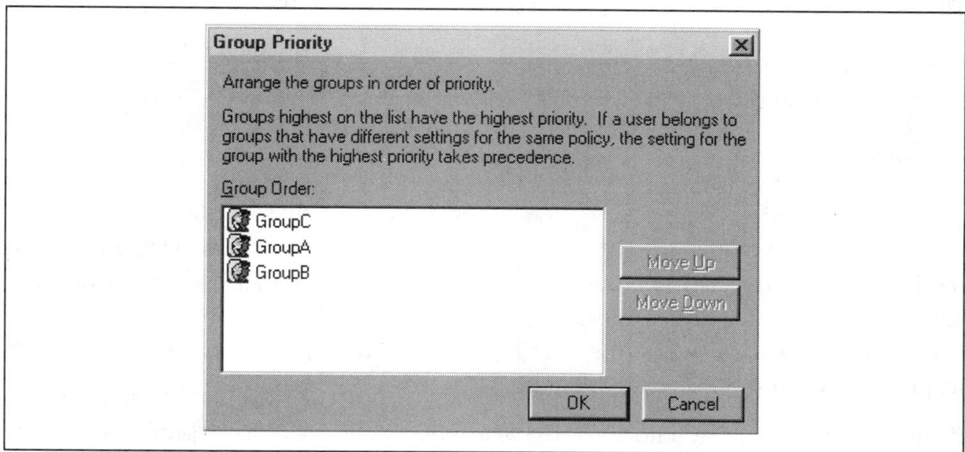

Figure 3-5. Setting group priority

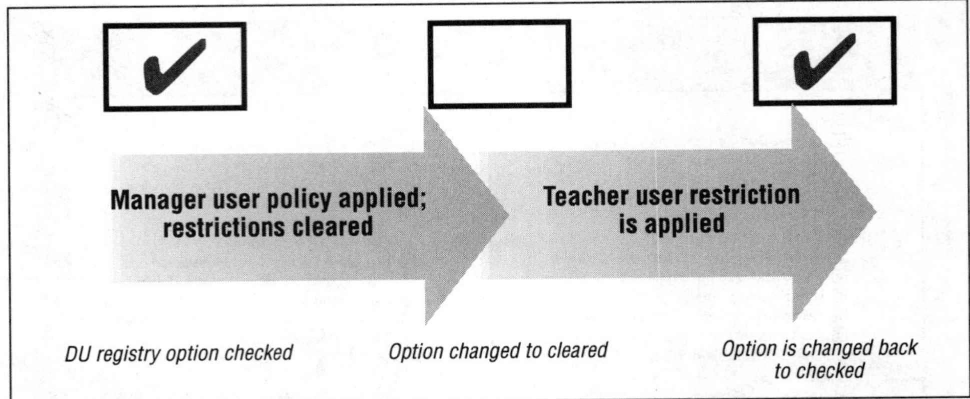

Figure 3-6. Group policy application order

Shared workstation

Policy conflicts happen when users share a communal workstation (see Chapter 1, *The Hidden Cost of Computers*, for a discussion on communal workstations). This is not often a recognized source of conflict, since a conflict occurs only if a number of separate conditions are met, and then only if the conditions occur in a specific order. The problems with conflicting policies on a shared workstation are traced to the presence of grayed template option states, and the absence of a user profile directory on the workstation. If the *C:\Windows\Profiles\User* (or *C:\WinNT\Profiles\User*) subdirectory on the local hard drive is unavailable when the user logs off, Windows will save the modified *user.dat* back to the default profile. This overwriting of the default profile is the root cause of the conflict.

Shared workstation conflicts seldom occur on Windows NT4 workstations, and are far more common on Windows 9x.

How does a user wind up without a local profile directory on which to save the modified *user.dat*? Two conditions must be met. First, either the user must not have previously used the workstation or the user's profile subdirectory must have been deleted. Second, when the user logged onto the workstation, she must have responded No to the message in Figure 3-7.

If the user responds by choosing No, she effectively prevents a profile subdirectory from being created on the local hard drive. In addition, since she apparently didn't intend on saving any settings, Windows does not copy her roaming profile from the network; instead, it uses the local default *user.dat*. When the user logs

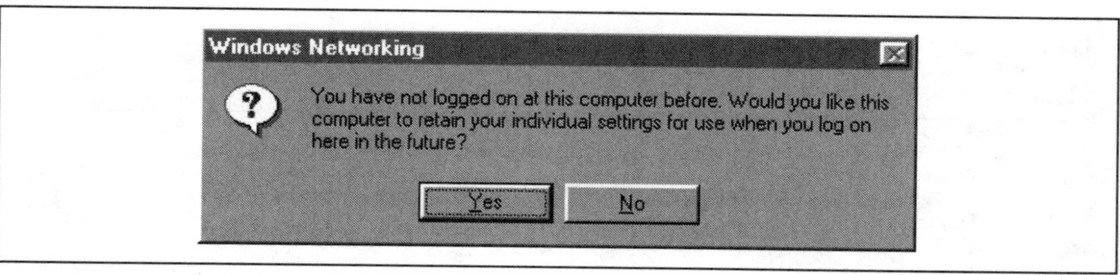

Figure 3-7. The save settings question

off, Windows saves the modified *user.dat* back to the main Windows directory. This then becomes the new local default profile.

Let's consider how this problem would present itself by looking at three users of a communal workstation who share one particular policy. Depending on the order in which they use the workstation after the policy file becomes active, a problem may or may not emerge.

Les, Rachel and Ivan share the same workstation. All three have specific user policies created with the *common.adm* template. By setting the template option to the cleared state, Les has been given access to the Run command. Rachel has that option grayed, and Ivan has been restricted from using the Run command by having that option checked. Figure 3-8 shows how each user's policy would appear in Poledit.

Let's assume that Ivan, whose user policy prevents him from using the Run command, logs onto the workstation for the first time. He receives the question asking, "Would you like this computer to retain your individual settings?" He chooses No, preventing the creation of the *C:\Windows\Profiles\Ivan* subdirectory. The default *user.dat* from the Windows root directory is loaded into the registry. His user policy is then downloaded and merged with the local registry. The resulting *user.dat* is then saved back to the Windows root directory. The default workstation profile, which had no restrictions, is now changed to disable the Run command (see Figure 3-9).

Now let's assume that Les logs onto the workstation in exactly the same way, answering No to retaining settings. Even though he loads the now modified *user.dat*, since his user policy specifies a cleared setting, Les will have access to the Run command. There would not appear to be any problem. Consequently, if only Les and Ivan used the workstation, a conflict would never be apparent.

The problem becomes evident when Rachel used that workstation. Depending on whether she logs on following Les or following Ivan, it may appear to the administrator that sometimes she has a Run command, while other times she does not.

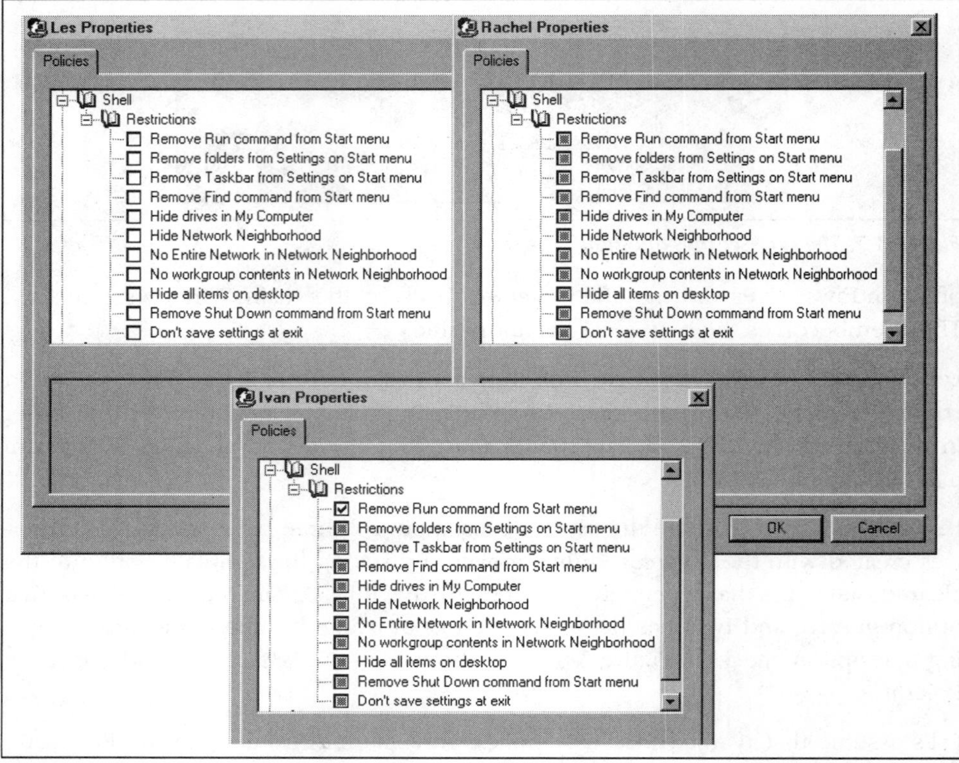

Figure 3-8. Communal workstation policy conflict

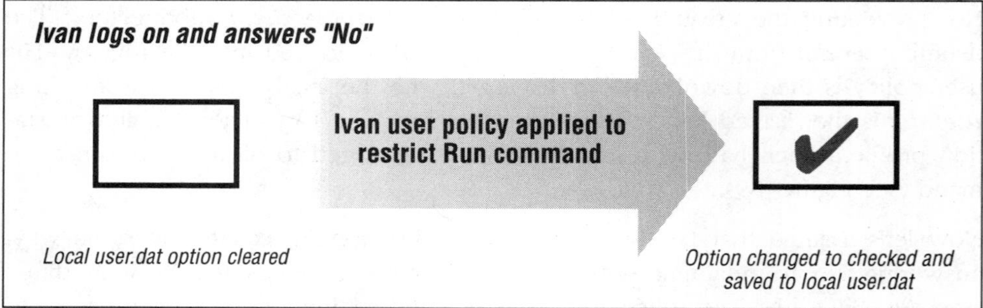

Figure 3-9. Communal workstation conflict—single user

Rachel *will not* have access to the Run command if she logs in following Ivan (see Figure 3-10).

However, Rachel *will* have a Run command if she logs in following Les (Figure 3-11).

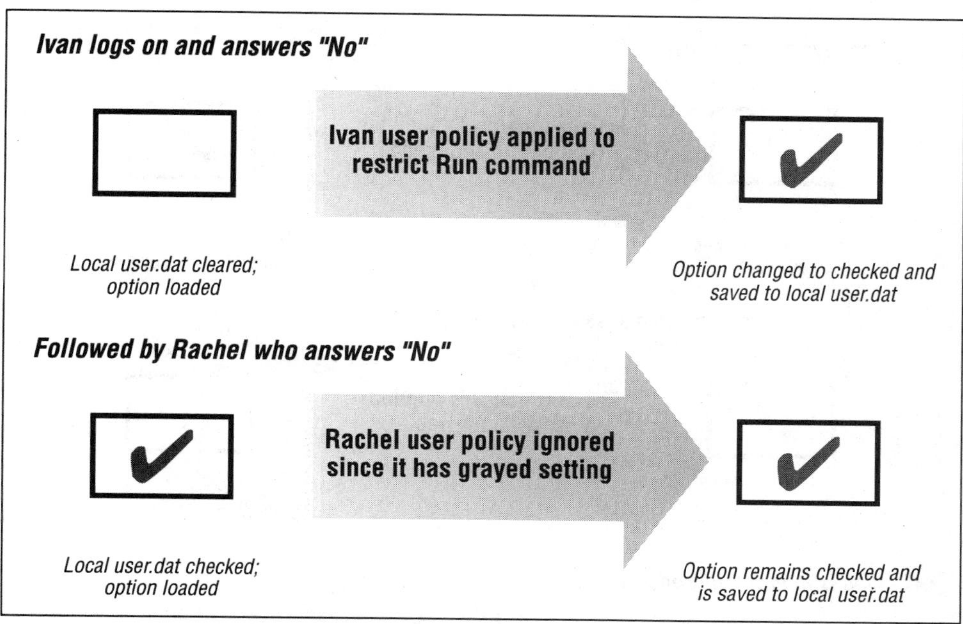

Figure 3-10. Communal workstation conflict—two users

A further complication will occur if Rachel *does* answer Yes to the question of retaining settings. In this case, if she logs on following Ivan the restriction that prevents the Run command will be saved to the *user.dat* in her network directory. Restricted access to the Run command will remain until her profile is specifically changed to remove the restriction (the grayed option setting is changed to cleared).

A conflict arising from a shared workstation can be avoided in one of four ways. One is by making sure that restrictions are either grayed for all users, or appropriately checked/cleared for all users. The second method is by making sure that all users answer Yes when asked if they would like to retain their settings. Answering Yes causes a specific profile subdirectory to be created on the local hard drive, and a network profile (if one exists) to be loaded. When the modified profile is saved, it is saved to the profile subdirectory and/or the network directory rather then overwriting the *user.dat* in the main Windows directory. However, being able to rely on users answering Yes to this question is dubious at best, so I wouldn't suggest depending on this method. The third technique is to create a batch file that edits the registry when the user logs on. This produces the same end result as would have occurred if the user had answered Yes. The fourth method uses the Microsoft Family Logon client. See Chapter 4 for more information on these possible solutions.

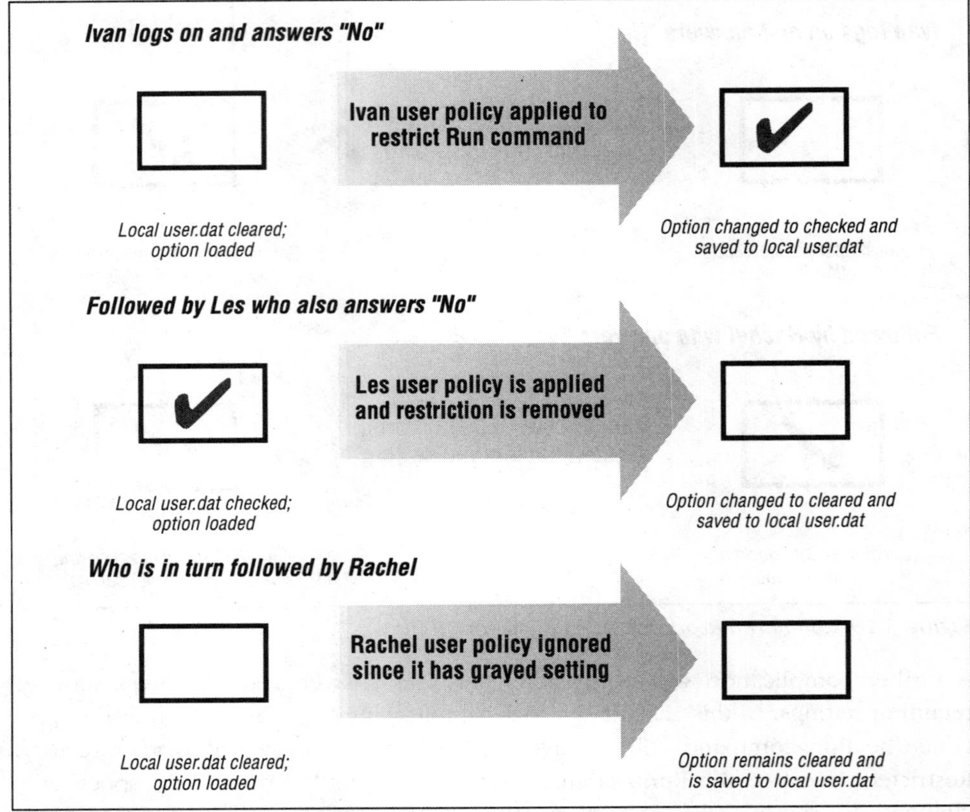

Figure 3-11. Communal workstation conflict—three users

Conflict Resolution Lists

If you still find unforeseen user or computer policies emerging, the following flowcharts and lists will aid you in tracking down the source of the policy conflict.

Conflict Resolution for User and Group Policies

The following list tracks the procedure (depicted in Figure 3-12) that is followed by Windows for editing a user's registry in the presence of user and group policies:

1. The user logs on to the network from a workstation with profiles and remote update enabled.
2. The most recent copy of the profile (*user.dat*), local or network version, is loaded into the registry.

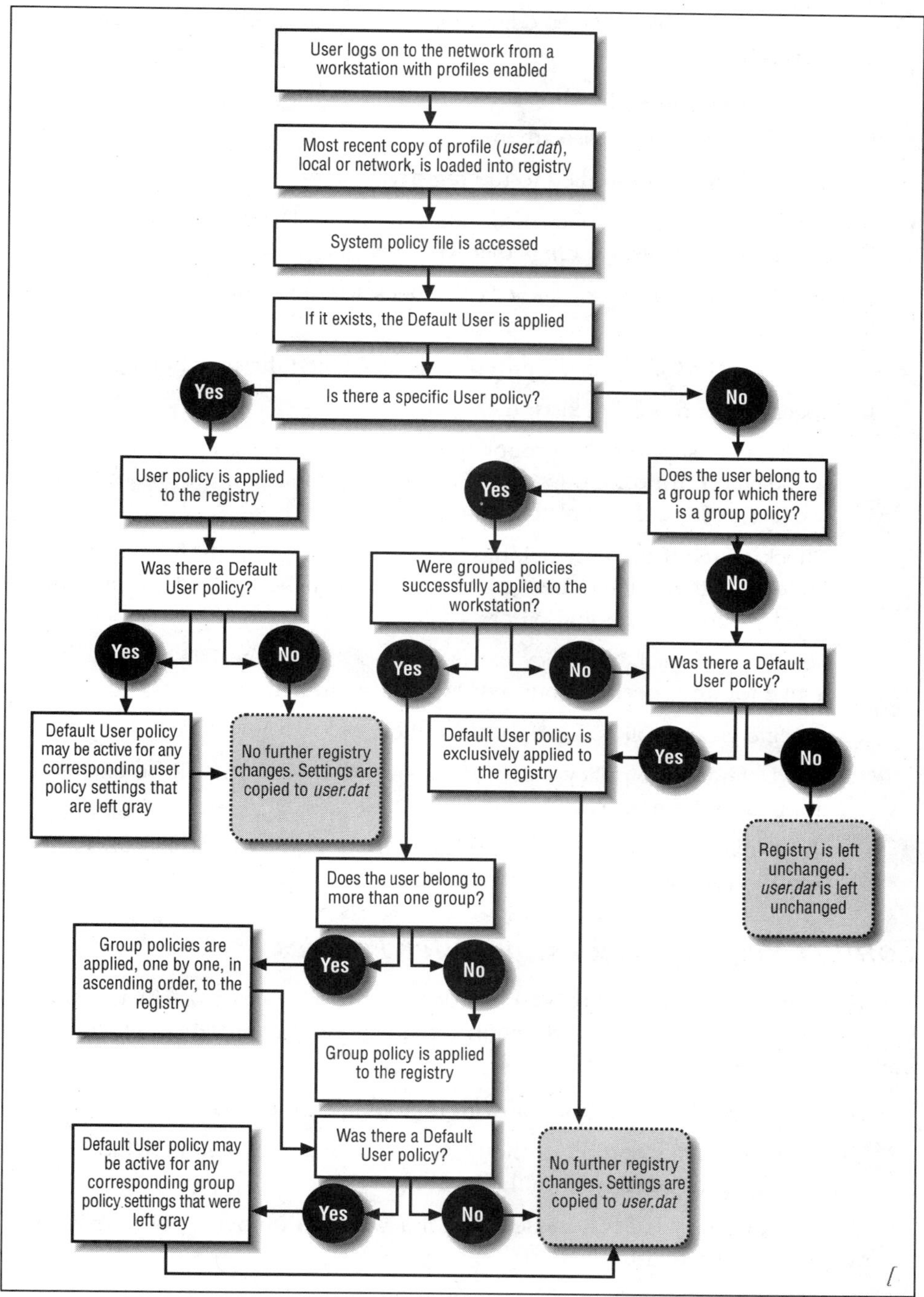

Figure 3-12. Conflict resolution for user policies

3. The system policy file is accessed, and if a Default User exists it is merged into the registry first.
4. Windows checks for a specific user policy.

   If a specific user policy exists, then:

   a. The user policy is applied to the registry.
   b. If the Default User policy also exists, then the DU settings will be active for any specific user settings that were left gray.

   If a specific user policy does *not* exist, check for any group policies to which the user belongs.
5. Windows checks for a specific group policy to which the user belongs.

   If a specific group policy exists, then:

   a. Verify that support for group policies was successfully installed on the workstation. If not, group policies will be ignored and the Default User, if it exists, will be the only active policy.
   b. Check to see if the user belongs to more than one group for which a policy exists. If he does, then group policies will be applied to the registry one by one in ascending order.
   c. See if a Default User policy exists; if it does, then the DU settings will be active for any specific group settings that were left gray.

   If a specific group policy does *not* exist, then:

   a. If a Default User policy exists, then those DU settings will be exclusively applied to the registry.
   b. If a Default User policy does *not* exist, the registry will be left unchanged, and the *user.dat* will remain unchanged.

Conflict Resolution for Computer Policies

The following list tracks the procedure (depicted in Figure 3-13) that is followed by Windows for editing a workstation's registry in the presence of computer policies:

1. The user logs onto a workstation with remote update enabled.
2. The local computer portion of the registry *system.dat* (*system* in Windows NT) is loaded into the registry from the local hard drive.
3. The system policy file is accessed, and if a Default Computer policy exists it is merged into the registry first.
4. Windows checks for a specific computer policy.

If a specific computer policy exists, then:

a. That computer policy is applied to the registry.

b. If the Default Computer policy also exists, then the DC settings will be active for any specific computer settings that were left gray.

If a specific computer policy does *not* exist, then:

a. If a Default Computer policy exists, those DC settings will be exclusively applied to the registry.

b. If a Default Computer policy does *not* exist, then the registry will be left unchanged, and the *system.dat (system)* will remain unchanged.

Case Studies

Hopefully when you reviewed your system you discovered that, with perhaps only a few modifications, you have all the platform requirements to fully use system policies. Now you are also aware of most of the possible conflicts, and are ready to deal with them. Your choices are wide open—perhaps a little *too* wide open. The next step is to start asking some specific questions to narrow down what sort of policies and restrictions you will need to use for your network. Do you want to restrict most users or only a few? Will you have group policies only or a mixture of groups and users? Is the risk of users hacking into your system low or high? Do you need desktop control (consistent desktops) or will the users be allowed to modify their desktops?

It's not an easy task to know where to begin, but reviewing the following case studies should give you an idea of how other administrators have approached this challenge. The case studies deal only with broad types of restrictions. To see exactly what settings and restrictions are available to you, examine Chapter 9; it reviews the most commonly used templates and their settings.

Case Study 1

Case study 1 is a public high school (this scenario could also apply to a public library or any other location with publicly accessed computers). The majority of computers in the school are communal. These communal workstations are in several different computer labs and are shared by both students and faculty. The network administrator has had problems with students changing the desktop and removing devices deliberately and accidentally. All users are frustrated with the high incidence of inoperative computers resulting from this tampering. The faculty is generally frustrated because each computer has a slightly different desktop, which creates difficulties in finding program icons when they move from one computer to another.

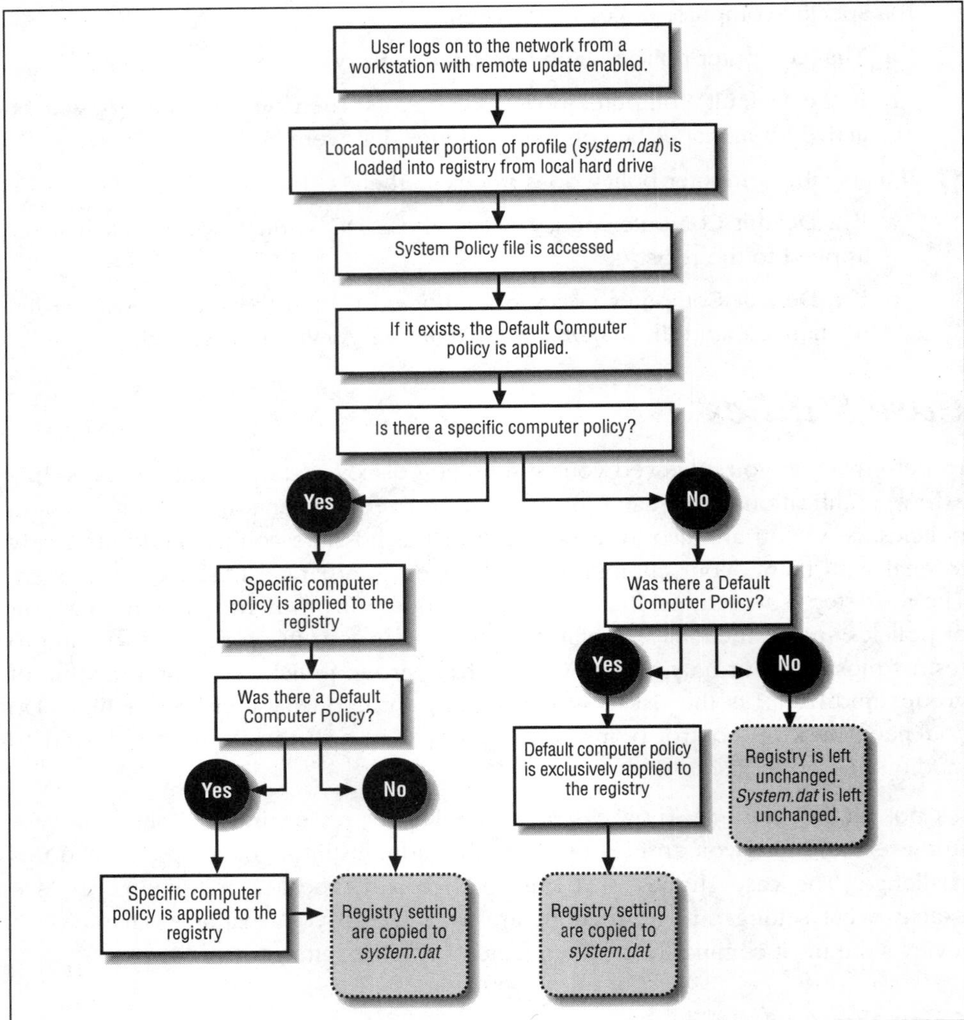

Figure 3-13. Conflict resolution for computer policies

Since a school may have thousands of students and faculty, the purpose is to keep the policy file as simple as possible by minimizing the number of user, group and computer policies. The maximum level of security is required for student users, with a more flexible policy for faculty users. Finally, some consistency in desktops from workstation to workstation is desired.

The motto of this case study could be "Lock it or lose it." The policy requirements for this case study are summarized in Table 3-6.

Table 3-6. Case Study 1

Requirement	Impact	Comment
Need for hack-risk prevention	High	The disposition of students makes the risk of malicious attempts to change the workstation configuration high.
Need for curiosity-risk prevention	High	The disposition of students and faculty makes the risk of accidental changes to the workstation configuration high.
Need for Default User	Yes	The majority of students can be restricted using the DU, eliminating the need for numerous individual user policies.
Need for user policies	Yes	For the Admin user, as well as department heads who are required to do some network troubleshooting.
Need for group policies	Yes	Most of the faculty can be given more relaxed restrictions than the DU, hence a Faculty group may be added. A Student group is also possible, rather than using the DU.
Need for computer policies	Maybe	Since computers are separated into labs, it would be possible to make computer policies, that affect only the computers in Lab 1, while computers in Labs 2 and 3 are unaffected.
Need for Default Computer	Yes	A DC should be set up to configure basic computer settings, such as disabling password caching and setting a preferred server (see Chapter 4 for more information).

The DU could cause conflicts for user or group policies from overlapping settings that are set to the grayed state. For example, if you wanted to allow UserA to customize her own wallpaper by setting it to the grayed position, but had the DU set with a specific wallpaper graphic, UserA will end up with the DU's graphic. Shared workstation conflicts can appear among users of the same workstation. The Microsoft Family Logon would not be useful, as each user is not assigned a specific workstation but may roam among many different computers. Finally, the user of any workstation with user profiles and remote update enabled could be unexpectedly affected by the DC or DU policies.

Case Study 2

Case study 2 is a newspaper office with several departments and city locations. Many of the computers are communal since employees are shift workers and share computers. There have been a few incidents with curious users changing device settings. Also, the network administrator has had problems relating to existing versions of the word processing program. Employees who share documents are saving a document in several different file formats. Telephone helpdesk support is difficult since each person has a different desktop and helpdesk personnel cannot easily direct the user to a specific program or shortcut.

In addition to setting minimal security, such as locking Control Panel applets, the purpose is to create uniformity across departments. This can be achieved by using consistent desktops, as well as computer policies to regulate file save formats, MS NetMeeting home pages, or network paths for Windows setup files. Users may be permitted some flexibility with settings such as wallpaper. In the past the network administrator may have used mandatory profiles to achieve some of this customization. However, as discussed in Chapter 2, system policies allow more flexibility and control and are now preferred.

The motto of this business could be "Replace mandatory profiles and ease telephone helpdesk woes." If mandatory profiles are used, replacing them would be practical since system policies provide much more flexibility. The policy requirements for this case study are summarized in Table 3-7.

Table 3-7. Case Study 2

Requirement	Risk	Comment
Hack risk	Low	The disposition of these long-time employees makes the risk of malicious attempts to change the workstation configuration low.
Curiosity risk	Low–medium	The disposition of these employees makes the risk of accidental attempts to change the workstation configuration low to medium.
Need for Default User	No	The majority of employees can be restricted using groups. Removing the DU removes one possible source of conflict for group policies.
Need for user policies	Yes	Minimal Admin user inclusion is recommended.
Need for group policies	Yes	To keep policies consistent, each department can be put into a group with its own policy settings.
Need for computer policies	Yes	Computer policies can be used to set such things as clipart gallery locations, default save-to formats, Microsoft NetMeeting home pages.
Need for Default Computer	Maybe	A DC could be set up to install basic computer settings, such as disabling password caching and setting a preferred server for the computers that do not have a specific computer policy.

Conflicts can crop up with users who are members of more than one group. In addition, the DC causes conflicts for specific computer policies from overlapping settings that are set to the grayed position. Shared workstation conflicts may occur if users from one departmental group use a workstation from another departmental group. However, since there are only a few users per workstation, using the Microsoft Family Logon may help prevent the shared workstation conflicts. See Chapter 4 for more information.

Case Study 3

Case study 3 is a business with a school/work co-op. Only a few of the computers are communal, with the majority being single-user workstations. The established employees are highly computer literate and regularly customize their workstations. The network administrator may have had problems with the transient workers in the co-op program changing settings, or he may simply be uneasy with a stranger using the workstation.

The purpose is to create a policy file that will affect only the transient workers while leaving the other employees completely unrestricted. In addition, the maximum level of security is desired for the co-op workers.

The motto of this business could be "Caution is prudent." The policy requirements for this case study are summarized in Table 3-8.

Table 3-8. Case Study 3

Requirement	Risk	Comment
Hack risk	High	Since the co-op workers are an unknown element, it is safest to assume a high risk.
Curiosity risk	High	Even though the curiosity risk from the permanent employees has been low, the risk from the co-op workers is unknown. Thus it is safest to assume a high risk.
Need for Default User	No	There is no need for restrictions for the permanent employees; the DU can be deleted.
Need for user policies	Yes	Minimal Admin user and specific user logons inclusion for the co-op workers is recommended.
Need for group policies	No	There is no need for restrictions for the permanent employees.
Need for computer policies	Maybe	A specific computer policy for those workstations used by the co-op workers may be desirable to set network directory paths.
Need for Default Computer	No	There is no desire for restrictions or settings for the majority of employees; the DC can be deleted.

Since there are no DU or DC policies, conflicts are minimized. However, shared workstation conflicts can appear among the co-op users, unless they share a "Guest" logon. In this case, using the Microsoft Family Logon with a single Guest user account would help prevent shared workstation conflicts. To completely prevent the permanent employees from becoming affected by the policy file, each user's workstation should have remote update turned off (set to the cleared state; see Chapter 4 for more information).

Case Study 4

Case study 4 is a small business with a limited number of employees. None of the workstations are communal, and all of the users are permanent employees. The network administrator may have had a few curious people changing system settings, but no major hacking problems.

The purpose is to create a nonintrusive policy that will restrict all workers from specific system areas while still allowing full desktop customization.

The motto of this business could be "You don't need to look there." The policy requirements for this case study are summarized in Table 3-9.

Table 3-9. Case Study 4

Requirement	Risk	Comment
Hack risk	Low	None of the workers are apt to deliberately destroy their workstation.
Curiosity risk	Medium	The curiosity risk from the employees has been causing some problems, so it can be classified as medium.
Need for Default User	Yes	It is desirable to restrict all employees from some system areas.
Need for user policies	Yes	Minimal Admin user inclusion is recommended.
Need for group policies	No	There are no groups set up on the network.
Need for specific computer policies	No	Workstations are not organized into any identifiable groups.
Need for Default Computer	Yes	Basic computer settings such as disabling password caching are desired.

Conflicts are unlikely since only DU and DC policies are used, and there are no shared workstations. Problems with the downloading of the policy file or user policies may arise for workstations that have not had either remote update or user profiles enabled.

Worksheet for Your Own Organization

The following worksheets (Figures 3-10 and 3-11) can be used to gather the necessary information prior to creating your own policy file. The "Comment" field has been left blank so that you may include your own notes in this section. Chapter 4 contains detailed information about creating the policy file, while Chapter 9 reviews the settings for the most commonly available templates. You may wish to read both of these sections before returning to these worksheets.

Table 3-10. Policy Worksheet A

Requirement	Impact	Comment
Hack risk Your hack risk is determined by such factors as age (seniors are less likely to be a hack risk than teenagers) and transient quality of users. A transient user is likely to be untraceable after an attack, and may likely feel invulnerable.	Low, medium or high	
Curiosity risk The risk can be determined by such factors as age and computer "comfortability": users more comfortable with computers are likely to attempt more customization.	Low, medium or high	
Need for Default User Do you want to easily restrict most users? Will most be requiring the same restrictions?	Yes or No	
Need for user policies You need at least one user policy: the Admin user. In addition, you may only want to restrict a few users or exempt others from group/DU policies.	Yes	
Need for group policies This is the policy to use if you have numerous users that require a few different policies. It is good for regulating desktops among members of a departmental group. Not universally supported by all network platforms, however.	Yes or No	
Need for computer policies Do you want to enable different settings for groups of computers, perhaps by location or use?	Yes or No	
Need for Default Computer At minimum, the DC is used to set the domain name or preferred server, and to enable remote update.	Yes or No	
Possible conflicts These may arise if you have a DU, DC, users that are members of multiple groups, or shared workstations.	Yes or No	

Table 3-11. Policy Worksheet B

Requirements	Impact	Comment
Groups List your group names. Order them according to the group requiring the least restrictions to the group requiring the most restrictions. List any users that should be exempt from the group policy. Also list these people under the Users list. (List the full NDS group name for groups on any NetWare servers using NDS.)	Group	Exempt user(s)
	Highest priority (fewest restrictions)	
	Lowest priority (greatest restrictions)	
Users List the users who will not be included in the Default User policy or who need to be exempt from a group policy. Always include an Admin user.	User Name	Does user share a workstation?
	Admin	Yes
Computers List the computers that require their own specific computer policy separate from the default computer policy.		

Preparing Your Users

You have prepared your network, but don't forget to prepare your users. Simply rolling out policies without some clarification will strike many people as draconian. Users in the habit of changing their wallpaper and icons will not look favorably upon a network administrator who snatches that feature away without some sort of justification. What you tell your users may depend on which case study most closely resembles your workplace. The following are suggestions only; use your own judgment regarding what is most appropriate in your situation.

Case Study 1

This involves the highest level of security, and thus the most restrictions. You may not have an obligation to explain your security to temporary users (such as public library users). However if these users are students, then a simple explanation may be best. Explain that they do not "own" the computer, but that it is there for the use of all students and staff. Mention how, due to the few who would cause intentional damage, you are forced to protect all of the workstations. For the less transient users (perhaps teachers or library employees), you could give examples of how often you had to restore the operating system, or how many hours a week you were spending fixing malicious attacks on the workstation. Point out how annoying it is for them to have different desktops on each PC, how hard it can be to find programs when the shortcut is missing, or how frustrating it is to go to use a workstation only to find it inoperative. Highlight the ease of use that will come with consistent desktops, how they will be able to go to any computer and feel comfortable.

Case Study 2

If you are simply replacing mandatory profiles with policies, your users will not need much preparation. They will be used to a low level of customization and not notice much change with system policies. If, however, you are just beginning to implement policy-based security, give them some preparation. Since your users are most likely business people, a quick discussion of TCO (see Chapter 1) will fit in nicely here. Highlight the time wasted by technicians fixing user-induced problems. Unless you want a lot of hostile stares, make sure that you always emphasize that the problems are caused more by curiosity than any malicious attempt to damage the system. Finally, tell them how much more rapidly the helpdesk should be able to respond to their problems now that user-induced problems have been reduced. If you have telephone helpdesk support, mention that the helpdesk people will be more efficient since they will know exactly what the desktop will look like for each department, making it quicker to guide users through troubleshooting.

Case Study 3

Fortunately for you, the users who will be working within a secure policy are likely grateful to be able to use the system at all. If they ask, a simple explanation of protecting the system from malicious hacker attacks should suffice. The permanent employees should be warned that the communal workstations are secured, in case they try to use those systems.

Case Study 4

With this minimal level of security, most of your users will likely not even realize that it exists. You are still allowing full customization of the desktop, but restricting Control Panel utilities—an area most users do not use. Sometimes in this case it is easiest to simply warn the users that you are using a new network utility, and for them to let you know if they experience any problems.

Acceptable-Use Policy

In any organization in which computers are widely used, consideration should be given to the implementation of an acceptable use policy. The use of such a policy ensures that each user is forewarned of the expectations of administration, as well as the penalties if the policy is violated. The acceptable use policy outlines the rules that must be abided by to maintain access to the network. In many locations, it is impossible to punish an offender without having first warned them that what they were attempting was prohibited. A sample acceptable use policy can be found in Appendix A. Although it is tailored to schools, it could easily be adapted to any organizational situation.

Summary

The key to successful use of system policies is preparation. Knowing your own system's limitations will prevent disappointment when you try to implement an unsupported policy type, particularly group policies, which are less widely supported by various network platforms than user and computer policies.

Policy conflicts are possibly the most frequent cause of an administrator abandoning the use of system policies. Understanding two things can eliminate this frustration: first, the three policy template option states and, second, the most common causes of policy conflicts—the Default User, the Default Computer, users belonging to multiple groups and shared workstations. Armed with knowledge of these causes, it is possible for an administrator to avoid these conflicts, or at least to deal with them quickly.

How other administrators have employed system policies was reviewed through four case studies. These case studies can be used as a model for your own organization when filling out the planning worksheets provided. Finally, the topic of user preparation was discussed with suggestions on the best way to present the policy change to users.

Chapter 4 moves on to the heart of the matter, the installation of the System Policy Editor and the specifics on creating a policy file.

4

Building the Policy File

Creating a policy file should not be a hit-or-miss procedure. Adding a user here, a group there, and editing the Default User off and on in between; to do so is to invite certain failure. Rather, if the file is created in a methodical manner, always with possible conflicts in mind, you will end up with a predictable policy file and a secure workstation. It's not as exciting, but it will save you from the frustration of an unreliable policy.

This chapter covers the installation of the System Policy Editor and the procedure for enabling remote registry editing and group policy support. Detailed instructions are given for creating and fully testing a sample Windows 9x policy file. Some final tips are included for techniques to add additional templates, customize the sample policy file, remove the "Do you want to save your settings" nag, and automate workstation setup using REG files in the logon script.

Installing the System Policy Editor

The System Policy Editor (SPE) should be installed only on the administrator's computer, and not on any workstation that will have restrictions imposed. The SPE is used only to create and edit the policy file, and so is not required to properly implement the policies.

To install the SPE on a Windows 9x workstation, complete the following steps.

1. In the Control Panel, open the Add/Remove Programs applet.
2. Select the Windows Setup tab. Since System Policy Editor is not on any of these lists, choose the Have Disk button.
3. In the window headed "Copy manufacturer's file from," type in the location of the *poledit.exe* program and *poledit.inf* file. See Chapter 3, *Preparation and Planning*, for the suggested version of the SPE.

4. Select the System Policy Editor checkbox. If you would like to use your workstation to test group policies, check this box as well. Then select the Install button (see more on installing group policies later in this chapter).
5. Finally, select OK to exit Add/Remove Programs.

This procedure will copy the program *poledit.exe* into your main *\Windows* directory and the *admin.adm* and *common.adm* templates into the *\Inf* subdirectory. It also adds the registry key HKCU\Software\Microsoft\Windows\CurrentVersion\Applets\PolEdit, which contains the list of the most recently opened policy files, as well as the most recently opened templates. Finally it adds a shortcut to the SPE in the Start menu under Programs → Accessories → System Tools.

The SPE is installed by default on Windows NT4 and Windows 2000 servers under Start → Programs → Administrative Tools → System Policy Editor. To install the SPE on a Windows NT workstation run *setup.bat* located on the Windows NT4 CD-ROM in the *\clients\svrtools\winnt* directory.

Is This Necessary?

No, it is not necessary to go through this procedure to successfully use the SPE on any given workstation. It is possible to simply run the SPE from a floppy disk containing the following files:

- *poledit.exe*
- *poledit.hlp*
- *common.adm*
- *winnt.adm* (if you are using an NT workstation)
- *windows.adm* or *admin.adm* (if you are using a Windows 9x workstation)
- Any other templates (**.adm*) you would like to use

Remote Registry Editing

The SPE can be used to remotely edit the registry of another workstation on the network. Generally remote registry editing is used to fix user-induced problems or to make systemwide changes such as the network location of Word templates. However, remote registry editing has limitations that are not inherent in policy files, and in my opinion using the SPE to remotely edit a registry has limited (if any) advantages to an organization that uses a policy file. You can edit a registry only one workstation at a time, and then only if the computer is on and the user is logged onto the network. It is simply more convenient and requires much less time to set up a user or computer policy that includes the changes you wish to make. Policies can be created and edited even without the users being logged on, and changes can be made for entire groups rather than for only individual users. Finally, remote registry editing requires that each workstation have a unique computer name. If you have chosen one of the case studies from Chapter 3 that suggested the use of computer policies for a group of workstations, you will not be able to use remote registry editing. In this case a choice would have to be made between group computer names (Windows 9x workstations with a common computer name) and remote registry editing, which requires a unique computer name for each workstation. However, since it is a capability of the SPE program (as well as the Registry Editor, System Monitor and Net Watcher programs), and may be useful for organizations that do not want to use a policy file, I will review the procedure for enabling remote registry editing.

Playing It Safe—Back up Your Registry

This chapter deals with procedures that edit the registry. Keep in mind that with computers, it is best to assume that, one way or another, something is likely to go wrong. So before continuing, you should back up the registry files. For Windows NT workstations you can use *regback.exe* or *ntbackup.exe;* both have options to back up the local registry. To make registry backups on a Windows 95 workstation you can use the utility *cfgback.exe* (found on the Windows 95 CD-ROM), which allows you to make up to nine compressed copies. On a Windows 98 workstation you can use *scanregw.exe* or *msbackup.exe.* Finally, you can use the good old DOS method for any Windows 9x workstation. Restart the workstation in DOS mode (available as a choice in the Shutdown window), change to the Windows root directory and use the Attrib command to remove the system, hidden and read-only attributes from the *user.dat* and *system.dat* registry files:

```
ATTRIB -s -h -r user.dat
ATTRIB -s -h -r system.dat
```

Then use the Copy command to copy these files to a backup version:

```
COPY user.dat user.bak
COPY system.dat system.bak
```

Finally, restore the original attributes to the files before restarting the workstation:

```
ATTRIB +s +h +r user.dat
ATTRIB +s +h +r system.dat
```

If you want to back up the entire registry to a very large, single file, you can use the following DOS command:

```
REGEDIT /e registry.txt – to export the registry to a file
REGEDIT /c registry.txt – to copy the file into the registry
```

Since the System Policy Editor itself works through local file I/O, and is not RPC (remote procedure call) enabled, an application with RPC support must be installed on both the administrator and user workstations. This application is the Remote Registry Service (RRS), and it enables communication between two computers across the network. Windows NT workstations support remote registry editing by default, however Windows 9x workstations require the installation of an RRS. In addition to the RRS itself, there are several other settings that are required for Windows 9x to successfully edit a remote registry (see Table 4-1). All of these settings are enabled by default on a Windows NT workstation, with the possible exception of defined remote administrators if the workstation is not a member of an NT domain. The remote administrator list must be manually enabled if it does not already exist.

Table 4-1. Windows 9x Requirements for Remote Registry Editing

Administrator's Workstation	Remote User's Workstation
User-level security must be enabled. Microsoft remote registry services must be installed. A common network protocol such as IPX, TCP/IP, or NetBEUI must be installed.	File sharing must be allowed. User-level security must be enabled. Remote administrators must be defined. Microsoft remote registry services must be installed. A common network protocol such as IPX, TCP/IP or NetBEUI must be installed.

Allowing File Sharing on Windows 9x

Even if you don't intend to share local files or directories with other users, it is necessary to enable file sharing on the remote workstation. Remote registry editing is not dependent on file sharing per se, but when remote administration is enabled on a workstation, several hidden shared directories are created. These are:

ADMIN$
: Gives administrators access to the file system, which includes the registry. In Windows NT this resolves to the *\winnt* system directory.

C$
: Provides access to the root of the C drive; if other drives are available they will also have a hidden share designated as X$ where X is the drive letter.

IPC$
: Provides an interprocess communication (IPC) channel between the workstation and the administrator's computer.

File sharing is enabled using the Network applet in the Control Panel, under the Configuration tab. Selecting the Print and File Sharing button will install the protocol *File and Printer Sharing for MS Networks.* For NetWare networks, you should add the protocol *MS File and Printer Sharing for NetWare Networks.* File sharing is enabled by default on Windows NT workstations.

If you have enabled remote registry editing on any of the workstations, make sure that you do *not* disable file sharing in your user or group policies when you create your policy file.

Enabling User-Level Security on Windows 9x

Begin by opening the Network applet in the Control Panel. Choose the Access Control tab shown in Figure 4-1.

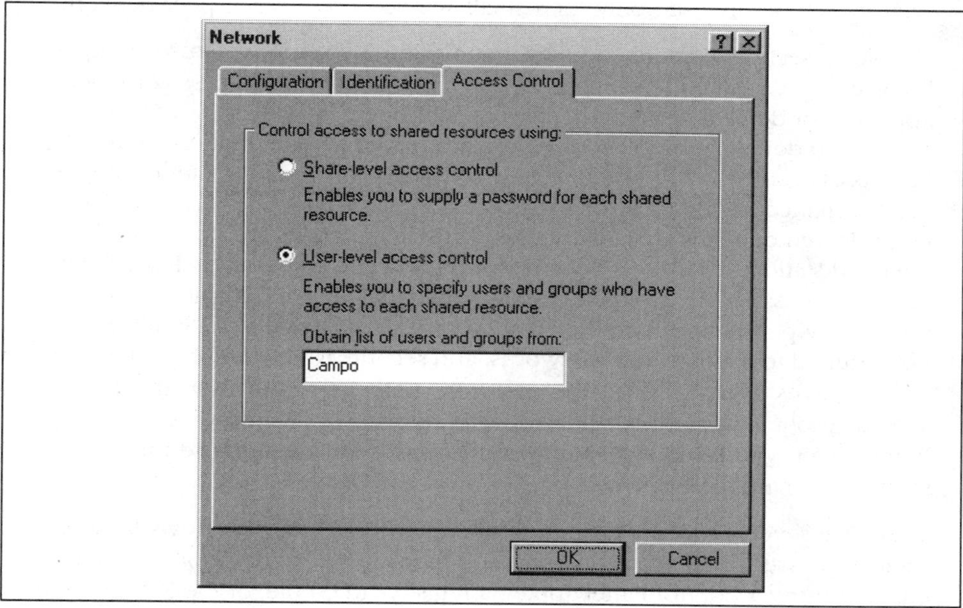

Figure 4-1. Enabling user-level access control

The name of a computer or domain, which is typed into the edit box under "Obtain list of users or groups from," is referred to as the authenticator. When you enter a name, *Campo* in the example, you will be asked to select the authenticator type from one of two options, either a Windows NT domain or Windows NT server. Choose Windows NT domain and type the name of your NT domain or Novell NetWare server as the authenticator. If you chose to use another NT server, such as an NT4 member server or an NT workstation, you will not get a complete list of users to add to the administrators list since the user list is taken from the authenticator's local user database.

After entering the authenticator name, select the OK button. You will now be prompted to reboot the workstation.

Share-Level Versus User-Level Security

When you want to share local resources, such as files on your hard drive or perhaps access to your printer over a network, you have two security options: *share-level* and *user-level* security.

Share-level security is the simplest type of security. Passwords are assigned to shared resources, also known as password-protected shares. User security information is stored on the local workstation, and all users providing the correct password will gain the same level of access to the resource. A password can be set for only one of two levels of access: full or read-only. Share-level security is typically used only for a small Windows 9x peer-to-peer network.

User-level security is more complex, but also far more robust. A user's request for access to a shared resource is not based solely on a password but is approved or denied via an authenticator, which can be a Windows NT or Windows 2000 domain controller or a NetWare server running bindery emulation. File access can be set to any one or a combination of read, write, create, list, delete, change attributes or change access rights. Although the user information is stored on the authenticator, the user's access rights are stored locally on the workstation. User-level security provides the ability to assign separate access permissions to groups or users, unlike share-level security, which can assign only permissions based on resources. The workstation's administrator is not required to manage any passwords, and security is not compromised when a user leaves a group since the password belongs to the user and not the shared resource. A network utilizing a Windows NT, Windows 2000 or NetWare server with Windows 9x or Windows NT clients would use this level of security to share local resources.

There are several ways to enable user-level security on a Windows 9x workstation (it is enabled by default on a Windows NT workstation). It can be enabled using a Control Panel applet, a registry (REG) file, or the SPE through the use of a computer policy.

If you previously had share level access enabled, changing the access control level will cancel any specific shared directories. These will need to be redefined after the workstation reboots.

After the workstation reboots, a new tab called Remote Administration (see Figure 4-2) will be available in the Passwords applet of the Control Panel. This tab is not available until user-level security has been enabled.

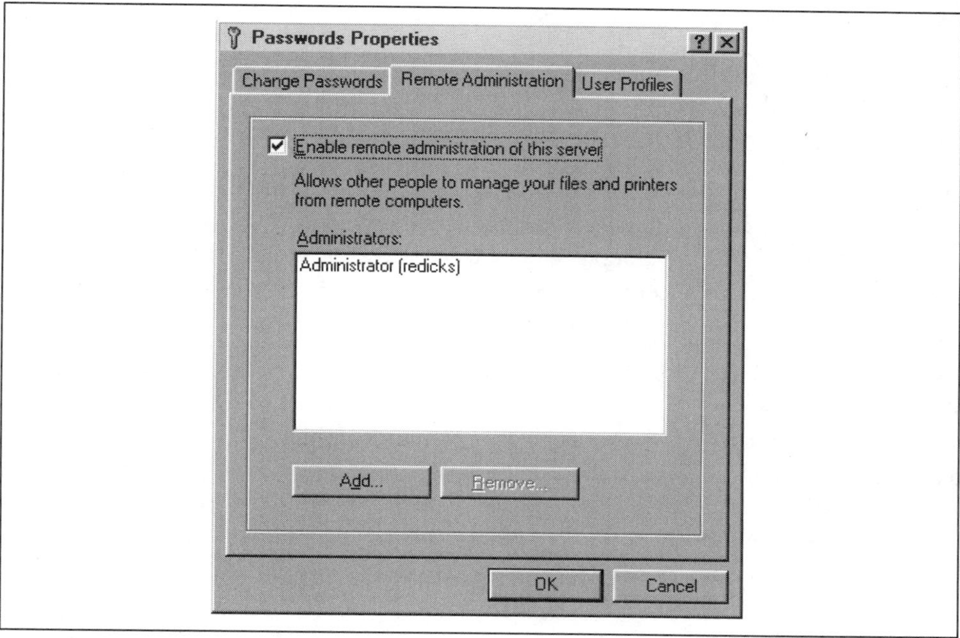

Figure 4-2. Adding administrators to the remote administration list

It is now possible to enable or disable remote administration of the server (in reality the local workstation) and to add additional administrators. By default, remote administration will have been enabled for the following groups:

Group	Administrator
Windows NT network	Domain Administrator group
Novell NetWare 3x network	Supervisor account
Novell NetWare 4x network	Administrator account

Installing the Windows 9x Remote Registry Service

The installation files for this service are in the *admin\nettools\remotreg* directory of the Windows 95 CD-ROM and the *tools\reskit\netadmin\remotreg* directory of the Windows 98 CD-ROM. To install the remote registry service:

1. Open the Network applet in the Control Panel and select Add.
2. The "Select Network Component Type" box appears. Select Service, and then select the Add button.
3. The "Select Network Service" box appears. Select the Have Disk button, and type the appropriate drive letter and directory path in the edit box that appears.

4. Select "Microsoft Remote Registry" in the Models box, and then click OK.

You will now be prompted to reboot the workstation.

Connecting to a Remote Registry

Once you have all the components installed on the remote and administrator workstations, you can try remotely editing a registry. Make sure that your administrator workstation and the remote workstation share the same OS. In other words, you cannot use Poledit to edit a remote Windows NT registry using a Windows 9x workstation due to the differences in registry structure between the two systems.

Open the SPE, select File → Connect. You will see a dialog box labeled Connect. Type the name of the computer you would like to connect to just as it appears on the Identification tab of the Control Panel Network applet. You can use the UNC name if there is more than one domain (such as *Campo\remotecomputer*), then select OK. The SPE titlebar will now read "System Policy Editor—Remote Registry." Note that most changes made to the registry will require the remote workstation to be rebooted before they take effect.

Creating a Policy File for a Windows 9x Workstation

I will create a sample policy file, based on the school of Case Study 1 in Chapter 3, *Preparation and Planning*. For this example I will concentrate on Windows 9x workstations, since Windows 9x requires a higher level of security than a Windows NT workstation. The template used will be the *admin.adm* template, which is available on the Windows 95 Resource Kit CD-ROM. This template can also be used to create a policy file for Windows 98 workstations, but not for NT workstations. The template options set for each policy is only briefly described here, but are examined in detail in Chapter 9, *The Policy Templates*, along with other available templates.

The policy file will include four user policies, one group policy and one computer policy:

Test user policy
: Used to test whether the policy file is being properly downloaded to a workstation.

Default User (DU) policy
: Used for all the students.

Admin user policy
: Used by the network administrator and allows full access to the workstation.

SuperR (super-restricted) user policy
: A completely restricted policy and is used to set the local default *user.dat* restrictions. This is achieved by exploiting the communal workstation policy conflict problem discussed in Chapter 3 (more on this later).

Teacher group policy
: Has fewer restrictions than the DU policy but more restrictions than the Admin user policy.

Default Computer (DC) policy
: Used for all communal computers.

These policies are created in a specific order, to utilize the template properties of the DU and to help prevent policy conflicts. Remember that since the SPE does not create user accounts, you must also add these users to your user database. The SPE policy names are not case sensitive, so you can use any combination of uppercase and lowercase letters in the policy file even if the username in your database does not.

On a NetWare network (which uses an NDS server), you must create and initially test the policy file while logged in as Administrator or as a user with supervisor rights to the system root. According to Microsoft, the first time that system policies are implemented on an NDS tree, the tree's database is modified. An NDS volume and path to the *config.pol* file must be supplied. This modification requires supervisor access rights to the NDS tree. See MS Knowledgebase Q149415 for more information.

Loading the Template

Before creating any user, group or computer policies, you must load a template. Begin by opening the SPE program. At this point if there were no templates previously loaded, and you did not install the SPE using the Add/Remove Programs applet, you may get the following error message:

```
"Unable to open template file C:\WINDOWS(WINNT)\INF\COMMON.ADM:
The system cannot find the file specified."
```

This error message can be safely ignored. When the SPE is installed, it copies *common.adm* to the Windows *\Inf* subdirectory and then tries to load this template by default. Once a template is loaded on the Current Policy Templates list, the error message will no longer appear. Alternately, you can make Poledit happy by copying the *common.adm* template into the *\Inf* subdirectory.

In the top menu bar, select Options → Policy Template. Select Add and browse to the location of the *admin.adm* template. Select Open and then OK. You now have the proper template loaded into the Policy Editor.

Briefly, the *admin.adm* template can be used to set the following user or group policy restrictions:

Control Panel
: Options to restrict the user/group from accessing Control Panel applets

Desktop
: Options to restrict the user/group to specific wallpaper or color schemes

Network
: Options to restrict file and print sharing

Shell
: Options to specify network directories to be used for custom desktop folders, to restrict access to aspects of the Start menu and other desktop options

System
: Options to restrict the use of DOS prompts and the registry editor, and to limit the user to specific applications

Creating a Test User

The Test user is used to test only whether the policy file is being properly accessed and downloaded by the workstation. It simply changes the user's wallpaper, a quick visual check, but it does confirm that the workstation is set for automatic remote update, user profiles are enabled, and the preferred server or domain is set correctly. You will notice as you create these user and group policies that wallpaper is the one setting that I consistently change. I do this for troubleshooting purposes because wallpaper is the only instantly visible indication of which particular group or user policy has become active on the workstation.

Choose File → New File to create the new policy file. The icons for Default User and Default Computer will automatically be added, and I will edit them later. All template options for both DU and DC are initially in the grayed position. Select the icon at the top that looks like a single head, or select Edit → Add User. The policy is labeled using the name the user would place in the username field of the logon window. In the list box, type the name of the user as TEST and select OK. A new user policy called TEST will now appear in the window. Since the DU was used as a model in the creation of this user, the TEST policy also has all the same template options set. Currently all of the DU settings are in the grayed position, so all of the Test user policy settings will also be grayed.

Open the newly created TEST policy by double-clicking on the icon. Select the "+" beside Desktop to expand the list. Change the selection beside Wallpaper (see Figure 3-1) from the grayed position to the checked position. At the bottom of the window you will now be able to type the directory location of the wallpaper; in this example it is the *sandstone.bmp* wallpaper in the main *windows* directory. Select OK to get back to the main SPE screen. Your Test user is now complete.

If you are using system policies loaded from a Novell server, your Test user *must* initially have Supervisor rights to the NDS tree. Since this is the first user to log on and test the policy file, this level of rights is necessary to make the required changes to the NDS. After the policy file is tested, the Supervisor rights can be removed from the Test user, or the Test user itself can be deleted.

Editing the Default User

The DU will be used as the default student policy, and in the school scenario it will require a high level of security. Most restrictions will be checked, although some will be cleared rather than left grayed to make sure that they don't cause a workstation conflict with the SuperR user policy restrictions. Figure 4-3 shows the suggested settings for Control Panel restrictions.

Each of the Control Panel restrictions, such as Restrict Display in Figure 4-3, have additional options that must be set to the checked position. These options are:

Restrict Display Control Panel

- Disable Display Control Panel
- Hide Background page
- Hide Screen Saver page
- Hide Appearance page
- Hide Settings page

Restrict Network Control Panel

- Disable Network Control Panel
- Hide Identification page
- Hide Access page

Restrict Passwords Control Panel

- Disable Passwords Control Panel
- Hide Change Passwords page
- Hide Remote Administration page
- Hide User Profiles page

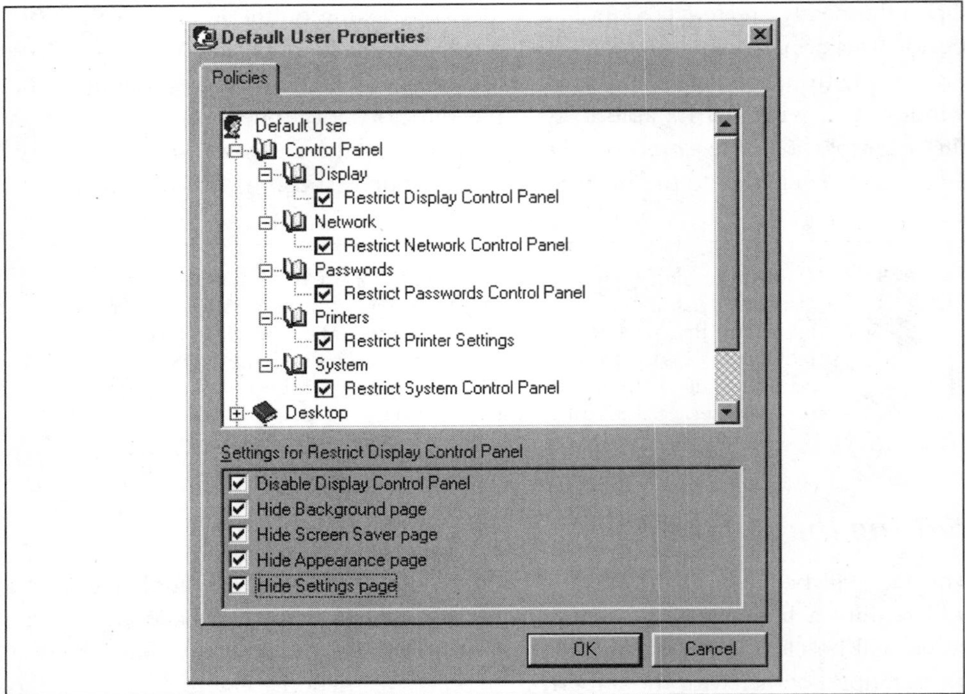

Figure 4-3. Control Panel restrictions for DU

Restrict Printer Settings

Hide General and Details pages

Disable Deletion of Printers

Disable Addition of Printers

Restrict System Control Panel

Hide Device Manager page

Hide Hardware Profiles page

Hide File System button

Hide Virtual Memory button

Figure 4-4 shows the suggested settings for Shell restrictions.

You may want to check the restriction Hide Drives in 'My Computer' although doing so would make it difficult (but not impossible) for the user to browse through files on A: drive or C: drive. Since I do not want them active, I'll leave the options "Hide all items on Desktop" and "Disable Shut Down" command in the cleared position. If these options are left in the grayed position the super-restricted

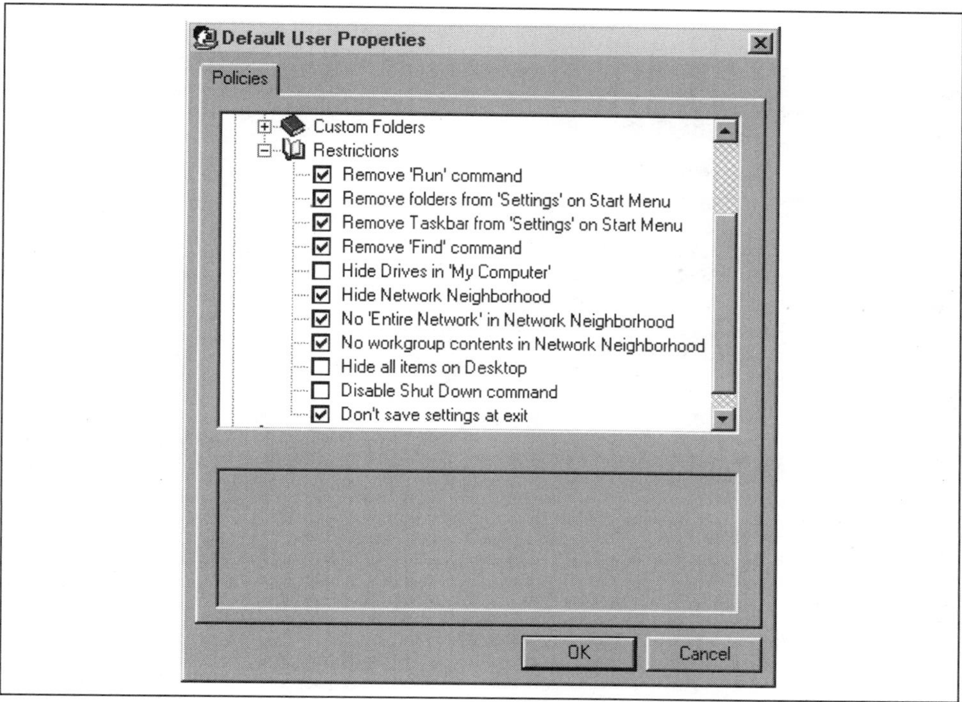

Figure 4-4. Shell restrictions for DU

user policy may cause a communal workstation conflict and overwrite them to the checked position. Figure 4-5 shows the suggested settings for system restrictions.

At this stage I would suggest clearing "Only run allowed Windows applications" since it can cause headaches if all applications required by the user are not on the list. It is better to first make sure that the policy is working as expected, and then restrict applications if you feel it is necessary. Note that restricting access to a DOS prompt, as in Figure 4-5, increases security. However, if your students use any non-Windows applications (i.e., DOS applications), do not check "Disable MS-DOS prompt," as this option does not disable just the prompt, but any DOS-based applications that might underlie a Windows application.

To provide a consistent desktop, you can set custom folders for programs (found in the Start menu) or desktop icons (**.lnk* and **.pif* shortcuts). I found that this was a valuable option, as the users would change icon names, delete icons or add programs to the Programs list. Since the custom folders are kept on a network directory, you are able to control access rights and to centrally configure the available shortcuts for all workstations. Figure 4-6 shows the options available for setting a consistent desktop.

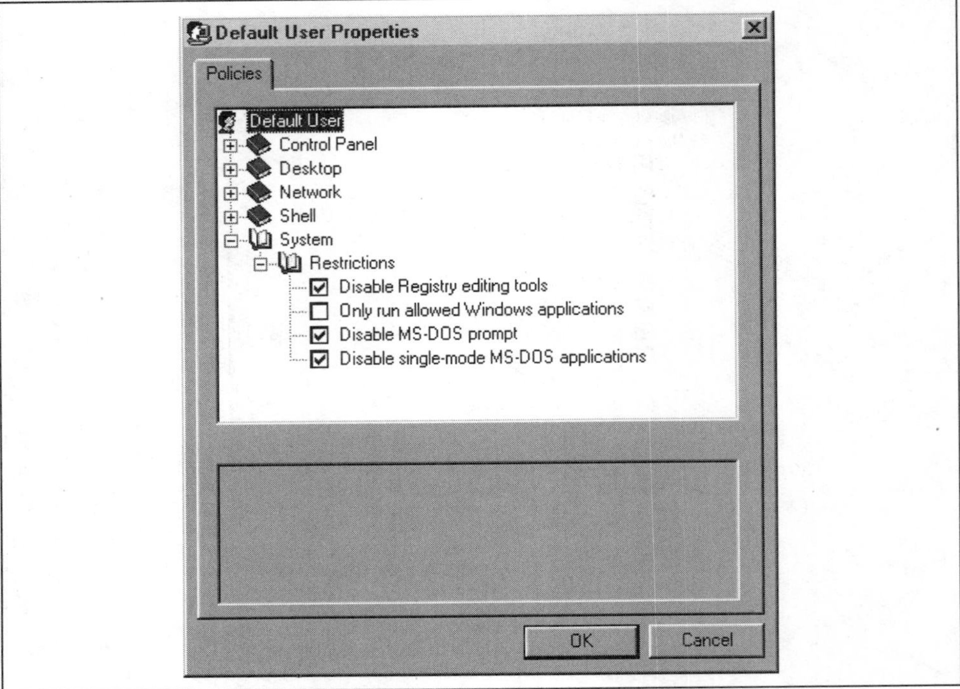

Figure 4-5. System restrictions for DU

For Windows 9x workstations, do not use folders in the Custom Network Neighborhood because Windows 9x does not support this feature. In addition, folder names cannot include environment variables such as *%username%*. Windows 9x cannot recognize and expand these variables within policy files.

Notice in this example that I did not use the UNC path for the Custom Programs Folder *(e.g., campo\sys\public\desktop),* but rather a mapped drive. This is because choosing Hide Network Neighborhood (a Shell policy option found in *admin.adm*) effectively disables the use of UNC pathnames. So whenever access to Network Neighborhood is restricted, mapped directories must be used for the network location of custom folders.

When you set permissions to the network directories used for custom programs Folders, make sure that you allow only Read access so that the users will not be able to alter the folder contents.

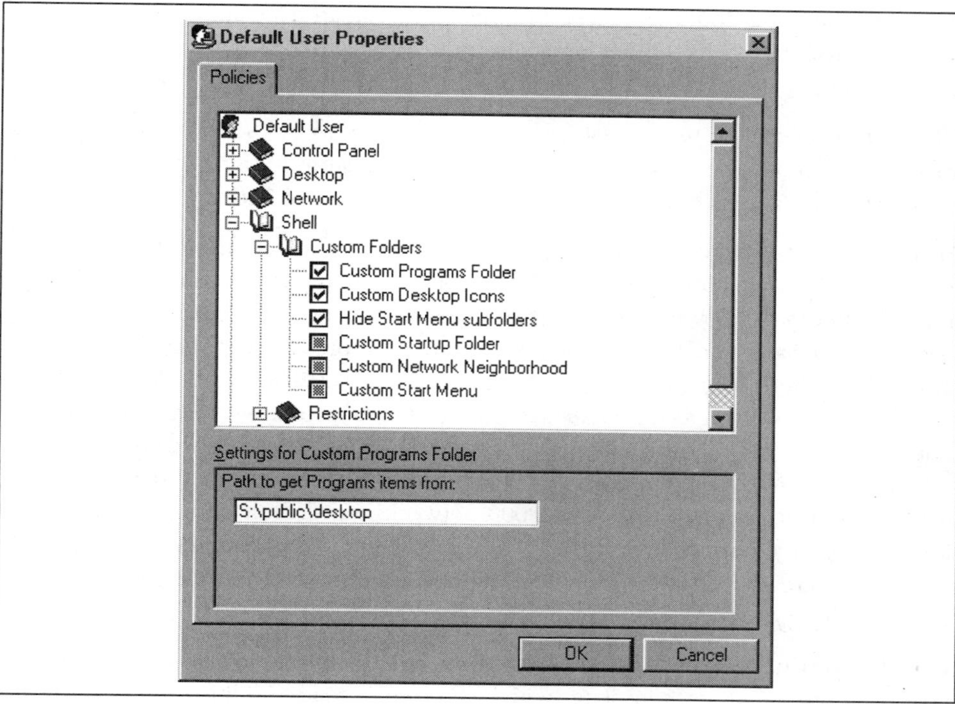

Figure 4-6. Custom folders for DU

When using mapped directories for custom folders, make sure that all users who share the folder have the same drive mappings.

Normally the local workstation folders become active for the custom folder options that are left in the grayed position. These local folders are found in Table 4-2.

Table 4-2. Custom Folders and Their Corresponding Local Folders

Custom Folder	Corresponding Folder on Local Drive
Programs folder	*C:\Windows\Start Menu\Programs*
Desktop icons	*C:\Windows\Desktop*
Startup folder	*C:\Windows\Start Menu\Startup*
Network Neighborhood	*C:\Windows\Nethood*
Start menu	*C:\Windows\Start Menu*

If another user or group policy had any specific custom folders set, however, grayed settings could be the source of a communal (shared) workstation conflict.

To avoid this, you could set these options to the cleared position to remove any previous custom folder settings and allow the local workstation folders to be the active folders.

Finally, to prevent the use of tasteless backgrounds, you can set the wallpaper to a specific bitmap on the network drive. As with the custom folders, the users should have read-only access to the bitmap so that it cannot be altered.

At this point, it is a good idea to save your policy file in the appropriate location for automatic downloading. Even if you want to eventually use manual downloading, use automatic downloading first to remove one possible cause of problems. Select File → Save and type in the name and location of the policy file. The file should be called *config.pol*. If you have a Novell NetWare network, you would save the file to *\\preferredserver\sys\public*. On a Windows NT4 network you would save the file to *%systemroot%\systemdrive>\WinNT\system32\repl\import\scripts* (which is the *Netlogon* directory) of each domain controller that participates in user authentication. On a Windows 2000 network, the default path is the *Netlogon* directory of any domain controller (*%systemroot%\sysvol\DomainName\scripts*). If the file was created on a Windows NT workstation/server, then the file should be called *ntconfig.pol* and saved to the same directories.

Now that you have set up the DU with the restrictions you will be using, you will have a more accurate template with which to create additional users. From Chapter 3 you will remember that the DU is loaded first, followed by any specific user policy. By configuring the DU first and then creating the specific user policy, you are mimicking this procedure—allowing any policy conflicts to become more apparent.

Be wary of editing the DU *after* creating other users. You may create user conflicts that did not exist previously.

Creating the Administrator User Policy

Again select the Add User button, this time creating a user based on whichever logon name you use for your Administrator account. The network client passes the name placed in the GUI logon Username window on the logon screen to the operating system as the username. This name is then used by Windows to search for a specific user policy. So, for example, if you enter Manager in this screen, the user policy object should also be called Manager. For this example, I will use Admin as the username. Since the Admin user is also created using the DU template, you must systematically go through each template option changing all restrictions with a check mark to the cleared state. This is by design, since by editing the DU before the Admin user you can now see where all of the DU restrictions were set. Do not change any option from the checked state to the grayed state, as you will be creating a conflict with the DU. If an option is already set to the grayed state, it is fine to leave it that way for now.

You can set your own custom desktop icons to allow quick access to your most frequently used administrator programs on the network. If you do, make this folder accessible only by the Admin user, and give yourself full access to make changes to the directory.

Before selecting the OK button, double-check that you do not have any of the Shell or System restrictions (Figures 4-4 and 4-5) in the checked state or you may find yourself locked out of a workstation.

If you are using a Novell NetWare 4.x or 5.x network, it is not considered prudent to log on as the Admin user from multiple client workstations. In this case, you may want to choose another logon name for your administrator user policy.

Creating the Super-Restricted User Policy

One problem with policy-based security on a Windows 9x workstation occurs when a user disconnects the network cable before logging on. This effectively prevents the policy file from downloading and the active restrictions will then depend on the default local *user.dat* restrictions. Depending on whom the last person was to log onto that workstation (see Chapter 3), the security can be adequate to nonexistent. How do you leave a workstation with the highest default restriction level, especially since when you choose not to save your settings during logon you overwrite the default local *user.dat*? One solution is to exploit workstation conflicts by creating a super-restricted user, and use this user to automatically create a restricted *user.dat*. When you log on as SuperR, as long as you answer No when asked if you'd like to save your settings, you will automatically create a restricted local default profile. Then to make sure that this default restricted profile remains and does not get overwritten, use the batch file (or Perl program) found later in this chapter ("Stopping the Save Settings Question") to automatically create a user directory and bypass the "Do you want to save your settings" logon question.

To create this policy, select the Add User button and name the user SuperR. Open the SuperR user and systematically expand each restriction under Control Panel, Shell Restrictions and System and set each to the checked position (see Figure 4-7). Set all restrictions *except* for Disable Shut Down, since you want even an intruder to be able to shutdown properly.

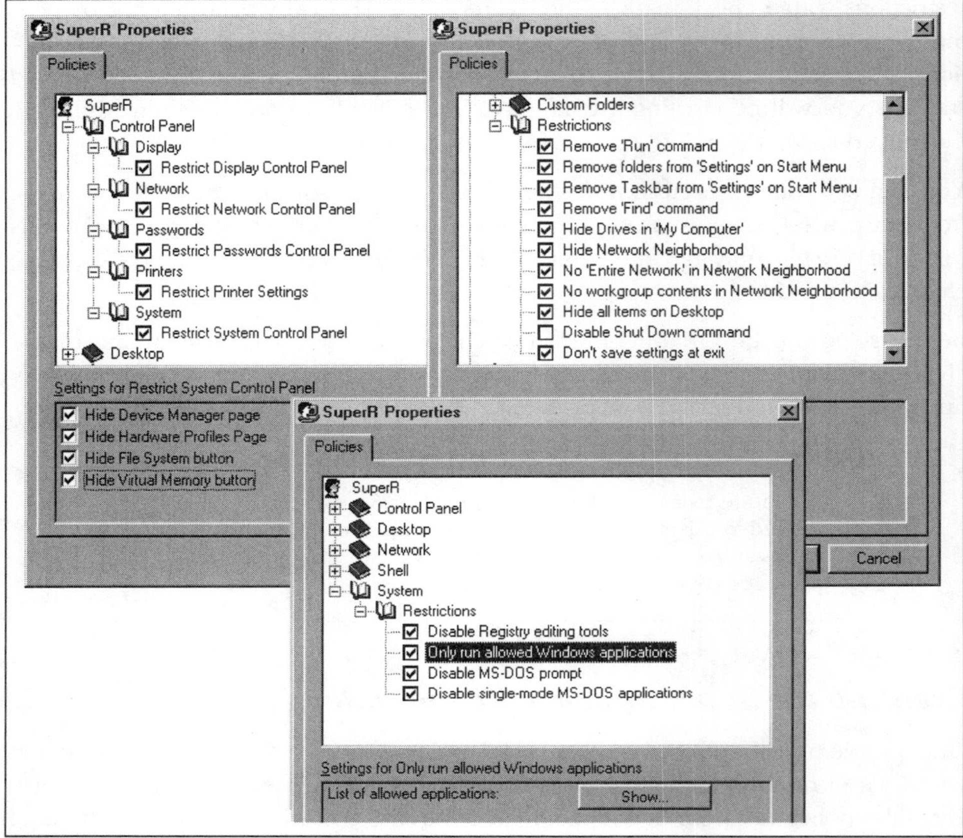

Figure 4-7. Super-restricted user settings

The Shell restriction "Hide all items on Desktop" will hide all shortcuts and folders (even the Recycle Bin, My Computer and the Internet Explorer shortcuts) on the desktop, leaving it totally blank. In Figure 4-7, "Only run allowed Windows applications" is shown in the checked position. Use caution with this option. If it is left checked, but no programs are specified, no programs will be allowed to run on the workstation. At the very least, I'd suggest putting *poledit.exe* on this list. Select the Show button, and you will see the window shown in Figure 4-8.

Allowed applications can be programs with an EXE, COM or BAT extension. Only the filename, and not the directory location, should be specified. Be cautious of the fact that the SPE checks only for a matching filename, regardless of the program's true *original* filename. This is a weakness in the program, since it is possible for a user to run any restricted program simply by renaming it to a filename on the allowed list. You will notice that I have not put the correct *poledit.exe* filename in the example. Malicious users may be aware of this security hole, expect

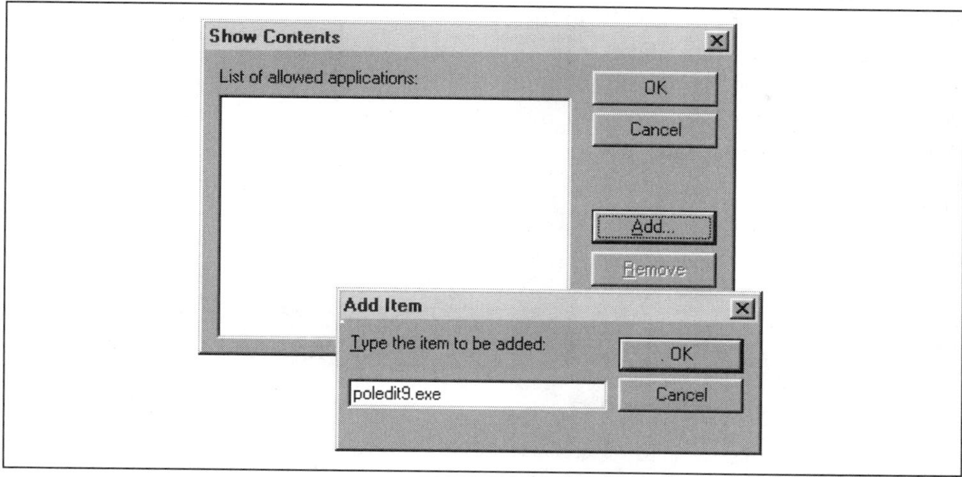

Figure 4-8. Allowed applications for super-restricted users

the SPE to be on the allowed programs list and try to run the program from a floppy. Listing the policy editor with some other filename (such as *poledit9.exe*) allows you, to some extent, to disguise the ability to run a program. This is especially true if you have only one program listed, and that program does not exist on the local hard drive. See Chapter 5, *It's Not Perfect* for more information on this security hole.

Creating the Teacher Group Policy

The teachers in this case study use the same computers as the students, but they require a more relaxed level of security. In addition, the Teacher group policy will set a separate wallpaper bitmap from that which was set for the students in the DU. This will allow the teacher who is monitoring the class to easily see if a student has logged into a workstation using a user account belonging to the teachers' group.

To create the Teacher group policy, select the two-headed icon, Add Group button, or select Edit → Add Group from the top menu bar. Enter the name of the group and then select OK. If you are logging in to a NetWare 4x server, you must use the fully qualified NDS group name (i.e., *TEACHER.STAFF.BEDROCK*) in *uppercase* letters or the bindery name if logging in as a bindery user. If the user is logging onto a Windows NT4 or Windows 2000 domain, use the global group name.

Unfortunately, the Teacher group is not created using the DU as a template. All template options will initially be in the grayed position, and so it is not possible to see where conflicts with the DU may occur. It would be possible to leave a restriction that was checked in the DU in the grayed position for the Teacher group, thus letting the DU restrictions take over. This is not a safe practice however, because you are likely to find yourself changing the DU several times after initially creating the policy file. Doing so, you may unknowingly create policy conflicts from DU settings by overwriting the grayed Teacher group settings. Therefore, when setting the Teacher policy options you should always set restrictions to either the checked or cleared positions as required (see Figure 4-9).

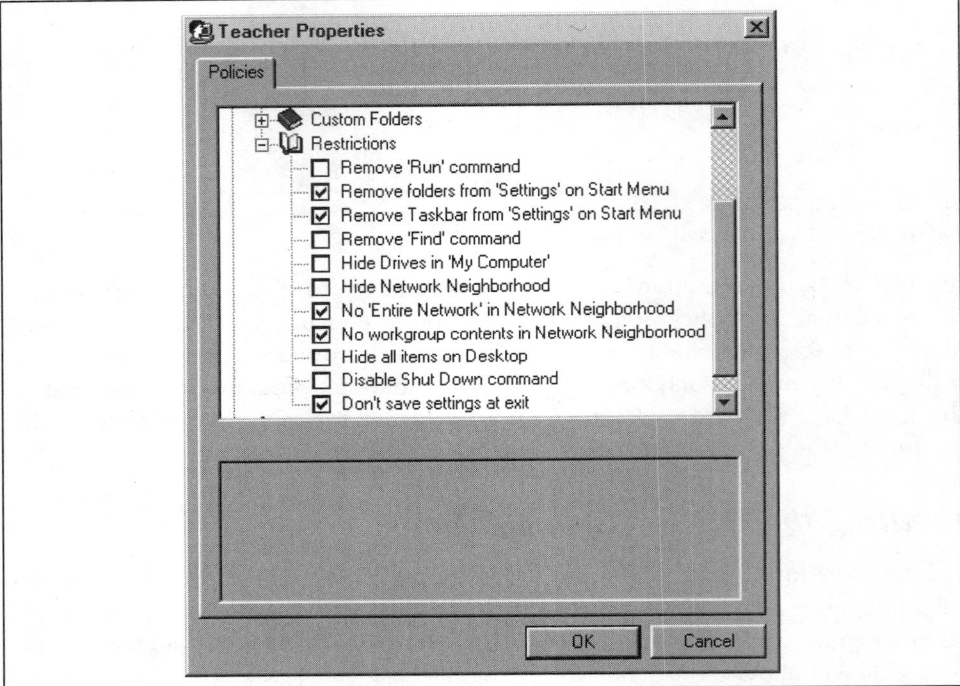

Figure 4-9. Teacher group policy Shell restrictions

Note that it is necessary to set policy options to the checked or cleared positions, only if they are true restrictions (they limit user access in some way, such as Hide All Drives). Indiscriminately setting *all* template options to the cleared or checked positions may remove required settings found in the local workstation's registry.

The Teacher group has all the same restrictions checked as the DU for Control Panel (Figure 4-3) and System (Figure 4-5). However, for Shell (Figure 4-4), I will allow the teachers access to the Run and Find commands. I will also allow them to view the Network Neighborhood. Notice that none of these settings are left in the grayed state.

The teachers have access to network programs and directories that are not available to the students. Therefore, the Teacher group policy also requires custom folders (see Figure 4-6) that are different from those specified for the students in the DU policy.

If these custom folder settings were left in the grayed position, the teachers would get the same custom folders as the DU since the DU policy is applied first, followed by the group policy. If the options are set to the cleared setting, then the local workstation folders in the *C:\Windows* directory become active rather than the DU's custom folders.

Finally, to allow monitoring teachers to see if a student is using a teacher account, set the wallpaper (see Figure 3-1) to a bitmap on the network drive. When you are looking at an entire computer room full of cloud wallpaper, an individual monitor with different wallpaper stands out quite dramatically. As with the custom folders, this bitmap should have read-only access.

Editing the Default Computer Policy

Now that the user and group policies have been set up, namely the settings for *user.dat*, it is time to work on the computer settings—the settings for *system.dat*. Computer settings are typically not restrictions as such, but setup options. There are numerous template options for computer settings, but I will review only the most common settings here. Although some of these settings will be configured during the workstation setup, it is a good idea to repeat them in the DC policy in case the user ever accidentally or maliciously changes the local settings. If that were to happen, the correct settings would be restored at the next boot-up when the policy file was downloaded by the workstation.

Unlike the user and group restriction policies, it is safe to leave many of the DC options in the grayed position. In this case study there are no other computer policies, and so there is no threat of computer policy conflicts. Also, most of the options are settings rather than true restrictions, and any option in the grayed position will allow the local *system.dat* setting to become active.

Open the DC policy, under Default Computer → Network → Access Control (Figure 4-10) and change Logon Banner to the checked position. This option will display a default message (which can be customized) warning the user that unauthorized access is not allowed. Check user-level security only if you have enabled remote registry editing, else leave it grayed. Under Network → Logon settings, require a valid network logon for access to Windows. Only users verified by the network will be able to use Windows. This will increase security but, depending

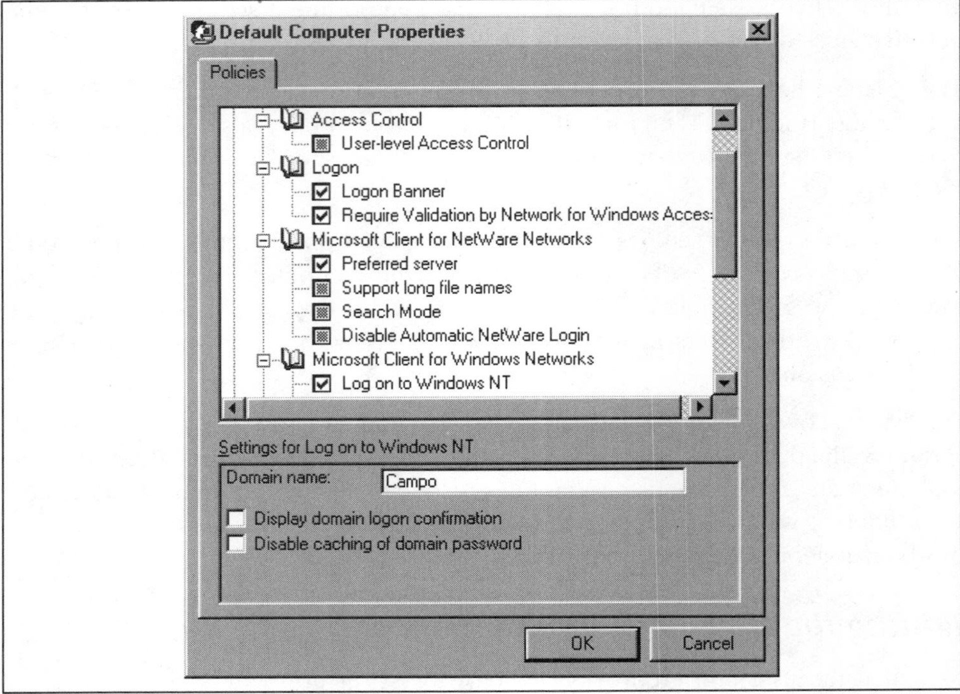

Figure 4-10. Default Computer network settings

on the workstation's default profile, it may make the workstation unusable if the network is down.

In many areas, before legal action can be brought against a person, they must have been warned that accessing a particular computer without permission is not allowed. Because of this, a logon banner should always be used if you are concerned about unlawful access to your workstations.

For a NetWare network, under Network → Microsoft Client for NetWare Networks, the preferred server should be set. For a Windows NT or Windows 2000 network, under Network → Microsoft Client for Windows Networks, the Domain (*Campo* in this example) should be specified. Set only the option that relates to your particular network, and leave the other grayed.

Under Network → Passwords (Figure 4-11) you can disable password caching. This will stop Windows from verifying the Windows password for each new user, and no *<username>.pwl* password files will be saved on the local drive. Additional security is provided as well since the user must log on separately to each network resource. Remote update (Network → Update) *must* be set to the checked position, and under "Settings for Remote Update" the update mode should be set to automatic and "Load balancing" should be enabled. "Display error messages" should be checked as displaying error messages may help if the policy file fails to download properly.

If you leave remote update in the cleared position, the workstation will be set to *not* download the policy file after the next reboot. Consequently, the policy file will no longer be effective on the workstation.

Under System settings, "Enable User Profiles" should be set to the checked position. If you missed enabling user profiles on any workstation, this option will enable profiles at the next reboot as long as the workstation was set to allow automatic remote update. Finally, if you have a network copy of the Windows CAB files, specify the location (for example, *S:\Win98*) in the System settings under "Network Path for Windows Setup." Even if you do not have network copies of the CAB files, specifying this setting is one safe way of checking to see if a specific computer policy has been downloaded by the workstation (see "Testing the Policy File" later in this chapter).

Select OK to finish the DC edits. Now save your policy file by selecting File → Save. Although it seems counterintuitive, do not choose Save As when saving the policy file. When you choose Save As and use the filename *config.pol*, a new policy file will be created with only the policy changes from the *current* template—overwriting your old policy file. You will lose all previous policy settings from other templates. Always choose Save to properly append new template options to your current policy file.

Your SPE window should now show the same policy icons that appear in Figure 4-12.

Preparing a Workstation

There are various registry settings required for the workstation to properly use the policy file. Remote update must be enabled, the preferred server or Domain must be specified and on a Windows 9x workstation user profiles and group policy support must be enabled. Before you begin, however, check that the workstation you will be using to test the policy file is working properly and clean out any erroneous files.

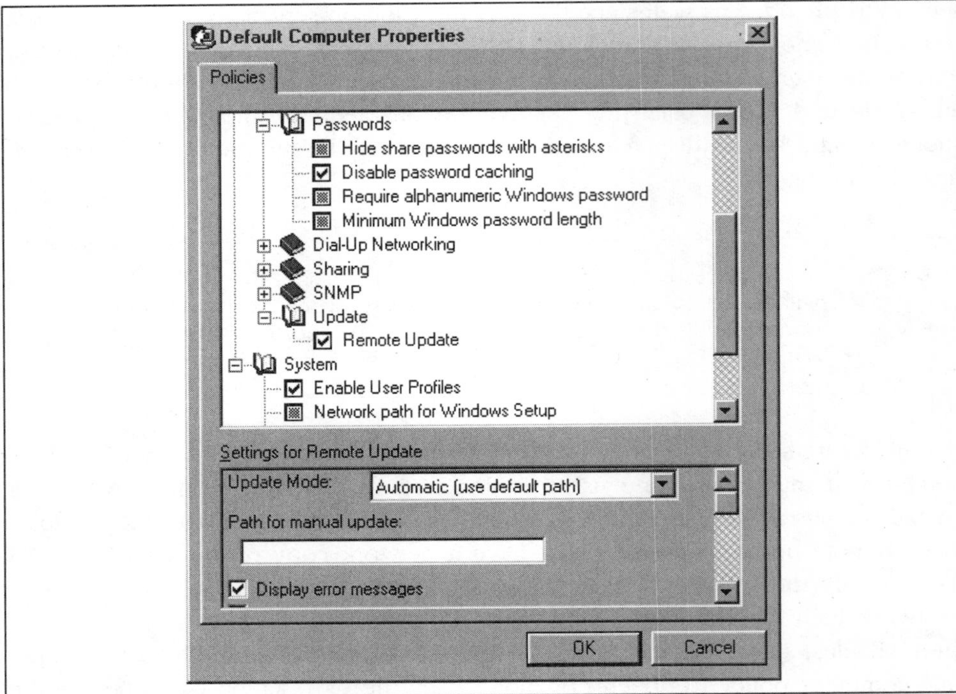

Figure 4-11. , Default Computer password, update and system settings

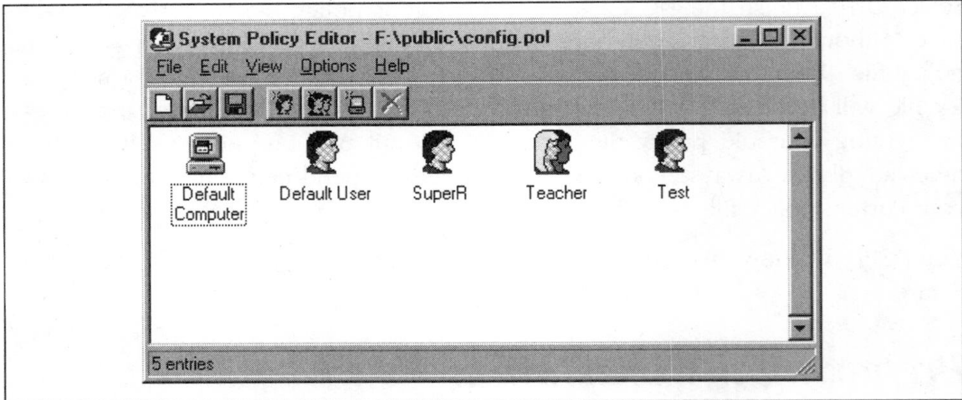

Figure 4-12. Complete policy file

Cleaning Up the Workstation

Initially, use a single client workstation to test your policies and have this workstation as perfectly configured as possible. This will minimize possible errors and give you a true test of how well your policies are working. To do it right, consider doing a fresh install of the Windows OS. Since the local *user.dat* will be used as a template to which the policy file will be merged and then copied as a profile for each new user, you will want it as flawless as possible. Although a full install may seem like a waste of time, you otherwise may find yourself pointlessly trying to fix a policy file when in fact the problem lies with the workstation's local profile.

Whether you do a fresh install or use an existing workstation, work through the following list on your test workstation:

To be sure that you are checking and fixing the local default user profile, initially set the workstation *not* to use user profiles (see Chapter 2, *A System Policies Primer*).

1. Check the Start menu. Are all necessary shortcuts listed under Programs, and do they all link correctly to their specific applications? Do you have access to the Settings, Find and Run commands? Make sure that all options are available.
2. Check the desktop. Are all necessary shortcuts on the desktop, and do they all link correctly to their specific applications? The Test user policy I created uses the *sandstone.bmp* wallpaper as a visual check, so make sure that that file exists on the local drive. Remove any current wallpaper settings, since a specific wallpaper setting is one of the tests for correct downloading of the policy file.
3. Check the Control Panel applets, especially Display, Passwords, System and Network. Do you have full access to all of them?
4. On Windows 9x workstations, check for existing profiles in the main Windows directory. If any exist, delete the entire profile subdirectory to clear all previous *user.dat* files. You may want to do this after rebooting into MS-DOS mode and using the Deltree command to quickly delete all subdirectories. At the DOS prompt, type:

   ```
   Echo Y | Deltree C:\Windows\profiles
   ```

   On Windows NT workstations, excess profiles can be removed through Control Panel → System → User Profiles, or by using NT Explorer to delete the *username* subfolders from *\Winnt\Profiles*. Additionally, a utility called *delprof.exe* is available from the Windows NT4 Resource Kit. This utility can be used on a local or remote computer running Windows NT to remove unwanted profiles. To prevent the NT workstation from caching any further profiles, use the "Delete cached copies of roaming profiles" policy found in the *winnt.adm* template.

5. Check for cached password (PWL) files in the Windows root directory, removing any that are found. You cannot verify the "Disable password caching" policy option unless these files are removed. After removing the cached passwords, you will be required to retype any previously saved passwords to shared resources.

Optionally, you can remove any existing users from the registry. In the Control Panel, use the Users applet and delete any users. Alternately, you can directly edit the registry and delete any subkeys below HKLM\Software\Microsoft\Windows\CurrentVersion\ProfileList. Finally, you may want to clear the *Documents* folder (*\recent* subdirectory in the main *\Windows* directory) and the IE cache.

Now your local profile should be shipshape and free of possibly conflicting registry settings.

Enabling User Profiles and Remote Update

Since your policy file will not download otherwise, check that remote update is enabled and set to automatic. You can verify this by using Regedit to examine the registry key HKLM\System\CurrentControlSet\Control\Update. UpdateMode should be set to a value of 1. If it is not, use the *admin.adm* template and the SPE in local registry mode (Chapter 2). Edit the Local Computer to change Remote Update just as you edited the DC earlier. Don't forget to re-enable user profiles using either the Passwords applet in the Control Panel or by using the SPE (Figure 4-11), again in local registry mode.

Enabling Group Policy Support for Windows 9x

Group policy support is built into Windows NT; therefore it needs to be installed only on a Windows 9x workstation. To successfully install the files and registry entries for group policies, follow the same procedure for adding new programs outlined in the "Installing the System Policy Editor" section. This time, however, do *not* choose to install the System Policy Editor, but only check off the group policies option.

Installation of group policy support using the Add/Remove Programs applet copies *grouppol.dll* to the *C:\Windows\System* subdirectory and creates the following registry entries (found in *grouppol.reg*):

Registry Key	Value Name (string)	Value Data
HKLM\Network\Logon	PolicyHandler	GROUPPOL.DLL, Process-Polices
HKLM\System\CurrentControlSet\Services\MSNP32\NetworkProvider	GroupFcn	GROUPPOL.DLL, NTGet-UserGroups
HKLM\System\CurrentControlSet\Services\NWNP32\NetworkProvider	GroupFcn	GROUPPOL.DLL, NWGet-UserGroups

Novell Group Policy Support for Windows 9x

Novell group policy support is installed automatically with the client software. Installation of the client places the *nwgroup.dll* file in the *C:\Windows\System* subdirectory and makes the required registry setting. To verify that this is complete, you can run Regedit and check the following registry key:

Registry Key	Value Name (string)	Value Data
HKLM\System\CurrentControlSet\Services\NOVELLNP\NetworkProvider	GroupFcn	NWGROUP.DLL, NWGetUserGroups

Automating the Windows 9x Setup

If you have many Windows 9x workstations, completing this setup process for all of them may seem overwhelming. However, many of the registry settings and some of the workstation cleaning can be completed remotely through the network logon script. Once you have fully tested the policy file (see the next section, "Testing the Policy File"), it is not as important to meticulously tidy each workstation. You can create a batch file (called *setup.bat*) run from the logon script to copy any necessary file from the network to the workstation. This same batch file could merge the necessary registry settings, in the form of a file called *setup.reg*, into the local registry. Then, upon the next boot-up, the workstation should be ready for full policy support. As always, back up your registry first before any testing and test this procedure on a few workstations before rolling it out to the entire network.

Using a text editor such as Notepad, type the following code and save it to a file called *setup.reg*:

```
REGEDIT4

[HKEY_LOCAL_MACHINE\Network\Logon]
; ENABLES USER PROFILES FOR WIN9x
"UserProfiles"=dword:00000001
; GROUP POLICY SUPPORT FOR WIN9x
"PolicyHandler"="GROUPPOL.DLL, ProcessPolicies"

[HKEY_LOCAL_MACHINE\System\CurrentControlSet\control\Update]
; SETS AUTOMATIC REMOTE UPDATE MODE FOR Win9x OR NT
"UpdateMode"=dword:00000001
; GROUP POLICY SUPPORT FOR WIN9x
[HKEY_LOCAL_MACHINE\System\CurrentControlSet\Services\MSNP32\NetworkProvider]
"GroupFcn"="GROUPPOL.DLL, NTGetUserGroups"
[HKEY_LOCAL_MACHINE\System\CurrentControlSet\Services\NWNP32\NetworkProvider]
"GroupFcn"="GROUPPOL.DLL, NWGetUserGroups"
```

The batch file (*setup.bat*) used to complete the setup is called from the logon script and could look something like this:

```
@echo off
C:
cd/Windows
;MERGE THE PROFILE REGISTRY SETTINGS SILENTLY WITH THE SYSTEM.DAT
Regedit /s \\servername\publicdirectory\profiles.reg
;COPY THE GROUP POLICY DLL TO SYSTEM DIRECTORY
copy \\servername\publicdirectory\grouppol.dll c:\windows\system
;DELETE ANY CURRENT WINDOWS 9x PROFILE FOLDERS
echo y | deltree c:\windows\profiles
;DELETE ANY PASSWORD FILES
del c:\windows\*.pwl
```

Again, Notepad could be used to create and save this batch file. Both *setup.reg* and *setup.bat* should be in a publicly accessible directory with read-only access.

Testing the Policy File

Before you roll out the policy file, thoroughly test all user and computer policies. If possible, test when there are no other users on the network. Since you will have to make the policy file publicly accessible to test all the user policies you created, anyone logging in during this test phase may also download the policy file. You could find yourself inundated with panicked users before you've even begun your testing.

Remember that this testing phase will edit the workstation registry. Start by making backup copies of the registry files (see the earlier sidebar, "Playing It Safe—Back up Your Registry"), and then confirm that you are ready to test the file by working through the following checklist.

1. Does the workstation have remote update and user profiles enabled? If using group policies on a Windows 9x workstation, has group policy support been installed? If the workstation is a member of a Windows NT domain, was load balancing enabled?
2. Are all the users (Admin, Test, SuperR) legitimate users in the network user database? Is the Teacher group also in the database? If the policy file is on a Windows NT or Windows 2000 network, is the Teacher group a global group?
3. Is the policy file (*config.pol* or *ntconfig.pol*) in the correct network directory for automatic download? Does this directory have read-only public access?
4. If you're using custom folders, are they in a network directory accessible by the user and do they have read-only access?
5. If you're using a wallpaper bitmap from a network drive, is the BMP file accessible by the user with read-only access?

6. Do you have a user logon name and password from the Teacher group to test that group policy? Do you have another user logon name and password to test the DU policy? This user obviously must not be a member of the Teacher group.

Once you have completed this checklist, move on to testing each policy. Test the user policies in the exact order suggested. You will want to check for possible policy conflicts and changing the testing order could actually conceal, rather than reveal, these conflicts.

As you verify each user, select the No button when you are asked the question, "You have not logged on to this computer before. Would you like this computer to retain your individual settings for use when you log on here in the future?" This will allow you to replicate possible shared workstation conflicts.

Step 1: Verifying the Test User Policy

Begin by logging in as the Test user. Since the Test user was created before I edited the DU, all of its options, except for wallpaper, are set to the grayed position. I can check the downloading of the policy file without changing 99% of the local drive's default profile settings. When Windows asks, you can safely say No to saving personalized settings without worrying about overwriting the default local profile.

When you log on as Test, does the wallpaper change? If it does, then you know that the policy file is being read, downloaded and merged properly by that workstation. If it does not change, then there are several possible reasons why:

The workstation does not have remote update enabled.

You can check this using a copy of *poledit.exe* and the *admin.adm* template on a floppy disk, and edit the registry using the SPE in local registry mode.

The workstation does not have user profiles enabled.

If remote update was enabled, then the Default Computer policy (which was set to enable user profiles) should have been downloaded and merged. Since this change would not activate until the next reboot, try shutting down the workstation and then logging on again. If user profiles are now active, then the wallpaper will change.

The wallpaper bitmap may not exist in the location specified, or it may not be accessible to the Test user.

Check that the BMP does in fact exist, that you perhaps did not misspell it in the policy file and that the Test user has sufficient rights to the file.

The user does not have sufficient access to the policy file.

Ensure that the *config.pol* file has read access for all users. If the Windows 9x workstation is a member of a Windows NT domain, ensure that load balancing was enabled.

Assuming that everything worked as expected (you got a wallpaper change), you can move on to the next test.

Step 2: Verifying the Default User

The Default User will be the sole policy for any user who is not otherwise specified in the policy file. In other words, if you log on as anyone besides Admin, SuperR, or a member of the Teacher group, you should get the DU policy. In this case study, it will be any student.

When you log on, do you have the custom icons on your desktop? Do you have a custom program list under the Start menu? If not, check that the user has sufficient rights to the network directory containing these files. If you do, try changing the name of a shortcut. You should get an error message saying that you do not have sufficient rights for that procedure.

Check each restriction. Can you access the Control Panel? Do you have the Settings, Run or Find commands in the Start menu? Can you access a DOS prompt? If you right-click on the desktop, do you have access to the display properties (such as screensaver settings)? If you browse the hard drive, can you run the registry editor? You shouldn't be able to do any of these things.

If any of these restrictions are not active, go back and double-check your DU policy for settings left in the grayed or cleared positions.

Step 3: Verifying the Teacher Group Policy

Log on to the workstation as a member of the Teacher group. Since you are logging in after the DU, the local default profile should contain all of the DU's restrictions. This will allow you to check to see if you left any unwanted restrictions in the grayed position.

Check that you have the Teacher group's custom icons on your desktop. Is the proper custom program list under the Start menu? If not, check first that the user is actually a member of the Teacher group. Also check that the user has sufficient rights to the network directory containing these shortcuts. Finally, make sure that the workstation has group policy support properly installed (see "Enabling Group Policy Support for Windows 9x" earlier in this chapter). If the proper desktop icons are available, try changing the name of a shortcut again. You should get a message saying that you do not have sufficient rights to do so, unless you have given the group more than read access to that directory.

Note that the Novell Windows NT client does not support the use of group policies.

As with the DU, ensure that the restrictions you want active actually *are* active. Check for access to the Control Panel applets, for example. Conversely, check that the user does have access where you intended to allow access. For example, do you have access to all drives or the Run and Find commands in the Start menu? If you do not have access to these commands, double-check the Teacher group policy for restrictions left in the grayed or checked positions.

Step 4: Verifying the Admin User

Log on to the workstation as the Admin user. Since you are logging in after a Teacher group member, the local default profile should contain all of that group's restrictions. This will allow you to check to see if you possibly left any unwanted restrictions in the grayed position for the Admin policy. Thoroughly check that you have no restrictions anywhere, since this log on will be your gateway into even the most restricted computer. Check that you have complete access to all the Control Panel applets, to the Network Neighborhood, to all drives, to the DOS prompt, to the registry editor and to the Find, Run and Settings commands on the Start menu.

If you find any restrictions active, double-check your Admin user policy for settings left in the grayed or checked positions. Remain logged in as Admin to continue testing the DC policy.

Step 5: Verifying the Default Computer Policy

While you are still logged in as the Admin user, test the DC policy. It is not possible for a workstation to properly download the user policies without properly downloading the DC policy. However, if you want to double-check for your own peace of mind, use the registry editor (assuming that your setup was the same as the DC example) to check that the registry key HKLM\Software\Microsoft\Windows\CurrentVersion\Setup\Sourcepath is set to *S:\Win98*.

Changing only the network path for Windows setup is a safe, quick check that can also be used to test for proper downloading of a specific computer policy. If you set a path in the DC different from that set for a specific computer policy, then checking the registry key will tell you which of the two was the active computer policy.

Step 6: Verifying the Super-Restricted (SuperR) User Policy

Use this policy cautiously! Never log on as SuperR until you are sure that your Admin policy and logon are working properly, or you may find your workstation unusable due to the extreme level of restrictions.

Log on to the workstation as the SuperR user. Ensure that you have a totally blank desktop: no Run, Find or Settings options in the Start menu; no access to Control Panel applets; and no access to any programs. You should effectively not be able to do anything but shut down. Power the workstation off, disconnect the network cable, and then power the workstation back on. When Windows starts up with no network available, select the Cancel button on the logon window and again check that the SuperR restrictions are still in place.

Logging on as SuperR will leave the workstation with the highest level of default policy security in the event that the workstation cannot download the policy file. Be aware that it is unlikely that the default profile will remain this highly restricted unless you bypass the "Do you want to save your settings" question. As soon as a user answers No to retaining personalized settings, the default local profile will be overwritten. To avoid this problem, use the batch file (or Perl program) mentioned in the later section "Stopping the Save Settings Question" in your logon scripts.

Many administrators of public Windows 9x workstations regularly delete the *\Windows\Profiles* subdirectory to save hard drive space. In this case, it is important to note that if the network is ever legitimately unavailable, workstations with the SuperR profile as the default local profile may not be usable unless the users are allowed to retain a local copy of their *user.dat*.

The Microsoft Family Logon

In some situations, this Windows 9x network client can be used in addition to system policies to increase workstation security. The Microsoft Family Logon client, as shown in Figure 4-13, was first introduced with Internet Explorer 4.0, and subsequently included with Windows 98 and Windows 98SE. It allows an administrator to create a predefined list of local users, which is then displayed at logon. The user chooses a logon name from the list; new usernames cannot be added.

The benefit of this network client is that new users and profile directories cannot be added without access to the Control Panel. Also, if the user tries to bypass the

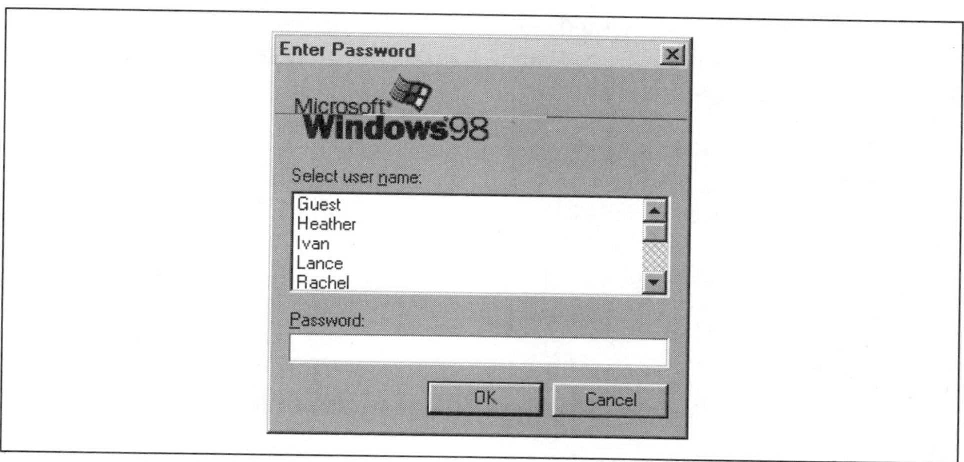

Figure 4-13. Microsoft Family Logon window

logon screen by pressing the Cancel button, she will receive the error message shown in Figure 4-14.

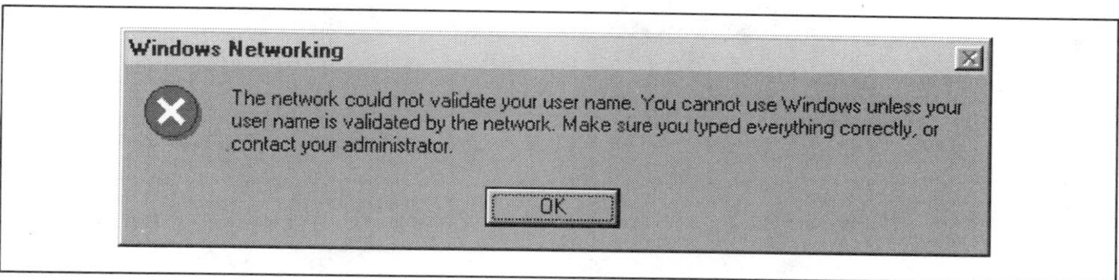

Figure 4-14. User must be validated

This client is best used in situations with a specific number of known user accounts, such as Case Studies 2 and 3 from Chapter 3. In this chapter's school example, with students roaming among multiple computers, the Family Logon client would likely not be useful.

Installation

On a Windows 98 workstation, if user profiles have not been enabled, open the Users Control Panel applet. A wizard will lead you through adding a new user. Once this user is added, the wizard will automatically enable user profiles and install the Microsoft Family Logon client.

On a Windows 95 workstation, or Windows 98 if user profiles have previously been enabled, open the Network Control Panel applet and select the Add button. In the Select Network Component Type window choose Client and select Add. Under Manufacturers choose Microsoft and then choose Microsoft Family Logon.

The primary network logon should now be set to Microsoft Family Logon. Choose OK to close the Network Control Panel applet. The workstation will need to be rebooted for the changes to take effect.

Note that a Windows 95 workstation requires the installation of IE 4.x before the choice of Microsoft Family Logon will be available.

Managing User Accounts

Users can easily be added or deleted through the Users Control Panel applet, as seen in Figure 4-15.

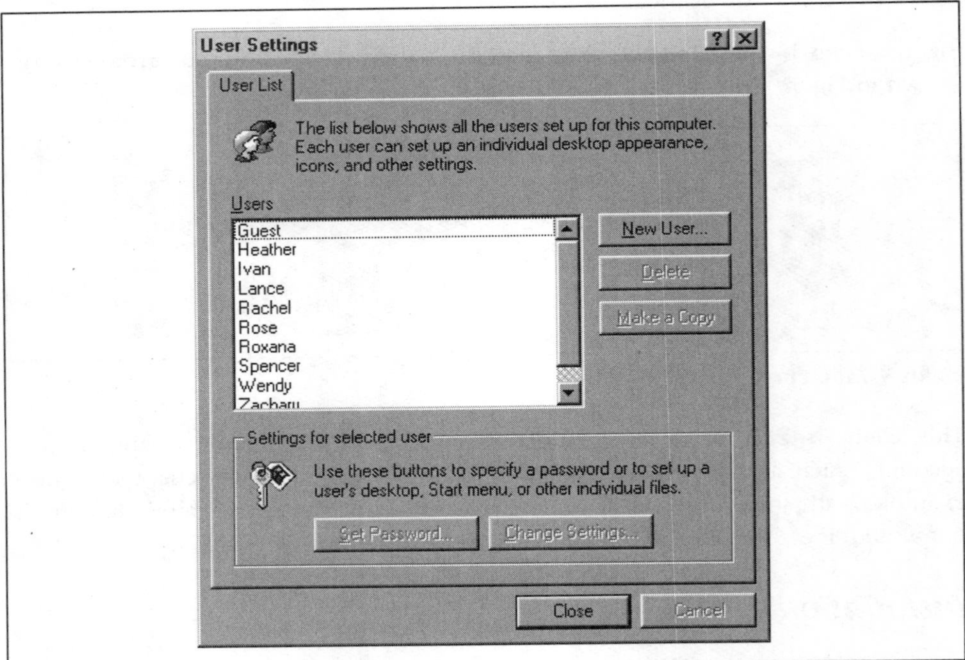

Figure 4-15. Managing users for the Microsoft Family Logon

There are a number of notes and cautions you should be aware of before using the MS Family Logon:

- Although it does co-exist with other network clients, the MS Family Logon must be the primary network logon.
- Password caching must be *enabled*; if it is not enabled, all users will receive an "incorrect password" error when they attempt to logon.

- The username and password used for the Family Logon can be the same as that used for the network. If the passwords are not the same, the user will have to perform a separate workstation and network logon. If the passwords are the same, the network logon will occur invisibly as a background process.
- If a password has not been set up for a user using the Users applet, if the local password file (**.pwl*) has been deleted, or if the *windows\profiles* `username` subdirectory is missing, then the password list box (Figure 4-13) will be grayed out. In this case, the Family Logon can be completely bypassed by selecting OK. However, as long as the computer policy "Require Validation by Network for Windows Access" is active, the user will still be required to enter his network logon password before obtaining access to the desktop. This computer policy is available in the *admin.adm* and *windows.adm* templates.

Miscellaneous Advice

There are a few miscellaneous points regarding building and using the policy file that were not previously discussed. These issues, as well as some final tips, are discussed next.

Expedite Processing of the Policy File

The more policy options that you have set to the cleared or checked position, the longer Windows will take to process the policy file. To speed up log on time, make sure you have as many options as possible set to the grayed position, since Windows will not bother to process grayed options.

Excluding Users and Computers

Whenever a policy file is used, there will be users who must be excluded, either from groups or from the Default User policy. To exclude users from a group, create a specific user policy for each person. Using the Copy and Paste commands, you can easily duplicate a user policy. In the SPE, highlight the user you want to copy. Select Edit → Copy to copy the user policy to the clipboard. Now highlight the new user and select Edit → Paste. The new user will now have the exact same policy restrictions.

If you find that you are excluding an inordinate number of users from the DU policy, either create an excluded group or delete the DU policy entirely. Try to keep your policy file to a minimum number of policies. Remember that the larger the policy file, the longer it will take to download, parse and merge with the workstation registry.

To exclude an entire workstation from the policy file, use the SPE in local registry mode to set the remote update option to the cleared position. The policy file will now be ignored by that workstation.

Adding Additional Templates

Once you are aware of the other template options, it is unlikely that you will be using only the *admin.adm* template to create your policy file. Although the templates have a 64 K restriction on their size, and so cannot be saved together as one large file, you can load multiple templates. When adding templates, follow the procedure outlined in "Loading the Template" earlier in this chapter, but continue to add all the templates you will be using.

There is one possible source of conflict using this method that can occur when you load more than one template containing exactly the same option. For example, if you load the *windows.adm* template included with Windows 98 and the *admin.adm* template included with Windows 95, both have the option of setting custom folders. The DU policy will appear as in Figure 4-16, with two Custom Desktop Icons options.

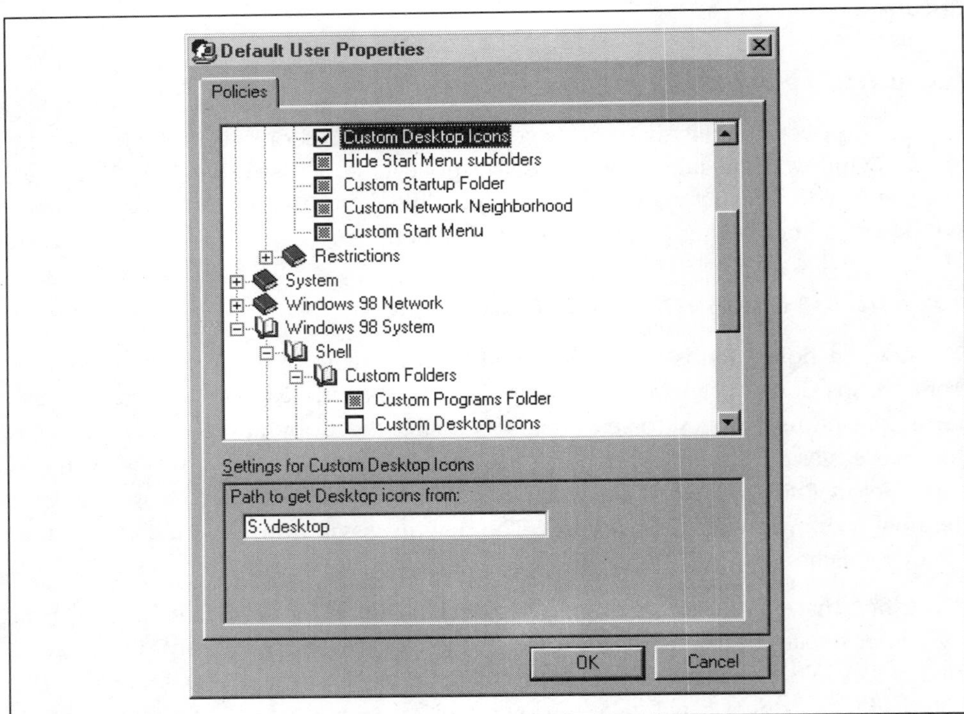

Figure 4-16. Using multiple templates with common options

The first instance of custom desktop icons comes from the *admin.adm* template, which is listed first in the SPE Current Policy Template(s) list box (Options → Policy Template). The second instance comes from the *windows.adm* template. With these two templates loaded, it is possible to specify two different custom icon folders for the same user. In this case, the policy file would be merged in much the same way as seen in Figure 4-16. The custom desktop icon folder will first be set to *S:\desktop*, and then be reset to the cleared position—allowing the icon folder on the local drive to be active. Use multiple templates cautiously, always checking that two instances of the same restriction do not have conflicting settings.

If you choose to load templates individually, closing the policy file between loading each template, make sure that you always save the policy file by choosing Save rather than Save As. If you choose Save As the settings from the second template will not be appended to the policy file, but will rather overwrite it.

Adding Specific Computer Policies

Specific computer policy entries in Poledit can be created based on the workstation's computer name, which is set in the Network applet of the Control Panel under the Identification tab.

In Figure 4-17, the computer name is Les; thus, a computer policy could be created with the name *Les*. The workstation's computer name (not the workgroup) could also be set to reflect group membership. This method could be used to give all of the computers in a particular group the same computer policy.

Note that if the computer name is ever changed, the computer policy will no longer be active, and the Default Computer policy (if one exists) will become active for that workstation.

Manual Update Mode

In some cases, such as when a network client does not support automatic downloading of system policies, you will need to use manual rather than automatic remote update. Microsoft cautions, however, that manual update works only after the policy file has been automatically downloaded at least once. This is because most workstations are set for automatic download by default. Rather than manually entering the location of the policy file on each workstation, it is easier to first store the policy file in the automatic remote update location with the option for manual remote update set in the policy file. The first download of the policy file will edit the registry to include the correct location to be used for manual downloading. The workstation will now be configured to subsequently download the policy file from the manual remote update location.

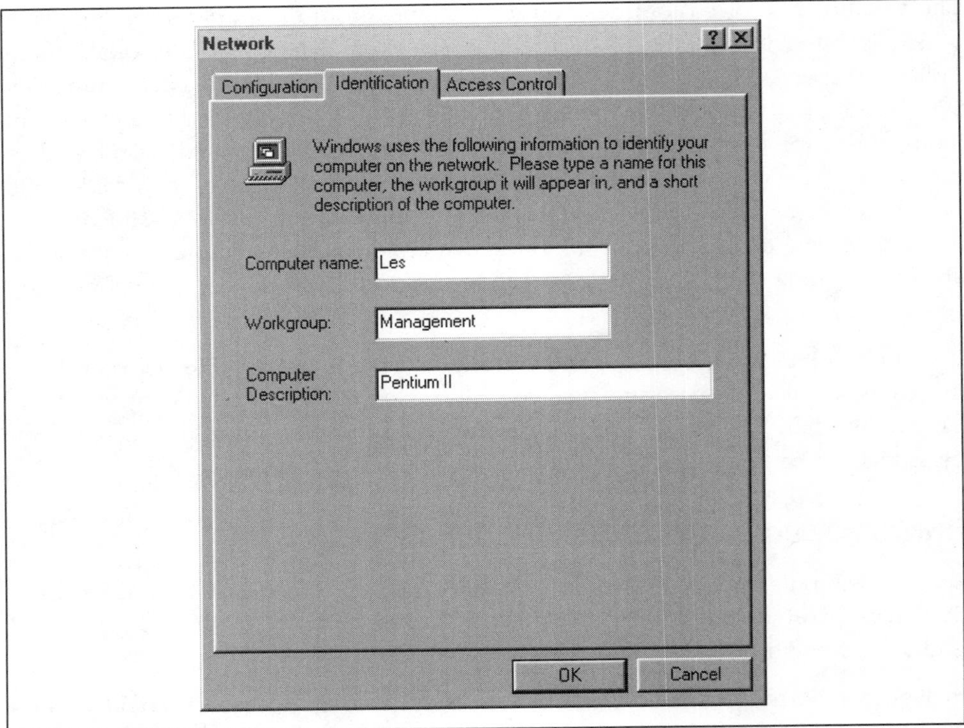

Figure 4-17. Setting the computer name

Manual update can be specified in the Default Computer policy (Figure 4-11) using the *admin.adm* or *windows.adm* templates in Network → Update. Use the drop-down menu to change Update Mode from automatic to manual. In the path list box, put the full pathname as well as the policy filename. This can be expressed as a mapped drive (e.g., *S:\Policy\config.pol*) or as a UNC path (*\\server\share\ntconfig.pol*). Note that the Windows NT *%LogonServer%* environment variable is not supported in the manual update pathname. This policy file setting will change the workstation to manual update after logging in the first time using automatic update.

On a Windows NT4 network, manual update could be used to specify any network server (such as a Windows Terminal Server) for the location of a Windows 9x policy file, rather than the validating domain controller. On a Windows 2000 network, a directory location other than the Netlogon share could be specified. On a NetWare network, a directory other than *Sys\public* on the preferred server could be specified.

Stopping the Save Settings Question

Many administrators of communal Windows 9x workstations routinely delete the entire Windows *\profiles* subdirectory using a command in the logon script. Some do it because the *user.dat* can become corrupted, causing unpredictable network errors. Others do it simply to prevent the local hard drive from becoming cluttered with profiles and folders. For whatever reason, all have the same complaint—how do you stop the annoying "Do you want to save your settings?" question?

It is possible to stop this nag by using a relatively simple batch file that is called from the logon script. The batch file creates the necessary profile subdirectory each time the user logs on, and uses the *%username%* environment variable and *Regedit* to save the required registry entries to a file called *profiles.reg*, which is then merged into the registry.

The username environment variable does not typically exist by default in a NetWare network, but adding the following line to the user's or container's logon script can easily create it:

```
SET USERNAME=login_name
```

Since the Windows NT logon processor does not support setting environment variables in Windows 9x workstations, use the utility *winset.exe* (available in the Windows 98 Resource Kit). The syntax is the same as for the MS-DOS Set command. To set the username variable, you can use the following command in the Windows NT logon script or from a batch file:

```
WINSET USERNAME=%USERNAME%
```

A text editor like Notepad can be used to create and save the following batch file, called *profiles.bat*. Included in this batch file are some optional workstation cleanup commands (line indents indicate that the line is too long for this book's margins and is a continuation of the previous one):

```
@echo off
C:
;DELETE THE WIN9X PROFILES SUBDIRECTORY (OPTIONAL)
ECHO Y | DELTREE C:\WINDOWS\PROFILES
;RECREATE THE PROFILES SUBDIRECTORY (OPTIONAL)
MD C:\WINDOWS\PROFILES
;CHANGE TO THE WINDOWS DIRECTORY
CD\WINDOWS
;DELETE ANY PREVIOUS COPIES OF PROFILES.REG FROM OTHER USERS
del profiles.reg
;ADD THE LINE WHICH IDENTIFIES PROFILES.REG AS A REGISTRY FILE
echo REGEDIT4 >> profiles.reg
;ADD THE REGISTRY KEY WHICH APPENDS THE USER TO THE PROFILE LIST
```

```
echo [HKEY_LOCAL_MACHINE\SOFTWARE\Microsoft\Windows\CurrentVersion\ProfileList\
      %username%] >> profiles.reg
;ADD THE LOCATION OF THE USER'S LOCAL PROFILE TO THE REGISTRY KEY
echo "ProfileImagePath"="C:\\WINDOWS\\Profiles\\%username%">> profiles.reg
;CREATE THE LOCAL SUBDIRECTORY FOR THE USER'S PROFILE
MD C:\WINDOWS\PROFILES\%USERNAME%
;MERGE THE REGISTRY FILE TO THE LOCAL REGISTRY
REGEDIT /S PROFILES.REG
```

If the user already existed in the registry, the key will not be duplicated but simply rewritten.

As an alternative to Regedit, you could use the *reg.exe* utility to create these same registry entries (see the "The reg.exe Utility" section later on).

If you prefer to use Perl, this same process can be replicated using the following Perl script, saved as a file called *profiles.pl.* The Perl binaries and libraries can be placed on a central network file share and then the scripts can be run from there:

```
`echo off`;
`c:`;

# delete c:\windows\profiles
`deltree /y c:\\windows\\profiles`;

#recreate the profiles subdirectory
`md c:\\windows\\profiles`;

#delete any previous copies of profiles.reg in c:\windows
`del c:\\windows\\profiles.reg`;

#add the line  which identifies profiles.reg as a registry file
`echo REGEDIT4 >> c:\\windows\\profiles.reg`;

#add the registry key which appends the user to the profile list
`echo [HKEY_LOCAL_MACHINE\\SOFTWARE\\Microsoft\\Windows\\CurrentVersion\\
         ProfilesList\\$ENV{username}] >> c:\\windows\\profiles.reg`;

#add the location of the user local profile to the registry key
`echo "ProfileImagePath"="C:\\\\WINDOWS\\\\Profiles\\\\$ENV{username}" >> c:\\
          windows\\profiles.reg`;

#create the local subdirectory for the users profile
`md c:\\windows\\profiles\\$ENV{username}`;

#merge the registry file to the local registry
`regedit /S c:\\windows\\profiles.reg`;

`echo on`;
exit;
```

The script could be run from the logon script by inserting the following command:

```
perl profiles.pl
```

Perl must be on an accessible network directory, or on the local hard drive.

Other Registry Edits

There are other useful registry settings that you may want to include when running the *profiles.bat* batch file. For example, you may not want the user's profile to be copied to their home network directory, but only saved to the local drive. Or perhaps you would like to turn off annoying profile error messages such as:

```
"Your local profile was created when the home directory was disconnected. Do you
want to use the local profile to overwrite your home directory profile?"
```

Finally, to increase security you can make sure that remote update and user profiles are re-enabled every time a user logs on.

To change these settings, you can add any or all of the following lines to the registry file, *profiles.reg,* after the line reading **REGEDIT 4**. Note that these edits will work for both Windows NT4 and Windows 9x workstations:

```
; RESTRICT SAVING PROFILE TO THE LOCAL DRIVE ONLY
Echo [HKEY_LOCAL_MACHINE\Network\Login] >> profiles.reg
Echo "UseHomeDirectory"=dword:00000000 >> profiles.reg
; STOP PROFILE ERRORS FROM BEING DISPLAYED
echo [HKEY_USERS\.Default\Software\Microsoft\Windows\CurrentVersion] >> profiles.
     reg
echo "DisplayProfileErrors"=dword:00000000 >> profiles.reg
; SETS AUTOMATIC REMOTE UPDATE MODE
Echo [HKEY_LOCAL_MACHINE\System\CurrentControlSet\Control\Update] >> profiles.reg
Echo "UpdateMode"=dword:00000001 >> profiles.reg
```

Cleaning Out the Profile List Registry Key

If you want to clean up the profiles list in the Windows registry, it is possible to use an INF file to remove the registry key that contains the list of users who have logged on to a particular workstation. This registry key is HKEY_LOCAL_MACHINE\SOFTWARE\Microsoft\Windows\CurrentVersion\ProfileList. To automate the removal of this registry key you must first create an INF file, which I will call *delreg.inf.* This file would contain the following lines:

```
[version]
signature="$CHICAGO$"

[DefaultUnInstall]
delreg=Reg.Delete.Keys

[Reg.Delete.Keys]
  HKLM,"Software\Microsoft\Windows\CurrentVersion\ProfileList"
```

The Windows 9x command to install this file is:

```
Rundll.exe setupx.dll,InstallHinfSection DefaultUninstall 132 N:\public\delreg.inf
```

The Windows NT command to install this file is:

```
Rundll32.exe syssetup.dll,SetupInfObjectInstallAction DefaultUninstall 132 N:\
      public\delreg.inf
```

Make sure that you include the full pathname of the *delreg.inf* file, and then this too could be included in the *profiles.bat* utility.

The reg.exe Utility

The *reg.exe* utility allows you to execute various registry edits either from the command prompt or a batch file, and is bundled with both the Windows NT4 and Windows 98 Resource Kits. *reg.exe* can be used to delete, add, or change registry entries. For example, instead of using an INF file to delete the profiles list registry key you could use the following single command line in a batch file:

```
REG DELETE HKLM\Software\Microsoft\Windows\CurrentVersion\ProfileList
```

The valid *reg.exe* commands are as follows:

REG /?
: Lists the valid commands and syntax.

REG ADD
: Adds a registry value for a specified registry key.

REG COPY
: Copies a registry entry to a new specified location in a local or remote registry.

REG DELETE
: Deletes a registry key or entire hive. It cannot be used to delete top-level registry keys, and—unlike the INF file method—on a remote workstation it can be used only to delete keys in the HKLM and HKU.

REG LOAD
: Used mainly for troubleshooting, this option temporarily loads a registry key or entire hive into the registry root from a REG file.

REG QUERY
: Lists the subkeys and values for a specified registry key.

REG RESTORE
: Restores the registry entries contained in a valid REG file.

REG SAVE or REG BACKUP

Saves a registry key, value or entire hive into a specified ASCII file (named **.reg*).

REG UNLOAD

Removes the registry entries loaded with the REG LOAD command.

REG UPDATE

Changes the value of a registry key only if that key exists in the registry.

To use this utility rather than Regedit to stop the "save settings" nag, include the following in a batch file to create the required registry entries replacing the *profiles.reg* file:

```
Echo Y | Reg delete HKLM\SOFTWARE\Microsoft\Windows\CurrentVersion\ProfileList >
         nul
Reg add HKLM\SOFTWARE\Microsoft\Windows\CurrentVersion\ProfileList\%username% >
         nul
Reg add HKLM\SOFTWARE\Microsoft\Windows\CurrentVersion\ProfileList\%username%\
         ProfileImagePath="C:\WINDOWS\Profiles\%username%" > nul
```

The addition of the > nul command directs the command responses to a null device, preventing them from displaying on the screen and allowing for silent operation of the batch file.

Summary

Creating a predictable policy file, one where you can be sure of a user's resulting restrictions, is a matter of careful workstation preparation as well as proper creation and testing of the policy file. I have given you an example of a precise method, intended to minimize the creation of policy conflicts while maximizing the ability to test for possible problems. The "Miscellaneous Advice" section should give you an idea of how you can customize this method for your own policy file, plus how to use registry files to automate some of the workstation setup and fix particular annoyances like the "save settings" nag.

Hopefully, you now find that your policy file works perfectly. You have your user, group and computer policies ready—but are your workstations really secure? Chapter 5 will discuss security holes in the SPE, and additional methods of securing your workstations.

5

It's Not Perfect

There is possibly nothing more frustrating (and more than a little embarrassing) than having someone break into your computer system just to destroy the system setup or system files. Just when you thought you had a secure system, you discover how wrong you were. The Windows System Policy Editor cannot be viewed as a perfect security tool. Existing security holes can be exploited by anyone with the patience and determination to do a modest amount of research, since the methods are easily found on the Internet by searching for such terms as hack, crack, cracking, hackz or hacker.

The term "hacker" has generally been used by the media to define any person who attempts to gain unauthorized access to a computer. However, the online computer encyclopedia Webopedia (*http://webopedia.internet.com*) says that the correct term for such a person is "cracker."

> The pejorative sense of *hacker* is becoming more prominent largely because the popular press has co-opted the term to refer to individuals who gain unauthorized access to computer systems for the purpose of stealing and corrupting data. Hackers, themselves, maintain that the proper term for such individuals is cracker.

Often a true hacker is not attempting anything malicious, but is trying to satisfy an unrelenting curiosity. Since a hacker tends to do little damage, and often restores a system to its original state when she is done, it is not the hacker who is responsible for causing a workstation to fail. Nor is it really a true computer cracker, whose purpose is typically high-tech burglary. A good cracker will also leave no evidence that he has tampered with a computer. Probably the best term for a person who destroys a workstation is *computer vandal.* Unlike a hacker, a vandal is bent on doing as much damage as possible. Curiosity is not a computer vandal's goal; chaos and possibly fulfillment of a god complex are. To avoid the computer vandal on a communal workstation, or at least to not be surprised by when she strikes, an admin should know something about bypassing computer security.

This chapter discusses some very basic methods of circumventing security on a Windows workstation. Although there is not complete agreement on the use of the term, I will refer to these methods as *cracking*. I will also discuss ways to prevent cracking attempts, plus some specific security problems with the SPE itself. I am not including this information because I in any way condone its use, but rather because I have often been the victim of a computer vandal's activities. I discovered that they only way to prevent some of the attacks was to expect them, and the only way to do that was to know exactly how the attack could be accomplished. Not all security holes can be plugged, but then no computer system is completely secure. A system administrator should simply do the best she can, and then utilize agreements such as acceptable use policies (see Appendix A, *Sample Acceptable-Use Policy*) to deal with successful computer vandals and to deter future attempts. In many areas, before legal action can be brought against a computer vandal, that person must have been warned that accessing a particular computer without permission was not allowed. So in addition to the acceptable use policy, a logon banner should always be used if you are concerned about unlawful access to your workstations (see Chapter 4, *Building the Policy File*).

Lack of Security in Windows 9x

If I were asked which Windows operating system was best suited for communal workstations, my answer would have to be either Windows NT or Windows 2000. However, many organizations with public workstations, such as schools or libraries, are instead using Windows 9x as their operating system. Windows 9x likely became the operating system of choice in these locations for various reasons. Both Windows NT and Windows 2000 require a faster processor than Windows 9x, and so do not run on the old hardware that some schools are still forced to use. Windows NT and Windows 2000 both have a far more strict hardware compatibility list, again meaning that many patchwork systems will not run them. Finally, many old DOS programs that are still in use in these organizations will not run on either Windows NT or Windows 2000.

As a result of the NTFS filesystem, both Windows NT and Windows 2000 are considered far more secure operating systems than Windows 9x. Consequently, this chapter will concentrate on increasing security in a Windows 9x workstation, which, although less secure, is frequently found in areas requiring a high level of workstation security.

FAT and NTFS

The filesystem of a hard disk contains information concerning where and how files are stored on the partition, as well as the attributes (or properties) of those files. The two most common filesystems are FAT (File Allocation Table) and NTFS (New Technology File System). Unlike the FAT system, NTFS has no file allocation table, but rather a Master File Table (MFT), which acts like an index to all of the files on the NTFS partition. The FAT format can be used by both DOS and Windows (versions 3x, 95, 98 and NT) operating systems. Only with Windows NT or Windows 2000 is there the choice of using either the FAT system or the more secure NTFS. Because of this difference in filesystems, an NTFS-partitioned drive is not visible if you boot the computer with either a DOS or Windows 9x boot disk. Since the required system files are typically too large to format a 1.44-MB floppy as an NTFS boot disk, third-party programs such as NTFSDOS (Winternals Software *http://www.winternals.com* or Sysinternals Software *http://www.sysinternals.com*) are required to create an NTFS boot disk.

What makes Windows 9x a less-secure operating system? Although there are many differences between the Windows operating systems, the most significant difference affecting security is their filesystems. Windows 9x uses the FAT filesystem, which supports simply read-only, hidden, system, and archive file attributes—for all intents and purposes, FAT doesn't have file-level security. The Windows NT and Windows 2000 NTFS filesystem, on the other hand, allows an administrator to assign a range of permissions for files and directories. Groups or individual users can have file or directory access ranging from no access through Read, Write, Execute, Delete or Full access permissions. See the Windows NT or Windows 2000 Resource Kits for more information on assigning file and directory permissions. Plus, the NTFS 5.0 filesystem available with Windows 2000 provides on-the-fly data encryption and decryption.

Passwords: Your First Line of Defense

You can implement every security procedure under the sun, but if your passwords are not secure nothing will save your system. Make sure that your users are aware that they must keep their passwords secret and not write them down. Check all monitors for sticky notes—unfortunately that's not a joke. Review the four rules of good passwords with your users:

- Don't use words found in the dictionary, because password cracking programs will try all words found in a standard dictionary. Even dictionary words with a number added to the beginning or end (such as secret1) can be broken using cracking programs.

- Don't use your name, your child's name, your pet's name, your user ID, your birthday or any other personal information. Anyone who knows anything about you could guess these passwords.
- Don't create passwords with fewer than four characters—try to make them at least six or eight characters long.
- Don't use letters only, but include numbers and special characters such as @, #, &, or * in your passwords.

A good password could be a phrase, such as MYFAVORITECOLOR, or better yet a phrase separated by numbers or characters, such as MY#FAVORITE2COLOR. A password like this may be harder to remember than your logon ID, but it would be almost impossible to crack.

You can also use the server security features found in NetWare, Windows NT and Windows 2000 to set a maximum password life span. If a user is forced to change his password regularly, it is less likely to be discovered by a cracker. Requiring the user to use unique passwords at each change will also prevent her from toggling between a few favorite passwords.

Hardware Vulnerabilities

Many cracking methods rely on a person having physical access to the computer, so if you allow this level of access, you must assume that your workstation is not secure. One of the first things you can do to increase security is to minimize physical contact. The computer case can be locked away so that a user cannot open the chassis, power the computer down or disconnect cabling. Only the monitor, keyboard and mouse should be accessible. This can easily be achieved by creating locking cabinets under the desktop. There are many options available from various businesses specifically for this purpose. One thing to note: if you do have closed locked cabinets, you must install venting fans to allow airflow so that the workstation does not overheat.

If you do not have the ability to physically lock your workstation, expect the cracking attempts that follow.

Protecting the BIOS Settings

The BIOS (Basic Input/Output System) contains optional user-defined system settings such as hard drive type, preferred boot device and so on. These settings are stored on the CMOS (Complementary Metal Oxide Semiconductor), a semiconductor chip located on the computer motherboard. The BIOS can retain settings even when the system is powered off because of the electrical backup provided by the CMOS battery. How the BIOS settings are accessed depends upon the BIOS manufacturer, but typically most are accessed while the computer is booting up by pressing a key during the power-on self-test (POST). For example, the AwardBIOS by Phoenix technologies is accessed by pressing the Delete key during the POST and after seeing the following message:

```
TO ENTER SETUP, PRESS DEL KEY
```

The BIOS is often a target for vandals since incorrect settings can cause the computer to fail to boot. Typically, an administrator will set-up a password in the BIOS to restrict access to the settings and prevent this malicious tampering. However, if the computer case is opened and the battery is removed for a period of time, the CMOS will lose any new settings and default back to the factory settings. This in effect causes the password to be lost, leaving the BIOS free to be altered. Sometimes the CMOS has a jumper, which if set to the closed position will also cause the CMOS to default to the factory settings when the computer is powered back on. Usually motherboard diagrams are required to find the appropriate jumper, though these diagrams are often available on the Internet.

Access to the BIOS can be gained even without physical access to the computer chassis. There are several BIOS password-cracking programs available on the Internet and given enough time to run the program, a user can crack the BIOS password. Only vigilant supervised access can prevent vandals from successfully using such a program.

Access to A: Drive

If a user has access to *A:* drive, there are multiple ways in which to tamper with the computer. Using a boot disk (a disk that contains the computer operating system) the person can gain access to a command prompt (DOS prompt). From a command prompt he can delete files, alter the startup files (*autoexec.bat, config.sys, win.ini* or *system.ini*), run the registry editor to merge changes from a REG file or delete security programs. Even if the floppy disk used is not a boot disk, unwanted files such as cracking programs, viruses or third-party registry editing programs can be brought in.

There are a number of things you can do to minimize access to *A:* drive:

Change the BIOS settings so that the computer does not attempt to boot from A: drive
: The typical BIOS settings allow you to choose to boot from various drives or combinations of drives (such as boot from *C:* then *A:* if *C:* is unavailable). The default is usually *A:* then *C:*. Change this to *C:* only (if *C:* is your boot drive). Users will then no longer be able to boot from a floppy disk and gain access to a command prompt.

Use the BIOS to disable A: drive altogether

The BIOS will allow you to choose a floppy drive type such as 3.5" 1.44-MB, 3.5" 720-K, and so on. One of the choices will be None. If you choose this, *A:* drive will no longer be available for use by any user.

Purchase a floppy disk lock

Locks can be purchased to restrict access to the floppy disk drive. These are usually plastic inserts with a swivel hook that locks onto the inside of the drive. The problem is that the keys are usually all exactly the same, in much the same way as a keyboard lock. If someone gains access to one key, she will have access to all the floppy locks.

Put the entire computer case into a locked cabinet

With the entire case locked away, even if *A:* drive is accessible via software, it will not be physically accessible.

The first three solutions are effective in many cases, however as I mentioned previously, even a password cannot keep your BIOS secure. Probably the most effective solution is to lock the entire computer case in a cabinet, the success of which is dependent on the quality of the cabinet and lock.

Vulnerability During System Boot

System policies and third-party programs provide a degree of protection for a Windows 9x workstation, yet these typically rely on the Windows operating system to be fully loaded. It is possible to interrupt this process and gain access to a command prompt. Since DOS inherently has no security, every vandal will try to get access to a DOS prompt.

There are many ways to obtain a command prompt during the boot process:

When the computer is booting, pressing Ctrl-Break or Ctrl-C repeatedly will bring up the message "Terminate batch job (Y/N)?". If the user responds with a Yes, *autoexec.bat* will terminate and Windows will fail to load. The user will be left with a DOS prompt. You can prevent this from happening by:

— Not using an *autoexec.bat* or *config.sys* file. These files are not required by Windows 9x and Windows will load perfectly fine if they do not exist, *unless* you have hardware which specifically requires settings to be loaded from the startup files. In this case, review the next three options below.

— Adding the line `switches = /F /N` to the *config.sys* file. The `/F` option skips the delay after displaying the "Starting Windows" message, and the `/N` option disables the use of F5 and F8 to bypass the startup files.

— Adding the line `@CTTY NUL` to the very beginning of the *autoexec.bat* and the line `CTTY CON` to the very end. The first command redirects input to the batch file to a null device and the second command redirects input back to the console when the batch file is complete. This effectively allows no user input until the batch program has completed.

— Add the line `Break Off` to the beginning of the *autoexec.bat*. This will minimize the number of opportunities for Ctrl-C to break the batch processing.

Boot menu

Just before Windows loads, and just after the POST, pressing the F5 key will bypass the startup files completely, while pressing the F8 key (or Ctrl in Windows 98) will bring up the boot menu. With this menu the user can choose from the following boot options:

- Normal
- Logged (*\BOOTLOG.TXT*)
- Safe mode
- Safe mode with network support
- Step-by-step conformation
- Command prompt only
- Safe mode command prompt only

The boot menu gives the options to selectively disable commands from the *config.sys* or *autoexec.bat* files or to bypass those files totally, to boot to a command prompt or boot to Windows Safe Mode, which allows varying degrees of access depending on the default profile settings (see Chapter 4).

To disable the boot menu, edit the file *msdos.sys* (found in the root directory of the boot disk) using a text editor such as Notepad. Since this file is typically hidden and read-only, if you edit the file from the command prompt you must first remove these attributes by typing the command **`ATTRIB MSDOS.SYS -S -H -R`**. Then add one or more of these switches to the `[Options]` section of the file:

`BOOTKEYS=0`
: With this entry, pressing the F4, F5, F6, F8 or Ctrl keys at bootup will have no effect.

`BOOTDELAY=0`
: This will minimize the delay between the POST and the loading of Windows 95—the time period in which pressing F5 or F8 is effective. Setting `BOOTKEYS=0` will override this switch. Note that this option is not supported in Windows 98.

`BOOTSAFE=0`

This will remove the option of safe mode from the boot menu.

`NETWORK=0`

This will remove the option safe mode with network from the boot menu.

Do not remove any text (such as the multiple rows of Xs) from the *msdos.sys* file. This file needs to be greater than 1024 bytes to provide backward compatibility with other software programs. When you are done editing the file set the appropriate attributes of hidden and read-only either by right-clicking on the file, choosing properties and checking the appropriate boxes or by typing the following command from the command prompt: `ATTRIB MSDOS.SYS +S +H +R`.

System Policy Editor Policies and Vulnerabilities

As I have already mentioned, the SPE is not a perfect tool. In fact it is much like the *Titanic*, it looks big and secure but it's full of annoying little holes. I will first examine the holes in the SPE based on the policy affected. Then I will try to point out any possible solutions using available Windows tools, although typically if these security holes are a problem, the best solution may be third-party security programs in addition to the SPE. Appendix B lists several of these available programs, many of which are compatible with the concurrent use of system policies.

Run Only Allowed Windows Applications

This policy is found in the user properties of many templates such as *admin.adm*, *common.adm*, *windows.adm* or the *shell.adm* templates. It allows the administrator to restrict a user's access to specified 32-bit Windows programs, or to DOS programs if they are listed as an associated PIF file, or a BAT file. Due to a bug in the SPE, DOS programs cannot be listed as their associated EXE or COM file.

Unfortunately, programs are restricted only if they are called through the shell namespace. If a program bypasses the shell namespace, the applications called from within this program will not be monitored by the SPE and so will not be restricted. See the section titled *msinfo32.exe* further on in this chapter for an example of just such a program. In addition some programming applications can be used to bypass this policy by adding an execute command into the script. Be aware of this if you allow your users to use programming applications such the popular school program Logo (by Harvard Associates).

A secondary problem with this policy is that the SPE checks only the application's current filename, rather than the *original* filename. An application's original filename can be viewed by right-clicking on the file and choosing Properties → the tab labeled Version → Original Filename (see Figure 5-1). The use of the current filename creates a problem because any prohibited application can be renamed to any application found on the allowed list, and then executed. For example, if a user knows she is allowed to run Internet Explorer, he will be able to run another program simply by renaming it to *iexplore.exe*. You can disguise this ability to some extent by renaming the allowed programs (for example renaming *iexplore.exe* to *iexplore2.exe*), and then listing this new filename in the allowed applications list. However, this provides only limited protection because if the user searches the local drive for the file, he will realize that it has been renamed.

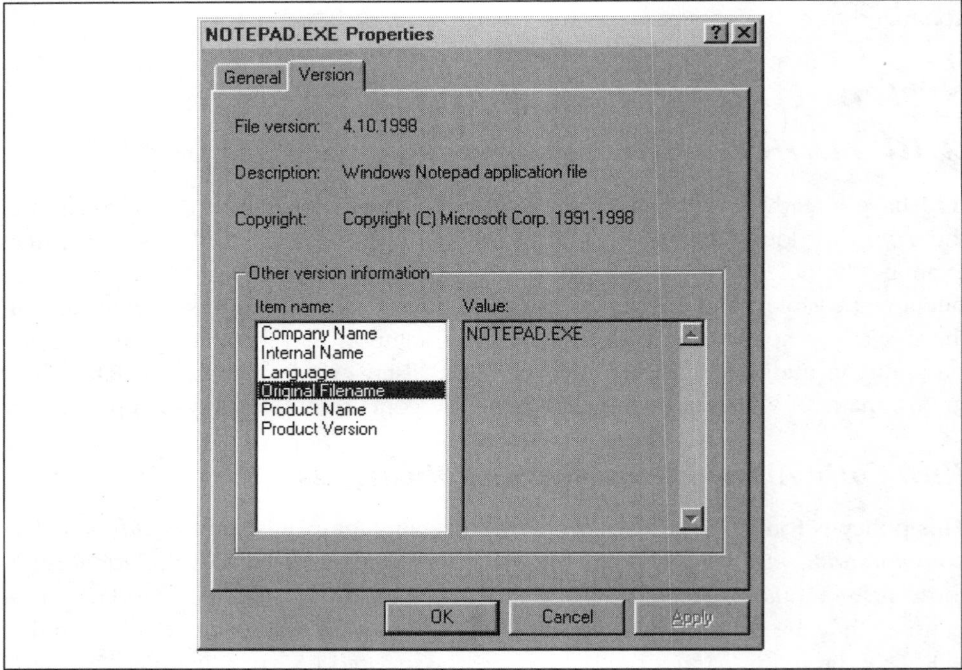

Figure 5-1. Locating the original filename

Right-click context menus and allowed programs

From the Windows desktop, right-clicking on a file will produce a context menu containing various options such as Open, Delete or Rename. Utilities such as Winzip or Norton Utilities may add additional choices to this menu. Any utility called from the context menu will be unaffected by this policy, and the associated program will be allowed to run.

To avoid this problem, disable right-click context menus. The relevant templates are called *shell.adm, sp1shell.adm* and *winnt.adm* and the policy is called "Disable context menu in shell folders." This policy does not work in Windows 95, in which case you could use a mouse utility program that allows the right mouse button to be reassigned to equal the left mouse button. In Windows NT4 this policy can still be bypassed, and the context menus displayed, by using Alt-Enter. Microsoft has a downloadable fix for this; contact Microsoft Technical Support for more information.

Remove Run Command

The option to remove the Run command from the Start menu is found in the user properties of many templates such as *admin.adm*, *common.adm*, *windows.adm* or the *shell.adm* templates. This policy does not remove the ability to run programs from other locations; thus a program can be run by double-clicking on it when browsing the drive or by double-clicking on it in the Find results window.

If you want to restrict access to a specific program in Windows 9x, you have a number of options:

- Choose the policy option Run Only Allowed Windows Applications (see previous section for holes in this policy).
- Hide drives to minimize the ability to browse for executables.
- Use a third-party software package to restrict access to files on the local drives (see Appendix B for a list of some of these programs).
- Remove the program completely from the local drive and place it on a network folder. Then grant appropriate permissions to that folder.

Hide Network Neighborhood

This policy is found in the user properties of many templates such as *admin.adm*, *common.adm*, *windows.adm* or the *shell.adm* templates. Network Neighborhood allows a user to browse through available network resources such as servers, shared drives, folders and printers. Shared network folders can be mapped to a drive letter that will then appear in My Computer, or printer ports can be captured (Novell) allowing the user to print to a network printer. To increase security, you may not want the user to freely browse though all available resources, and so Network Neighborhood can be hidden using this policy.

However, users will still be able to browse network resources by choosing the Map Network Drive option available by right-clicking on My Computer either from the desktop or from within Explorer. In Windows NT a user would still be able to browse network resources through the use of the `NET VIEW` and `NET USE` commands issued from the command prompt.

The only way to hide the My Computer icon and avoid this problem would be to use the policy Hide All Items on Desktop, which is available in the same five templates mentioned previously. An alternative would be to use the Hide Drives option in addition to Hide Network Neighborhood. Although the Map Network Drive option will still show a list of servers, any mapped drives will not be visible in Explorer, on My Computer, or at the DOS prompt. Note that there are ways around the Hide Drives option too (see the "Hide Drives in My Computer" section later in this chapter).

It is not possible to safely disable the Explorer command without the use of third-party software. To avoid the use of **NET USE** and **NET VIEW** in Windows NT, set user permissions to disable access to the command prompt (restrict access to *cmd.exe*) or do not allow execute permission for these commands.

Require Validation by Network for Windows Access

This policy is found under the computer properties in the *admin.adm* and *windows.adm* templates. If this policy is not used, then at the logon window the user could simply choose Cancel, and get the default user profile with its possibly more relaxed level of restrictions. If this policy *is* active, the user will not be allowed to progress beyond the logon screen, unless she provides a valid network username and password. If a user tries to cancel out of the logon screen, she will get the message displayed in Figure 5-2.

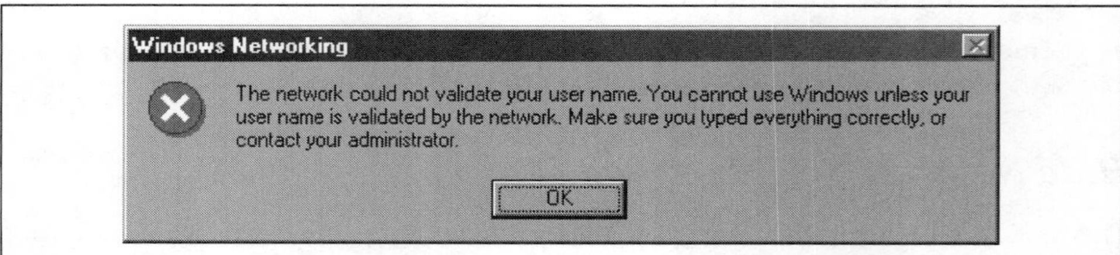

Figure 5-2. Network could not validate username message

This policy can be bypassed in three situations:

The computer is booted in safe mode
: If the user boots to safe mode, the logon screen will not appear at all since network support is not loaded. The user will have a limited degree of access to the workstation. The level of access will depend upon the default local user profile.

The workstation uses the Novell client and the user disconnects the network interface card (NIC) from the network by unplugging the network cable
: For Microsoft clients, this policy will be active even if the user disconnects the NIC from the network by unplugging the network cable. However, when using Novell clients, the policy will not be active if the NIC is unplugged, and the user will still be able to access the workstation by selecting Cancel at the

logon window. This is because if the NIC doesn't bind with Novell's GINA (Graphical Identification and Authentication dynamic link library), the client does not load. Since system policies are loaded by the client, the user is allowed to log on even without network confirmation. The user's level of access will again depend upon the default local user profile.

The user enters an incorrect NT domain name in the network dialog box on a Windows 9x or Windows NT workstation

If the domain name in the dialog box is changed to have one or more spaces appended to the end, or if it is a nonexistent domain name, system policies will not be applied. When Windows attempts to verify that the server is in the correct domain, the verify process fails due to the added space or nonexistent name. Consequently policies are not merged with the registry and no error message appears to warn the user. The user is instead prompted with a local Windows logon box that can be bypassed by pressing Esc, giving him access to the workstation.

The first problem, booting into safe mode, can be remedied by disabling the Boot menu (see "Vulnerability During System Boot") and by creating a severely restricted default local user profile. The second problem can be avoided by either using the Microsoft client for Novell networks, creating a restricted default user profile, or physically locking the computer chassis to prevent access to the network cables. The third problem is fixed with updated *msnp32.dll* and *msnet32.dll* files available from Microsoft (see Knowledgebase articles Q237923 and Q178979 for more information).

Control Panel Restrictions

Various control panel applets can be restricted using policies found in the *admin.adm, windows.adm, common.adm, shell.adm,* and *sp1shell.adm* templates. There are methods for circumventing these policies, since policies restricting Control Panel access only hide the applets from within the Control Panel rather than disabling their use. Even with the restrictions active, applets can still be accessed in four ways:

- Through the use of help files
- From Find results
- Through a command prompt
- By re-enabling the registry key

Help files

If you search for "password" in Windows help you will be given helpful information on how to change your password—including a link to the password control applet. There is no way to disable the use of Windows help files using the SPE, but there are a few options:

- You could rename the *winhlp32.exe* file, although this will also disable Contents and Index help in programs such as Office 97. However, removing this file will not disable the Help option in the Start menu in Windows 98. You must rename the file *hh.exe* to disable the Help option in the Start menu.
- For Windows 95 and Windows NT, you could replace the *windows.hlp* file with another innocuous help file such as *winmine.hlp*—the Minesweeper help file. This file would then be displayed by default when the Help option is chosen from the Start menu.
- You can delete specific **.hlp* files themselves. Most help files can be found in the *\Windows\Help* subdirectory.
- You could remove the **.cpl* files from the hard drive, and then access them from a restricted network folder or from a floppy disk as required.

Find: All files

Control Panel applets can also be accessed simply by using the Start menu → Find → Files or Folders, or by pressing F3 and searching for **.cpl*, and then double-clicking on the file when it is found. To minimize this access, the Find command can be disabled from the Start menu (using the *admin.adm* and *windows.adm* templates), and although the F3 shortcut cannot be removed, it can be reassigned so that it no longer brings up the Find window. See the "Other Tips to Increase Workstation Security" section later in this chapter for more information.

Command prompt

From a command prompt, Control Panel applets can be accessed by typing the following command:

```
CONTROL applet_name.cpl
```

To minimize this problem you could:

- Remove the *control.exe* program from the local drive.
- Remove the applets from the local drive (see the "Hiding Specific Control Panel Applets" section later in this chapter for a list of applet filenames).
- Restrict access to a command prompt (using the *admin.adm*, and *windows.adm* templates).

Re-enable registry keys

Since registry keys are used to hide Control Panel applets, a REG file can be used to remove the policy and make them visible again (see Chapter 4 for information on using a REG file). The REG file can be merged into the registry from a DOS prompt or a DOS shell since the Regedit command-line options work even in 32-bit mode. This method requires that the user know the registry key that is used to disable the applet, and so it isn't as likely to occur as the other three methods.

To prevent a REG file from being used in this manner, delete *regedit.exe* or *regedt32.exe* from the local hard drive, restrict the use of command prompts, and disable access to floppy drives. See earlier in this chapter for a discussion on limiting access to a DOS shell and restricting access to floppy drives.

An additional protection is to disable the ability to edit specific registry keys. Although registry keys cannot be locked in Windows 9x, they can be locked if you are using a Windows NT workstation. To restrict access to specific registry keys on an NT workstation, run *regedt32.exe*. For each subkey you wish to lock choose Security → Permissions → Replace Permissions on Existing Subkeys. Then choose Everyone, change Type of Access to Read and then choose OK.

Before changing permissions on registry keys read the Microsoft Knowledgebase article Q13934, "Incorrect Permission in Registry Cause Unpredictable Results." Another useful KB article is Q153183, "How to Restrict Access to NT Registry from a Remote Computer."

If you have a NetWare server, you may want to look into using ZENworks instead of Microsoft policies. With ZENworks, policies are stored in the NDS rather than the local registry. Changes cannot easily be made to prevent the policy from being applied since the NDS resides on the network server. However, since ZEN policies are dependent upon the Workstation Manager service, removing this service from the network properties will disable ZEN policies.

Hiding Specific Control Panel Applets

If you would like to remove key applets, or copy them to a network drive for Admin-only use, Table 5-1 lists some of the common Control Panel applet filenames. These applets can be found in the *\Windows\System* subdirectory.

Table 5-1. Control Panel Applets

Filename	Windows 9x Control Panel Applet
access.cpl	Accessibility properties
appwiz.cpl	Add/Remove programs
desk.cpl	Display properties
findfast.cpl	MS Office Find Fast

Table 5-1. Control Panel Applets (continued)

Filename	Windows 9x Control Panel Applet
inetcpl.cpl	Internet properties-Internet Explorer
intl.cpl	Regional settings properties
joy.cpl	Game controllers
main.cpl	Mouse properties
mlcfg32.cpl	Internet mail properties
mmsys.cpl	Multimedia properties and devices
modem.cpl	Modem properties
netcpl.cpl	Network properties-protocols, clients and devices
odbccp32.cpl	ODBC data source administrator
password.cpl	Passwords properties
powercfg.cpl	Power management properties
sticpl.cpl	Scanners and cameras
sysdm.cpl	System properties (equal to right-click context menu from My Computer)
telephon.cpl	Dialing properties
themes.cpl	Desktop themes
timedate.cpl	Time/date properties
wgpocpl.cpl	Microsoft workgroup postoffice admin

It is also possible to hide certain Control Panel applets using the *control.ini* file rather than a registry entry. This method is not as commonly known, and so may be effective—although relying on a method that presumes a lack of knowledge is the weakest method of security. To hide applets in this manner, add the following lines to the *control.ini* file found in the Windows main directory:

```
[Don't Load]
applet_name.CPL=NO
```

If you would like to limit access to individual applets not listed in the standard policy templates, you can create your own custom template to restrict access using the following registry key entry:

```
HKCU\Control Panel\Don't Load
VALUENAME "applet_name.cpl"
```

To allow the applet to load use a DWORD value of 0, to stop it from loading use a string value of NO. See Chapter 8, *Creating a Custom Template*, for information on creating a custom template.

Object Linking and Embedding

Most Windows programs (such as Write, Excel, Word, WordPerfect, and so on) allow you to embed or link objects into a file. This is a security problem because these objects can be any kind of file, even an executable. Programs can be run, or hidden drives displayed by inserting an OLE object. This object can be displayed as an icon, and then selected from within the document to run the desired program (for example, *command.pif* to access a DOS shell).

There is no way to completely avoid this issue as OLE is a fundamental element of Windows programs. The program *packager.exe* could be renamed or deleted, or a customized toolbar could be created to remove the ability to link an object. However, this greatly reduces the ability to make complex documents, such as presentations that incorporate sound and video. The best choice would be to restrict access to specific programs through the "Run Only Allowed Windows Applications" policy, or to use third-party software.

Problems Related to Microsoft Office

MS Office 97 and MS Office 2000 bypass much of the typical Windows shell namespace, and so create security issues not found in other office suites. Specific security problems with Office 97 and Office 2000 are discussed in this section.

msinfo32.exe

As I mentioned previously, the policy 'Run only allowed windows applications' only restricts programs called through the shell namespace. Office includes a Windows shell program called *msinfo32.exe,* which runs outside of this namespace. This program is used by Microsoft technical support to aid in troubleshooting and can be accessed directly by browsing the drive, or by selecting from any Office toolbar Help → About Microsoft X (Word, Excel, etc.) → System Info.

Unfortunately from a security viewpoint, Msinfo also allows the user to run various system management tools. In addition, the System Information toolbar has a Run option (File → Run). The Run option can be used to access programs such as Regedit directly or to browse drives for an executable. A version of this program is also bundled with Windows 98, and although it does not have the Run option like the Office 97 version, it also allows INI files and startup files such as *autoexec.bat* to be altered.

Msinfo will not execute programs if a policy exists to restrict them, such as the policies that restrict registry tools or access to the MS-DOS prompt. However, since it can be used as a replacement for the Run command, you may want to remove it if it exists on your system. For most users the simplest solution is to delete the *msinfo.exe* or *msinfo32.exe* program files from the local drive. If you have not yet installed Office, use custom installation options to choose not to install Msinfo.

Hyperlinks

By default, typing a URL such as *http://www.ora.com* in a Word document will result in a live hyperlink. Double-clicking this link will launch the default browser, even if the appropriate shortcuts and icons are not otherwise available.

To avoid this problem in Word 2000, use the *word9.adm* template to set the policy Internet and Network Paths with Hyperlinks to the cleared position. This policy is found in the user properties: Microsoft Word 2000 → Tools | AutoCorrect... → AutoFormat As You Type → Replace As You Type. Unfortunately, this menu option cannot be similarly changed in Office 97 since the registry entry (located in HKCU\software\microsoft\office\8.0\word\data) is a binary value, and binary values cannot be altered using system policies.

Hide Drives in My Computer

While browsing drives, a user can right-click on a file and perhaps delete or rename it. So to prevent browsing, drives can be hidden. Although this policy hides drives within Explorer and My Computer, these drives are still available in any Office program. From the toolbar in Office 97 choose File → Open. You will note that in the list box labeled Look In, the drives are still effectively hidden. However if you type any hidden drive letter (such as *C:*) in the list box labeled "File to Open" you will be able to freely browse that drive. The same basic problem also exists in Office 2000 under File → Open. If you type any hidden drive letter (such as *C:*) in the list box labeled "File name," and then select the button labeled Open, you will be able to freely browse that drive. Microsoft reports that MS Office 2000 Service Release 1 resolves this problem (see KB article Q249949). Another method to browse a hidden drive in both Office versions is to choose Insert → Object → Create From File → Browse. You will again be able to browse the hidden drives.

Since Office does not use Explorer to access the directory structure of the drives, policies cannot be used to disable the ability to browse hidden drives. However, the mouse right-click context menus can be disabled, at least minimizing this problem. The relevant templates are called *shell.adm, sp1shell.adm* and *winnt.adm* and the policy is called "Disable context menu in shell folders." This policy does not work in Windows 95, in which case you could use a mouse utility program that allows the right mouse button to be reassigned to equal the left mouse button. In Windows NT4 this policy can still be bypassed, and the context menus displayed, by using Alt-Enter. Microsoft has a downloadable fix for this; contact Microsoft Technical Support for more information.

On a Windows NT workstation, the user can still access the drives by using the Tools menu in Explorer unless the user policy Remove Tools → Goto Menu From Explorer, in the *winnt.adm* template, is used in with to the Hide Drives policy.

Hide Network Neighborhood

In addition to the problems with this policy mentioned previously, Office programs have an added weakness. Even with this policy active, a network drive can still be mapped by choosing File → Save As. In the Office 97 Save As window, a button is available in the upper-right corner called Commands and Settings. Selecting this button produces options including Map Network Drive. In the Office 2000 Save As window there is a menu selection called Tools that when chosen produces a drop-down list containing the option to map a network drive. Although the network cannot be browsed, using the server name and path any available network folder can be mapped to a drive letter.

This problem can be avoided either by creating a macro that displays a custom Save As dialog box or by using a resource editor to edit the program menu (see "Custom Macro Solution" and "Resource Editors" later in this chapter).

Find Fast and Office Startup

In Office 97 and Office 2000, Find Fast is used to build an index of files that speed up finding documents from the Open dialog box in any Microsoft Office program. Office Startup (*osa.exe*) initializes the shared code used by Office programs allowing those programs to start faster. *osa.exe* is also the application used when you select the option Open Office Document or New Office Document from the Start menu or Office Shortcut Bar.

Since it is outside of the shell namespace, Find Fast is not affected by the policies Hide Drives in My Computer or Remove Find Command. In addition, if you choose Open Office Document from the Start menu, hidden drives will be available for browsing. If you want to use the Hide Drives policy, remove the Office Startup and Find Fast icons from the Startup folder. These two options tend to slow down overall Windows performance anyway. Find Fast is a Control Panel applet and can be removed by running the Office setup program using the Add/Remove Programs applet, or by simply deleting the *findfast.cpl* file. The Office Startup application can also be deleted from the local drive, but note that removing *osa.exe* will make the Start menu and Microsoft Office Shortcut Bar options Open Office Document and Open New Document unavailable.

Custom Macro Solution

Some of the Office 97 security problems mentioned can be avoided by creating macros that customize certain dialog boxes, such as Open, Save or Save As. These macros would then be loaded into the user's default Word template, *normal.dot*. A sample macro called File Open/Save Restrictor is available on the *Windows Magazine* web site at *http://www.winmag.com*, in the August 1999 issue. This macro controls which files and drives a user may view or edit by presenting a customized File/Open dialog box. Other customized dialogs can be created for Office applications using UserForms in Visual Basic for Applications. For more information, read the help topic: Microsoft Word Visual Basic Reference.

Other Vulnerabilities

There are many other security vulnerabilities found in Windows 9x. Although it is not possible to cover them all, some of these vulnerabilities are reviewed here.

Internet Explorer and Active Desktop

IE is actually a Windows shell program, operating much like the default shell program Explorer. In the address list box, where you normally type a URL, you can type a program name and launch any program. This makes it an effective replacement for the Start menu Run command if this command is hidden using system policies. The use of Active Desktop also displays the address toolbar at the top of any open folder.

Programs will not run if they have been disabled using the policies Run Only Allowed Windows Applications or Disable MSDOS Prompt, and so these policies should be used in addition to the Hide Run Command policy. Optionally the IE address toolbar can be removed by right-clicking on the IE toolbar and unchecking the address bar option. Then the policy "Disable Customizing Browser Toolbars," found in the *inetres.adm* template, can be used to prevent the address bar from being re-enabled. However, removing the address toolbar will also remove the ability to manually enter a URL.

On the desktop, the policy "Disable Active Desktop" can be applied to remove the open folder address listbox. This policy can be found in either the *shell.adm* or *sp1shell.adm* template.

Task Manager

The Windows Task Manager is a security problem because it can be used to run programs, to close programs or to browse drives (even if they are hidden). Within the Task Manager program, choose File → Run Application. You can type the name of any executable in the Open list box and so, like the IE address toolbar, this makes it a replacement for the Run command.

For Windows 95 and 98 workstations an even greater risk occurs before the user logs on. Since the taskbar has not yet loaded, Ctrl-Esc will launch Task Manager (it normally launches the Start menu). A user could gain a DOS prompt this way since system policies will not yet have loaded. In this instance the only way to prevent access to a command prompt is to use the *admin.adm* or *windows.adm* template to make sure the default profile does not allow access to a MS-DOS prompt. An alternative is to upgrade to Windows 98SE, which does not show this behavior.

The easiest fix on a Windows 9x workstation for the security hole caused by Task Manager is to delete *taskman.exe* from the local drive. On Windows NT there are three solutions:

- The following registry key can be used to disable the task manager: HKEY_USERS\{account_name}\Software\Microsoft\Windows\CurrentVersion\Policies with a REG_DWORD valuename of DisableTaskManager and a value of 1.
- Change NT permissions so only the Admin account has privileges to run *taskmgr.exe.*
- Remove the Task Manager program file (*taskmgr.exe*) from the local drive.

Registry Editing

In Windows 9x or NT the following registry entry disables registry tools such as Regedit:

```
[HKCU\Software\Microsoft\Windows\Current Version\Policies\System]
 "DisableRegistryTools"=dword:00000001
```

The policy Disable Registry Editing Tools depends upon an application actually checking for the presence of this DisableRegistryTools registry value. Third-party registry editing tools that do *not* check for this key may allow the user to edit the registry even if the administrator has restricted access.

The only solution to this problem is to try to minimize the user's access to outside programs. This can be done using third-party programs to prevent unauthorized applications from being installed, and by disabling the *A:* drive so that programs cannot be brought in on a floppy.

Using the policy "Disabling Registry Editing Tools" does not disable the use of the System Policy Editor. A user can still edit the registry using *poledit.exe*.

Access to the Local Hard Drive

There is no way to restrict access to directories or files in Windows 9x. This means that files on the local drive can be changed, removed or altered by any user. You can try to minimize this by using the Hide Drives policy, but the only truly effective way is to use a third-party program, Windows NT or Windows 2000.

Backdoors

Backdoors are malicious remote control tools that allow an intruder (usually running a client version of the backdoor software) to have control over your workstation. The amount of control the intruder has can vary depending on which backdoor program is used. On a Windows 9x system, backdoors can initialize from one of two registry keys:

The HKLM\Software\Microsoft\Windows\CurrentVersion\Run registry key
: An example of this kind of backdoor is NetBus, a trojan horse program which allows an intruder access to your system via TCP/IP.

The HKLM\Software\Microsoft\Windows\CurrentVersion\RunServices registry key
: An example of this kind of backdoor is Back Orifice 2000 (or BO2K), a trojan horse program that allows an intruder almost full access to your system over the Internet.

The best way to avoid backdoor trojans is to use a virus protection program and regularly update the virus data files. Set the virus scanner to automatically delete or clean infected files. Don't depend on user input for removal, as the user may be deliberately trying to infect the system.

System policies can also provide a small measure of protection from backdoors by editing these two registry keys, thus overwriting any changes made by a virus or backdoor trojan. For method one, the computer policy Run (templates *admin.adm*, *windows.adm* and *common.adm*) can be used to specify which programs are allowed to run at startup. For method two, the computer policy Run Services (templates *admin.adm*, *windows.adm*) can be used to specify which services are run at startup.

Choosing a Third-Party Security Program

I have mentioned several times the possibility of using third-party software to increase the security of your Windows 9x workstation, but what should you look for when choosing from many similar types of programs? The following checklist will help in this decision:

- Does the program load from the *autoexec.bat* or *config.sys* startup files? If so, these lines are easily edited out, or the startup files can be deleted entirely.
- If you press Ctrl-Alt-Del, displaying the Close program dialog box, does the program show up on the task list? Fortunately, most security programs will also disable this key sequence. If they do not, and the program appears, it may be simply disabled by choosing End Task.
- Does the program load from the *win.ini* file? If so, the `LOAD=` and `RUN=` lines are easily edited out from a command prompt.
- Does the program use an easily identifiable DLL or VXD file? If so, these files can be deleted or corrupted causing the program to fail to initialize.
- Does the program turn off with a hotkey combination that cannot be disabled? It's amazing how many key combinations a determined vandal will try if she is bored enough.
- Does the program load from the Startup folder in the Start menu? Such a program is easily removed.
- Can the program be unloaded using the Add/Remove programs applet, or a specific control applet (**.cpl*)? If it can, make sure that you remove these applets from the local drive.
- Does the program load from the registry key HKLM\Software\Microsoft\Windows\CurrentVersion\Run? If so, this key can be exported from a command prompt, then merged back as a REG file with that program missing.

As a final check, search the Internet for the program name plus the word "hack" or "crack" to see if there are programs available to circumvent the security program. You may be unpleasantly surprised.

Other Tips to Increase Workstation Security

The following tips can be used in addition to the SPE to increase security on your workstation. Just how secure your workstation needs to be depends on the type of user you have. A communal workstation in a public library will require far more security measures than the typical shared office computer.

Reassign the F3 shortcut

Although the F3 shortcut to the Find command cannot be removed, it can be reassigned. Create a shortcut on the desktop to an innocuous program such as Calculator. Right-click on this shortcut and choose Properties. In the Shortcut Key list box, enter F3. Now when F3 is entered, the calculator will appear rather then the Find window. If this shortcut is stored on a network directory with other custom desktop icons, a user will not be able to alter or delete it.

Replace the shell program

The default shell program for Windows 9x and Windows NT is *explorer.exe*. This can be replaced with another shell program such as *progman.exe* (the Windows 3x shell) or *iexplore.exe* (the Internet Explorer shell). Iexplore could be used as a shell program on a workstation used only for Internet browsing. If the browser is closed, the user is left with a blank desktop without so much as a toolbar. The hotkey combination Ctrl-Alt-Del would have to be used to properly shut down the workstation.

To change the shell, edit the *system.ini* file in the main Windows directory. The line in the `[Boot]` section that reads **`Shell=Explorer.exe`** can be changed to reflect whichever shell you choose to use. Note that the filename must be in 8.3 format (i.e., *Shell=Progra~1\Intern~1\Iexplore.exe*). For Windows NT4, use the Custom Shell policy found in the *winnt.adm* template.

Use registry files in the logon script

Since it is possible to completely stop the downloading of the policy file through a registry entry, it may be a good idea to use the logon script to continually replace this registry key. If users are turning off remote update, you can enable it with every logon with the following REG file which sets remote update to automatic mode:

```
Regedit4
HKEY_LOCAL_MACHINE\System\CurrentControlSet\Control\Update
"Updatemode"=dword:00000001
```

Standardize web browser wallpaper

To help prevent users from creating wallpaper from web browsers, save an acceptable BMP to the following names: *Internet Explorer Wallpaper.bmp* and *Netscape Wallpaper.bmp*. Then make these files read-only. However, this will work only until the users realize that they can remove the read-only attribute. Alternately, use the policy "No HTML Wallpaper" in the user properties of the *shell.adm* templates.

Use Windows NT

On Windows NT, prohibit the Guest account from writing or deleting any files, directories or registry keys (with the exception of any home directory for Guest). Alternately, you can disable the Guest account altogether.

It is possible for a user to authenticate to a validating DC that doesn't contain the policy file, thus bypassing the policy restrictions. Therefore, it is necessary to run directory replication between all domain controllers that participate in user authentication. The policy file *%systemroot%\netlogon\ntconfig.pol* should either be copied to the *%systemroot%\system32\repl\export* subdirectory for replication to all domain controllers or manually copied to all *Netlogon* directories. See the Microsoft KB article Q101602 for more information.

There is one additional disconcerting security flaw on Windows NT networks relating to domain names. See "Other Vulnerabilities" earlier in this chapter for more information.

Use server setup of Windows 9x

If your network server can handle the greatly increased demand, use a server-based setup (shared installation) of Windows 9x. This keeps most or all of the system files on the server and prevents key Windows files from being deleted, altered or corrupted. For more information on using a server-based setup see the Microsoft KB article Q133349 and the Windows 95 or 98 Resource Kit.

Watch for keylogging programs

Keylogging programs can be used to record usernames and passwords. Consider using the policy 'Items to Run at Startup' to set the RUN registry key so that these programs cannot be loaded from the registry. This policy is found in the *admin.adm*, *common.adm* and *windows.adm* templates.

Keylogging programs can also be loaded in the *Win.ini* file. In the `[Windows]` section, check the `Run=` line for suspicious programs.

Remove hazardous executables

The following applications can be used maliciously, so consider removing them from the local hard drive:

- **.cpl* (Control Panel applets)
- *attrib.exe*
- *deltree.exe*
- *fdisk.exe*
- *format.com*
- *msinfo32.exe*
- *regedit.exe*
- *regedt32.exe*
- *taskman.exe*
- *winfile.exe*

Get the latest software patches

New security holes are being found as you read this, and typically (at least for the major software vendors) as each problem is found, a patch fixing it is released. Regularly check for the latest software security patches for all of your major software applications, including Windows (*http://www.windowsupdate.microsoft.com*).

Secure the startup files

It's not a perfect solution since it is easy to bypass, but it is still a good idea to make sure that your startup files (*config.pol, autoexec.bat, system.ini, and win.ini*) have the read-only attributes set.

Resource Editors

It is possible to customize program menus using a resource editor. A resource editor can be used to remove menu options, disable functions or change the default action of those functions.

There are a number of resource editors available, such as:

Borland's Resource Workshop

It is available by itself, or as part of the Borland's C++ and Turbo C compiler packages.

Microsoft's Resource Editor

It is available as part of the Microsoft Visual C compiler.

When making changes to part of a copyrighted software program, you should always write the software manufacturer first for permission to do so.

Policy Options to Increase Security

Table 5-2 lists the templates that contain policies to increase workstation security.

Table 5-2. Policies to Increase Workstation Security

ADM File	Policy Names
Admin.adm *Windows.adm*	Control Panel—all restrictions Shell restrictions—all restrictions Disable registry editing tools Run Only Allowed Windows applications Disable MS-DOS prompt Logon banner Require validation by network for Windows access Disable automatic NetWare login Disable caching of domain password Password options—all options
WinNT.adm	Shell restrictions—all restrictions Custom shell Disable Task Manager Logon banner Disable context menus Do not display last logged on username
Shell.adm *Sp1shell.adm*	Disable adding/deleting active desktop items Disable selecting HTML wallpaper Start menu restrictions, such as Clear Recently Opened Documents List, Disable Logoff, Disable Shutdown, Disable File menu in Internet Explorer Shell restrictions, such as Disable right-click context menus and Hide Floppy drives Do not allow computer to restart in MS-DOS mode
ZAK95.adm *ZAK98.adm*	Custom shell Use secure custom Task Manager
Off97nt4.adm *Off97w95.adm* *Off97w98.adm*	Setting the Options6 policy to a value of 8 in the user properties under Excel 97 → Tools_Options will enable macro virus protection. See MS Knowledgebase Q169811 for more information.

Internet Security Sites

The following are a number of sites that discuss computer security:

- CERT® was formerly known as the Computer Emergency Response Team; CERT is located at Carnegie Mellon University. It provides incidence response, researches the causes and prevention of security vulnerabilities, and offers advice on system security improvement. The organization provides CERT advisories about security problems and their impact on typical systems. (*http://www.cert.org*)
- Shields UP! is an excellent page by Steve Gibson; it benignly probes your computer for security holes that can be exploited through an Internet connection. If security problems are found, advice is also provided to help you plug those holes. (*http://grc.com/x/ne.dll?bh0bkyd2*)

- Xforce bills itself as the "World's #1 resource for computer threats and vulnerability." The site contains a searchable database of security vulnerabilities by platform type. (*http://xforce.iss.net*)
- The Microsoft security adviser site provides security bulletins, a discussion of technologies such as CryptoAPI, and various resources such as white papers, presentations and books for all Windows platforms. (*http://www.microsoft.com/security/default.asp*)
- To check for critical security updates for your Windows workstation, use the Microsoft Windows update site. (*http://windowsupdate.microsoft.com*)
- NT Security provides the latest Windows NT and Windows 2000 security alerts, including virus information, books, security tools, FAQs and a security newsletter. (*http://www.ntsecurity.net*)
- This site offers a brief discussion on Windows 98 security versus Windows NT security. (*http://msdn.microsoft.com/library/partbook/win98dh/html/windows-98securityversusntsecurity.htm*)
- Microsoft provides a paper on maintaining NT registry security. (*http://msdn.microsoft.com/library/winresource/dnwinnt/s847a.htm*)
- Antivirus information can be found on these sites:

  http://www.antivirus.com/vinfo/default.asp
  http://www. f-secure.com
  http://www.mcafee.com
  http://www.norton.com

Summary

Remember that no computer application or platform is perfectly secure. Remember also that the typical user is almost completely unaware of how to take advantage of this situation. Fortunately, the two tend to balance each other. Unfortunately, this balance can make most administrators complacent about security. That is, until after their first experience with a computer vandal.

Don't be discouraged. Knowledge of the most common security holes and some methods of blocking those holes is the administrator's best defense. This chapter discussed not only the problems with specific system policies, but also basic security flaws in the Windows 9x operating system. Some of the suggestions to improve security were:

- Use the four rules for creating a good password.
- Since Windows NT and Windows 2000 have an inherently more secure filesystem than Windows 9x, consider using one of them as your operating system if your workstation is especially susceptible to vandals.

- Restrict physical access to the computer chassis and to the *A:* drive.
- Restrict a user's free or unsupervised time. Most vandals are quite persistent in their attacks, which is typically due to the amount of spare time available to the average computer vandal.
- Minimize vulnerabilities during system boot.
- Be aware of the problems with various system policies and ways to minimize these problems.
- Minimize the security problems with Office97 using methods such as custom macros. Alternately, you can upgrade to Office 2000, which offers more restrictions via the Office 2000 templates.
- Any nonessential files and applications that can be used by a computer vandal should by removed from the local drive and stored on a restricted network folder.
- Get a virus protection program. This is a must for any workstation.
- If you need increased security for Windows 9x workstations, consider a third-party program in addition to system policies. However, depending on your workstation setup, these programs may cause unexpected general protection faults, so use them on a test workstation first.

6

Troubleshooting

No matter how carefully you plan the creation and implementation of your policy file, unforeseen problems can still occur. Fortunately, most problems have been experienced, solved and documented by others. This chapter deals with those error messages, problems and solutions.

I have provided four tables: the first contains specific error messages, the second lists problems specific to a Windows 9x or Windows NT workstation, the third lists problems specific to Novell NetWare networks and the fourth table lists problems specific to Windows NT and Windows 2000 domains.

Troubleshooting Tables

While many of the problems listed in these tables can have more than one possible cause, I refer only to those created by the implementation of system policies. Although sometimes I didn't concur with the suggested causes or solutions, I have added any relevant Microsoft Knowledgebase (numbers beginning with Q) and Novell Support (numbers beginning with TID) articles.

Microsoft Knowledgebase articles can be found by searching for the article number (for example, Q150687) in the search form found at *http://search.microsoft.com*. The Novell articles can be found by searching for the article number without the TID prefix (for example, 2944437) in the search form found at *http://support.novell.com*.

Error Messages

Occasionally when system policies do not work properly there is actually an error message displayed. Typically, by itself, this error gives you absolutely no clue as to what is the true problem. To help decipher these messages, Table 6-1 lists the errors with an explanation of why the error occurred, plus possible solutions.

Table 6-1. System Policy Error Messages

Error Message	Explanation and Solution
A required privilege is not held by the client.	This error occurs if you attempt to use the version of *poledit.exe* that shipped with Windows 95 on an NT workstation. Use the version of Poledit with a modification date of May 1, 1997, or later.
Access violation error is recorded in Dr. Watson for *poledit.exe*.	An extremely large number of applications have been listed for the policy "Run Only Allowed Windows Applications" using an older version of the Policy Editor. Reduce the number of applications listed, or use the recommended version of *poledit.exe*. Reference: Q179553
Cannot access this folder. Path is too long.	This error occurs on a Windows 9x workstation if you use a policy that tries to map a drive to the network server, and the server is unavailable. Reference: Q247877
Clip Gallery encountered an error. Try restarting Windows, or restarting Microsoft applications.	This error occurs if you have the Office 2000 policy "Always install with elevated privileges" in the checked position. Apply the MS Office 2000 Service Release 1. Reference: Q228593
Error 2007. Expected a numeric value. Found –1. The file cannot be loaded.	This error occurs if you use the version of *poledit.exe* that shipped with Windows 95 on an NT workstation. Use the version of Poledit with a modification date of May 1, 1997, or later.
Error 2011: the corresponding string was not found in the [strings] section. The file could not be loaded.	The size of the custom policy template exceeds 64 K, or a string is not properly defined in the [strings] section. Split the custom template into two or more smaller files. Make sure all strings are defined in the [strings] section. Reference: Q159992
Insufficient system resources exist to complete the requested service.	This error appears when users establish a SAMR (security accounts manager service) connection with the DC to verify global group membership for group policies, and the open pipes to the SAM database are not all released. Eventually the client processes exceed 2048 and any further SAMR requests fail. This bug was fixed in Windows NT Service Pack 4. The updated *userenv.dll* should be copied to all workstations. For users who log on to both an NT domain and an NDS tree, the same bug was fixed with the Novell client 4.5 for Windows NT. Rebooting the DC will temporarily relieve the problem. Reference: Q191634, TID2939557

Table 6-1. System Policy Error Messages (continued)

Error Message	Explanation and Solution
Internet Explorer cannot open the Internet site *http://<site name>*. The site was not found. Make sure the address is correct, and try again.	Policies to set the proxy server exist in the following templates: *ieak.adm, off97nt.adm, off97w95.adm* and *off97w98.adm*. More than one template may have been used to set the proxy URL, causing conflicts in the policy file. Enable this policy in only one template, while setting the policy to the grayed setting for the others. Reference: Q170602
Pagefault at ***address*** in *comctl32.dll*.	The policy Run Only Allowed Windows Applications is active in a policy created with an old version of Poledit. Use the version of Poledit with a modification date of May 1, 1997, or later. Reference: Q153469
Password required to connect to *<resource>* (for example, a shared network printer).	The SPE has been used to disable password caching. Re-enable password caching; this option is found in the templates *admin.adm, off97nt4.adm, off97w95.adm, off97w98.adm* and *windows.adm*.
Poledit: This program has performed an illegal operation and will be shut down. Poledit caused an invalid page fault in module <unknown> at 0000: 00000013.	This error occurs if you try to load a corrupted template, or a template that is not saved in ASCII format, or if the *poledit.exe* application is corrupt. Use a text editor such as Notepad or Wordpad to open and check the template. If it is corrupted, restore your backup copies. If not, try restoring a backup copy of *poledit.exe*.
That password is incorrect.	Windows 9x workstations using the Microsoft Family Logon client will not work with password caching disabled. Use the *admin.adm* and *windows.adm* templates to set the computer policy "Disable Password Caching" to the cleared position (to enable caching of passwords). Reference: Q178361
The configuration registry database is corrupt.	This error can occur if you try to read a *ntconfig.pol* file using a Windows 9x workstation or a *config.pol* file using a Windows NT workstation. Create and edit the policy file using the same platform for which it is intended. For example, the policy file *config.pol* must be created and edited on a Windows 9x workstation since it will be used by other Windows 9x workstations.
The file or folder *<filename>* that this shortcut refers to cannot be found.	Windows NT desktop shortcuts in custom folders created for mapped drives resolve to the UNC path instead. Creating a shortcut automatically embeds a UNC path in the *.lnk* file. Apply the latest Windows NT service pack to update the *shell32.dll* file, and then set the policy "Do Not Track Shell Shortcuts During Roaming" found in the *shell.adm, shellm.adm, sp1shell.adm* and *winnt.adm* templates to the checked position. Reference: Q158682

Table 6-1. System Policy Error Messages (continued)

Error Message	Explanation and Solution
The following error occurred while loading the device VNETSUP: Error 6102: The string specified by the WORKGROUP keyword in the registry was not found.	This error occurs if the workgroup name or computer name is not properly specified or if it was set to the cleared position in the policy file. Use the template *admin.adm* or *windows.adm* to set the workgroup name in the Microsoft Client for Windows Networks policy. This sets the workgroup name found in the Identification tab of the Network properties.
The password you typed for Microsoft Networking is not correct. Please type the old password.	This error message may appear if your workstation and NT network passwords are different, and the SPE has been used to disable password caching. Re-enable password caching;, this option is found in the templates *admin.adm, off97nt4.adm, off97w95.adm, off97w98.adm,* and *windows.adm.* Otherwise, make the passwords for both resources the same. Reference: Q137826
The path *http://windowsupdate.microsoft.com* does not exist or is not a directory.	The error occurs when the user tries to use Windows update from the Start menu and the policy restriction Hide Internet Explorer Icon was used. Set this user policy, found in the *shell.adm* and *sp1shell.adm* templates, to the cleared position. Reference: Q190414
The User Template folder *\\servername\sharename\%username%* was not found. Do you want to create this folder?	Microsoft Office 97 cannot expand environment variables read from the registry. Use similarly mapped drives for all users when specifying folder locations in the Office templates. For example, *\\servername\sharename\%username%* may be mapped to drive *H*: for all users, and then this drive letter can be used in the template to define the location of the custom folder (see Figure 4-6.). Reference: Q170264
This installation is forbidden by system policy. Contact your system administrator.	This error occurs while running setup for Office 2000 if the computer policy "Disable Browse Dialog Box for New Source" is in the checked position. Set this policy, found in the *instlr1.adm* template, to the cleared position. Reference: Q234041
This operation has been cancelled due to restrictions in effect on this computer. Please contact your system administrator.	• The program the user is trying to run is not on the list of allowed programs. Check and edit the list of programs using the template *admin.adm, common.adm* or *windows.adm.* The policy "Run Only Allowed Windows Programs" is found in the user properties by expanding System → Restrictions. • The policy restriction "Hide Drives In My Computer" is used and the client has been upgraded to Windows NT Service Pack 4 or 5. Contact Microsoft Product Support Services to obtain an updated *shell32.dll* file for Windows NT workstations. Reference: Q140355, Q156432, Q238218

Table 6-1. System Policy Error Messages (continued)

Error Message	Explanation and Solution
Unable to browse the network, the network is not accessible.	When you double-click Entire Network in Network Neighborhood, this error appears if the policy Alternate Workgroup policy was used. The workgroup name for this policy, found in *admin.adm* and *windows.adm*, must be entirely IN CAPITAL LETTERS. Reference: Q190648
Unable to open <*path\config.pol (ntconfig.pol)*>: Error 3 occurs. Or the blue Stop screen occurred.	Windows NT workstations using clients 4.11 through 4.6 cannot save directly to a NetWare volume. Client 4.10 does not have this problem. Save the policy file to the local drive, and then copy it from the drive onto the NetWare volume. Reference: TID2934916
Unable to open <*path\filename.adm*>: the configuration registry database is corrupt.	This error can occur if you try to load a corrupted template, or a template that was edited using a word processing program, and subsequently not saved in ASCII format. Use a text editor such as Notepad or Wordpad to open and check the template. If it is corrupted, restore your backup copies.
Unable to open *config.pol (ntconfig.pol)*: An I/O operation initiated by the Registry failed unrecoverable. The registry could not read in, or write out, or flush, one of the files that contain the system's image of the registry.	This error can occur if you try to edit a *ntconfig.pol* file using a Windows 9x workstation, or a *config.pol* file using a Windows NT workstation. Create and edit the policy file using the same platform for which it is intended. For example, the policy file *config.pol* must be created and edited on a Windows 9x workstation since it will be used by other Windows 9x workstations.
Unable to open *ntconfig.pol*: A required privilege is not held by the client. *Or*: the configuration registry database is corrupt.	The policy file has a file size of 0, or you are logged in to a Windows NT domain using an administrator-equivalent account. Create the policy file only while logged in as a user who is a member of the Administrators group. Reference: Q167900
Unable to open *public\config.pol:* Error 1317 occurred.	This occurs when a Windows NT workstation, using File and Print Services for NetWare, attempts to save a policy file to a NetWare 4.11 server. Update to Windows NT Service Pack 4 or later. Reference: Q181928
Unable to open template file *C:\Windows\Inf\common.adm* (or *C:\WinNT\Inf\common.adm*): The system cannot find the file specified.	The SPE will try to load the template *common.adm* by default. If it cannot be found in the default location, this error message will be displayed. Copy this template to the *C:\Windows\Inf* or *C:\WinNT\inf* subdirectory, or ignore the error message. Once any template is loaded, the error will no longer display.

Table 6-1. System Policy Error Messages (continued)

Error Message	Explanation and Solution
Unable to save *config.pol*: Error 1010 occurred.	The group policy name for a NetWare NDS group has more than 39 characters. Change the group name in the NDS so that the fully qualified group policy name has fewer than 39 characters. Reference: Q192938
Unable to save the registry: Error 1243220 *or* Error 1243216 occurred.	While using the SPE in remote registry mode, you use a template specific to a different platform, or you do not use a workstation with the same OS as the remote workstation. Only a Windows 9x workstation can be used to remotely edit another Windows 9x workstation. The same holds true for Windows NT. In addition, templates meant for Windows NT workstations cannot be used to remotely edit the registry of a Windows 9x workstation (and vice versa). Reference: Q177295
Unable to save to registry: Error code 1243516 occurred.	The user, who is attempting to use the policy editor to edit the local registry, does not have full control permissions to all of the affected registry keys. Also, this can occur with an Administrator account if the registry has become corrupt. If the user is a member of the Administrator account, you may need to repair the registry or restore it from backup. Read the reference article for more information. Reference: Q184009
Unable to update configuration from <*\path*> Error 5: Access is denied. You may need to contact your administrator.	Manual remote update is used, but the location indicated for the *config.pol* file is incorrect. Check the path using the template *admin.adm, common.adm* or *windows.adm*. Open the computer properties, expand Network → Remote Update and verify that Path for Manual Update is correct. Reference: Q139705
Word cannot find the required registry information. To restore the registry, run Setup again. Make sure Web Page Authoring (HTML) is selected, even if you already installed it.	The Web Page Wizard may not be fully functional when the *off97nt4.adm, off97w95.adm* or *off97w98.adm* templates are used to set Office user policies. Update to MS Office97 Service Release 2. Reference: Q166096

In Windows NT workstations, it is possible to create a log file that is useful in debugging not only system policies, but also profiles. The Microsoft Knowledgebase article Q154120 includes instructions on how to do this. Unfortunately, there is nothing comparable for a Windows 9x workstation, although you should make sure that the display of policy error messages is active. To do this, set the option to Display Error Messages, in the computer policy Remote Update, to the checked position. This option is available in the templates *admin.adm, common.adm* and *windows.adm.*

Workstation Problems

Table 6-2 lists problems that affect Windows 95, Windows 98 and Windows NT4 workstations.

Table 6-2. Troubleshooting Workstation Problems

Problem	Explanation and Solution
A custom Network Neighborhood (NN) folder still displays the Entire Network icon and the default workgroup.	These icons must be hidden using additional separate policies. Use the template *admin.adm, windows.adm,* or *winnt.adm* to enable the user policies "No Entire Network in NN" and "No Workgroup Contents in NN" in addition to setting up a custom NN folder. Reference: Q138766
A policy was removed, but the old setting did not return.	Generally, policies with edit boxes set to the cleared position will wipe out any previous settings in the local registry. If this is a computer policy, it will be removed for all users. See Chapter 9 for more information on specific policies. When removing this type of policy, set the box to the grayed rather than the cleared position to allow the default profile settings to take effect.

A Start menu policy does not work properly when using the *shellm.adm* template.	An error in this template prevents the Start menu Windows NT policy "Add Run Dlg CheckBox for New Memory Space" from taking effect.
	Edit the template (see Chapter 8) to reverse two of the part lines in the `!!Startmenu` policy section, so that the `keyname` is after the `Part` statement as follows:
	`PART !!MemCheckBoxInRunDlg CHECKBOX`
	`KEYNAME Software\Microsoft\Windows\`
	`CurrentVersion\Policies`
	`VALUENAME MemCheckBoxInRunDlg`
	`END PART`
	Reference: Q199013

A user's customized desktop settings (e.g., appearance, background) are not saved, despite the fact that they are not restricted using system policies.	The user must be allowed to save settings when he exits, as well as having these desktop settings unrestricted. Set the policy "Don't Save Settings at Exit" found in the user properties of the *admin.adm, common.adm* and *windows.adm* templates to the cleared position.
A value beyond 9999 cannot be entered into a numeric box in the SPE.	Attempting to type a value such as 10000 into a numeric box causes the value to be truncated to 1000 (or 4 digits). Use the spin dial to increase the value beyond 9999 rather than entering a value into the edit box. Reference: Q190928
Anti-virus programs.	Some anti-virus programs, such as Eliashim's Virusafe, may prevent the dynamic modification of the registry. Contact the manufacturer of the anti-virus programs for possible updates and fixes.

Table 6-2. Troubleshooting Workstation Problems (continued)

Problem	Explanation and Solution
Automatic remote update does not work.	The policy file must be in the correct location on the NetWare, Windows NT or Windows 2000 server (see Chapter 3). The network client must be a 32-bit client. Real-mode clients do not support automatic remote update.
Desktop shortcuts in custom folders created for mapped drives resolve to the UNC path instead (Windows NT).	Creating a shortcut automatically embeds a UNC path in the *.lnk* file. Apply the latest Windows NT service pack to update the *shell32.dll* file, and then set the policy" Do Not Track Shell Shortcuts During Roaming" found in the user properties of the *shell.adm*, *shellm.adm*, *sp1shell.adm* and *winnt.adm* templates to the checked position. Reference: Q158682
Despite using the Additive template keyword, the entries in the listbox replace those already in the registry.	This keyword does not work for Windows NT 4 workstations. Do not use the `Additive` keyword in custom policy templates for Windows NT workstations.
DOS applications will not run.	The policy Disable MS-DOS Prompt is checked This policy will disable all DOS applications, not just the command prompt,so it cannot be used if you want the users to be able to run a DOS application. Uncheck the user restriction using the *admin.adm* or *windows.adm* template.
Environment variables used in custom folders do not expand.	Windows 9x cannot recognize and expand environment variables used in policy files. Use similarly mapped drives for all users when specifying folder locations. For example, *\\servername\sharename\%username%* may be mapped to drive *H:* for all users, and then this drive letter can be used in the template to define the location of the custom folder (see Figure 4-6).
Icons on a Windows NT Start menu, mapped to NetWare drives, are unstable.	NetWare login scripts are used, and the user desktop loads before the NetWare login script finishes. Check the policy Run Logon Scripts Synchronously in the computer properties of the *winnt.adm* template. This forces the system to finish running the script before loading the desktop. Reference: Q186475
In Office 97, Step 1 of the Web Page Wizard is blank.	The Web Page Wizard may not be fully functional when the *off97nt4.adm*, *off97w95.adm* or *off97w98.adm* templates are used to set Office user policies. Update to MS Office97 Service Release 2. Reference: Q166096
In Lantastic 7.0 network, policies are set to manual remote update, but they still do not download.	System policies are not supported on Lantastic networks. Reference: Q187220

Table 6-2. Troubleshooting Workstation Problems (continued)

Problem	Explanation and Solution
Microsoft Plus! For Kids Protect It! conflict.	Protect It! settings conflict with system policies. Do not use the two together. Reference: Q163170
Microsoft Visual C++ does not work properly.	A developer using Visual C++ requires unrestricted access to the workstation. On Windows 9x the user cannot have restrictions imposed by the SPE. Reference: Q190317
Microsoft Word template icons are displayed as question marks inside balloons.	The policy Hide Network Neighborhood (NN) is active, and the templates are located on a network drive. The templates will still work correctly despite this problem. Clear this policy and instead use the policies No Entire Network in NN, No Workgroup Contents, Disable File Sharing and Disable Printer Sharing. These polices are available in the *admin.adm, common.adm* and *windows.adm* templates. Although the NN icon will be visible, network resources cannot be browsed and network drives are hidden. Reference: Q153821
Only the Entire Network icon appears in Network Neighborhood, and double-clicking it results in an error message.	The SPE was used to set an alternate workgroup policy. The workgroup name for this policy, found in *admin.adm* and *windows.adm*, must be entirely UPPERCASE. Reference: Q190648
Policies do not completely restrict access in Office 97 programs.	See Chapter 5 for more information on security holes in Office 97 programs. Reference: Q175683, Q178720, Q178720
Program Control Group (Microsoft Systems Management Server) does not properly configure the user's desktop.	SPE was used to define a custom program folder that can prevent the PCG (which needs a local program folder) from successfully configuring the desktop. Configure a custom Start menu instead of a custom program folder. Also, do not check the policy Hide Start Menu Subfolders or the custom group will not appear. Reference: Q173793
Remote administration operates erratically.	This can occur if the policy file Disable File Sharing Controls is checked for specific users or groups. If you want to remotely administer a workstation, allow file sharing using the user properties of either *admin.adm* or *windows.adm*. See Chapter 4 for more information.
The Channel Bar for IE4 shows folder icons instead of the correct icons.	The policy Disable Cached Copies of Roaming Profiles is enabled. Set this policy to the cleared position using the computer properties of the *winnt.adm* template.
The computer name can still be changed even when the Control Panel Network restriction policies are active.	The computer contains an infrared device and the infrared Control Panel applet allows the computer name to be changed. Remove this Control Panel applet, or create a custom template to hide it (see Chapter 8). Reference: Q184221

Table 6-2. Troubleshooting Workstation Problems (continued)

Problem	Explanation and Solution
The custom folder is empty or contains the wrong list.	The location specified in the SPE for the custom folder is incorrect, missing or in UNC format. Double-check all custom folders for the correct locations. If the policy Hide Network Neighborhood is used, a UNC path cannot be specified for these folders;, a mapped drive and path must be used instead. Reference: Q176988
The DOS application is added to the Run Only Allowed Windows Applications list, but the application still is not allowed to run.	DOS applications cannot be listed according to their associated EXE or COM file. Create a shortcut to the application and include this PIF file in the list of allowed programs. A batch file can also be created, and the associated BAT file included in the list. Also make sure that the policy Disable MS-DOS Prompt is not in the checked position using the *admin.adm* or *windows.adm* template. Reference: Q165224
The network contains more than one policy file, and the wrong file is being applied.	The user logs onto both a NetWare server and a Windows NT or Windows 2000 domain. The Primary Network Logon specified in Network properties will determine which policy file is applied to the workstation registry.
The password box in the Microsoft Family Logon screen is grayed out.	The password box will be grayed out if one of the following two conditions occur: • The *username.pwl* password file is missing or corrupt. Use the Users Control Panel applet to set a new user password. • The *\windows\profiles\username* directory is missing. Using the Users applet, recreate the user. Reference: Q195440
The policy file downloaded once, but then never again.	The computer policy Remote Update is set to the cleared position in the policy file. For policies to download at all, this setting must be in the checked position in the policy file. See Chapter 4 for more information.

The policy Hide Drives in My Computer becomes active for all users, even when you specifically uncheck the policy.	An error in the *admin.adm* and *common.adm* templates sets this policy to default to the checked position.
	Edit the template (see Chapter 8) to add a `Valueoff` statement, so that the Hide Drives policy appears as follows:
	`POLICY !!HIDEDRIVES`
	`VALUENAME "NoDrives"`
	`VALUEON NUMERIC 67108863`
	`VALUEOFF NUMERIC 0`
	Reference: Q153000 and Q169634

Table 6-2. Troubleshooting Workstation Problems (continued)

Problem	Explanation and Solution
The text in the logon banner is truncated.	Using the SPE, the logon banner can be a maximum of 255 characters. Even if the template is modified to create a longer edit box, the SPE will pass only the first 255 characters entered to the registry. You must modify the registry directly to have a banner that exceeds this length. For Windows 9x, the registry key is HKLM\ Software\Microsoft\Windows\CurrentVersion\ Winlogon, for Windows NT the registry key is HKLM\ Software\Microsoft\WindowsNT\CurrentVersion\Winlogon. For both, the string values are `LegalNoticeCaption` and `LegalNoticeText`. Microsoft has a reported fix that allows a banner up to 2048 characters. This fix works only if the text is edited directly in the registry. Reference: Q173385
The user logs off of a server using Network Neighborhood, then logs on again a second time, but Windows does not prompt him for a password.	The password is being cached, and this cached password is being used to log on to the server the second time. Use the policy Disable Password Caching so that you are prompted for a password each time you access a network resource. This option is found in the templates *admin.adm, off97nt4.adm, off97w95.adm, off97w98.adm* and *windows.adm*. Reference: Q130521
The Windows NT shell loads before the user's logon script completes. Reference: Q186475	The policy Run Logon Scripts Synchronously, found in the *winnt.adm* template, is in the cleared position. Note that this policy exists in both the user and the computer properties. If it is cleared in the computer properties, even if it is checked in the user properties, the computer setting will take priority.
UNC path for custom folders does not work. Custom folders work for some but not all users.	The user policy Hide Network Neighborhood is in the checked position for all or some of the users. This policy effectively disables the use of UNC pathnames. Use similarly mapped drives for all users when specifying folder locations. For example, *\\servername\sharename\%username%* may be mapped to drive *H:* for all users, and then this drive letter can be used in the template to define the location of the custom folder (see Figure 4-6).
User profiles continually become enabled on the workstation, even after they are disabled using the Passwords Control Panel applet.	The Default Computer policy Enable User Profiles, found in the *admin.adm, common.adm* or *windows.adm* template, is set to the checked position in the policy file. See Chapter 4 for more information on how to permanently exclude computers from the policy file.
Using the Network Control Panel applet, a new service cannot be added because the Service network component type is missing.	Either of the user policy restrictions Disable File Sharing Controls or Disable Print Sharing Controls is checked using the *admin.adm* or *windows.adm* templates. Set these restrictions to the cleared position. Reference: Q192924

NetWare Networks

Table 6-3 lists problems that affect either Windows 9x or Windows NT4 workstations logging into a NetWare server.

Table 6-3. Troubleshooting Problems on NetWare Networks

Problem	Explanation and Solution
Group policies do not work.	• Older versions of the Novell client (below Version 2. 11) do not support group policies. Update to the latest Novell client. • The group name in the policy file must be a fully qualified NDS group name such as *TEACHER.STAFF. BEDROCK* and completely uppercase • The preferred NetWare server was not specified, only the preferred tree. Specify the preferred server in the computer properties using one of the following templates: *admin.adm, client32.adm, nwnt.adm* or *windows.adm*. • The workstation is Windows NT. Novell NT clients do not support group policies. Use the Microsoft client for NetWare networks, or ZENworks group policies. Reference: TID2908467, TID2928729, TID2921251, TID2921674, TID2928060, TID2928515
Manual remote update does not work for Windows NT4 workstations.	The location for the policy file was set using the *common. adm* template. This template creates registry settings that conflict with those set by the Novell client Workstation Manager. Use automatic remote update an NT configuration object (see TID2921251 for information on how to do this) to specify the manual update path, rather than using the policy template or the client advanced logon settings. Reference: TID2928984
MPREXE GPF error occurs.	The group name for a group policy has more than 39 characters. Older versions of the *nwgroup.pol* only allocated a buffer size of 39 characters per group name (there are many other reasons for MPREXE errors unrelated to system policies; see the following TIDs). Update to the latest Novell client, or rename the NDS group so that the fully qualified group name has fewer than 39 characters. Reference: TID2907849, TID2936820, Q192938
NAL Explorer cannot change the user's desktop shortcuts.	The Custom Folders policy has been set using the *admin. adm, windows.adm* or *winnt.adm* template. The user has been given only Read and File scan access to these custom network folders. The administrator can manually add the required desktop shortcuts, or temporarily give the user Write permission to this folder so that NAL can add the shortcuts. Reference: TID2944437

Table 6-3. Troubleshooting Problems on NetWare Networks (continued)

Problem	Explanation and Solution
Policies are inconsistently applied to a Windows NT4 workstation.	The DNS properties tab (in the network TCP/IP properties window) lists an NT domain in the Domain listbox. Enter a valid Internet domain name in this listbox. Reference: TID2931552
Policies do not download properly using Client 3.0 for Windows 9x.	If an NDS Workstation or ZEN user policy exists, the Microsoft policy file will not be loaded at all. An updated *novellnp.dll*, which allows the MS policies to load as well as the ZEN policies to load, is available in Client 3.02 or later client versions. Reference: TID2942751

The computer policy Disable Default Policy Support stays active even when you specifically uncheck the policy.	An error in the *client32.adm* template does not allow this policy to be reset to the cleared position from the checked position.
	Edit the template (see Chapter 8) to add **VALUEON** and **VALUEOFF** statements, so that the PolicySupport policy appears as follows:
	`POLICY !!PolicySupport`
	`KEYNAME "Software\Novell\Workstation Manager\`
	`Policy Support"`
	`VALUENAME "Check Default"`
	`VALUEON NUMERIC 0`
	`VALUEOFF NUMERIC 1`
	`PART !!PolicyPath EDITTEXT`
	`KEYNAME "Software\Novell\Workstation Manager\`
	`Policy Support"`
	`VALUENAME "Policy Path"`
	`MAXLEN 255`
	`END PART`
	`END POLICY`

The NetWare search mode is set incorrectly using the SPE.	The templates *admin.adm* and *windows.adm* incorrectly create a DWORD value instead of the required binary value. The SPE cannot be used to create binary values. The following registry key may be edited manually, or a REG file can be created to import it from the logon script: HKLM\System\CurrentControlSet\Services\VxD\Nwredir. Create a Binary value called SearchMode with the correct value (see reference for list of values). Reference: Q138744
The network Logon dialog box does not appear after starting Windows.	Automatic NetWare Login is enabled. Using the *admin.adm* or *windows.adm* template, in computer properties, expand Microsoft Client for NetWare Networks and check Disable Automatic NetWare Login. Reference: Q141858
The policy file cannot be saved to the NetWare volume: an error message occurs or the Windows blue Stop screen appears.	Windows NT workstations using Clients 4.11 through 4.6 cannot save directly to a NetWare volume. Client 4.10 does not have this problem. Save the policy file to the local drive, and then copy it from the drive onto the NetWare volume. Reference: TID2934916

Table 6-3. Troubleshooting Problems on NetWare Networks (continued)

Problem	Explanation and Solution
The policy Require Validation by Network for Windows Access does not work.	The NIC was unplugged from the network, causing the client to fail to load. If the NIC doesn't bind, the client does not load. Since system policies are loaded by the client, the user is allowed to log on even without network confirmation. See Chapter 5 for more information. Reference: TID2920541
The user saves a file with a long filename to a Novell server. However the file is saved in 8.3 format despite the fact that the server supports LFN and the policy Support Long Filenames was enabled. Trying to access a file on a NetWare 3.11 server produces an error message such as File not found, File not accessible, or Sharing violation.	The templates *admin.adm* and *windows.adm* incorrectly create a DWORD value instead of the required binary value. The SPE cannot be used to create binary values. The following registry key may be edited manually, or a REG file can be created to import it from the logon script: HKLM\System\CurrentControlSet\Services\VxD\Nwredir and create a binary value called SupportLFN with a value of 2. Otherwise, add the following line into the *system.ini* in the `[Nwredir]` section: `SupportLFN=`*X* X=1 for all servers 3.12 and above X=2 for all servers that support LFN Reference: Q137275, Q130710
User policies fail to load when a user logs on by using a desktop shortcut to the client32 logon EXE.	Windows 9x fails to run its own logon process using this method, and so fails to reload the user policies into the *user.dat* portion of the registry. Log on using the Windows Start menu option Logoff (Windows 98), or Shutdown → Close all programs and log on as another user (Windows 95). Reference: TID2920904
Microsoft Service for NetWare Directory Services (MSNDS) group policies no longer work.	MSNDS allows the user name to be submitted in either upper-, or lowercase letters. NetWare 3.1x servers require the username to be in uppercase only, and if it is submitted in lowercase, group policies will not work. Obtain the updated *grouppol.dll* dated 3/25/96 from Microsoft Technical Support. Reference: Q149415
When the policy file is opened, group names have random symbols appended at the end.	The group policy name for a NetWare NDS group has more than 39 characters. Change the group name in the NDS so that the fully qualified group policy name has less than 39 characters. Reference: Q192938
When the Windows 9x workstation is logged in without user intervention (autologon disabled), system policies are not applied.	When autologon is set to off (to allow logging in without the user inputting a password), the *user.dat* is read and merged with the registry before the user is logged in—effectively bypassing system policies. Even if the user's logon does not require a password, system policies can only operate with autologon enabled. Reference: TID2912469

Table 6-3. Troubleshooting Problems on NetWare Networks (continued)

Problem	Explanation and Solution
ZENworks policies do not work properly.	If a system policy file containing a Default User exists on the preferred server, those policies will overwrite any changes made by a ZENworks policy file. The Microsoft policy file will take precedence. Remove the Default User from the system policy file, or set affected policies to the grayed position in the policy file so that the ZEN policies become active. Reference: TID2942751

Windows NT and Windows 2000 Domains

Table 6-4 lists problems which affect either Windows 9x or Windows NT4 workstations that are part of a Windows NT4 or Windows 2000 domain.

Table 6-4. Troubleshooting Problems on Windows NT and Windows 2000 Domains

Problem	Explanation and Solution
A custom shell is loaded rather than the Independent Computing Architecture (ISA) application interface.	ISA clients, such as Citrix's Winframe and Metaframe software, will not load if a custom shell is defined using system policies. Using the *winnt.adm* template, set the user policy custom Shell to the cleared position. Reference: Q256171
Desktop shortcuts referencing an URL do not work.	This problem may occur under the following conditions: the system policy Run Only Allowed Windows Programs is used, IE is on the allowed programs list, and the client has been upgraded to Service Pack 4 or 5. Contact Microsoft Product Support Services for an updated *shell32.dll* file. Reference: Q234255
Directory replication problem: the policy file is not replicated from BDC to PDC, or PDC to BDC.	If the policy file in the export folder is changed and saved using Poledit, it may not be flagged for replication. Rename the policy file keeping the POL extension, allow replication to take place, and then rename the policy file back to its original name. Normal replication should then occur. Note that replication cannot occur from different file system;, that is, a NTFS partition cannot replicate to a FAT partition. Reference: Q172445

Table 6-4. Troubleshooting Problems on Windows NT and Windows 2000 Domains

Problem	Explanation and Solution

Disabling the policy Automatically Detect Slow Connections does not stop the workstation from continuing to detect slow connections.	Older versions of *winnt.adm* (up to the version included with Service Pack 5) do not have `VALUEON` and `VALUEOFF` statements for this policy.
	A text editor such as Notepad can be used to modify the template so that this policy section reads as follows:
	`Policy !!EnableSlowLinkDetect`
	`Valuename "SlowLinkDetectEnabled"`
	`Valueon Numeric 1 Valueoff Numeric 0`
	`End Policy`
	Reference: Q176966

Group policies are not applied at all, although user policies are applied.	• The domain controller has a computer name longer than 13 characters. Obtain the latest Windows NT service pack. • The user is a member of a local rather than a global group. Users must be members of global groups. See Chapter 2 for more information. • The global group name is longer than 20 characters. Limit the global group name to 20 characters. Reference: Q163875, Q131417

Hidden administrative shares are no longer available.
Installation of the Microsoft Systems Management Server (SMS) fails.
SMS no longer operates properly.
	The polices Create Hidden Drive Shares (Windows NT server and workstation) are set to cleared by default in older versions of the *winnt.adm* template. The ADMIN$ share will no longer be available.
	Manually check these policies each time you use the SPE, obtain a later version of the *winnt.adm* template (Service Pack 3 and up), or edit this template manually using a text editor such as Notepad or Wordpad so the policy statements appear as follows:
	`POLICY !!WorkstationShareAutoCreate`
	`        (!!ServerShareAutoCreate)`
	`VALUENAME "AutoShareWks"`
	`          ("AutoShareServer")`
	`VALUEON NUMERIC 1 VALUEOFF NUMERIC 0`
	Reference: Q156365, Q158292, Q161710

Network performance is slow while Windows 9x clients are downloading the policy file.	On large networks with many users, performance can suffer if the policy file is downloaded from only one location. Enabling the load-balancing policy (found under the Default Computer properties in the *windows.adm* and *common.adm* templates) will help resolve this bottleneck. Load balancing allows the policy file to be downloaded from any validating domain controller instead of only the PDC. Directory replication must be active so that the policy file exists on all possible validating controllers. Also, the client's workgroup name must be equal to the domain name.

Table 6-4. Troubleshooting Problems on Windows NT and Windows 2000 Domains

Problem	Explanation and Solution
Policies are not applied if the domain name in the network dialog box has a space appended to the end or if the domain name is a nonexistent domain.	If the domain name in the dialog box is changed to have one or more spaces appended to the end, or if it is a nonexistent domain name, system policies will not be applied. When Windows attempts to verify that the server is in the correct domain, the verify process fails due to the added space or nonexistent name. Consequently, policies are not merged with the registry and no error message appears to warn the user. The user is instead prompted with a local Windows logon box that can be bypassed by pressing Esc, giving him access to the workstation. Contact Microsoft Product Support Services for updated *msnet32.dll* and *msnp32.dll* files. Reference: Q237923, Q178979
SNMP community names and permissions are not set properly by the policy file.	Windows NT Service Pack 4 created changes in the registry to support enhanced SNMP community security. The old registry settings created by the SPE are now ignored. This problem can be resolved with the latest service pack or by an individual software update available from Microsoft Product Support Services. Reference: Q228543
The policy Enable Shutdown From the Authentication Dialog Box was checked, however the Shutdown button is still missing. Or, the policy was unchecked, however the shutdown button is still present.	This policy is set using the *winnt.adm* template; if it is changed, the template does not have the ability to restore the previous default setting. By default, the Shutdown button is present on a Windows NT workstation, but absent on a Windows NT server. The default setting must be restored by manually editing the registry. The registry key is HKLM\Software\Microsoft\Windows NT\CurrentVersion\Winlogon. The REG_SZ Valuename "ShutdownWithoutLogon" should have a value of 1 to enable the button and a value of 0 to disable it. Reference: Q155956, Q200863
The policy file is not downloaded.	• The DC name is longer than 13 characters. This problem was solved in Service Pack 3. Update to the latest service pack. • The user inappropriately requires read and write access to *ntconfig.pol*. This problem was solved in Service Pack 3. Update to the latest service pack. Reference: Q157673
The policy Hide Drives is active, but users can still access drives in Explorer.	The user can still access the drives by using the Tools menu in Explorer. The user policy Remove Tools → Goto Menu From Explorer, found in the *winnt.adm* template, should be used in addition to the Hide Drives policy.

Table 6-4. Troubleshooting Problems on Windows NT and Windows 2000 Domains

Problem	Explanation and Solution
The user's desktop does not contain the custom desktop shortcuts and folders.	If the server containing the custom folder shortcuts is unavailable, the user's desktop will not contain these shared items. Investigate using the Windows NT4 or Windows 2000 server distributed file system (Dfs). Reference: *http://www.microsoft.com/WINDOWS2000/library/planning/fileandprint/dfssteps.asp*
The *winnt.adm* template does not have policies for disabling the Lock Workstation, Change Password or Task Manager buttons.	Older versions of the *winnt.adm* template did not have these user policy options. Obtain the template version found in Service Pack 4 and up. Reference: Q174840
User policies from a Windows 2000 domain are not applied when using a Windows NT workstation.	This problem occurs with Windows NT4 workstations and users who are part of a global group on the Windows 2000 domain. This problem is resolved by updating the workstation to Service Pack 6. Reference: Q240076
Using manual remote update, user policies are not immediately taking effect.	The directory used to store the policy file should allow unvalidated connections, since the policy file is downloaded before the user is authenticated.
Windows 95 group policies are not applied at logon, and the user instead acquires the Default User policies.	Users are authenticated by a BDC, or the PDC is not available at logon. Since Windows 95, SR1, and SR2x will only try to query the global groups on the PDC for group membership (even with load balancing enabled), when none can be found the Default User policy is applied instead. Contact MS Technical Support for an updated *grouppol.dll* dated 1/27/97 (11,776 bytes) or later. Reference: Q150687

Locked Out

Despite the recommendation to back up the registry before using the SPE, accidents happen and people get locked out of their workstations. Almost 100% of the time it is a Windows 9x workstation and the policy Run Only Allowed Windows Applications has been checked off without any programs specified in the allowed list. This effectively prevents the user from running any programs, even Poledit.

If you are one of these unlucky users, the following steps will help you unlock your workstation. I'll begin with the easiest method and progress to editing the registry. Specifically, the user profile, or *user.dat,* is the area of the registry that contains these restrictions.

Are all users locked out?
Try logging in as other users to see if you can run Poledit or any other programs. To see which users may have less restricted profiles on this workstation, look at the subdirectories below *C:\Windows\Profiles*. Each subdirectory will be named according to the user's logon name.

Boot up into safe mode.
This will allow you to use the default local user profile, which may contain fewer restrictions. If you can run any program at all, simply rename the SPE to this program name to run Poledit. For example, if you can run Notepad rename the SPE from *poledit.exe* to *notepad.exe*. You will now be able to use Poledit in local computer mode to remove the default restrictions.

Assuming that the first two suggestions failed, you must progress to editing the registry. Since no programs can be run, Regedit and Poledit cannot be used in 32-bit mode. However, Regedit can still be used in real mode (DOS mode) using the following instructions:

1. Use a Windows 9x boot disk to boot to a command prompt.
2. Change to the Windows main directory by typing:

   ```
   Cd C:\Windows
   ```

3. If possible, remove all local profiles by typing either of the following commands:

   ```
   Deltree /y C:\Windows\Profiles or
   Echo Y | Deltree C:\Windows\Profiles
   ```

   If you want to retain some of the user's local profiles, temporarily rename any *user.dat* file in the individual profile subdirectories. You need to either rename or delete these files to allow the default profile (which you will edit in the next few steps) to be copied to your profile directory when you log on in Step 7, enabling you to run Poledit.

4. If the Run command is also missing from the Start menu, edit the *win.ini* file to automatically load Poledit when Windows loads. Add the following line, with the appropriate path, to the `[Windows]` section of this file:

   ```
   Load=C:\Windows\Poledit.exe
   ```

5. Create the registry file below using a real-mode text editor such as *edit.exe*. Save this file as *C:\Windows\restrict.reg*:

   ```
   REGEDIT4
   [HKEY_USERS\.Default\Software\Microsoft\Windows\CurrentVersion\Policies\Explorer\
   RestrictRun]
   "1"="poledit.exe"
   "2"="regedit.exe"
   ```

   This registry file will add the programs Poledit and Regedit to the allowed program list.

6. While still in the *C:\Windows* directory, type the following command to merge this registry file into the default user profile registry (located in the main Windows directory):

```
Regedit /s C:\Windows\restrict.reg
```

7. Reboot the computer and allow Windows to load. Then to make sure that you use the now unrestricted default *user.dat,* either cancel the network logon, or answer No to the question, "You have not logged onto this computer before, Would you like this computer to retain your individual settings for use when you log on here in the future?".
8. Poledit should now automatically start up, allowing you to remove the rest of the restrictions using File → Open Registry and editing the Local User. Once you have made the appropriate changes, save the local registry by choosing File → Save. At this time you may also want to disable user profiles, just until you are sure that all unwanted restrictions have been removed. Do this only if you do not want to retain any of the user profiles from Step 3.
9. The removal of all the restrictions will not be apparent until the workstation is rebooted one last time.

Summary

There are a number of basic points to remember when debugging system policy files:

- Policies will not download at all if remote update is not enabled on the workstation. In addition, the network client must be a 32-bit client for automatic remote update to occur.
- User policies will not be active unless user profiles are enabled, and group policies will not be active on a Windows 9x workstation until group policy support has been installed (see Chapter 4). Review Table 3-1 for other group policy requirements.
- Some policies will not be available (or restrictions will not be active) until the workstation is rebooted. Most notably, this is true of computer policies, since the *system.dat* portion of the registry is not reloaded until the workstation is restarted.
- The policy file must be created, saved and edited on the platform for which the file is intended. If you are going to be using the policy file on a Windows 9x workstation, it must be created on a Windows 9x workstation.
- The policy file will not automatically download from the network if it is not in the correct network folder. On a NetWare server it should be in the *Public* directory of the preferred server *(\\preferred server\sys\public),* on a Windows

NT network it should be in the *Netlogon* directory of all validating domain controllers *(%Systemroot%\winnt\system32\repl\import\scripts).* On a Windows 2000 network it should be on the *Netlogon* directory of any domain controller *(%Systemroot%\sysvol\DomainName\scripts)* for replication to other domain controllers. For other network operating systems, remote update must be in manual mode and the full pathname of the policy file specified.

- The policy file must be named appropriately and have Read and File scan permissions, for automatic remote update to occur. A policy file used on a Windows NT workstation must be called *ntconfig.pol,* while a policy file used on a Windows 9x workstation must be called *config.pol.*
- If the policies are not as expected for a particular user, suspect a user or group conflict. See Chapter 3 for more information on possible conflicts.
- Many problems can be solved by staying up to date. This means installing the latest recommended service packs, obtaining the most recent version of the policy templates and using the latest version of the System Policy Editor itself.

7

Standalone Windows 9x Workstations

Simply stated, a *standalone workstation* is one that is not connected to a local or wide area network. This does not include workstations with Internet access via a dial-up connection or cable modem. On a standalone Window 9x workstation the SPE provides only minimal security because the FAT file structure fails to protect the most crucial file, the *config.pol* (see Chapter 5, *It's Not Perfect*). Despite this, the SPE may provide adequate security on workstations with users, such as young children or trusted employees, who are unlikely to attempt to bypass security. In this case the SPE can provide cheap security, with no fear of software conflicts.

Windows NT4 Workstations

Although policies can be used on a standalone Windows NT4 workstation, they are rarely used because of the built-in security of Windows NT. As with a networked NT workstation, it is necessary to have at least Service Pack 3 installed for proper operation of the policy file. A *Netlogon* share can be created for *%SystemRoot%\System32\Repl\Import\Scripts* with Read permissions for everyone and full control for the Administrators group. The policy file should be named *ntconfig.pol* and unlike Windows 9x, Remote Update can be set to automatic.

Standalone Versus Networked

What follows is a brief review of some basic differences between using the SPE on a standalone Windows 9x workstation versus a networked client:

Installation of the SPE

The SPE should not be installed on any of the workstations but should only be saved to and used from some removable media such as a floppy disk. Installing the SPE on the workstation would only make it easier for a user to remove or change any imposed restrictions.

Remote update

Only manual Remote Update is supported on a standalone Windows 9x workstation, and setting Remote Update to automatic will in fact disable the policy file. Any location on the local hard drive can be used to store the policy file.

Group policies

Group policy support does not have to be installed on a Windows 9x workstation since group policies are not supported on a standalone workstation. Group policies can be used only in an environment that supports user groups, such as a server-based network. Peer-to-peer networks do not support the type of groups necessary for defining policy groups, even a peer-to-peer Windows NT network, since NT groups must be global and not local (see Chapter 2, *A System Policies Primer* for more information).

User Conflicts

Chapter 3, *Preparation and Planning*, contains a thorough discussion of conflicts that occur when using the SPE. The two conflicts most likely to occur on a standalone workstation are discussed in the "Default User" and "Shared workstation" sections of Chapter 3.

Knowing where conflicts are likely to occur is necessary to the successful use of system policies. Therefore, I'll take a look at the three logon situations a user will face on a standstalone workstation, how the policy file would be applied in each case, and where a conflict may take place. Note that in these examples *default Windows profile* refers to the *user.dat* located in the main *Windows* directory, while *individual profile* refers to the *user.dat* located in a *\Windows\Profiles\Username* subdirectory.

A User Policy Exists

The user has a specific user policy in the *config.pol* file. However, since the user's individual profile may or may not exist, there are two possible logon conditions:

The user has an existing individual profile

When the user logs on, the *user.dat* from his *Profiles* subdirectory is applied, then the DU policy is applied, and finally the user's specific user policy is applied.

No workstation conflict will occur, but the DU can create a conflict for any grayed settings in the user's policy.

The user has never logged on before, or a \Windows\Profiles\<Username> subdirectory does not exist for the user

The default Windows profile is applied, then the DU policy, and finally the specific user policy. Since the user does not have a *Profiles* subdirectory, he will be asked the save settings question. If he answers No, a shared workstation conflict will occur with a modified *user.dat* becoming the new default Windows profile. If he answers Yes to saving the settings, the *user.dat* will be saved to the user's newly created Profiles subdirectory. Although a workstation conflict will not occur, any restrictions in the DU or the default Windows profile can create conflicts for any grayed settings in the user's policy.

When considering the possibility of workstation conflicts, remember that any time a user enters his logon name incorrectly, he is essentially logging on as a new user. When he realizes that he has logged on incorrectly, he may very well respond No to the "retain settings" question, overwriting the default Windows profile.

A User Policy Does Not Exist

The user does not have a user policy specified in the *config.pol* file. Again because an individual profile may or may not exist, two logon conditions are possible:

The user has an existing individual profile

When the user logs on the *user.dat* from her *Profiles* subdirectory is applied, followed by the DU policy.

No workstation conflict will occur, but any checked settings in the DU can create a conflict with the user's profile.

The user has never logged on before, or a *Windows**Profiles*\<*Username*> subdirectory does not exist for the user.

The default Windows profile is applied followed by the DU policy.

Since the user does not have a Profiles subdirectory, she will be asked the save settings question. If she answers No, a shared workstation conflict will occur with a modified *user.dat* becoming the new default Windows profile. If she answers Yes to saving the settings, the *user.dat* will be saved to the user's newly created *Profiles* subdirectory. Although a workstation conflict will not occur, any grayed settings in the DU can create a conflict if the default Windows profile is more restrictive than the DU.

The User Is Unaffected by the config.pol File

The user may or may not have a user policy, but because he cancels the logon by selecting the Cancel button on the Windows logon screen, or boots to safe mode only one logon condition is possible.

Neither a specific user policy nor the DU policy will be applied, the policy file will be ignored, and only the default Windows profile will be loaded.

> The level of security in this case will depend upon the restrictions active in the default *user.dat.* Although this may at one time have been adequate, if any shared workstation conflicts have occurred the security may no longer be acceptable.

Avoiding User Conflicts

Conflicts created by the DU and shared workstations can be avoided by:

- Giving proper consideration to the creation of the user policies.
- Removing any profiles that were created before the policy file was implemented.
- Once the policy file is active, performing the initial logon for each specific user to make sure that their *Profiles* subdirectory is created. This will avoid further instances of the save settings question.
- Creating the DU and the local default Windows profile with exactly the same restrictions and settings.
- Using the Microsoft Family Logon to prevent the addition of new user profiles. See the "Microsoft Family Logon" section later in this chapter for more information.

Unless you are using the Microsoft Family Logon, there is really no benefit to having the local default Windows profile any more restrictive than the DU. An unknown user is a security risk whether the user logs on properly with an unknown name or whether she simply cancels the logon.

Planning the Policy File

Planning the policy file for a standalone workstation is much simpler than for a networked workstation, mainly because group policies and specific computer policies cannot be used. Consequently, the typical utilization of a standalone workstation can be simplified into two examples.

Example 1: The Workstation Is Used by Many New Users

This workstation may be used in an elementary school library to browse the Internet. Each student could potentially log on using a different name each time, so no specific user policies can be defined. In this case, the default security would need to be high. A DU policy would be used, plus one Administrator user policy. Since the user can easily cancel the logon process, the default Windows profile should have the same restrictions as the DU policy.

Example 2: The Workstation Is Used by One or a Few Regular Users

This workstation may be shared by two secretaries in an office and would require only a minimal level of security. Two specific user policies would be defined, as well as a single Administrator user policy. The DU would be used only if the secretary logged in incorrectly and could be set up with essentially no option but to shut down. This would encourage the user to log in again with his correct username and avoid the problem of "lost files" due to the user creating several similar logon names.

Prepare the Workstation

There are only two registry settings required for a standalone workstation to properly use the policy file:

- Remote update must be enabled and set to manual.
- User profiles must be enabled on a Windows 9x workstation.

However, begin by verifying that the workstation is working properly, and clean out any unnecessary files. You will want the workstation as perfectly configured as possible, and you should even consider doing a fresh install of the Windows OS. The *user.dat* in the main *Windows* directory will be used as a template to which the policy file is merged and then copied as a profile for each user; therefore, you will want the default Windows profile as flawless as possible. Work through the "Cleaning Up the Workstation" section in Chapter 4, *Building the Policy File*. To be sure that you are checking and fixing the default Windows profile, it is a good idea to initially set the workstation *not* to use user profiles (see Chapter 4). When you are confident that you have a good quality default Windows profile, you can then re-enable user profiles.

Back Up the Registry

I can't impress this point strongly enough—you must somehow back up the workstation's registry before implementing the policy file (see the sidebar, "Play It Safe—Back up Your Registry" in Chapter 4. The best time to backup the registry is after completing the default Windows profile clean up, and it is easiest to back up to another location on the local drive. If you want to keep a local copy of the unrestricted registry, the files can be "hidden" by giving them a false name. For example the *user.dat* could be saved to *C:\windows\reguser.dll* and the *system.dat* to *C:\windows\regsystm.dll.*

Create a Policy File

I will create a simple Windows 9x standalone policy file, much like the policy file from Chapter 4. Again, the template used will be the *admin.adm* template, which is available on the Windows 95 Resource Kit CD-ROM.

The policy file will include four user policies and one computer policy:

A Default User (DU) policy
: Used to ensure that the default Windows profile (*user.dat*) in the main Windows directory remains unchanged. There will be two DU options, one for Example 1 mentioned earlier and the other more restrictive option for Example 2.

An Admin user policy
: Used by the administrator and allows full access to the workstation.

Two specific user policies
: These have fewer restrictions than the DU policy but more restrictions than the ADMIN user policy.

A Default Computer (DC) policy
: Used to ensure that the local computer settings (*system.dat*) remain unchanged.

These policies are created in a specific order, to utilize the template properties of the DU and to help prevent policy conflicts.

Load the Template

Before creating any user policies, you must load a template. In the top menu bar of the SPE, select Options → Policy Template. Select Add and browse to the location of the *admin.adm* template. Select Open and then OK. You now have the proper template loaded into the policy editor.

Edit the Default User

The DU will be used as the default secure logon; it will require a high level of security. Choose File → New File to create the new policy file. The icons for the Default User and Default Computer will automatically be added. Begin by editing the Default User.

Example 1 (the workstation is used by many users)
Most of the same restrictions that were used in Chapter 4 for the DU will be checked. These include the Control Panel restrictions found in Figure 4-3, the Shell restrictions found in Figure 4-4, and finally the System restrictions found in Figure 4-5.

Example 2 (the workstation is used by one or a few regular users)
In addition to the restrictions used in Example 1, add the restrictions Hide Drives in 'My Computer' and Hide all items on Desktop to encourage the secretaries to log on using their correct logon name. You can also add the restriction Run Only Allowed Windows Applications, but use this restriction with care. Put at least one allowed program on this list, even if it is a fictional program name such as *nothing.exe*. This will allow you to still run the Poledit program simply by renaming it as *nothing.exe* (see Chapter 5). When the user logs on and receives this DU policy, there will be essentially no choice but to shut down and log on as another user.

At this point, it is a good idea to save the policy file. Select File → Save and type in the name and location of the policy file. The file can be called *config.pol*, although since you will be using manual update any filename is acceptable as long as it is in 8.3 format and has the POL extension (e.g., *C:\windows\policy.pol*).

Now that you have set up the DU with the restrictions you will be using, it will provide a more accurate template with which to create additional users. From Chapter 3 you will remember that the DU is loaded first, followed by any specific user policy. By configuring the DU first, and then creating the specific user policy, you are mimicking this procedure—allowing any policy conflicts to become more apparent.

Be wary of editing the DU *after* creating other users. You may create user conflicts that did not exist previously.

Create the Administrator User Policy

Select the Add User button and create a user based on whichever logon name you use for your Administrator account. For this example I will use Admin. Since the Admin user is also created using the DU template, you must systematically go through each template option changing all restrictions with a check mark to the cleared state. Since you are editing the DU before the Admin user you can now see where all of the DU restrictions were set. Do not change any option from the checked state to the grayed state, as you will be creating a conflict with the DU. If an option is already set to the grayed state, it is fine to leave it that way for now.

Before selecting the OK button, double-check that you do not have any of the Shell or System restrictions (Figures 4-4 and 4-5) in the checked state or you may find yourself locked out of the workstation.

Create a Specific User Policy

Using Example 2 (a workstation shared by two secretaries), I will create two specific users with a far more relaxed level of security than the DU. For Control Panel (Figure 4-3) and System (Figure 4-5) both users have the same restrictions as the DU. However, for Shell (Figure 4-4), I will allow the users access to the Run and Find commands and allow them to Save Settings at Exit. I will leave the custom folder option grayed (Figure 4-6) so that the custom folders in the user's *C:\Windows\Profiles\<Username>* subdirectory will be used.

I will call my first user Rose. Once I have created Rose's user policy, I will again click the Add User button and call my second user Gabriel. Since I want Gabriel to have exactly the same restrictions as Rose, I can copy and paste Rose's settings to Gabriel by highlighting Rose and selecting Edit → Copy. Then I select and highlight Gabriel and choose Edit → Paste. The two users now have identical settings.

Edit the Default Computer Policy

Now that you have completed the user policies, namely the settings for *user.dat*, move on to the computer settings or the settings for *system.dat*. It is a good idea to set some policies in the DC in case the user ever accidentally or maliciously changes the default settings. If that were to happen, each time the policy file was merged by the workstation, the correct settings would be restored.

Open the DC policy, under Default Computer → Network → Access Control (Figure 4-10) and change Logon Banner to the checked position. This option will display a default message (which can be customized) warning the user that unauthorized access is not allowed.

Remote update (Network → Update, Figure 4-11) *must* be set to the checked position, and under "Settings for Remote Update" the update mode must be manual. In the "Path for Manual Update" edit box, type the full pathname of the policy file including the name of the policy file itself (i.e., *C:\windows\config.pol*).

If you leave Remote Update in the cleared position or set to automatic, the workstation will be set to *not* download the policy file after the next reboot. In effect, the policy file will no longer be active on the workstation.

Under System settings, Enable User Profiles should be set to the checked position. If you missed enabling user profiles, this option would enable them at the next reboot as long as the workstation was set to allow manual Remote Update.

Select OK to finish the DC edits. Now save the policy file by selecting File → Save. Your SPE window should now show the same policy icons that appear in Figure 7-1.

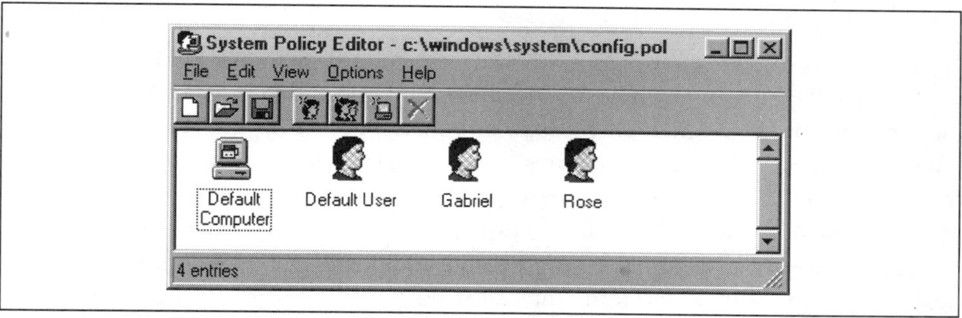

Figure 7-1. Complete policy file

Edit the Local Computer Policy

Most OEM versions of Windows 9x will have Remote Update enabled; however it will be set to automatic update. This must be changed to manual update with the location of the policy file specified or the workstation will not load the policy file. Although this was set in the DC policy, it must also be set in the default Windows registry.

If the policy file is still open, choose File → Close to close it. Now choose File → Open Registry to open the local registry files. Choose Local Computer, and set Remote Update to manual, specifying the location of the policy file as you did when editing the DC policy. As well, check the policy Enable User Profiles (see Figure 4-11). Finally choose File → Save to save the changes to the default *system.dat*.

Test the Policy File

Before you leave the workstation, thoroughly test all user and computer policies. To enable the policy file you will need to power down and restart the workstation. Again, make sure you have a backup of the unrestricted registry before completing this final step. Once the computer is restarted and the policies are tested, the registry will be permanently altered.

Verify the Default User

The Default User will be the active policy for any user who is not otherwise specified in the policy file. In other words, if you log on as anyone besides Admin or a specified user, you should get the DU policy. For Example 1, all users would receive the DU policy.

Log on with any unknown name. When asked the "Do you want to retain your individual settings?" question, answer No. This will cause the DU settings to be copied to the default Windows profile. This is a quick way to set the default Windows profile without having to use the SPE in local registry mode to set all the Local User options.

Check each restriction. If you used the DU setup from Example 1, can you access the Control Panel? Do you have the Settings, Run and Find commands in the Start menu? Can you access a DOS prompt? If you right-click on the desktop, do you have access to the Display Properties (such as wallpaper settings)? If you browse the hard drive, can you run the registry editor? You shouldn't be able to do any of these things. If you used the DU setup from Example 2, as well as all of the restrictions listed for Example 1, you should additionally have a completely blank desktop. If you checked the Run Only Allowed Applications restrictions, verify that you indeed cannot run any application.

If any of these restrictions are not active, go back and double-check the DU policy for settings left in the grayed or cleared positions.

Verify the User Policies

Log on to the workstation as either of the specified users, this time answering Yes to the save settings question. If you answer negatively, you will overwrite the default Windows profile. Answering Yes will allow you to create the individual *Profiles* subdirectory for each user, preventing the question from being asked when the user next logs on.

As with the DU, ensure that the restrictions you want active are actually active. Check for access to the Control Panel applets for example. Conversely, check that you do have access where you want it. For example, do you have access to all drives or the Run and Find commands in the Start menu? Since you are logging in after the DU, the local default Windows profile (which was used as a template to create the user's profile) contained all of the DU's restrictions. If you do not have access to some commands, double-check the specific user policy for restrictions left in the grayed position that were possibly overwritten by the DU.

Verify the Admin User

Log on to the workstation as the Admin user, again answering Yes to the save settings question. If you answer negatively, you will overwrite the default Windows profile with a completely unrestricted profile. This is probably the greatest dilemma when using system policies on a standalone workstation, and so is something you must be aware of. See "Using the System Policy Editor Without User Profiles" later in this chapter. The *hidereg.bat* file mentioned here could be run from the *autoexec.bat*, offering a possible solution to this dilemma.

Once you are logged in, thoroughly check that you have no restrictions anywhere, since this logon will be your gateway into the workstation. Check that you have complete access to all the Control Panel applets, to the Network Neighborhood, to all drives, to the DOS prompt, to the registry editor and to the Find, Run and Settings commands on the Start menu.

If you find any restrictions active, double-check the Admin user policy for settings left in the grayed or checked positions.

Verify the "Cancel Logon" User

At the Windows logon screen, select the Cancel button. The logon process will bypass the policy file completely and load only the default Windows profile. Verify that this profile has the same restrictions as the DU. If it does not, you likely did not answer No to the save settings question when you tested the DU, or you did not answer Yes to this question when testing each specific user or the Admin user. To rectify this, log on with a new and unknown username, and answer No to the save settings question.

Copying the Policy File to Other Workstations

The policy file you have just created can be copied to a floppy disk and from that to other workstations as long as the operating systems match. In other words, a Windows 98 policy file can be copied to another Windows 98 workstation. On each workstation, complete the hard drive cleanup and ensure that the new workstation has manual Remote Update enabled. The location to which the policy file is copied must match the location specified in the Default Computer policy. If it does not match, the policy file will not be active after the next reboot. Finally to set the default user profile, log on as an unknown new user answering No to the save settings question. The restrictions in the default Windows profile will now equal the DU policy restrictions.

Microsoft Family Logon

Consider using the Microsoft Family Logon client (Chapter 4) on a standalone workstation as an initial line of defense. If many different users are using the workstation as in Example 1, a single Guest user account could be created in addition to the SuperR default level of user restrictions found in Chapter 4. This would prevent a glut of new user profile accounts from being created on the local drive, as well as providing security in the event that the workstation were booted into safe mode. In Example 2, the users would be able to choose their name only from the predefined list and incorrect username entries would be avoided.

Be cautious though; by itself this client does not provide sufficient security. If a password has not been set up for a user using the Users applet, if the password file (**.pwl*) has been deleted, or if the *Windows\Profiles\<Username>* subdirectory is missing, then the password listbox (Figure 4-13) will be grayed out. In this case, full access to that user's profile can be obtained simply by choosing the user name and clicking OK. When using the Microsoft Family Logon don't include an Administrator account in the user; since access to this account is easily obtained.

The Microsoft Family Logon client requires the use of user profiles, and password caching must be enabled.

Using the System Policy Editor Without User Profiles

If you are only interested in creating a DU without any specific users, it is possible to use the SPE to secure only the default Windows profile without ever enabling user profiles. This may be preferential in some circumstances (such as a Windows 9x workstation in a public library), as it would prevent numerous profile subdirectories from being created and filling up the hard drive. Use the SPE with the appropriate template to edit the Local User, setting the desired restrictions. If you use the SPE to edit the Local Computer, do not check off the option Enable User Profiles.

The one drawback with this method is that restrictions have to be manually removed before system settings can be altered. Alternately, a local copy of the unrestricted user profile could be saved (see the earlier section, "Back Up the Registry"). The unrestricted profile could be restored to the *Windows* directory from the command prompt whenever system settings needed to be changed. This process of moving and renaming the registry files could be automated by using batch files such as:

restoreg.bat renames the restricted profile and restores the unrestricted profile:

```
@echo off
Cd\Windows
Attrib -s -h -r user.dat
Ren user.dat user.bak
Copy C:\Windows\Regsystm.dll C:\Windows\user.dat
Attrib +s +h +r user.dat
Echo Now reboot the computer
```

hidereg.bat removes the unrestricted user profile and restores the restricted profile:

```
@echo off
Cd\Windows
Attrib -s -h -r user.dat
Del user.dat
Ren user.bak user.dat
Attrib +s +h +r user.dat
Echo Now reboot the computer
```

Final Tips

A few miscellaneous points, as well as some final tips, are discussed in this section.

Caution Regarding Template States

Use caution when changing some policy options to the cleared state. For example, if the option Custom Desktop Icons for a specific user was set to cleared, that user would get the same desktop icons as the default Windows profile. If this policy option were then switched back to grayed, the user's old desktop icons would not be restored. This is because each user of a workstation with user profiles enabled has custom folders already specified in the registry, located in his or her *Windows\Profiles\<Username>* subdirectory. Setting Custom Desktop Icons to the cleared state deletes that registry entry, but returning to the grayed state cannot restore that specific registry value. The only way to restore the user's registry entry would be to set the Custom Desktop Icons option to the checked position again, and specify the folder location.

Cleaning Out the Profile List Registry Key

It is possible to automatically remove the registry key that contains the list of all users who have ever logged on to the workstation. For information on how to do this, see "The reg.exe Utility" in Chapter 4. These commands may be saved to a batch file and run as a regular maintenance option. This batch file can be executed automatically when the user logs off by using the utility Wrapup by Tessler's Nifty Tools (*http://ourworld.compuserve.com/homepages/NIFTY_TOOLS/*), or ShutUp from PC Magazine (*http://www.zdnet.com/pcmag/pctech/content/16/15/ut1615.001.html*). In much the same way that Windows executes any program in the Startup folder, Wrapup and ShutUp will execute any program copied to a logoff folder.

Using Multiple Templates

Once you are aware of the other template options, it is unlikely that you will only be using the *admin.adm* template to create the policy file. Although the templates have a 64 K restriction on their size, and cannot be saved together as one large file, you can load multiple templates. When adding templates, follow the procedure outlined in the "Loading the Template" section in Chapter 4, but continue to add all the templates you will be using.

There is one possible source of conflict using this method that occurs when you load more than one template with the same option. See the "Adding Additional Templates" section in Chapter 4.

Summary

Using the SPE for security on a Windows 9x standalone workstation can provide only minimal protection at best, with any knowledgeable computer user easily bypassing the security. However in some situations in which the users are quite young or very inexperienced, the SPE (in addition to tips provided in Chapter 5) can provide adequate security.

The best option for a standalone workstation is to use one of the other Windows operating systems with built-in file-level security, such as Windows NT or Windows 2000. For Windows 9x workstations, a third-party security software package (see Appendix B) is another viable option.

8

Creating a Custom Template

Perhaps one of the most versatile functions of the SPE is the ability to create a custom template for just about any program that utilizes the Windows registry. This is particularly useful if an organization uses in-house software programs and needs to gain some measure of consistency across workstations. This consistency can be achieved using the SPE and a custom template.

This chapter will first examine the structure of a template, breaking it down into its smallest components while giving a full explanation and example of each. I will then go through the creation of a unique template, one that uses many popular Windows registry hacks. While creating this template, I will point out the information required and emulate the decision-making process for choosing the appropriate syntax and keywords.

The Four Zones

A template consists of four nested zones: class, category, policy and part. parts nest within policies; policies nest within categories; and categories nest within one single class. Figure 8-1 displays this basic structure.

Two of the four zones are really organizational in nature. class separates computer and user policies, while category organizes policy options into logistical areas. It is policy and part that are the working parts of the template, and it is these two zones that contain the elements that allow the registry to be edited.

Information within each zone is displayed in a specific area of the computer or user properties page of the SPE, as shown in Figure 8-2. I will examine each zone in more detail in the following sections.

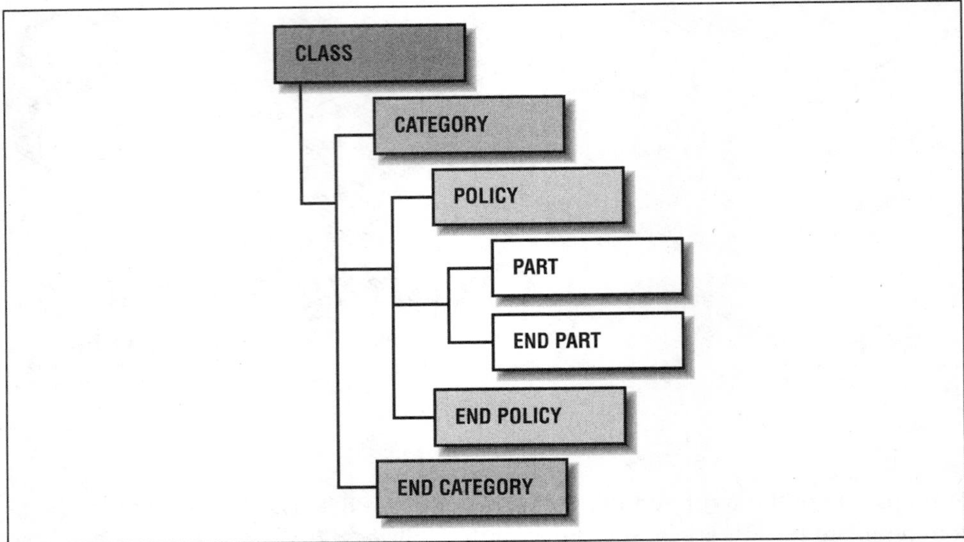

Figure 8-1. Basic template structure

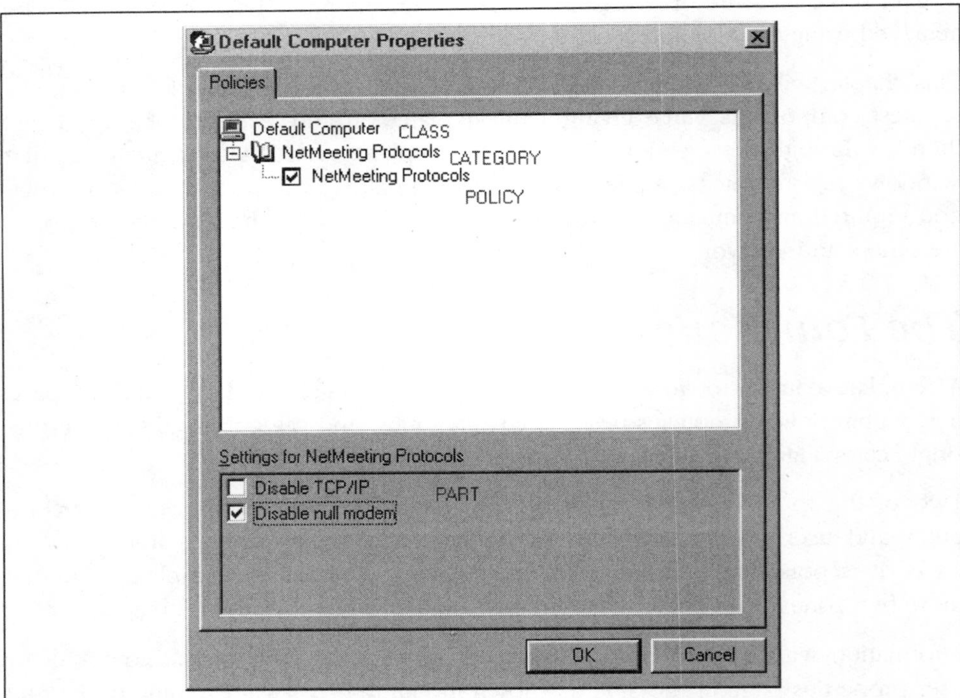

Figure 8-2. Template zones in the conf.adm template

In each of the four zones there are a number of available keywords. While most keywords are specific to their own areas, there are three that can be used anywhere within the four zones:

KEYNAME "value"

Indicates a full registry key path. Unless elsewhere specified, it will be inherited by all child areas of the template. The top-level key, HKLM or HKCU, does not need to be specified as it is assumed depending on which class type precedes the KEYNAME. Additional KEYNAME statements can be subkeys of a previously mentioned key. For example, the class statement could mention the key "Software\Microsoft\Windows\CurrentVersion" while a policy statement would only have to mention "Policies\Network." For example:

```
KEYNAME "Control Panel\Colors"
```

!!string

Indicates a string that will be replaced with a text label in the SPE properties window. This is used for labels on categories, policies, and parts, or for help text. Using this, a text label only has to be defined once. A section at the end of the template labeled `[strings]` contains the string definitions. For example:

```
!!Wallpaper1 !!Wallpaper2
[strings]
Wallpaper1="Black Thatch.bmp"
```

; comment

Comments can be entered anywhere in the template by preceding them with a semicolon. Any line beginning with a semicolon will not be processed by the SPE. For example:

```
;template version 2.1
```

The use of the `!!` keyword for text labels is not absolutely necessary. Text entered without the `!!` keyword will be used as is, but any text containing spaces would have to be enclosed within quotes.

Each of the four zones has a basic syntax and its own specific keywords, which I cover in the next sections.

Class

There are only two valid classes: Machine and User (see Table 8-1). They define one or the other of the two registry keys that can be edited by a template, either HKCU or HKLM. HKCU will appear as a user or group policy and is referred to as class `USER`. HKLM will appear as a computer policy and is referred to as class `MACHINE`.

Basic Syntax	CLASS *class_type*
Examples from *conf.adm*	CLASS MACHINE CLASS USER

Category

On the SPE properties page, the text captions that appear beside the book icons are the categories (see Figure 8-2). They are included on either the computer or user/group properties page, depending on which class statement they follow. If they follow Class Machine, they will be on the computer properties page; if they follow Class User, they will be on the user or group properties page. Categories are used to give the template organizational structure and can be nested within each other to create main categories and subcategories.

Basic Syntax	CATEGORY !!*string* KEYNAME *"value"* *[policy and part statements go here]* END CATEGORY
Example From *conf.adm*	CATEGORY !!NetMeeting2 KEYNAME "Software\Microsoft\Conferencing" *[policy and part statements]* END CATEGORY

KEYNAME is optional. If it is not specified here, it can be taken from the parent category, or it can be specified in the subsequent policy or part statements. If a KEYNAME *is* specified, it can be used by all child subcategories, policies and parts. This inheritance of keywords allows the template to be simplified by removing the necessity of repeating the oftentimes lengthy registry keywords.

Policy

The essence of the template is the policies that exist within a category. They are the familiar checkboxes that can be set to one of three positions: cleared, grayed or checked. While the class and category statements have no direct effect on the registry, changing a policy option will alter a registry key or value. The basic policy syntax is as follows:

```
POLICY !!string
KEYNAME "value"
    [optional keyword(s)]
    [optional PART statement(s)]
END POLICY
```

As with category, KEYNAME is optional and can be inherited from preceding policies or categories.

A policy can contain several optional keywords, listed here. They may be included within the part statements instead.

`VALUENAME "value"`
: The `VALUENAME` of the registry key. It is optional *only* if the policy contains additional part statements. A `VALUENAME` containing spaces must be enclosed within quotes, although all valuenames may be enclosed in quotes for consistency. For example:

```
VALUENAME "Background"
```

`VALUE value`
: The value of the registry entry specified by `VALUENAME`. If there is no `VALUE` statement, the default value when the policy box is checked is a DWORD of 1, and the default value when the policy box is cleared is to remove the value entirely.

If a value is specified, the default is for that value to be interpreted as a string (REG_SZ) value. Strings with spaces must be enclosed in quotes. To create specific DWORD values, the value must be preceded with the word `NUMERIC`. To totally remove a `VALUENAME/VALUE` registry pair, use a value of `DELETE`. For example:

```
VALUENAME "Background"      VALUE "128 128 192"
VALUENAME "Platform_Type"   VALUE NUMERIC 0
VALUENAME "StaticVxD"       VALUE DELETE
```

`DEFCHECKED`
: The policy box is initially checked.

`VALUEON value`
: Overrides the checked position default of the `VALUE` keyword (DWORD value of 1) to another specified value. As with the `VALUE` keyword, values default to a string (REG_SZ) value unless preceded by the word NUMERIC. For example:

```
VALUEON "1"
VALUEON DELETE
```

`VALUEOFF value`
: Overrides the default behavior to set a specified value when the box is in the cleared position. It follows the same rules as `VALUEON`.

`ACTIONLISTON`
: Optional actions (other registry keys to be changed) if a policy box is set to the checked (on) position. For example, in the *admin.adm* template there is an option to choose a desktop color scheme by name (e.g., Rainy Day). The `ACTIONLIST` would then be used to change the color of each individual control panel item to achieve the Rainy Day color scheme.

ACTIONLISTOFF

Optional actions (other registry keys to be changed) if policy box is in the cleared (off) position. The syntax for both **ACTIONLISTON** and **ACTIONLISTOFF** is as follows:

```
ACTIONLISTOFF (or ACTIONLISTON)
   KEYWORD value
   VALUENAME "value" VALUE value
END ACTIONLISTOFF (or END ACTIONLISTON)
```

Any number of policies can exist under any one category or subcategory.

For Windows 9x there can be only two types of **VALUE** entries: string or DWORD. Binary values are not supported by the SPE templates. For Windows NT, only REG_DWORD, REG_SZ, and REG_EXPAND_SZ registry values are supported.

An example of a simple policy from the *conf.adm* template is as follows:

```
POLICY !!PreventAnswering
     PART !!PreventAnswering CHECKBOX
     VALUENAME "NoAnswering"
     END PART
END POLICY
```

You will notice in this example that the **VALUENAME** does not need to be specified immediately after the policy statement, as it is included within the **PART** statement instead. In addition, since a value is not specified, it will default to a DWORD value of 1.

Part

If there are policy options in addition to enabled and disabled (cleared and checked), then these can be identified in a part statement. Once the policy checkbox is set to the checked position, the part options become available in the lower gray portion of the user or computer property sheet. There are seven part types, and these types allow for the data to be presented in various forms such as text boxes, spin dials and so on (see each specific part type for more information).

The basic **PART** syntax is as follows:

```
PART !!string part_type
part_type optional_keyword
KEYNAME "value"
VALUENAME "value" VALUE value
END PART
```

The string is the label that appears beside the actual part type in the properties box. The available optional keywords will depend on the specific part type.

KEYNAME is again optional, as it can be inherited from the parent policy or category. **Value** is also optional, and if it is not specified, it will default to a DWORD value of 1. However, **Valuename** must be specified for most part types (see each part type for further information).

An example of a simple policy from the *conf.adm* template is as follows:

```
PART !!EnableNullModem CHECKBOX
    DEFCHECKED
    KEYNAME "Software\Microsoft\Conferencing\Transports\DIRCB"
    VALUENAME "Disabled"
END PART
```

In this example the part type is a checkbox, and the part type optional keyword is **DEFCHECKED** (the checkbox will be in the checked position by default).

A simple policy (without any part statements) shares much in common with the part type **CHECKBOX**, as they both use the same syntax and optional keywords.

Putting It Together

Putting together the four zones (class, category, policy and part), the entire Machine portion of the *conf.adm* template displayed in Figure 8-2 appears like this:

```
CLASS MACHINE

CATEGORY !!NetMeeting2
KEYNAME "Software\Microsoft\Conferencing"
    POLICY !!NetMeeting2
        PART !!EnableTCPIP CHECKBOX
         KEYNAME "Software\Microsoft\Conferencing\Transports\TCPIP"
         VALUENAME "Disabled"
        END PART

        PART !!EnableNullModem CHECKBOX
         DEFCHECKED
         KEYNAME "Software\Microsoft\Conferencing\Transports\DIRCB"
         VALUENAME "Disabled"
        END PART
    END POLICY
END CATEGORY
```

If you examine this class example, you see that there is only one category, as well as a single policy within which are two part statements. Although this category specifies a keyname, it is not necessary as each of the two parts also specify keynames. In both parts, the valuename is specified although the Value is not, indicating that the default DWORD value of 1 will be used.

Part Types

The true flexibility of a custom template comes from the individual part types, of which there are seven:

- `TEXT`
- `EDITTEXT`
- `CHECKBOX`
- `NUMERIC`
- `DROPDOWNLIST`
- `COMBOBOX`
- `LISTBOX`

Each part shares the same universal keywords shown in the four zones universal keyword list, in addition to their own unique keywords.

TEXT

The `TEXT` part type does not edit the registry, as it is merely descriptive text with no associated registry key or value. It allows you to put in explanatory text for your policy or parts as shown in Figure 8-3.

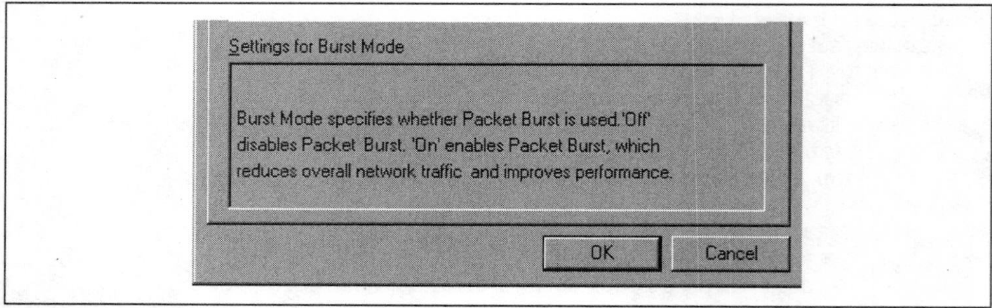

Figure 8-3. TEXT part option from nwnt.adm

The **TEXT** part that is displayed in Figure 8-3 is created by the following template statements:

```
PART !!BurstMode_TIP1 TEXT END PART
PART !!BurstMode_TIP2 TEXT END PART
PART !!BurstMode_TIP3 TEXT END PART

[strings]
BurstMode_TIP1="Burst Mode specifies whether Packet Burst is used.'Off'"
BurstMode_TIP2="disables Packet Burst. 'On' enables Packet Burst, which"
BurstMode_TIP3="reduces overall network traffic and improves performance."
```

The text is broken up into three lines so that it does not run off the edge of the properties window. Approximately 65 characters can be used before the text runs off the edge of the window.

EDITTEXT

EDITTEXT allows you to make a box for alphanumeric text input, as shown in Figure 8-4.

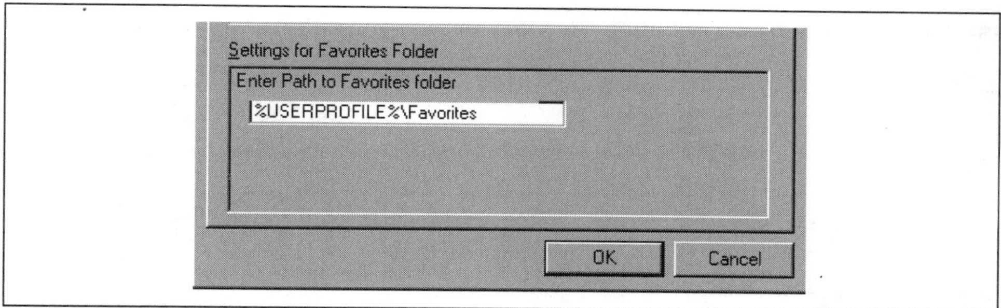

Figure 8-4. EDITTEXT part type from zakwinnt.adm

This part will have an associated registry keyname, which will either be specified or inherited from a parent policy or category. The **EDITTEXT** statement may also include one or more of the optional keywords shown in Table 8-1.

Table 8-1. EDITTEXT Keywords

Optional Keywords	Details
`VALUENAME "value"`	This keyword is *not* optional. See policy optional keyword list for details.
`VALUE value`	See policy optional keyword list for details.
`DEFAULT value`	Specifies the initial text string. The default is a blank box. The value is set in the registry as a string (REG_SZ) type.
`EXPANDABLETEXT`	Allows use of environment variables by writing the value to the registry with the datatype REG_EXPAND_SZ.

Table 8-1. EDITTEXT Keywords (continued)

Optional Keywords	Details
MAXLEN value	Maximum length of the text, to a maximum of 255 characters.
REQUIRED	The policy cannot be set to the checked position until something is entered into the listbox. If nothing is entered, the user is prompted to do so by an error message.
OEMCONVERT	Sets the **ES_OEMCONVERT** style in the edit field so that typed text converts from the ANSI character set to the installed OEM character set.

The **EDITTEXT** part that is displayed in Figure 8-4 is created by the following template statements:

```
Part !!UserProfiles_FavoritesPathEDITTEXT REQUIRED EXPANDABLETEXT
    Default !!UserProfiles_FavoritesPathDefault
    Valuename "Favorites"
End Part
```

You will notice that the edit box allows the use of environmental variables through the use of the keyword **EXPANDABLETEXT**. In addition, the use of the second keyword **REQUIRED** will not allow the user to leave the edit text box blank.

A custom template can be made that has an edit box of more than 255 characters; howeve,r only the first 255 characters will be passed onto the registry by the SPE.

CHECKBOX

A **CHECKBOX** can have two positions in a template, checked or unchecked (on or off). By default, if the box is checked, the value will be a REG_DWORD of 1. If the box is cleared, the value entry is set to zero.

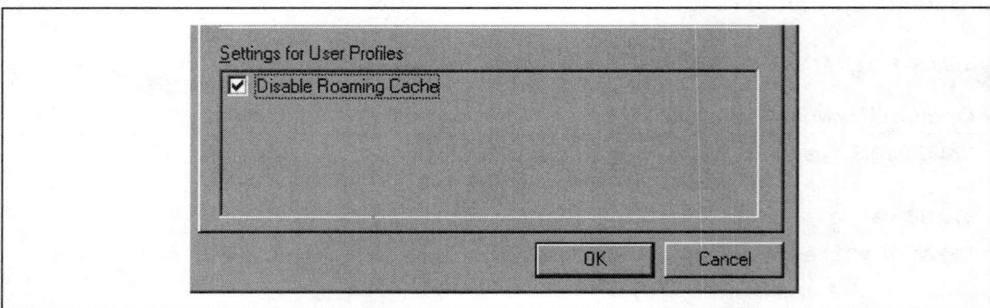

Figure 8-5. CHECKBOX part option

This part will have an associated registry keyname, which will either be specified or inherited from a parent policy or category. The **CHECKBOX** part type uses the same optional keywords as the basic policy (see the policy optional keyword list for more information), as shown in Figure 8-5. These keywords are:

- VALUENAME
- VALUE
- DEFCHECKED
- VALUEON/VALUEOFF
- ACTIONLISTON/ACTIONLISTOFF

The **CHECKBOX** part that is displayed in Figure 8-5 is created by the following template statements:

```
PART !!DisableCache CHECKBOX
    VALUENAME "UserProfiles"
    VALUEON NUMERIC 0
    VALUEOFF NUMERIC 1
ACTIONLISTON
    KEYNAME "Software\Microsoft\Windows\CurrentVersion\Internet Settings\5.0\
         Cache\Content"
    VALUENAME "PerUserItem" VALUE NUMERIC 0
END ACTIONLISTON
ACTIONLISTOFF
    KEYNAME "Software\Microsoft\Windows\CurrentVersion\Internet Settings\5.0\
         Cache\Content"
    VALUENAME "PerUserItem" VALUE NUMERIC 1
END ACTIONLISTOFF
END PART
```

You will notice that when the **CHECKBOX** is in the checked position, the **ACTIONLISTON** statement allows an additional registry edit to occur. Also, the **ACTIONLISTOFF** statement allows for an additional registry edit when the checkbox is in the cleared position. Typically **ACTIONLISTON** and **ACTIONLISTOFF** do not occur independently of each other, even if **ACTIONLISTOFF** does nothing else but delete the **VALUENAME/VALUE** registry pair created by the **ACTIONLISTON**.

NUMERIC

The **NUMERIC** part type allows you to type in a numeric value, or use a spin dial (the up and down arrows) to choose a value. The spin dial can have an optional specified range and increment value.

This part will have an associated registry keyname, which will either be specified or inherited from a parent policy or category. The **NUMERIC** statement may also include one or more of the optional keywords in Table 8-2.

Figure 8-6. NUMERIC part option from winnt.adm

Table 8-2. NUMERIC Optional Keywords

Optional Keywords	Details
`VALUENAME "value"`	This keyword is *not* optional. See the policy optional keyword list for details.
`VALUE value`	See the policy optional keyword list for details. This value will be read as a binary (REG_DWORD) value.
`DEFAULT value`	Specifies the initial numerical value; the default is a blank box.
`MIN value`	Minimum value, default is 0.
`MAX value`	Maximum value, default is 9999.
`SPIN value`	An increment for spin control; default is 1. Spin 0 removes the control arrows.
`TXTCONVERT`	Writes values as strings (REG_SZ) rather than DWORD values.
`REQUIRED`	The policy cannot be set to the checked position until something is entered into the list box. If nothing is entered, the user is prompted to do so by an error message.

The `NUMERIC` part that is displayed in Figure 8-6 is created by the following template statements:

```
PART !!ProfileSize      NUMERIC REQUIRED SPIN 100
     DEFAULT 30000
     MAX    30000
     MIN    300
     VALUENAME "MaxProfileSize"
END PART
```

Notice that the spin dial will increase by increments of 100, from a minimum of 300 to a maximum of 30,000—which also happens to be the default value.

Due to a bug in Poledit, the maximum value that a user can type directly into a numeric box is 9999 (or 4 digits), although a spin dial can be used to increase the value beyond this number.

DROPDOWNLIST

A `DROPDOWNLIST` (see Figure 8-7) presents the user with a number of options from which to choose. The user is not free to type in any other choices.

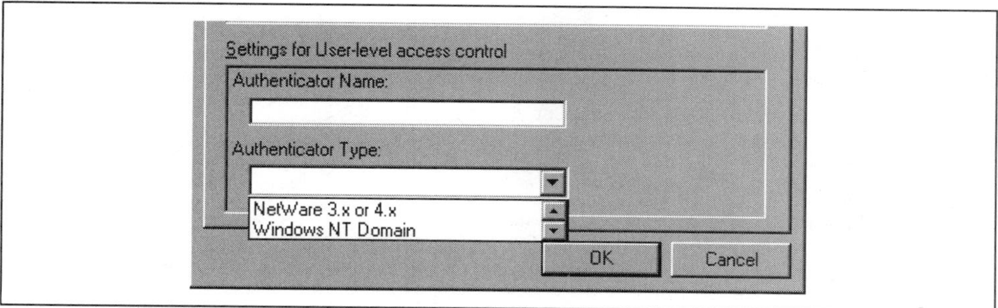

Figure 8-7. DROPDOWNLIST part option from windows.adm

This part will have an associated registry keyname, which will be either specified or inherited from a parent policy or category. The `DROPDOWNLIST` statement may also include one or more of the optional keywords in Table 8-3.

Table 8-3. DROPDOWNLIST Optional Keywords

Optional Keywords	Details
VALUENAME *"value"*	This keyword is not optional, see the policy optional keyword list for details.
VALUE *value*	See the policy optional keyword list for details.
NOSORT	Will not sort data alphabetically. Default is to sort.
REQUIRED	The policy cannot be set to the checked position until something is entered into the list box. If nothing is entered, the user is prompted to do so with an error message.

ITEMLIST	The list of items to be included in the drop-down list.
	The syntax is as follows (see the policy optional keyword list for VALUENAME and VALUE options):
	`ITEMLIST`
	`    NAME !!string  VALUE value`
	`ACTIONLIST`
	`  KEYNAME "value"`
	`    VALUENAME "value" VALUE value`
	`END ACTIONLIST`
	`END ITEMLIST`

The `ITEMLIST` allows each choice, labeled by the `!!string`, and any associated additional registry edits, to be listed separately. In this situation, `ACTIONLIST` functions in much the same way as the `CHECKBOX` keyword `ACTIONLISTON` (policy optional keyword list).

The DROPDOWNLIST part that is displayed in Figure 8-7 is created by the following template statements:

```
PART !!AuthenticatorType DROPDOWNLIST
KEYNAME Security\Provider
VALUENAME "Platform_Type" REQUIRED
ITEMLIST
    NAME !!AT_NetWare      VALUE NUMERIC 3
ACTIONLIST
    KEYNAME System\CurrentControlSet\Services\VxD\NWSP
    VALUENAME "StaticVxD" VALUE nwsp.vxd
    VALUENAME "Start"        VALUE NUMERIC 0
    KEYNAME Security\Provider
    VALUENAME "Address_Book"  VALUE nwab32.dll
END ACTIONLIST
    NAME !!AT_NTAS          VALUE NUMERIC 2
ACTIONLIST
    KEYNAME System\CurrentControlSet\Services\VxD\MSSP
    VALUENAME "StaticVxD"    VALUE mssp.vxd
    VALUENAME "Start"        VALUE NUMERIC 0
    KEYNAME Security\Provider
    VALUENAME "Address_Book"  VALUE msab32.dll
END ACTIONLIST
    NAME !!AT_NT            VALUE NUMERIC 1
ACTIONLIST
    KEYNAME System\CurrentControlSet\Services\VxD\MSSP
    VALUENAME "StaticVxD" VALUE mssp.vxd
    VALUENAME "Start"        VALUE NUMERIC 0
    KEYNAME Security\Provider
    VALUENAME "Address_Book"  VALUE msab32.dll
END ACTIONLIST
END ITEMLIST
END PART
```

Notice that there are three NAMEs, indicating that there will be three options on this drop-down list. The value specified beside each name will be applied to the VALUENAME listed on line three (Platform_Type). Also notice that each name has an associated ACTIONLIST with additional registry edits.

COMBOBOX

The COMBOBOX (shown in Figure 8-8) is basically a combination of the part types EDITTEXT and DROPDOWNLIST. Like EDITTEXT you can type in alphanumeric text, or like DROPDOWNLIST you can choose from a list of suggestions.

This part will have an associated registry keyname, which will be either specified or inherited from a parent policy or category. The COMBOBOX statement may also include one or more of the optional keywords in Table 8-4.

Figure 8-8. COMBOBOX part option from admin.adm

Table 8-4. COMBOBOX Optional Keywords

Optional Keywords	Details
VALUENAME *"value"*	This keyword is *not* optional. See the policy optional keyword list for details.
VALUE *value*	See the policy optional keyword list for details.
DEFAULT *value*	Specifies the initial text string. Default is blank.
EXPANDABLETEXT	Allows use of environment variables by writing the value to the registry with the datatype REG_EXPAND_SZ.
MAXLEN *value*	Maximum length of the text.
REQUIRED	The policy cannot be set to the checked position until something is entered into the list box. If nothing is entered, the user is prompted to do so with an error message.
OEMCONVERT	Sets the ES_OEMCONVERT style in the edit field so that typed text is mapped from ANSI to OEM and back.
NOSORT	Do not sort data alphabetically. The default is to sort.
SUGGESTIONS	Lists suggestions to be included in the drop-down box. Each suggestion is separated from the next by a space. Suggestions with a space are enclosed by quotes: SUGGESTIONS !!*string1* !!*string2* !!*string3* END SUGGESTIONS

The COMBOBOX part that is displayed in Figure 8-8 is created by the following template statements:

```
PART !!WallpaperName COMBOBOX REQUIRED
  SUGGESTIONS
      !!Wallpaper1 !!Wallpaper2 !!Wallpaper3 !!Wallpaper4 !!Wallpaper5
      !!Wallpaper6 !!Wallpaper7 !!Wallpaper8 !!Wallpaper9 !!Wallpaper10
  END SUGGESTIONS
  VALUENAME "Wallpaper"
END PART
```

You will notice that in this example VALUENAME appears after the suggestion list. It is not necessary for the valuename to follow the line containing the part type, although it is easier to debug your template if you use a specific keyword order.

LISTBOX

LISTBOX is the only part type which allows the addition and removal of multiple values under one registry key. One example of this type of registry key (Figure 8-9) is the key which lists all the programs that are run when Windows loads.

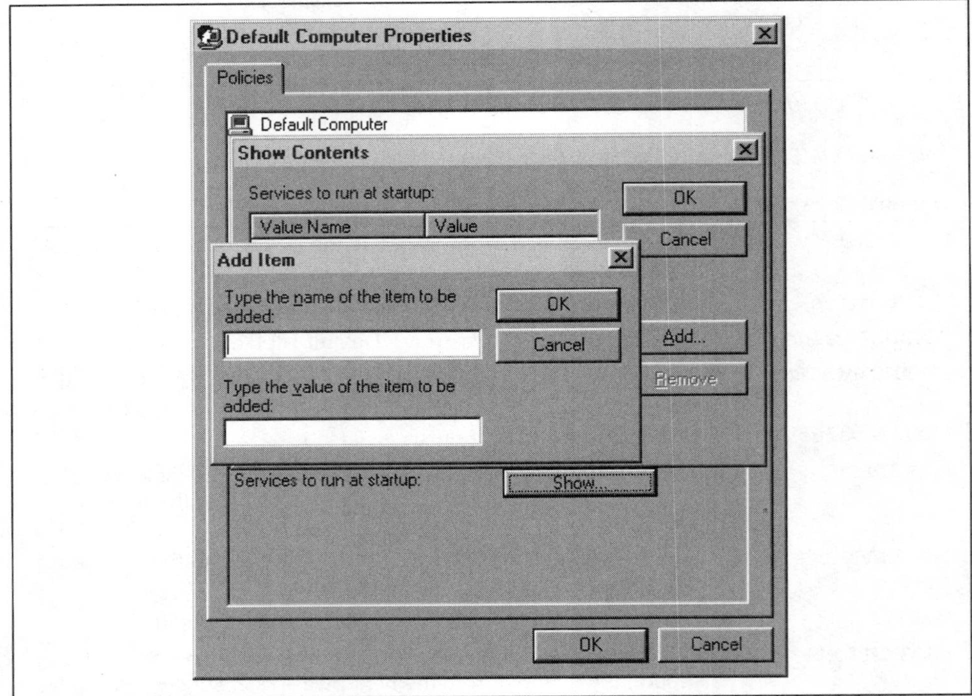

Figure 8-9. LISTBOX part option from admin.adm

This part will have an associated registry keyname, which will either be specified or inherited from a parent policy or category. However, unlike most of the other part types, `VALUENAME` and `VALUE` are not supported. There can be no single registry valuename or value possible for an option that allows multiple entries.

The `LISTBOX` statement may also include one or more of the optional keywords in Table 8-5.

Table 8-5. LISTBOX Optional Keywords

Optional Keywords	Details
`VALUEPREFIX "value"`	The prefix is added to an incremental number to create the `VALUENAME`. For example the prefix "Directory" will result in data named "Directory1" , "Directory2", and so on. Empty quotes "" will result in only the numerals. This keyword cannot be used with `EXPLICITVALUE`.
`EXPLICITVALUE`	Displays two columns in the Show Contents listbox, and provides the user with a place to enter both a valuename and value data. By default the valuename is identical to the value data. This keyword cannot be used with `VALUEPREFIX`.
`ADDITIVE`	Values entered will be appended to the existing registry entry. Default is that the values will overwrite what exists in the registry. NOTE: this keyword is not supported in ADM files for NT4; the values will still be overwritten.

The `LISTBOX` part that is displayed in Figure 8-9 is created by the following template statements:

```
PART !!RunListbox LISTBOX EXPLICITVALUE
END PART
```

Although `LISTBOX` has one of the most complex interfaces, its syntax is one of the simplest.

Part Type Keyword Summary

Table 8-6 can be used as a quick check to see if a part type supports a particular keyword. If a keyword is supported, this is indicated by an X in the table.

Table 8-6. Part Type Keyword Summary

Keyword	CHECKBOX	COMBOBOX	DROPDOWNLIST	LISTBOX	NUMERIC	EDITTEXT	TEXT
!!	✗	✗	✗	✗	✗	✗	✗
KEYNAME	✗	✗	✗	✗	✗	✗	
VALUENAME	✗	✗	✗		✗	✗	
VALUE	✗	✗	✗		✗	✗	
DEFCHECKED	✗						
VALUEON/ VALUEOFF	✗						

Table 8-6. Part Type Keyword Summary (continued)

Keyword	CHECKBOX	COMBOBOX	DROPDOWNLIST	LISTBOX	NUMERIC	EDITTEXT	TEXT
ACTIONLISTON/ ACTIONLISTOFF	✗						
DEFAULT		✗			✗	✗	
MIN					✗		
MAX					✗		
SPIN					✗		
Txtconvert					✗		
Required		✗	✗		✗	✗	
Expandabletext		✗				✗	
Maxlen		✗				✗	
Oemconvert		✗				✗	
Nosort		✗	✗				
Suggestions		✗					
Itemlist			✗				
Actionlist			✗				
Valueprefix				✗			
Explicitvalue				✗			
Additive				✗			

#if version

To provide backward compatibility, you can perform logic testing for a specific version of *poledit.exe*. The original version of Poledit did not support the keywords `NOSORT` or `EXPANDABLETEXT`. If you would like your custom template to be available for wide distribution, you can prevent some error messages in older Poledit versions by performing version checking.

The Poledit shipped with Windows 95 is assumed to be Version 1. The versions shipped with Windows 98, NT4 Service Packs and Office 2000 are Version 2.

The syntax is very simple:

```
#if version operator poledit_version
part_keyword
#endif
```

There are five operators:

- < less than
- > greater than
- <= less than or equal to
- >= greater than or equal to
- == equal to

If the statement being tested is false, then processing will skip past the **endif** statement and continue.

An example of a policy that contains version checking from the *off97NT4.adm* template follows:

```
PART !!MyDocText EDITTEXT
    VALUENAME "Personal"
    #if VERSION > 1
       EXPANDABLETEXT
    #endif
    REQUIRED
END PART
```

This example will test to see if the version of Poledit is greater than Version 1, and if it is, will allow environment variables to be expanded.

Make a Template

I will cover the creation process of a Windows 9x template which incorporates a few popular registry hacks. Specifically these hacks are:

- Changing the Windows program registration names
- Changing the tips of the day
- Changing the system Start and Exit sound events
- Changing the cascading menus delay
- Hiding drives in My Computer

Hiding specific drives will conflict with "Hide All Drives" in the *common.adm* and *admin.adm* templates. Do not enable this particular policy if you want to hide specific drives.

Creating the Policies and Parts

To begin creating the policies and parts you will need certain information about each of these registry changes, specifically:

- The class type (Machine or User)
- The specific registry key affected
- The registry key VALUENAME
- The registry key VALUE(s)
- The value type (string or DWORD)

Tracking Registry Changes

Sometimes it is possible to find documentation on the registry key you wish to change, and other times it is not. When you are unsure of which registry keys are affected when you customize program options, you can use a registry tracking program. One such shareware program is called xSnapShot from JAS Concepts (*http://www.jasconcepts.com*). This utility is very similar to the Windows NT4-only utility, *sysdiff.exe*. xSnapShot runs on Win9x as well as WinNT, and allows the user to specify exactly which registry keys to scan and which to exclude. A snapshot of the registry can be made before and after setup changes or software installation. These two snapshots can be compared, and an INF file containing all registry changes is generated. This information can then be used to create a custom policy template.

The following tables itemize what is required for each proposed registry change. Once you have the required information, it is necessary to decide how you need to control the user's input. In other words, which part type would be best, or would a simple policy checkbox suffice?

Windows registration names

Under the General tab of the 'My Computer' properties window is the name and organization of the registered owner. You may want to change this if workstations are moved from one department to another, or if you just want consistency across workstations. The information for this portion of the template is in Figure 8-7.

Table 8-7. Windows Registration Names

Class	Machine (HKLM)
Registry Key	`Software\Microsoft\Windows\CurrentVersion`
Valuename Owner **Organization**	RegisteredOwner RegisteredOrganization

Table 8-7. Windows Registration Names (continued)

Value	Entered by user
Value Type	String (REG_SZ)

The user will enter a varying text string, so obviously a simple policy checkbox will not suffice, and you will need to use a part. The part types that allow for text to be entered are `EDITTEXT`, `COMBOBOX` and `LISTBOX`. As there are no standard owner or organization names, there are no possible suggestions; therefore, `COMBOBOX` is not a good choice. `LISTBOX` (which does not support the use of `VALUENAME`) is not a good choice either as there are specific valuenames. This leaves me with `EDITTEXT`. Of our `EDITTEXT` options (Table 8-1), only `REQUIRED` is applicable since blank text would defeat the purpose of having this option.

It is always helpful to add some explanatory text, and in this case I could simply explain where the changes would be visible (My Computer properties). This section of the template could then appear like this:

```
KEYNAME "Software\Microsoft\Windows\CurrentVersion"
POLICY !!Changereg
   PART !!Changereg1 EDITTEXT REQUIRED
   VALUENAME "RegisteredOwner"
   END PART
   PART !!changereg2 EDITTEXT REQUIRED
   VALUENAME "RegisteredOrganization"
   END PART
   PART !!changeregtext1 TEXT END PART
   PART !!changeregtext2 TEXT END PART
END POLICY
```

These statements will create one policy with four parts. One part changes the owner's name, while a second changes the organization name. The remaining two parts add explanatory text. By splitting the text across two parts you prevent it from running off the end of the properties window.

Tips of the day

You can change the tips that display each time Windows 95 loads so that they are specific to your particular organization. These tips display with the Windows welcome screen, beneath the words "Did you know?". The welcome screen on a Windows 98 workstation is not compatible, and so this registry modification will only work with Windows 95. Despite this, it is still a good example to review. The information required for this portion of the template is summarized in Table 8-10.

Table 8-8. Tips of the Day

Class	Machine (HKLM)
Registry key	Software\Microsoft\Windows\CurrentVersion\Explorer\Tips
Valuename	Variable, tips are numbered sequentially
Value	Tip is entered by user
Value Type	String (REG_SZ)

The user will enter a varying text string. Again, a simple policy checkbox will not suffice. The part types that allow for text to be entered are `EDITTEXT`, `COMBOBOX` and `LISTBOX`. `COMBOBOX` is not a good choice as the tips will be at the discretion of the user, and there are no likely suggestions. `EDITTEXT` is not an option as there are no specific valuenames. The only part that allows for multiple valuenames is `LISTBOX`. For `LISTBOX` options (Table 8-5), I do not need to use `VALUEPREFIX`, since the tips are simply numbered. `ADDITIVE` could be used if the user wanted to append the tips to the pre-existing list. `EXPLICITVALUE` could be used if I wanted to allow the user to number the tips. In that case, the value would be the tip number, while the valuename would be the tip itself. This section of the template could then appear like this:

```
POLICY !!tips
    KEYNAME "Software\Microsoft\Windows\CurrentVersion\Explorer\Tips"
    PART !!tips LISTBOX
    END PART
    END POLICY
```

One thing to note is that the tips will not display if the option to show tips is turned off. Since this registry key has a hex value (REG_BINARY), it is not possible to change it using a policy template. However, a registry file could be used from the logon script (see Chapter 4, *Building the Policy File*) to append the change to the user's registry. This REG file would include the following lines:

```
[HKCU\Software\Microsoft\Windows\CurrentVersion\Explorer\Tips]
"Show"=hex:01,00,00,00
```

A hex value of 00,00,00,00 turns the tips off. Alternately, you could use the *admin.adm* template to run the program *welcome.exe* at startup. Doing so will also change the appropriate registry keys.

Sound events

Sound files (WAV files) from the local drive or from the network drive can be used as the system start and exit sound events. The information required for this portion of the template is summarized in Table 8-9.

Table 8-9. Sound Events

Class	Machine (HKLM)
Registry Key Start Shutdown	 AppEvents\Schemes\Apps\.Default\SystemStart\.Current AppEvents\Schemes\Apps\.Default\SystemExit\.Current
Valuename	[Default]
Value	WAV filename is entered by user
Value Type	String (REG_SZ)

The user will enter a varying text string, so a simple policy checkbox will not suffice. The part options that allow for text to be entered are `EDITTEXT`, `COMBOBOX` and `LISTBOX`. `LISTBOX` is not an option as there are specific valuenames. There could be suggestions, as there are some standard Windows WAV files; therefore, `COMBOBOX` is a possible option. I also could choose `EDITTEXT`, if I did not want to include suggestions or were unsure of which sound files might be available on the local drive. Since it's easiest, I will go with `EDITTEXT`. Of our `EDITTEXT` options (Table 8-3), none are really required. Finally, I could choose to have the options displayed as two policies with one part each, or one policy with two parts. This is an individual choice; I chose to display it as two policies. This section of the template could then appear like this:

```
POLICY !!changestart
    KEYNAME "AppEvents\Schemes\Apps\.Default\SystemStart\.Current"
        PART !!wavfile EDITTEXT
        VALUENAME ""
        END PART
END POLICY

POLICY !!changeexit
    KEYNAME "AppEvents\Schemes\Apps\.Default\SystemExit\.Current"
        PART !!wavfile EDITTEXT
        VALUENAME ""
        END PART
END POLICY
```

Note that although the `VAULENAME` is displayed in the registry as `[Default]`, you do not use this as the actual `VALUENAME`. If you did, the template would add a second `[Default]` `VALUENAME` rather than editing the true default value. To edit the `[Default]` `VALUE` you must use a `VALUENAME` consisting only of empty quotes.

Menu delay

On the Windows desktop, any associated submenus automatically open when the mouse cursor hovers over a menu. It is possible either to speed up this process or to slow it down so much that it seems to stop completely. In the latter case, a mouse click would be required to open the submenu. The information required for this portion of the template is summarized in Table 8-10.

Table 8-10. Cascading Menus Delay

Class	User (HKCU)
Registry key	Control Panel\Desktop
Valuename	MenuShowDelay
Value	0 to 10,000 milliseconds (Default 400)
Value Type	String (REG_SZ)

The value is a number with a range of 0 to 10,000. The part type that best displays numerical entries is **NUMERIC**. However, if you look at the value type you see that it is not DWORD, but string. It will be necessary to use the **NUMERIC** optional keyword (Table 8-2) **TXTCONVERT** to convert the value to a string. The Windows default delay is 400 milliseconds, so I should use the **DEFAULT** option and give it this value. Adding a spin dial will make it easier for the user to enter a value, and because increments of less then 500 milliseconds will make very little visible difference, I will set the dial for that incremental value. Finally, I can add a minimum value of 0 and a maximum value of 10,000.

Explanatory text could be added as not many people will be familiar with this setting. It is necessary to explain that lower numbers indicate faster cascading. This section of the template could then appear like this:

```
POLICY !!menudelay
    KEYNAME "Control Panel\Desktop"
        PART !!menudelay NUMERIC SPIN 500
          VALUENAME "MenuShowDelay"
          TXTCONVERT
          DEFAULT 400
          MIN 0
          MAX 10000
        END PART
        PART !!MENUTEXT TEXT END PART
END POLICY
```

Hiding drives

Specific drives can be hidden from Explorer and My Computer. A program that bypasses Explorer may still show the contents of these drives, so this policy should not be relied upon to keep out malicious users (see Chapter 6, *Trouble-*

shooting for more information). The information required for this portion of the template is summarized in Table 8-11.

Table 8-11. Hidden Drives

Class	User (HKCU)
Registry key	Software\Microsoft\CurrentVersion\Policies\Explorer
Valuename	NoDrives
Value	A: 1, B: 2, C: 4, D: 8, E: 16, F: 32, G: 64, H: 128, I: 256, J: 512, K: 1024, L: 2048, M: 4096, N: 8192, O: 16384,P: 32768, Q: 65536, R: 131072, S: 262144, T: 524288, U: 1048576, V: 2097152, W: 4194304, X: 8388608, Y: 16777216, Z: 33554432, ALL 67108863 To hide more than one drive, sum the value of each drive. For example, to hide A:, B:; and C:, add 1 + 2 + 4 =7
Value Type	Binary (REG_DWORD)

A simple policy checkbox could be used for each drive letter; however, to include all drives would necessitate having 26 policy checkboxes under one category. It would not appear as cluttered if you use one of the part types that allow the user to make a choice from a list of suggestions. part types fitting this description are `COMBOBOX` and `DROPDOWNLIST`. `COMBOBOX` is not a good choice as it allows user input and the user probably won't have any idea of which value to enter. This leaves me with `DROPDOWNLIST`. Of the `DROPDOWNLIST` options (Table 8-3), you may want to use `NOSORT` to display the drive optionS in a specific order. I will also use a Default value of 0 (no hidden drives), in case the option is checked inadvertently.

Only one drive, or a single combination of drives can be chosen. It would not be possible to display all 26 drive letters and allow the user to check off more than one drive to hide, as there is no template syntax to allow additive values. The last drive checked would be the hidden drive, while the others would simply be ignored. To allow the user to hide more than one drive, I must create specific options to do this in the drop-down list. In addition, explanatory text could mention that the drives would be hidden only in certain program areas. This section of the template could then appear like this:

```
POLICY !!HideDrives
    KEYNAME Software\Microsoft\Windows\CurrentVersion\Policies\Explorer
        PART !!HIDEDRIVES DROPDOWNLIST REQUIRED
        #if version > 1
        NOSORT
        #endif
        VALUENAME "NoDrives"
            ITEMLIST
            NAME !!A VALUE NUMERIC 1
            NAME !!B VALUE NUMERIC 2
            NAME !!C VALUE NUMERIC 4
```

```
            NAME !!AB VALUE NUMERIC 3
            NAME !!ABC VALUE NUMERIC 7
            NAME !!CLEARALL VALUE NUMERIC 0 DEFAULT
            END ITEMLIST
        END PART
        PART !!HIDEDRIVESTEXT1 TEXT END PART
        PART !!HIDEDRIVESTEXT2 TEXT END PART
```

In this example, I will allow the user the option to hide only drive A, only drive B, only drive C, both drive A and B, or all three drives A, B, and C.

Putting It Together

Once you have the policies and parts, you must group them into categories and then put those categories into their appropriate classes. I have already indicated in which class each policy belongs. Specifically, the policies in class **MACHINE** are those that change the Windows registration names and show daily tips. The other policies (sound events, menu cascade delay and hide drives) belong in **USER**.

Grouping the policies into categories is simply a process of deciding the most logical way to group them. In this example I will simply create one category for each of the Tables 8-11 through 8-11.

Finally, a Strings section must be created for each value preceded by `!!`, with the text definition of that string. The complete policy template would appear like this:

```
; chapter8.adm
;;;;;;;;;;;;;;;;;;;;;
CLASS MACHINE  ;;;;;;
;;;;;;;;;;;;;;;;;;;;;

CATEGORY !!changereg
KEYNAME "Software\Microsoft\Windows\CurrentVersion"
    POLICY !!Changereg
        PART !!Changereg1 EDITTEXT REQUIRED
        VALUENAME "RegisteredOwner"
        END PART
        PART !!changereg2 EDITTEXT REQUIRED
        VALUENAME "RegisteredOrganization"
        END PART
        PART !!changeregtext1 TEXT END PART
        PART !!changeregtext2 TEXT END PART
    END POLICY
END CATEGORY

CATEGORY !!TIPS
    POLICY !!tips
    KEYNAME "Software\Microsoft\Windows\CurrentVersion\Explorer\Tips"
    PART !!tips LISTBOX EXPLICITVALUE
    END PART
    END POLICY
END CATEGORY
```

```
;;;;;;;;;;;;;;;;;;;;;
CLASS USER   ;;;;;;;;
;;;;;;;;;;;;;;;;;;;;;

CATEGORY !!changesounds
     POLICY !!changestart
     KEYNAME "AppEvents\Schemes\Apps\.Default\SystemStart\.Current"
          PART !!wavfile EDITTEXT
          VALUENAME ""
          END PART
     END POLICY

     POLICY !!changeexit
     KEYNAME "AppEvents\Schemes\Apps\.Default\SystemExit\.Current"
          PART !!wavfile EDITTEXT
          VALUENAME ""
          END PART
     END POLICY
END CATEGORY

CATEGORY !!menudelay

     POLICY !!menudelay
     KEYNAME "Control Panel\Desktop"
          PART !!menudelay NUMERIC SPIN 500
          VALUENAME "MenuShowDelay"
          TXTCONVERT
          DEFAULT 400
          MIN 0
          MAX 10000
     END PART
          PART !!MENUTEXT TEXT END PART
          END POLICY
END CATEGORY

CATEGORY !!HIDEDRIVES
     POLICY !!HideDrives
     KEYNAME Software\Microsoft\Windows\CurrentVersion\Policies\Explorer
          PART !!HIDEDRIVES DROPDOWNLIST REQUIRED
          #if version > 1
          NOSORT
          #endif
          VALUENAME "NoDrives"
               ITEMLIST
               NAME !!A VALUE NUMERIC 1
               NAME !!B VALUE NUMERIC 2
               NAME !!C VALUE NUMERIC 4
               NAME !!AB VALUE NUMERIC 3
               NAME !!ABC VALUE NUMERIC 7
               NAME !!CLEARALL VALUE NUMERIC 0 DEFAULT
               END ITEMLIST
          END PART
          PART !!HIDEDRIVESTEXT1 TEXT END PART
          PART !!HIDEDRIVESTEXT2 TEXT END PART
```

```
END POLICY
END CATEGORY

[STRINGS]
changereg="Change Registration"
changereg1="Registered Owner"
changereg2="Registered Organization"
changeregtext1="Change registration names under the "General" tab of"
changeregtext2=""My Computer" properties window"
tips="Write out your personalized "Tips of the Day""
changesounds="Change Windows Sound Events"
changestart="Change Windows Start Sound"
wavfile=".WAV file to use"
changeexit="Change Windows Exit Sound"
menudelay="Delay in milliseconds"
menutext="Change the delay before submenus automatically cascade open"
hidedrives="Hide Drives"
A="Restrict Drive A"
B="Restrict Drive B"
C="Restrict Drive C"
AB="Restrict Drive A and B"
ABC="Restrict Drive A, B, and C"
clearall="Do not restrict any drives"
hidedrivestext1="Hide one or more drives from My Computer and Explorer"
hidedrivestext2="Note: Do not use with other "hide drives" policies"
```

Debugging the Template

Debugging the template, at least as far as proper syntax is concerned, is amazingly simple. Once you have completed the text file, save it with the ADM extension. Then load the template into the SPE. If an error is found, the SPE will display an error message telling you the line that caused the error, the unexpected keyword or text and a list of suitable keywords for the problem area.

However, the SPE will not check to see if the KEYNAME or values are reasonable. That can be done only by actually setting the policy options to see if you get the expected result in the registry or your program. One thing to note, if you make changes to the template while the SPE is still open, you must reload the template again for those changes to be visible in the SPE. To do this, select Options → Template and then select the OK button. As an alternative, you can close the SPE, make the modifications to your template and then start the program up again. This will have the same effect since the template is reloaded automatically each time the SPE starts.

Always back up your registry before trying out your new template!

Summary

The template can be broken down into four main zones (class, category, policy and part). The class and category zones are mostly organizational in nature, while the policy and part zones contain the actual registry changes. The use of a template is made easier through the application of one or more of the seven part types (`TEXT`, `EDITTEXT`, `CHECKBOX`, `NUMERIC`, `DROPDOWNLIST`, `COMBOBOX` and `LISTBOX`). These part types allow the data to be collected in the most logical way based upon the value type and really account for the template's true versatility.

If you are like me, you will be eager to find all your favorite registry hacks to see if they can be incorporated into a custom policy template. If the hack is to a subkey of the HKCU or HKLM, and it has a value type of string (REG_SZ and REG_EXPAND_SZ) or DWORD (REG_DWORD) you probably can. Unfortunately, if the key is outside of the top-level keys HKCU and HKLM or if it has a Binary (REG_Binary) or other Windows NT registry value, those keys will still have to be edited by hand using the registry editor or a REG file. Despite these drawbacks, custom templates will extend the functionality of the SPE even into those organizations that use only in-house programs.

9

The Policy Templates

The System Policy Editor would not be the indispensable tool it is without the flexibility provided by the policy templates. This chapter is not only meant to be an exhaustive list of the policies available in the 47 most common templates, but also a listing of their respective registry keys and value names. Knowing the precise registry keys and value names for each policy is invaluable when troubleshooting policy files. Since many policies exist in more than one template, setting a policy one way in one template and another way in another template will cause difficulties. For example, the option to set a proxy server exists in the *ieak.adm* and all of the *off97*.adm* templates. If this option is set differently using one template from the way it was set using another, the following error message will appear:

> Internet Explorer cannot open the Internet site *http://<site name>*. The site was not found. Make sure the address is correct, and try again.

The ablility to check the value entered in the registry key for this policy would be helpful in tracking down the cause of this error message. Additionally, helpful comments are added for many of the policies, particularly for the more obscure policies.

The 47 templates included in this chapter are broken down into the following seven sections:

System templates
: Templates for the Windows 9x and Windows NT4 operating systems

NetWare templates
: Templates for the Windows NetWare clients

Zero Administration Kit (ZAK) templates
: Templates for use with the Windows ZAKs

Internet Explorer Administration Kit (IEAK) templates
: Templates for use with Internet Explorer Version 4 and Version 5, and associated programs such as NetMeeting

Office 97 templates
: Templates for use with the Office 97 suite of applications

Office 2000 templates
: Templates for use with the Office 2000 suite of applications

Miscellaneous templates
: A few templates that did not fit into other categories

How to Read This Chapter

Each template is organized in basically the same manner as the templates themselves (see Chapter 8, *Creating a Custom Template,* for more information on template structure), as follows:

Template Name

User or Computer Properties

Category → Subcategory

Comments (if applicable)

Registry Keyname: (if not defined later)

Policy

> *Can be checked, unchecked or grayed*
>
> Comments (if applicable)
>
> Registry Keyname: (if undefined elsewhere)
>
> Registry Valuename: (if undefined elsewhere)
>
> *Part*
>
> > Comments (if applicable)
> >
> > Input (Part) type (see Chapter 8 for types)
> >
> > Registry Keyname: (if undefined elsewhere)
> >
> > Registry Valuename:

The registry keynames can occur in any one of three places, as illustrated previously. If a keyname is not listed in an area, then the keyname from the previous section is used. For example, if no keyname exists in the Policy section, keyname from the Category section is used. If no keyname exists in a Part section, then the keyname from the Policy section is used. If no keyname exists in the Policy section, then the keyname from the Category section is used, and so on.

Each Comments section can come from one of two places: either it exists as an actual part of the template itself (see Figure 9-1), or I added it in areas that I felt required more explanation. While some policies are self-explanatory, the function of others is unclear and requires some additional clarification.

Figure 9-1 shows an example from the *client32.adm* template and how it translates into the format used in this chapter.

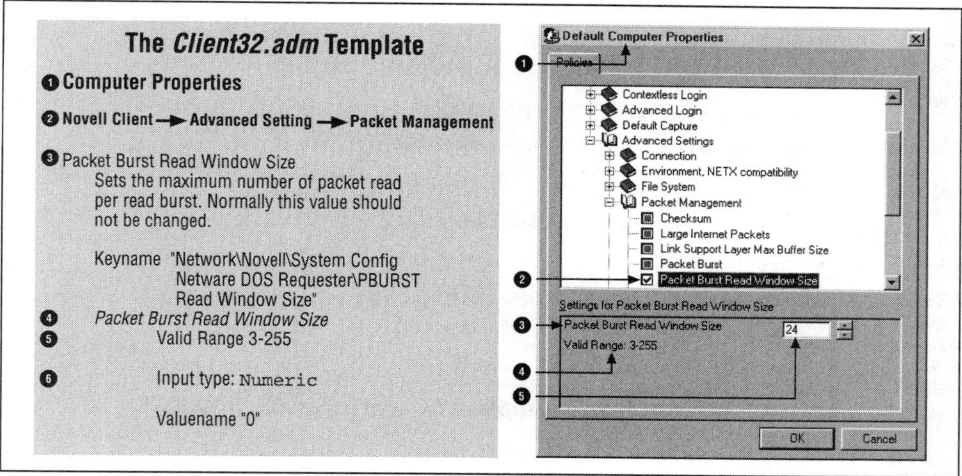

Figure 9-1. Adaptation of the client32.adm template

Actionlist Keynames and Valuename

Throughout this chapter you will see references to Actionlist keynames and valuenames. An Actionlist is a list of optional actions (additionally modified registry keys) that occur when a policy box is set to the checked (on) position. For example, in the *admin.adm* template there is an option to choose a desktop color scheme by name (e.g., Rainy Day). The Actionlist would then be used to change the color of each individual Control Panel item to achieve the Rainy Day color scheme. Therefore, the Actionlist keynames and valuenames referenced in this chapter refer to those additionally modified registry keys. To illustrate the use of actionlist statements see Chapter 8.

Policy Template Downloads

Listed here are the most common download locations for each set of templates. Since many of the templates are available in a number of different versions, check first for any relevant comments preceding each template description.

System templates
: These templates are included on the original Windows 9x or Windows NT server CDs.

NetWare templates
: *http://www.novell.com/download/#Clients*

Zero Administration Kit (ZAK) templates
: *http://www.microsoft.com/windows/zak/getzak.htm*

Internet Explorer Administration Kit (IEAK) templates
: *http://www.microsoft.com/windows/ieak/en/download/default.asp*

Office 97 templates
: *http://www.microsoft.com/office/ork/download/SetupPol.exe*

Office 2000 templates
: *http://www.microsoft.com/office/ork/2000/download/ORKTools.exe*

Miscellaneous templates
: *cpanel.adm*
: *http://support.microsoft.com/support/kb/articles/Q207/7/50.ASP*

: *date.adm*
: *http://support.microsoft.com/support/kb/articles/Q216/6/61.ASP*

: *scrsave.adm*
: *http://support.microsoft.com/support/kb/articles/Q195/6/55.ASP*

Other policy templates may be found by searching the Internet using terms such as "system policy templates" or "policy editor templates." One site containing a few public domain templates for programs such as Netscape is *http://www.schleipsoft.org/windowsnt/policies.asp.*

System Templates

The system templates allow extensive customization of Windows 9x and Windows NT4 computer and user options. Included in this section are the following templates:

Admin.adm
: This template is used to set a variety of policies and restrictions for Windows 9x workstations.

Appsini.adm

This template contains a policy to set the Windows 9x network location for an *Apps.ini* file. The *Apps.ini* file contains a list of applications and their network locations.

Common.adm

This template contains policies common to both Windows 9x and Windows NT4 workstations.

Shell.adm, Shellm.adm, and Sp1shell.adm

These templates contain policies for the Windows 9x and Windows NT system shell (*explorer.exe*) functions and Active Desktop settings. Since they are very similar to each other with only a few minor differences, they are incorporated into a single section.

Windows.adm

This Windows 9x template includes all of the policies that were in the original *Maple.adm* template—the Microsoft Service for NetWare Directory Services (MSNDS) policy file. This template is optimized for Windows 98, but most policies also apply to a Windows 95 workstation with Active Desktop installed.

WinNT.adm

This template contains policies specific to Windows NT4 workstations.

Admin.adm

Microsoft has distributed three versions of this template, the first with the Windows 95 CD-ROM, the second with the Windows 95 ZAK and the third with the ORK 2000. All versions are exactly the same, with each version unfortunately having the same error in the Hide Drives policy. This error causes the Hide Drives policy to be automatically set to the checked position for all users. See Chapter 6, *Troubleshooting*, for more information.

User Properties

Control Panel → Display

Restrict Display Control Panel

This policy restricts access to various display properties both from the Display Control Panel applet and from the desktop right-click context menu (under Properties).

Keyname: "Software\Microsoft\Windows\CurrentVersion\Policies\System"

Disable Display Control Panel

Input type: `Checkbox`

Valuename: "NoDispCPL"

Hide Background page

Input type: `Checkbox`

Valuename: "NoDispBackgroundPage"

Hide Screen Saver page

Input type: `Checkbox`

Valuename: "NoDispScrSavPage"

Hide Appearance page

Input type: `Checkbox`

Valuename: "NoDispAppearancePage"

Hide Settings page

Input type: `Checkbox`

Valuename: "NoDispSettingsPage"

Control Panel → Network

Restrict Network Control Panel

This policy restricts access to network properties both from the Network Control Panel applet and from the Network Neighborhood icon right-click context menu (under Properties).

Keyname: "Software\Microsoft\Windows\CurrentVersion\Policies\Network"

Disable Network Control Panel

Input type: `Checkbox`

Valuename: "NoNetSetup"

Hide Identification Page

Input type: `Checkbox`

Valuename: "NoNetSetupIDPage"

Hide Access Control Page

Input type: `Checkbox`

Valuename: "NoNetSetupSecurityPage"

Control Panel → Passwords

Restrict Passwords Control Panel

This policy restricts access to various password properties usually available through the Passwords Control Panel applet.

Keyname: "Software\Microsoft\Windows\CurrentVersion\Policies\System"

Disable Passwords Control Panel

Input type: Checkbox

Valuename: "NoSecCPL"

Hide Change Passwords page

Input type: Checkbox

Valuename: "NoPwdPage"

Hide Remote Administration page

Input type: Checkbox

Valuename: "NoAdminPage"

Hide User Profiles page

Input type: Checkbox

Valuename: "NoProfilePage"

Control Panel → Printers

Restrict Printer Settings

This policy restricts access to various printer properties usually available through the Printers Control Panel applet.

Keyname: "Software\Microsoft\Windows\CurrentVersion\Policies\Explorer"

Hide General and Details pages

Input type: Checkbox

Valuename: "NoPrinterTabs"

Disable Deletion of Printers

Input type: Checkbox

Valuename: "NoDeletePrinter"

Disable Addition of Printers

Input type: Checkbox

Valuename: "NoAddPrinter"

Control Panel → System

Restrict System Control Panel

This policy restricts access to various system properties usually available through the System Control Panel applet.

Keyname: "Software\Microsoft\Windows\CurrentVersion\Policies\System"

Hide Device Manager page

Input type: Checkbox

Valuename: "NoDevMgrPage"

Hide Hardware Profiles Page

Input type: `Checkbox`

Valuename: "NoConfigPage"

Hide File System button

Input type: `Checkbox`

Valuename: "NoFileSysPage"

Hide Virtual Memory button

Input type: `Checkbox`

Valuename: "NoVirtMemPage"

Desktop

If the user is given access to the Display properties, the wallpaper and color scheme can be temporarily changed, but it will revert back to the settings specified in these policies the next time the user logs on.

Wallpaper

Keyname: "Control Panel\Desktop"

Wallpaper name

Input type: `Combobox`

Valuename: "Wallpaper"

Tile wallpaper

Input type: `Checkbox`

Valuename: "TileWallpaper"

Color Scheme

Keyname: "Control Panel\Appearance"

Scheme name

Colors are in format X; for example, black is 0 0 0 and white is 255 255 255.

Input type: `Dropdownlist`

Valuename: "Current"

Itemlist Keyname: "Control Panel\Colors"

Itemlist Valuenames: "ActiveBorder", "ActiveTitle", "AppWorkspace", "Background", "ButtonDkShadow", "ButtonFace", "ButtonHilight", "ButtonLight", "ButtonShadow", "ButtonText", "GrayText", "Hilight", "HilightText", "InactiveBorder", "InactiveTitle", "InactiveTitleText", "Menu", "MenuText", "InfoText", "InfoWindow", "Scrollbar", "TitleText", "Window", "WindowFrame", "WindowText"

Network → Sharing

Enabling these policies will remove the sharing properties for directories or printers. The user will then not be able to alter which resources are shared on the workstation.

Keyname: "Software\Microsoft\Windows\CurrentVersion\Policies\Network"

Disable file sharing controls
Valuename: "NoFileSharingControl"

Disable print sharing controls
Valuename: "NoPrintSharingControl"

Shell → Custom Folders

See Chapter 4, *Building The Policy File* for more information on the use of custom folders. If Network Neighborhood is hidden, only mapped drives can be used for the network location of the custom folders (i.e., *M:\Desktop* rather than *//server/desktop*).

Keyname: "Software\Microsoft\Windows\CurrentVersion\Explorer\User Shell Folders"

Custom Programs Folder
Path to get Programs items from
Input type: `Edittext`

Valuename: "Programs"

Custom Desktop icons
Path to get Desktop icons from
Input type: `Edittext`

Valuename: "Desktop"

Hide Start menu subfolders
Check this if you use a custom Programs Folder or custom Desktop icons, otherwise two Programs entries will appear in the Start menu.

Keyname: "Software\Microsoft\Windows\CurrentVersion\Policies\Explorer"

Valuename: "NoStartMenuSubFolders"

Custom Startup Folder
Path to get Startup items from
Input type: `Edittext`

Valuename: "Startup"

Custom Network Neighborhood

Path to get Network Neighborhood items from

Windows 9x does not support the use of folders in a custom NN.

Input type: `Edittext`

Valuename: "NetHood"

Custom Start menu

Path to get Start menu items from

Input type: `Edittext`

Valuename: "Start menu"

Shell → Restrictions

These policies will remove various options from the Start menu on the taskbar.

Keyname: "Software\Microsoft\Windows\CurrentVersion\Policies\Explorer"

Remove "Run" command

See Chapter 5, *It's Not Perfect*, for a discussion of the limitations of this policy.

Valuename: "NoRun"

Remove folders from "Settings" on Start menu

Prevents access to any Settings submenus such as Control Panel or Printers.

Valuename: "NoSetFolders"

Remove Taskbar from "Settings" on Start menu

Valuename: "NoSetTaskbar"

Remove "Find" command

The Find command is removed from the Start menu. See Chapter 5 for a discussion of the limitations of this policy.

Valuename: "NoFind"

Hide Drives in "My Computer"

See Chapter 5 for a discussion of the limitations of this policy; see Chapter 6 for information on how to fix an error in this template option.

Valuename: "NoDrives"

Hide Network Neighborhood

If this policy is checked, the NN icon is hidden and UNC pathnames are disabled. Therefore custom folders must be set to mapped drives rather than UNC pathnames.

Valuename: "NoNetHood"

No "Entire Network" in Network Neighborhood

Keyname: "Software\Microsoft\Windows\CurrentVersion\Policies\Network"

Valuename: "NoEntireNetwork"

No workgroup contents in Network Neighborhood

Keyname: "Software\Microsoft\Windows\CurrentVersion\Policies\Network"

Valuename: "NoWorkgroupContents"

Hide all items on Desktop

None of the desktop shortcuts will be visible, only the taskbar.

Valuename: "NoDesktop"

Disable Shut Down command

The Shut Down command is removed from the Start menu.

Valuename: "NoClose"

Don"t save setting at exit

Settings are not saved to the *user.dat* file.

Valuename: "NoSaveSettings"

System → Restrictions

Disable Registry editing tools

See Chapter 5 for a discussion of the limitations of this policy.

Keyname: "Software\Microsoft\Windows\CurrentVersion\Policies\System"

Valuename: "DisableRegistryTools"

Run Only Allowed Windows Applications

To create a list of allowed applications, click Show then Add, and enter the application executable name (e.g., *winword.exe*, *poledit.exe*, *powerpnt.exe*). See Chapter 5 for a discussion of the limitations of this policy.

Keyname: "Software\Microsoft\Windows\CurrentVersion\Policies\Explorer"

Valuename: "RestrictRun"

List of allowed applications

Input type: `Listbox`

Keyname: "Software\Microsoft\Windows\CurrentVersion\Policies\Explorer\RestrictRun"

Disable MS-DOS prompt

Enabling this policy will not only disable a DOS prompt, but additionally any DOS-based programs.

Keyname: "Software\Microsoft\Windows\CurrentVersion\Policies\WinOld-App"

Valuename: "Disabled"

Disable single-mode MS-DOS applications

The computer is not allowed to restart in MS-DOS mode, preventing users from running DOS applications in DOS mode.

Keyname: "Software\Microsoft\Windows\CurrentVersion\Policies\WinOld-App"

Valuename: "NoRealMode"

Computer Properties

Network → Access Control

User-level Access Control

Enables user-level security on the workstation. See Chapter 4, *Building the Policy File*, for more information on user-level security.

Keyname: "System\CurrentControlSet\Services\VxD\FILESEC"

Valuename: "Start"

Actionliston Keyname: "System\CurrentControlSet\Services\VxD\FILESEC"

Actionliston Valuename: "StaticVxD"

Actionlistoff Keynames: "Security\Provider", "System\CurrentControlSet\Services\VxD\FILESEC", "System\CurrentControlSet\Services\VxD\NWSP", "System\CurrentControlSet\Services\VxD\MSSP"

Actionlistoff Valuenames: "Platform_Type", "StaticVxD", "Start"

Authenticator Name:

Input type: `Edittext`

Keyname: "Security\Provider"

Valuename: "Container"

Authenticator Type:

Input type: `Dropdownlist`

Keyname: "Security\Provider"

Valuename: "Platform_Type"

Actionlist Keynames: "System\CurrentControlSet\Services\VxD\NWSP", "Security\Provider", "System\CurrentControlSet\Services\VxD\MSSP"

Actionlist Valuenames: "Start", "Address_Book"

Network → Logon

Logon Banner

This policy allows a customized message to be displayed at logon and can be used to warn unauthorized users that access is prohibited. Do not set this policy to the cleared position, as it may delete the default registry settings. To disable the policy, set it to the grayed position.

Keyname: "Software\Microsoft\Windows\CurrentVersion\Winlogon"

Caption

Input type: `Edittext`

Valuename: "LegalNoticeCaption"

Text

Input type: `Edittext`

Valuename: "LegalNoticeText"

Require Validation by Network for Windows Access

When checked, this policy will allow access only if the user has been validated by a network server. See Chapter 5 for security issues with this policy on a NetWare network.

Keyname: "Network\Logon"

Valuename: "MustBeValidated"

Network → Microsoft Client for NetWare Networks

Keyname: "System\CurrentControlSet\Services\VxD\NWREDIR"

Preferred server

The preferred server must be specified for the policy file to download properly. Do not set this policy to the cleared position, as it may delete the default registry settings. To disable the policy, set it to the grayed position.

Keyname: "System\CurrentControlSet\Services\NWNP32\NetworkProvider"

Server name

Input type: `Edittext`

Valuename: "AuthenticatingAgent"

Support long filenames

Support long filenames on

Input type: `Dropdownlist`

Valuename: "SupportLFN"

Search Mode

This policy sets the mode for finding a file when it is not in the path or the local directory.

Search Mode

Input type: `Numeric`

Valuename: "SearchMode"

Disable Automatic NetWare Login

When checked, this policy prevents the user"s name, and network or Windows logon password, from being used to attempt to automatically log on to a NetWare server. This increases password security.

Keyname: "System\CurrentControlSet\Services\NWNP32\NetworkProvider"

Valuename: "DisableDefaultPasswords"

Network → Microsoft Client for Windows Networks

Log on to Windows NT

This policy allows the workstation to be part of an NT domain.

Keyname: "Network\Logon"

Valuename: "LMLogon"

Domain name

Input type: `Edittext`

Keyname: "System\CurrentControlSet\Services\MSNP32\NetworkProvider"

Valuename: "AuthenticatingAgent"

Display domain logon confirmation

This policy will display a message when the domain controller has validated the user"s logon. This dialog box lists the validating server, which may be helpful for troubleshooting network problems.

Input type: `Checkbox`

Keyname: "Network\Logon"

Valuename: "DomainLogonMessage"

Disable caching of domain password

When checked, the user will have to log on separately to each network resource. Automatic logon to these resources will be disabled.

Input type: `Checkbox`

Keyname: "Network\Logon"

Valuename: "NoDomainPwdCaching"

Workgroup

Do not set this policy to the cleared position, as it may delete the default registry settings. To disable the policy, set it to the grayed position.

Keyname: "System\CurrentControlSet\Services\VxD\VNETSUP"

Workgroup name

To enable load balancing, set this policy to be equal to the domain name.

Input type: `Edittext`

Valuename: "Workgroup"

Alternate Workgroup

Keyname: "System\CurrentControlSet\Services\VxD\VREDIR"

Workgroup name

The alternate workgroup name must be entirely in capital letters.

Input type: `Edittext`

Valuename: "Workgroup"

Network → File and printer sharing for NetWare Networks

Disable SAP Advertising

This policy should be checked. If it is enabled (cleared), a Windows 9x workstation would appear on the network as a NetWare server. This could cause problems by creating unwanted network traffic, or by causing DOS clients to attempt to log in to the Windows 9x client rather than the NetWare server.

Keyname: "System\CurrentControlSet\Services\NcpServer\Parameters"

Valuename: "Use_Sap"

Actionliston/off Keyname: "System\CurrentControlSet\Services\NcpServer\Parameters\Ndi\Params\Use_Sap"

Actionliston Valuenames: "Value '0'"

Actionlistoff Valuenames: "Value '1'"

Network → Passwords

Keyname: "Software\Microsoft\Windows\CurrentVersion\Policies\Network"

Hide share passwords with asterisks

Unchecking this option will allow the password characters typed for shared folders and printers to be displayed, rather than appearing as asterisks.

Valuename: "HideSharePwds"

Disable password caching

Password cache files (**.pwl*) for share-level resources or applications are no longer generated. Since it is possible to uncover a user"s password by cracking the password files, checking this policy increases security.

Valuename: "DisablePwdCaching"

Require alphanumeric Windows password

Increases security by requiring that the user's password have a combination of letters and numbers for their password.

Valuename: "AlphanumPwds"

Minimum Windows password length

Length

A good password should be a minimum of 6 characters.

Input type: `Numeric`

Valuename: "MinPwdLen"

Network → Dial-Up Networking

Disable dial-in

This policy prevents dial-in connections to the workstation.

Keyname: "Software\Microsoft\Windows\CurrentVersion\Policies\Network"

Valuename: "NoDialIn"

Network → Sharing

Keyname: "Software\Microsoft\Windows\CurrentVersion\Policies\Network"

Disable file sharing

File sharing is disabled on the workstation.

Valuename: "NoFileSharing"

Disable print sharing

Printer sharing is disabled on the workstation.

Valuename: "NoPrintSharing"

Network → SNMP

Communities

Keyname: "System\CurrentControlSet\Services\SNMP\Parameters\ValidCommunities"

Communities

Communities to which the workstation belongs that are allowed to query the SNMP agent.

Input type: `Listbox`

Permitted managers

Keyname: "System\CurrentControlSet\Services\SNMP\Parameters\Permitted-Managers"

Permitted managers

This policy specifies IP or IPX addresses that are allowed to query the SNMP agent.

Input type: `Listbox`

Traps for "Public" community

Keyname: "System\CurrentControlSet\Services\SNMP\Parameters\TrapConfiguration\Public"

Trap configuration

This policy specifies IP or IPX addresses of hosts in the public community to which the SNMP agent sends alerts (traps) following unusual events. To send traps to a community other than "Public", the registry must be edited manually.

Input type: `Listbox`

Internet MIB(RFC1156)

This policy will set the contact name and location of the Management Information Base (a database, created by an SNMP agent, containing information and statistics on each network device).

Keyname: "System\CurrentControlSet\Services\SNMP\Parameters\RFC1156-Agent"

Contact Name

Input type: `Edittext`

Valuename: "sysContact"

Location

Input type: `Edittext`

Valuename: "sysLocation"

Network → Update

Remote Update

This policy *must* be checked to allow the system policy file to download.

Keyname: "System\CurrentControlSet\Control\Update"

Actionlistoff Valuenames: "UpdateMode"

Update mode

The options are automatic or manual. If set to manual, the location of the policy file must be specified.

Input type: `Dropdownlist`

Valuename: "UpdateMode"

Path for manual update

Input type: `Edittext`

Valuename: "NetworkPath"

Display error messages

Checking this policy may help in troubleshooting problems with the policy file.

Input type: `Numeric`

Valuename: "Verbose"

Load balance

By default, a Windows client on an NT network will only query the PDC for the policy file. Checking this policy option will allow the client to receive the policy file from any validating domain controller, increasing security in the event that the PDC is not available. Note that the client"s workgroup name must be the same as the domain name.

Input type: `Numeric`

Valuename: "LoadBalance"

Network → System

Enable User Profiles

This policy *must* be checked to enable the policy file to be used.

Keyname: "Network\Logon"

Valuename: "UserProfiles"

Network path for Windows Setup

Keyname: "Software\Microsoft\Windows\CurrentVersion\Setup"

Path

This policy is useful for updating the workstations if you ever change the network location of the Windows setup files.

Input type: `Edittext`

Valuename: "SourcePath"

Network path for Windows Tour

Note that the path must end in *tour.exe* for Windows 95 (*discover.exe* for Windows 98).

Keyname: "Software\Microsoft\Windows\CurrentVersion\Setup"

Path

Input type: `Edittext`

Valuename: "TourPath"

Run

Keyname: "Software\Microsoft\Windows\CurrentVersion\Run"

Items to run at startup

This policy specifies applications and utilities that are run every time a user logs on.

Input type: `Listbox`

Run Once

This policy specifies applications and utilities that are run just once when a user logs on, and then the application is removed from the registry. However, if this option is checked in a policy file it will be run each time the user logs on until it is disabled in the policy file. Leave this option checked only long enough to be downloaded to the workstation, then clear the policy.

Keyname: "Software\Microsoft\Windows\CurrentVersion\RunOnce"

Items to run once at startup

Input type: `Listbox`

Run Services

This policy specifies services that are run at system startup.

Keyname: "Software\Microsoft\Windows\CurrentVersion\RunServices"

Services to run at startup

Input type: `Listbox`

Appsini.adm

This template is available on the Windows 98 CD-ROM.

Computer Properties

Network Install → Use apps.ini for Network Installs

Enable Add/Remove Programs, Network Install Tab

This policy will create a new tab in the Add/Remove Programs applet listing all of the applications in the *apps.ini* file.

Keyname: "Software\Microsoft\Windows\CurrentVersion"

Network path to apps.ini

Example: *MyServery\MyShare\Apps.ini*

Input type: `Edittext`

Valuename: "AppInstallPath"

Common.adm

Microsoft has distributed several versions of this template. One with the Windows NT4 client CD-ROM, one with the Windows 98 CD-ROM, one with the NT ZAK, and several with the various NT Service Packs. The version specified here is included with the Windows NT4 Service Pack 5. Older versions of the template had an error in the template, and were missing the `Valueoff` statement for the Hide Drives policy. See the *admin.adm* template and Chapter 6 for details.

User Properties

Control Panel → Display

Restrict display

This policy restricts access to various display properties both from the Display Control Panel applet and from the desktop right-click context menu (under Properties).

Keyname: "Software\Microsoft\Windows\CurrentVersion\Policies\System"

Deny access to display icon

Input type: `Checkbox`

Valuename: "NoDispCPL"

Hide Background tab

Input type: `Checkbox`

Valuename: "NoDispBackgroundPage"

Hide Screen Saver tab

Input type: `Checkbox`

Valuename: "NoDispScrSavPage"

Hide Appearance tab

Input type: `Checkbox`

Valuename: "NoDispAppearancePage"

Hide Settings tab

Input type: `Checkbox`

Valuename: "NoDispSettingsPage"

Desktop

If the user is given access to the Display properties, the wallpaper and color scheme can be temporarily changed, but it will revert back to the setting used in these policies the next time the user logs on.

Wallpaper

Keyname: "Control Panel\Desktop"

Wall paper Name

Specify location and name (e.g., *C:\winnt\winnt256.bmp*).

Input type: `Edittext`

Valuename: "Wallpaper"

Tile Wallpaper

Input type: `Checkbox`

Valuename: "TileWallpaper"

Color scheme

Keyname: "Control Panel\Appearance"

Scheme name

Colors are in format X; for example, black is 0 0 0 and white is 255 255. 255

Input type: `Dropdownlist`

Valuename: "Current"

Itemlist Keyname: "Control Panel\Colors"

Itemlist Valuenames: "ActiveBorder", "ActiveTitle", "AppWorkspace", "Background", "ButtonDkShadow", "ButtonFace", "ButtonHilight", "ButtonLight", "ButtonShadow", "ButtonText", "GrayText", "Hilight", "HilightText", "InactiveBorder", "InactiveTitle", "InactiveTitleText", "Menu", "MenuText", "InfoText", "InfoWindow", "Scrollbar", "TitleText", "Window", "WindowFrame", "WindowText"

Shell → Restrictions

These policies will remove various options from the Start menu on the taskbar.

Keyname: "Software\Microsoft\Windows\CurrentVersion\Policies\Explorer"

Remove Run command from Start menu

See Chapter 5 for a discussion of the limitations of this policy.

Valuename: "NoRun"

Remove folders from Settings on Start menu

Prevents access to any Settings submenus such as Control Panel or Printers.

Valuename: "NoSetFolders"

Remove Taskbar from Settings on Start menu

Valuename: "NoSetTaskbar"

Remove Find command from Start menu

The Find command is removed from the Start menu. See Chapter 5 for a discussion of the limitations of this policy.

Valuename: "NoFind"

Hide drives in My Computer

See Chapter 5 for a discussion of the limitations of this policy.

Valuename: "NoDrives"

Hide Network Neighborhood

If this policy is checked, the NN icon is hidden and UNC pathnames are disabled. Therefore custom folders must be set to mapped drives rather than UNC pathnames.

Valuename: "NoNetHood"

No Entire Network in Network Neighborhood

Keyname: "Software\Microsoft\Windows\CurrentVersion\Policies\Network"

Valuename: "NoEntireNetwork"

No workgroup contents in Network Neighborhood

Keyname: "Software\Microsoft\Windows\CurrentVersion\Policies\Network"

Valuename: "NoWorkgroupContents"

Hide all items on desktop

None of the desktop shortcuts will be visible, only the taskbar.

Valuename: "NoDesktop"

Remove Shut Down command from Start menu

The Shut Down command is removed from the Start menu.

Valuename: "NoClose"

Don"t save setting at exit

Settings are not saved to the *user.dat* file.

Valuename: "NoSaveSettings"

System → Restrictions

Disable Registry editing tools

See Chapter 5 for a discussion of the limitations of this policy.

Keyname: "Software\Microsoft\Windows\CurrentVersion\Policies\System"

Valuename: "DisableRegistryTools"

Run only allowed Windows applications

To create a list of allowed application, click Show then Add, and enter the application executable name (e.g., *winword.exe*, *poledit.exe*, *powerpnt.exe*). See Chapter 5 for a discussion of the limitations of this policy.

Keyname: "Software\Microsoft\Windows\CurrentVersion\Policies\Explorer"

Valuename: "RestrictRun"

List of allowed applications

Input type: `Listbox`

Keyname: "Software\Microsoft\Windows\CurrentVersion\Policies\Explorer\RestrictRun"

Computer Properties

Network → System policies update

Remote update

This policy *must* be checked to allow the system policy file to download.

Keyname: "System\CurrentControlSet\Control\Update"

Actionlistoff Valuename: "UpdateMode"

Update mode

The options are automatic or manual. If set to manual, the location of the policy file must be specified.

Input type: `Dropdownlist`

Valuename: "UpdateMode"

Path for manual update

Input type: `Edittext`

Valuename: "NetworkPath"

Display error messages

Checking this policy may help in troubleshooting policy file problems.

Input type: `Checkbox`

Valuename: "Verbose"

Load balancing

By default, a Windows client on an NT network will query only the PDC for the policy file. Checking this policy option will allow the client to receive the policy file from any validating domain controller, increasing security in the event that the PDC is not available. Note that the client"s workgroup name must be the same as the domain name.

Input type: `Checkbox`

Valuename: "LoadBalance"

System → SNMP

Communities

Keyname: "System\CurrentControlSet\Services\SNMP\Parameters\ValidCommunities"

Communities

Communities to which the workstation belongs that are allowed to query the SNMP agent.

Input Type: `Listbox`

Permitted managers

Keyname: "System\CurrentControlSet\Services\SNMP\Parameters\PermittedManager"

Permitted managers

This policy specifies IP or IPX addresses that are allowed to query the SNMP agent.

Input Type: `Listbox`

Traps for Public community

Keyname: "System\CurrentControlSet\Services\SNMP\Parameters\TrapConfiguration\Public"

Trap configuration

This policy specifies IP or IPX addresses of hosts in the public community to which the SNMP agent sends alerts (traps) following unusual events.

Input type: `Listbox`

System → Run

Run

Keyname: "Software\Microsoft\Windows\CurrentVersion\Run"

Items to run at startup

This policy specifies applications and utilities that are run every time a user logs on.

Input type: `Listbox`

Shell.adm, Sp1shell.adm and Shellm.adm

Microsoft has distributed three versions of basically the same template. The *shell.adm* template is included with the Windows 98 ZAK, the *shellm.adm* template is included on the Windows 98 CD-ROM, and the *sp1shell.adm* template is included with both IEAK5 and IEAK5.1. The *shell.adm* template has almost all of the listed policies. Some policies are not found in all Shell templates, and this is noted in the policy comments section. Most of these policies will also work on a Windows NT4 workstation. If the policies are specific to a particular platform, this is noted as well in the policy comments section. Note that these policies have no computer properties.

User Properties

Desktop

Desktop Restrictions

Keyname: "Software\Microsoft\Windows\CurrentVersion\Policies\Explorer"

Disable Active Desktop

Active desktop allows the user to place active content from the Web onto the desktop.

Valuename: "NoActiveDesktop"

Do not allow changes to Active Desktop

Input type: `Checkbox`

Valuename: "NoActiveDesktopChanges"

Hide Internet Explorer icon

Input type: `Checkbox`

Valuename: "NoInternetIcon"

Hide Network Neighborhood icon

This policy is not found in the *shellm.adm* template. If checked, UNC pathnames will be disabled. Therefore, custom folders must be set to mapped drives rather than UNC pathnames.

Input type: `Checkbox`

Valuename: "NoNetHood"

Hide all items on Desktop

This policy is not found in the *shellm.adm* template. If checked, none of the desktop shortcuts will be visible, only the taskbar.

Input type: `Checkbox`

Valuename: "NoDesktop"

Active Desktop Items

Keyname: "Software\Microsoft\Windows\CurrentVersion\Policies\ActiveDesktop"

Disable ALL desktop items

This policy is not found in the *sp1shell.adm* template.

Input type: `Checkbox`

Valuename: "NoComponents"

Disable adding ANY desktop items

Input type: `Checkbox`

Valuename: "NoAddingComponents"

Disable deleting ANY desktop items

Input type: `Checkbox`

Valuename: "NoDeletingComponents"

Disable editing ANY desktop items

Input type: `Checkbox`

Valuename: "NoEditingComponents"

Disable closing ANY desktop items

Input type: `Checkbox`

Valuename: "NoClosingComponents"

Desktop Wallpaper Settings

Keyname: "Software\Microsoft\Windows\CurrentVersion\Policies\ActiveDesktop"

No HTML wallpaper (or Disable selecting HTML as wallpaper)

Input type: `Checkbox`

Valuename: "NoHTMLWallPaper"

Disable changing wallpaper

Input type: `Checkbox`

Valuename: "NoChangingWallPaper"

Desktop Toolbars Settings

Keyname: "Software\Microsoft\Windows\CurrentVersion\Policies\ActiveDesktop"

Disable dragging, dropping and closing ALL toolbars (or Disable adding new toolbars)

Input type: Checkbox

Valuename: "NoCloseDragDropBands"

Disable resizing ALL toolbars

Input type: Checkbox

Valuename: "NoMovingBands"

Start menu

Start menu

Keyname: "Software\Microsoft\Windows\CurrentVersion\Policies\Explorer"

Remove Favorites menu from Start menu

Input type: Checkbox

Valuename: "NoFavoritesMenu"

Remove Find menu from Start menu

The Find shortcut key (F3) will still be active. See Chapter 5 for more information on disabling this shortcut.

Input type: Checkbox

Valuename: "NoFind"

Remove Run menu from Start menu

See Chapter 5 for a discussion of the limitations of this policy.

Input type: Checkbox

Valuename: "NoRun"

Remove the Active Desktop item from the Settings menu

Input type: Checkbox

Valuename: "NoSetActiveDesktop"

Remove the Windows Update item from the Settings menu

This policy is not found in the *shellm.adm* template.

Input type: Checkbox

Valuename: "NoWindowsUpdate"

Disable drag-and-drop context menus on the Start menu

Input type: Checkbox

Valuename: "NoChangeStartMenu"

Remove the Folder Options menu item from the Settings menu

Input type: Checkbox

Valuename: "NoFolderOptions"

Remove Documents menu from Start menu

Input type: `Checkbox`

Valuename: "NoRecentDocsMenu"

Do not keep history of recently opened documents

Input type: `Checkbox`

Valuename: "NoRecentDocsHistory"

Clear history of recently opened documents

Input type: `Checkbox`

Valuename: "ClearRecentDocsOnExit"

Disable Logoff

Input type: `Checkbox`

Valuename: "NoLogoff"

Disable Shut Down command (or Disable Shut Down from Start menu)

This policy is not found in the *shellm.adm* template. The Shut Down command is removed from the Start menu.

Input type: `Checkbox`

Valuename: "NoClose"

Disable changes to Printers and Control Panel Settings

This policy is not found in the *shellm.adm* template.

Input type: `Checkbox`

Valuename: "NoSetFolders"

Disable changes to Taskbar and Start menu Settings

Removes Taskbar from the Settings option of the Start menu.

Input type: `Checkbox`

Valuename: "NoSetTaskbar"

Disable context menu for Taskbar

If checked, right-click context menus are disabled for the taskbar, Start menu button, clock and other taskbar applications.

Input type: `Checkbox`

Valuename: "NoTrayContextMenu"

Hide custom Programs folders

This policy is not found in the *sp1shell.adm* template. Check this if you use a custom Programs folder or custom Desktop icons, otherwise two Programs entries will appear in the Start menu.

Input type: `Checkbox`

Valuename: "NoStartMenuSubFolders"

Hide common program groups in Start menu (Windows NT only)

This policy is not found in the *sp1shell.adm* template.

Input type: `Checkbox`

Valuename: "NoCommonGroups"

Add run Dlg checkbox for New Memory Space (Windows NT only)

This policy is not found in the *shell.adm* template, and it does not work properly in the *shellm.adm* template. See Chapter 6 for more information.

Input type: `Checkbox`

Keyname: "Software\Microsoft\Windows\CurrentVersion\Policies"

Valuename: "MemCheckBoxInRunDlg"

Shell

Keyname: "Software\Microsoft\Windows\CurrentVersion\Policies\Explorer"

Enable Classic Shell

This policy is not found in the *sp1shell.adm* template. Rather than the Windows update shell, included with IE4 and Win98 (among other things), the Start menu will appear as multiple columns rather than one scrollable column.

Input type: `Checkbox`

Valuename: "ClassicShell"

Disable File menu in Shell folders

The file menu in browser windows is disabled.

Input type: `Checkbox`

Valuename: "NoFileMenu"

Disable context menu in Shell folders

If checked, right-click context menus are disabled for the desktop.

Input type: `Checkbox`

Valuename: "NoViewContextMenu"

Allow only approved Shell extensions

Only shell extensions listed in the HKLM\Software\Microsoft\Windows\CurrentVersion\Shell Extensions\Approved registry key will be used.

Input type: `Checkbox`

Valuename: "EnforceShellExtensionSecurity"

Do not track Shell shortcuts during roaming

Shortcuts contain a static path as well as an embedded UNC pathname. If this policy is checked, only the static pathname is used.

Input type: `Checkbox`

Valuename: "LinkResolveIgnoreLinkInfo"

Hide Floppy Drives in My Computer (or Hide Drives in My Computer)

Same policy as "Hide drives in My Computer" in the *admin.adm* template. See Chapter 5 for a discussion of the limitations of this policy.

Input type: `Checkbox`

Valuename: "NoDrives"

Disable net connections/disconnections

The Map Network Drive and Disconnect Network Drive menus and the right-click option from My Computer are removed.

Input type: `Checkbox`

Valuename: "NoNetConnectDisconnect"

Printers

None of the printer policies is available in the *shellm.adm* template.

Keyname: "Software\Microsoft\Windows\CurrentVersion\Policies\Explorer"

Hide General and Details tabs in Printer Properties

Windows 9x only.

Input type: `Checkbox`

Valuename: "NoPrinterTabs"

Disable Deletion of Printers

Input type: `Checkbox`

Valuename: "NoDeletePrinter"

Disable Addition of Printers

Input type: `Checkbox`

Valuename: "NoAddPrinter"

System

System

Keyname: "Software\Microsoft\Windows\CurrentVersion\Policies\Explorer"

Valuename: "RestrictRun"

Run only specified Windows applications

This policy is not found in the *shellm.adm* template. To create a list of allowed applications, click Show then Add, and enter the application executable name (e.g., *winword.exe, poledit.exe, powerpnt.exe*). See Chapter 5 for a discussion of the limitations of this policy.

Input type: `Listbox`

Keyname: "Software\Microsoft\Windows\CurrentVersion\Policies\Explorer\RestrictRun"

Do not allow computer to restart in MS-DOS mode

Windows 9x Only. The computer is not allowed to restart in MS-DOS mode, preventing users from running DOS applications in DOS mode.

Input type: `Checkbox`

Keyname: "Software\Microsoft\Windows\CurrentVersion\Policies\WinOldApp"

Valuename: "NoRealMode"

Windows.adm

Microsoft has made available two versions of this template; the first is included on the Windows 98 CD-ROM and the second is included with the Windows 98 ZAK. The version listed here is from the Windows 98 CD-ROM, which includes all of the policies found in the ZAK 98 version, plus four additional policies.

User Properties

Windows 98 Network → Sharing

Enabling these policies will remove the sharing properties for directories or printers. The user will then be unable to change which resources are shared on the workstation.

Keyname: "Software\Microsoft\Windows\CurrentVersion\Policies\Network"

Disable file sharing controls

Valuename: "NoFileSharingControl"

Disable print sharing controls

Valuename: "NoPrintSharingControl"

Windows 98 System → Shell → Custom Folders

See Chapter 4 for more information on the use of custom folders. If Network Neighborhood is hidden, then only mapped drives can be used for the network location of the custom folders (i.e., *M:\Desktop* rather than *//server/desktop*).

Keyname: "Software\Microsoft\Windows\CurrentVersion\Explorer\User Shell Folders"

Custom Programs Folder

Path to get Program items from

Input type: `Edittext`

Valuename: "Programs"

Custom Desktop Icons

Path to get Desktop icons from

Input type: `Edittext`

Valuename: "Desktop"

Hide Start menu subfolders

Check this if you use a custom Programs Folder or custom Desktop icons, otherwise two Programs entries will appear in the Start menu.

Keyname: "Software\Microsoft\Windows\CurrentVersion\Policies\Explorer"

Valuename: "NoStartMenuSubFolders"

Custom Startup Folder

Path to get Startup items from

Input type: `Edittext`

Valuename: "Startup"

Custom Network Neighborhood

Note that Windows 9x does not support the use of folders in a custom NN.

Path to get Network Neighborhood items from

Input type: `Edittext`

Valuename: "NetHood"

Custom Start menu

Path to get Start menu items from

Input type: `Edittext`

Valuename: "Startmenu"

Windows 98 System → Shell → Restrictions

These policies will remove various options from the Start menu on the taskbar.

Keyname: "Software\Microsoft\Windows\CurrentVersion\Policies\Explorer"

Remove "Run" command

See Chapter 5 for a discussion of the limitations of this policy.

Valuename: "NoRun"

Remove folders from "Settings" on Start menu

Prevents access to any Settings submenus.

Valuename: "NoSetFolders"

Remove Taskbar from "Settings" on Start menu

Valuename: "NoSetTaskbar"

Remove "Find" command

The Find command is removed from the Start menu. See Chapter 5 for a discussion of the limitations of this policy.

Valuename: "NoFind"

Hide Drives in "My Computer"

See Chapter 5 for a discussion of the limitations of this policy.

Valuename: "NoDrives"

Hide Network Neighborhood

If this policy is checked, the NN icon is hidden and UNC pathnames are disabled. Therefore, custom folders must be set to mapped drives rather than UNC pathnames.

Valuename: "NoNetHood"

No "Entire Network" in Network Neighborhood

Keyname: "Software\Microsoft\Windows\CurrentVersion\Policies\Network"

Valuename: "NoEntireNetwork"

No workgroup contents in Network Neighborhood

Keyname: "Software\Microsoft\Windows\CurrentVersion\Policies\Network"

Valuename: "NoWorkgroupContents"

Hide all items on Desktop

None of the desktop shortcuts will be visible, only the taskbar.

Valuename: "NoDesktop"

Disable Shut Down command

The Shut Down command is removed from the Start menu.

Valuename: "NoClose"

Don"t save settings at exit

Settings are not saved to the *user.dat* file.

Valuename: "NoSaveSettings"

Windows 98 System → Control Panel → Display

Restrict Display Control Panel

This policy restricts access to various display properties both from the Display Control Panel applet and from the desktop right-click context menu (under Properties).

Keyname: "Software\Microsoft\Windows\CurrentVersion\Policies\System"

Disable Display Control Panel

Input type: `Checkbox`

Valuename: "NoDispCPL"

Hide Background page

Input type: `Checkbox`

Valuename: "NoDispBackgroundPage"

Hide Screen Saver page

Input type: `Checkbox`

Valuename: "NoDispScrSavPage"

Hide Appearance Page

Input type: `Checkbox`

Valuename: "NoDispAppearancePage"

Hide Setting page

Input type: `Checkbox`

Valuename: "NoDispSettingsPage"

Windows 98 System → Control Panel → Network

Restrict Network Control Panel

This policy restricts access to network properties both from the Network Control Panel applet and from the Network Neighborhood icon right-click context menu (under Properties).

Keyname: "Software\Microsoft\Windows\CurrentVersion\Policies\Network"

Disable Network Control Panel

Input type: `Checkbox`

Valuename: "NoNetSetup"

Hide Identification Page

Input type: `Checkbox`

Valuename: "NoNetSetupIDPage"

Hide Access Control Page

Input type: `Checkbox`

Valuename: "NoNetSetupSecurityPage"

Windows 98 System → Control Panel → Passwords

Restrict Passwords Control Panel

This policy restricts access to various password properties usually available through the Passwords Control Panel applet.

Keyname: "Software\Microsoft\Windows\CurrentVersion\Policies\System"

Disable Passwords Control Panel

Input type: `Checkbox`

Valuename: "NoSecCPL"

Hide Change Passwords page

Input type: `Checkbox`

Valuename: "NoPwdPage"

Hide Remote Administration page

Input type: `Checkbox`

Valuename: "NoAdminPage"

Hide User Profiles page

Input type: `Checkbox`

Valuename: "NoProfilePage"

Windows 98 System → Control Panel → Printers

Restrict Printer Settings

This policy restricts access to various printer properties usually available through the Printers Control Panel applet.

Keyname: "Software\Microsoft\Windows\CurrentVersion\Policies\Explorer"

Hide General and Details pages

Input type: `Checkbox`

Valuename: "NoPrinterTabs"

Disable Deletion of Printers

Input type: `Checkbox`

Valuename: "NoDeletePrinter"

Disable Addition of Printers

Input type: `Checkbox`

Valuename: "NoAddPrinter"

Windows 98 System → Control Panel → System

Restrict System Control Panel

This policy restricts access to various system properties usually available through the System Control Panel applet.

Keyname: "Software\Microsoft\Windows\CurrentVersion\Policies\System"

Hide Device Manager page

Input type: `Checkbox`

Valuename: "NoDevMgrPage"

Hide Hardware Profiles Page

Input type: `Checkbox`

Valuename: "NoConfigPage"

Hide File System button

Input type: `Checkbox`

Valuename: "NoFileSysPage"

Hide Virtual Memory button

Input type: `Checkbox`

Valuename: "NoVirtMemPage"

Windows 98 System → Desktop Display

If the user is given access to the Display properties, the wallpaper and color scheme can be temporarily changed, but it will revert back to the setting used in these policies the next time the user logs on.

Wallpaper

Keyname: "Control Panel\Desktop"

Wallpaper name

Fewer wallpaper options are available in the template version included with ZAK 98.

Input type: `Combobox`

Valuename: "Wallpaper"

Tile Wallpaper

Input type: `Checkbox`

Valuename: "TileWallpaper"

Color scheme

Keyname: "Control Panel\Appearance"

Scheme name

Colors are in format X; for example, black is 0 0 0 and white is 255 255 255. Fewer color options are available in the template version included with ZAK 98.

Input type: `Dropdownlist`

Valuename: "Current"

Actionlist Keyname: "Control Panel\Colors"

Actionlist Valuenames: "ActiveBorder", "ActiveTitle", "AppWorkspace", "Background", "ButtonDkShadow", "ButtonFace", "ButtonHilight", "ButtonLight", "ButtonShadow", "ButtonText", "GrayText", "Hilight", "HilightText", "InactiveBorder", "InactiveTitle", "InactiveTitleText", "Menu", "MenuText", "InfoText", "InfoWindow", "Scrollbar", "TitleText", "Window", "WindowFrame", "WindowText"

Windows 98 System → Restrictions

Disable Registry editing tools

See Chapter 5 for a discussion of the limitations of this policy.

Keyname: "Software\Microsoft\Windows\CurrentVersion\Policies\System"

Valuename: "DisableRegistryTools"

Run Only Allowed Windows Applications

To create a list of allowed applications, click Show, then Add, and enter the application executable name (e.g., *winword.exe*, *poledit.exe*, *powerpnt.exe*). See Chapter 5 for a discussion of the limitations of this policy.

Keyname: "Software\Microsoft\Windows\CurrentVersion\Policies\Explorer"

Valuename: "RestrictRun"

List of allowed applications

Input type: `Listbox`

Keyname: "Software\Microsoft\Windows\CurrentVersion\Policies\Explorer\RestrictRun"

Disable MS-DOS prompt

Enabling this policy will not only disable a DOS prompt, but additionally any DOS-based programs.

Keyname: "Software\Microsoft\Windows\CurrentVersion\Policies\WinOldApp"

Valuename: "Disabled"

Disable single-mode MS-DOS applications

The computer is not allowed to restart in MS-DOS mode, preventing users from running DOS applications in DOS mode.

Keyname: "Software\Microsoft\Windows\CurrentVersion\Policies\WinOld-App"

Valuename: "NoRealMode"

Computer Properties

Windows 98 Network → Access Control

User-level access control

Enables user-level security on the workstation. See Chapter 4 for more information on user-level security.

Keyname: "System\CurrentControlSet\Services\VxD\FILESEC"

Valuename: "Start"

Actionliston Keyname: "System\CurrentControlSet\Services\VxD\FILESEC"

Actionliston Valuename: "StaticVxD"

Actionlistoff Keynames: "Security\Provider", "System\CurrentControlSet\Services\VxD\FILESEC", "System\CurrentControlSet\Services\VxD\NWSP", "System\CurrentControlSet\Services\VxD\MSSP"

Actionlistoff Valuenames: "Platform_Type", "StaticVxD", "Start"

Authenticator Name

Input type: `Edittext`

Keyname: "Security\Provider"

Valuename: "Container"

Authenticator Type

Input type: `Dropdownlist`

Keyname: "Security\Provider"

Valuename: "Platform_Type"

Actionlist Keynames: "System\CurrentControlSet\Services\VxD\NWSP", "Security\Provider", "System\CurrentControlSet\Services\VxD\MSSP"

Actionlist Valuenames: "Start", "Address_Book"

Windows 98 Network → Logon

Logon Banner

This policy allows a customized message to be displayed at logon and can be used to warn unauthorized users that access is prohibited. Do not set this policy to the cleared position, as it may delete the default registry settings. To disable the policy, set it to the grayed position.

Keyname: "Software\Microsoft\Windows\CurrentVersion\Winlogon"

Caption

Input type: `Edittext`

Valuename: "LegalNoticeCaption"

Text

Input type: `Edittext`

Valuename: "LegalNoticeText"

Require validation from network for Windows access

When checked, this policy will allow access only if the user has been validated by a network server. See Chapter 5 for security issues with this policy on a NetWare network.

Keyname: "Network\Logon"

Valuename: "MustBeValidated"

Don't show last user at logon

The name of the last user to log on is not displayed in the logon window.

Keyname: "Network\Logon"

Valuename: "DontShowLastUser"

Don't show logon progress

The logon progress window is not displayed. This policy is not found in the template version included with Windows 98.

Keyname: "Network\Logon"

Valuename: "NoProgressUI"

Windows 98 Network → Password

Keyname: "Software\Microsoft\Windows\CurrentVersion\Policies\Network"

Hide share passwords with asterisks

Unchecking this option will allow the password characters typed for shared folders and printers to be displayed, rather than appearing as asterisks.

Valuename: "HideSharePwds"

Disable password caching

Password cache files (**.pwl*) for share-level resources or applications are no longer generated. Since it is possible to uncover a user"s password by cracking the password files, checking this policy increases security.

Valuename: "DisablePwdCaching"

Require alphanumeric Windows password

Increases security by requiring that users use a combination of letters and numbers for their password.

Valuename: "AlphanumPwds"

Minimum Windows password length

Length

A good password should be a minimum of 6 characters.

Input type: `Numeric`

Valuename: "MinPwdLen"

Windows 98 Network → Proxy Server

Disable automatic location of proxy server

Enable this policy to ensure that manual settings for the location of the proxy server are used. This policy is not found in the template version included with Windows 98.

Keyname: "Software\Microsoft\Windows\CurrentVersion\Internet settings"

Valuename: "DisableProxyServerAutoLocate"

Windows 98 Network → Microsoft Client for NetWare Networks

Preferred server

The preferred server must be specified for the policy file to download properly. Do not set this policy to the cleared position, as it may delete the default registry settings. To disable the policy, set it to the grayed position.

Keyname: "System\CurrentControlSet\Services\NWNP32\NetworkProvider"

Server name:

Input type: `Edittext`

Valuename: "AuthenticatingAgent"

Support long filenames

Keyname: "System\CurrentControlSet\Services\VxD\NWREDIR"

Support long filenames on:

Input type: `Dropdownlist`

Valuename: "SupportLFN"

Disable automatic NetWare login

When checked, this policy prevents the user"s name, and network or Windows logon password, from being used to attempt to automatically log on to a NetWare server. This increases password security.

Keyname: "System\CurrentControlSet\Services\NWNP32\NetworkProvider"

Valuename: "DisableDefaultPasswords"

Windows 98 Network → NetWare Directory Services

Keyname: "System\CurrentControlSet\Services\NWNP32\NetworkProvider"

Preferred Tree

The directory tree the client connects to at logon.

Keyname: "System\CurrentControlSet\Services\VxD\NWREDIR"

Tree name:

Input type: `Edittext`

Valuename: "PreferredNDSTree"

Default Name Context

Keyname: "System\CurrentControlSet\Services\VxD\NWREDIR"

Default Name Context:

Input type: `Edittext`

Valuename: "DefaultNameContext"

Load NetWare DLLs at startup

Valuename: "PreLoadNWRunTime"

Disable automatic tree login

Valuename: "DisableDefaultLogon"

Enable login confirmation

Valuename: "EnableLogonPopup"

Don"t show advanced login button

Valuename: "DisableAdvancedLogonSettings"

Default type of NetWare login

Default type of NetWare login

Input type: `Dropdownlist`

Valuename: "LogonType"

Don"t show servers that aren"t NDS objects

Valuename: "BrowseDisableBNDServers"

Don"t show peer workgroups

Valuename: "BrowseDisableWorkgroups"

Don"t show server objects
Valuename: "BrowseDisableServers"

Don"t show container objects
Valuename: "BrowseDisableContainers"

Don"t show printer objects
Valuename: "BrowseDisablePrinters"

Don"t show print queue objects
Valuename: "BrowseDisableQueues"

Don"t show volume objects
Valuename: "BrowseDisableVolumes"

Windows 98 Network → Microsoft Client for Windows Networks

Log on to Windows NT

This policy allows the workstation to be part of an NT domain.

Keyname: "Network\Logon"

Valuename: "LMLogon"

Domain name:

Input type: `Edittext`

Keyname: "System\CurrentControlSet\Services\MSNP32\NetworkProvider"

Valuename: "AuthenticatingAgent"

Display domain logon confirmation

This policy will display a message when the domain controller has validated the user"s logon. This dialog box lists the validating server, which may be helpful for troubleshooting network problems.

Input type: `Checkbox`

Keyname: "Network\Logon"

Valuename: "DomainLogonMessage"

Disable caching of domain password

When checked, the user will have to log on separately to each network resource. Automatic logon to these resources will be disabled.

Input type: `Checkbox`

Keyname: "Network\Logon"

Valuename: "NoDomainPwdCaching"

Workgroup

Do not set this policy to the cleared position, as it may delete the default registry settings. To disable the policy, set it to the grayed position.

Keyname: "System\CurrentControlSet\Services\VxD\VNETSUP"

Workgroup name

To enable load balancing, set this policy to be equal to the domain name.

Input type: `Edittext`

Valuename: "Workgroup"

Alternate Workgroup

Keyname: "System\CurrentControlSet\Services\VxD\VREDIR"

Workgroup name

The alternate workgroup name must be entirely in capital letters.

Input type: `Edittext`

Valuename: "Workgroup"

Windows 98 Network → File and Printer Sharing for NetWare Networks

Disable SAP Advertising

This policy should be checked. If it is enabled (cleared), a Windows 9x workstation would appear on the network as a NetWare server. This could cause problems by creating unwanted network traffic, or by causing DOS clients to attempt to log in to the Windows 9x client rather than the NetWare server.

Keyname: "System\CurrentControlSet\Services\NcpServer\Parameters"

Valuename: "Use_Sap"

Actionlist Keyname: "System\CurrentControlSet\Services\NcpServer\Parameters\Ndi\Params\Use_Sap"

Actionlist Valuename: ""

Windows 98 Network → File and Printer Sharing for Microsoft Networks

Enabling these policies will remove the sharing properties for directories or printers. The user will then not be able to alter which resources are shared on the workstation.

Keyname: "Software\Microsoft\Windows\CurrentVersion\Policies\Network"

Disable file sharing

Valuename: "NoFileSharing"

Disable print sharing

Valuename: "NoPrintSharing"

Windows 98 Network → Dial-In Networking

Disable dial-in

This policy prevents dial-in connections to the workstation.

Keyname: "Software\Microsoft\Windows\CurrentVersion\Policies\Network"

Valuename: "NoDialIn"

Windows 98 Network → Update

Remote Update

This policy *must* be checked to allow the system policy file to download.

Keyname: "System\CurrentControlSet\Control\Update"

Actionlistoff Valuename: "UpdateMode"

Update Mode

The options are automatic or manual. If set to manual, the location of the policy file must be specified.

Input type: `Dropdownlist`

Valuename: "UpdateMode"

Path for manual update

Input type: `Edittext`

Valuename: "NetworkPath"

Display error messages

Checking this policy may help in troubleshooting problems with the policy file.

Input type: `Checkbox`

Valuename: "Verbose"

Load balance

By default, a Windows client on an NT network will query the PDC only for the policy file. Checking this policy option will allow the client to receive the policy file from any validating domain controller, increasing security in the event that the PDC is not available. Note that the client"s workgroup name must be the same as the domain name.

Input type: `Checkbox`

Valuename: "LoadBalance"

Windows 98 System → User Profiles

Enable User Profiles

This policy *must* be checked to enable the policy file to be used.

Keyname: "Network\Logon"

Valuename: "UserProfiles"

Windows 98 System → Network Paths

Keyname: "Software\Microsoft\Windows\CurrentVersion\Setup"

Network path for Windows Setup

Path:

This policy is useful for updating the workstations if you ever change the network location of the Windows setup files.

Input type: `Edittext`

Valuename: "SourcePath"

Network path for Windows Tour

Path

The path must end in *discover.exe* (or *tour.exe* for Windows 95)

Input type: `Edittext`

Valuename: "TourPath"

Windows 98 System → SNMP

Communities

Keyname: "System\CurrentControlSet\Services\SNMP\Parameters\ValidCommunities"

Communities

Communities to which the workstation belongs that are allowed to query the SNMP agent.

Input type: `Listbox`

Permitted managers

Keyname: "System\CurrentControlSet\Services\SNMP\Parameters\Permitted-Managers"

Permitted managers:

This policy specifies IP or IPX addresses that are allowed to query the SNMP agent.

Input type: `Listbox`

Traps for "Public" community

Keyname: "System\CurrentControlSet\Services\SNMP\Parameters\TrapConfiguration\Public"

Trap configuration

This policy specifies IP or IPX addresses of hosts in the public community to which the SNMP agent sends alerts (traps) following unusual events. To send traps to a community other than "Public," the registry must be edited manually.

Input type: `Listbox`

Internet MIB (RFC 1156)

This policy will set the contact name and location of the Management Information Base (a database, created by an SNMP agent, that contains information and statistics on each network device).

Keyname: "System\CurrentControlSet\Services\SNMP\Parameters\RFC1156-Agent"

Contact Name:

Input type: `Edittext`

Valuename: "sysContact"

Location:

Input type: `Edittext`

Valuename: "sysLocation"

Windows 98 System → Programs to Run

Run

Items to run at startup

This policy specifies applications and utilities that are run every time a user logs on.

Input type: `Listbox`

Run Once

Keyname: "Software\Microsoft\Windows\CurrentVersion\RunOnce"

Items to run once at startup

This policy specifies applications and utilities that are run just once when a user logs on, and then the application is removed from the registry. However, if this option is checked in a policy file it will be run each time the user logs on until it is disabled in the policy file. Leave this option checked only long enough to be downloaded to the workstation, then clear the policy.

Input type: `Listbox`

Run Services

Keyname: "Software\Microsoft\Windows\CurrentVersion\RunServices"

Services to run at startup

This policy specifies services that are run at system startup.

Input type: `Listbox`

Windows 98 System → Install Device Drivers

Digital Signature Check

Driver files will be checked for a Microsoft digital signature before they are installed. This policy is not found in the template version included with Windows 98.

Keyname: "Software\Microsoft\Driver Signing"

Digital Signature Check

Level 0 allows all drivers to be installed, Level 1 checks to see if the driver has passed WHQL testing, and Level 2 blocks the installation of all drivers that do not have a digital signature.

Input type: `Dropdownlist`

Valuename: "Policy"

Windows 98 System → Windows Update

Disable Windows Update

Access to Windows Update is completely restricted, including removing the shortcut from the Start menu. Enabling this option ensures that the setup of all workstations remains consistent.

Keyname: "Software\Microsoft\Windows\CurrentVersion\Policies\Explorer"

Valuename: "NoWindowsUpdate"

Actionlist Keyname: "Software\Microsoft\Windows\CurrentVersion\RunOnce"

Actionlist Valuename: "WUCheckShortcut"

Override Local Web Page

The first time Windows Update is launched, the user is redirected to this URL.

Keyname: "Software\Policies\Microsoft\Windows Update"

Local Web Page

Input type: `Edittext`

Valuename: "Local URL"

Override Windows Update Site URL

Whenever Windows Update is launched, the user is redirected to this URL.

Keyname: "Software\Policies\Microsoft\Windows Update"

Site URL

Input type: `Edittext`

Valuename: "RemoteURL"

Winnt.adm

Microsoft has distributed several versions of this template: one with the NT4 ZAK, and several with the various NT Service Packs. The version specified here is included with Windows NT4 Service Pack 5. Older versions of the template had an error in the template, which set the policy "Create Hidden Drive Shares" to the cleared position. See Chapter 6 for more information on this error.

User Properties

Windows NT Shell → Custom user interface

Custom shell

Keyname: "Software\Microsoft\Windows NT\CurrentVersion\Winlogon"

Shell name (e g., explorer.exe)

A custom user interface, other than the default shell *explorer.exe*, may be set.

Input type: `Edittext`

Valuename: "Shell"

Windows NT Shell → Custom folders

See Chapter 4 for more information on the use of custom folders. See Computer Properties for custom *shared* folders.

Keyname: "Software\Microsoft\Windows\CurrentVersion\Explorer\User Shell Folders"

Custom Programs folder

Path to location of Program items

Input type: `Edittext`

Valuename: "Programs"

Custom desktop icons

Path to location of desktop icons

Input type: `Edittext`

Valuename: "Desktop"

Hide Start menu subfolders

Check this if you use a custom Programs folder or custom Desktop icons, otherwise, two Programs entries will appear in the Start menu.

Keyname: "Software\Microsoft\Windows\CurrentVersion\Policies\Explorer"

Valuename: "NoStartMenuSubFolders"

Custom Startup folder

Path to location of Startup items

Input type: `Edittext`

Valuename: "Startup"

Custom Network Neighborhood

Path to location of Network Neighborhood items

Input type: `Edittext`

Valuename: "NetHood"

Custom Start menu

Path to location of Start menu items

Input type: `Edittext`

Valuename: "Startmenu"

Windows NT Shell → Restrictions

Keyname: "Software\Microsoft\Windows\CurrentVersion\Policies\Explorer"

Use Only Approved Shell Extensions

Only shell extensions listed in the HKLM\Software\Microsoft\Windows\CurrentVersion\Shell Extensions\Approved registry key will be used.

Valuename: "EnforceShellExtensionSecurity"

Remove View → Options menu from Explorer

Valuename: "NoOptions"

Remove Tools → Goto Menu from Explorer

Valuename: "NoGoTo"

Remove File menu from Explorer

The file menu in browser windows is disabled

Valuename: "NoFileMenu"

Remove common program groups from Start menu

Valuename: "NoCommonGroups"

Disable context menus for the taskbar

If checked, right-click context menus are disabled for the taskbar, Start menu button, clock, or other taskbar applications.

Valuename: "NoTrayContextMenu"

Disable Explorer"s default context menu

If checked, right-click context menus are disabled for the desktop. This option is available only with Service Pack 2 or later.

Valuename: "NoViewContextMenu"

Remove the "Map Network Drive" and "Disconnect Network Drive" options

The Map Network Drive and Disconnect Network Drive menus and the right-click option from My Computer are removed.

Valuename: "NoNetConnectDisconnect"

Disable link file tracking

Shortcuts contain a static path as well as an embedded UNC pathname. If this policy is checked, only the static pathname is used.

Valuename: "LinkResolveIgnoreLinkInfo"

Windows NT System

Parse Autoexec.bat

When this box is checked, environment variables (such as *%USERNAME%*) declared in *autoexec.bat* are included in the user"s environment.

Keyname: "Software\Microsoft\Windows NT\CurrentVersion\Winlogon"

Valuename: "ParseAutoexec"

Run logon scripts synchronously

Wait for the logon scripts to complete before starting the user"s shell. If this value is also set in the computer section, that value takes precedence.

Keyname: "Software\Microsoft\Windows NT\CurrentVersion\Winlogon"

Valuename: "RunLogonScriptSync"

Disable Logoff

Keyname: "Software\Microsoft\Windows\CurrentVersion\Policies\Explorer"

Valuename: "NoLogoff"

Disable Task Manager

This button, which appears when the user presses Ctrl-Alt-Del, can be disabled.

Keyname: "Software\Microsoft\Windows\CurrentVersion\Policies\System"

Valuename: "DisableTaskMgr"

Disable Lock Workstation

This button, which appears when the user presses Ctrl-Alt-Del, can be disabled.

Keyname: "Software\Microsoft\Windows\CurrentVersion\Policies\System"

Valuename: "DisableLockWorkstation"

Disable Change Password

This button, which appears when the user presses Ctrl-Alt-Del, can be disabled.

Keyname: "Software\Microsoft\Windows\CurrentVersion\Policies\System"

Valuename: "DisableChangePassword"

Show welcome tips at logon

Keyname: "Software\Microsoft\Windows\CurrentVersion\Explorer\Tips"

Valuename: "Show"

Windows NT User Profiles

Limit profile size

With NT Service Pack 4 installed, it is possible to set this policy to set profile quotas. The amount of disk space a user profile uses can be limited.

Keyname: "Software\Microsoft\Windows\CurrentVersion\Policies\System"

Valuename: "EnableProfileQuota"

Custom Message

Message displayed when the profile exceeds the quota.

Input type: `Edittext`

Valuename: "ProfileQuotaMessage"

Max Profile size (KB)

Default is 30 KB; setting the value too low will cause problems. The user will not be able to log off if his profile is too large.

Input type: `Numeric`

Valuename: "MaxProfileSize"

Include registry in file list

Exceeding the quota produces an error icon. Double-clicking the icon lists the profile files, allowing the user to delete files and create more space. Checking this option includes the *ntuser.dat* in that list, although it cannot be deleted by the user.

Input type: `Checkbox`

Valuename: "IncludeRegInProQuota"

Notify user when profile storage space is exceeded

A dialog box appears as soon as the disk quota is exceeded. By default this dialog box only appears when the user attempts to log off.

Input type: `Checkbox`

Valuename: "WarnUser"

Remind user every X minutes

Input type: `Numeric`

Valuename: "WarnUserTimeout"

Exclude directories in roaming profile

You can enter multiple directory names, semicolon-separated, all relative to the root of the user"s profile.

Keyname: "Software\Policies\Microsoft\Windows\System"

Prevent the following directories from roaming with the profile

Input type: `Edittext`

Valuename: "ExcludeProfileDirs"

Computer Properties

Windows NT Network → Sharing

Keyname: "System\CurrentControlSet\Services\LanManServer\Parameters"

Create hidden drive shares (workstation)

Automatically creates <drive letters>$ and Admin$ shares when Windows NT Workstation starts.

Valuename: "AutoShareWks"

Create hidden driver shares (server)

Automatically creates <drive letters>$ and Admin$ shares when Windows NT Server starts.

Valuename: "AutoShareServer"

Windows NT Printers

Keyname: "System\CurrentControlSet\Control\Print"

Disable browse thread on this computer

When this box is checked, the print spooler does not send shared printer information to other print servers.

Valuename: "DisableServerThread"

Scheduler priority

Priority

Set the scheduler thread priority, which is used to assign jobs to ports.

Input type: `Dropdownlist`

Valuename: "SchedulerThreadPriority"

Beep for error enabled

A check in this box enables beeping (every 10 seconds) when a remote job error occurs on a print server.

Valuename: "BeepEnabled"

Windows NT Remote Access

Remote Access Server allows remote users to dial-in to the office server to access files and printers. These policies allow customization of that service.

Keyname: "System\CurrentControlSet\Services\RemoteAccess\Parameters"

Max number of unsuccessful authentication retries

Number of retries

Input type: `Numeric`

Valuename: "AuthenticateRetries"

Max time limit for authentication

Length in seconds

Input type: `Numeric`

Valuename: "AuthenticateTime"

Wait interval for callback

Length in seconds

Input type: `Numeric`

Valuename: "CallbackTime"

Auto Disconnect

Disconnect after (minutes)

Input type: `Numeric`

Valuename: "AutoDisconnect"

Windows NT Shell → Custom shared folders

See User Properties for custom folders.

Keyname: "Software\Microsoft\Windows\CurrentVersion\Explorer\User Shell Folders"

Custom shared Programs folder

Path to location of shared Program items

Input type: `Edittext`

Valuename: "Common Programs"

Custom shared desktop icons

Path to location of shared desktop icons

Input type: `Edittext`.

Valuename: "Common Desktop"

Custom shared Start menu

Path to location of shared Start menu items

Input type: `Edittext`

Valuename: "Common Start menu"

Custom shared Startup folder

Path to location of shared Startup items

Input type: `Edittext`

Valuename: "Common Startup"

Windows NT System → Logon

Keyname: "Software\Microsoft\Windows NT\CurrentVersion\Winlogon"

Logon banner

This policy allows a customized message to be displayed at logon and can be used to warn unauthorized users that access is prohibited.

Caption

Input type: `Edittext`

Valuename: "LegalNoticeCaption"

Text

Input type: `Edittext`

Valuename: "LegalNoticeText"

Enable shut down from Authentication dialog box

When this box is checked, you can click Shut Down in the Authentication dialog box to select options. Default: NT Server=Off, NT Workstation=On. If this policy is changed, the template does not have the ability to restore the previous default setting. See Chapter 6 for more information.

Keyname: "Software\Microsoft\Windows NT\CurrentVersion\Winlogon"

Valuename: "ShutdownWithoutLogon"

Do not display last logged-on username

When this box is checked, Windows NT does not automatically display the username of the last person to log on in the Authentication dialog box.

Keyname: "Software\Microsoft\Windows NT\CurrentVersion\Winlogon"

Valuename: "DontDisplayLastUserName"

Run logon scripts synchronously

Wait for the logon scripts to complete before starting the user"s shell. If this value is also set in the User section, this value takes precedence.

Keyname: "Software\Microsoft\Windows NT\CurrentVersion\Winlogon"

Valuename: "RunLogonScriptSync"

Windows NT System → File System

Keyname: "System\CurrentControlSet\Control\FileSystem"

Do not create 8.3 filenames for long filenames

If you do not need DOS-compatible filenames, enabling this option will improve performance on NTFS volumes.

Valuename: "NtfsDisable8dot3NameCreation"

Allow extended characters in 8.3 filenames

Short filenames with extended characters may not be viewable on computers that do not have same character code page.

Valuename: "NtfsAllowExtendedCharacterIn8dot3Name"

Do not update last access time

For files that are only being read, do not update the last access time. This will increase the file system"s performance.

Valuename: "NtfsDisableLastAccessUpdate"

Windows NT User Profiles

Keyname: "Software\Microsoft\Windows NT\CurrentVersion\winlogon"

Delete cached copies of roaming profiles

When users with roaming profiles log off, delete the locally cached profile (to save disk space).

Valuename: "DeleteRoamingCache"

Automatically detect slow network connections

Enable "slow network connection" errors. Older versions of *winnt.adm* (up to the version included with Service Pack 5) do not have `VALUEON` and `VALUEOFF` statements for this policy. See Chapter 6 for more information.

Valuename: "SlowLinkDetectEnabled"

Slow network connection timeout

Time (milliseconds)

Increasing this value can prevent a "slow network connection" error when the user"s profile is being downloaded from a busy network. The default is 2000 (2 seconds); the maximum is 120,000.

Input type: `Numeric`

Valuename: "SlowLinkTimeOut"

Slow network default profile operation

Default option

Use network or local profile.

Input type: `Dropdownlist`

Valuename: "SlowLinkProfileDefault"

Choose profile default operation

Default option

Use network or local profile

Input type: `Dropdownlist`

Valuename: "ChooseProfileDefault"

Timeout for dialog boxes

Time (seconds)

Input type: `Numeric`

Valuename: "ProfileDlgTimeOut"

NetWare Templates

These Novell templates allow customization of the NetWare client for Windows workstations. Included in this section are the following templates:

client32.adm

This template contains computer policies for Windows 9x Client Version 3.x.

novell.adm

This template contains computer policies for protocol settings such as IP, IPX, SPX, SNMP and TSA policies.

nwNT.adm

This template contains computer policies for Windows NT Client Version 4.x.

Client32.adm

Novell has distributed two versions of this template, one with the original Client 32 and the other with Client Version 3.1. The version specified here is Version 2.0 of the template included with Client Version 3.1. Note that this template has no user properties.

Computer Properties

Novell Client → Client

Preferred Server

Preferred NetWare server used to authenticate the user. Setting this causes the client to automatically attempt to create a connection to the server.

Keyname: "Network\Novell\System Config\Netware DOS Requester\Preferred Server"

Server name

Input type: `Edittext`

Valuename: "0"

Name Context

Default logon context in the NDS tree; only applies to NetWare 4 or NetWare 5 networks.

Keyname: "Network\Novell\System Config\Netware DOS Requester\Name Context"

Context name

Input type: `Edittext`

Valuename: "0"

Preferred Tree

The directory tree the client connects to at logon.

Keyname: "Network\Novell\System Config\Netware DOS Requester\Preferred Tree"

Tree name

Input type: `Edittext`

Valuename: "0"

First Network Drive:

The first available drive letter for network drives.

Keyname: "Network\Novell\System Config\Netware DOS Requester\First Network Drive"

First Network Drive

Input type: `Dropdownlist`

Valuename: "0"

Novell Client → Default Login

Enable or disable the display of certain options in the logon dialog box.

Display Connection Page

Keyname: "Network\Novell\System Config\Network Provider\Graphical Login"

Valuename: "Connection Tab"

Login to tree

Input type: `Checkbox`

Valuename: "Tree Login"

Login to Server

Input type: `Checkbox`

Valuename: "Server Login"

Bindery

Input type: `Checkbox`

Valuename: "Bindery Connections"

Clear Current Connections

Input type: `Checkbox`

Valuename: "Clear Connections"

Display Script Page

Keyname: "Network\Novell\System Config\Network Provider\Graphical Login"

Valuename: "Script Tab"

Script

Input type: `Edittext`

Keyname: "Network\Novell\System Config\Network Provider\Graphical Login\Scripts\1"

Valuename: ""

Profile

Input type: `Edittext`

Keyname: "Network\Novell\System Config\Network Provider\Graphical Login\Profiles\1"

Valuename: ""

Close Script Results Automatically

Input type: `Checkbox`

Keyname: "Network\Novell\System Config\Network Provider\Graphical Login"

Valuename: "Close Results"

Run login scripts

Input type: `Checkbox`

Keyname: "Network\Novell\System Config\Network Provider\Graphical Login"

Valuename: "Login Script"

Display Variables Page

Keyname: "Network\Novell\System Config\Network Provider\Graphical Login"

Valuename: "Script Variable Tab"

%2 through %5

Four variable scripts can be displayed from %2 through %5.

Input type: `Edittext`

Keyname: "Network\Novell\System Config\Network Provider\Graphical Login\Variables\2" through "Network\Novell\System Config\Network Provider\Graphical Login\Variables\5"

Valuename: ""

Save Setting on Login Exit

Keyname: "Network\Novell\System Config\Network Provider\Graphical Login"

Valuename: "Save On Exit"

Novell Client → Contextless Login

This policy option is available only when connecting to NetWare 5 servers.

Enable Contextless Login

Contextless login allows the user to log on without specifying an NDS context

Keyname: "Network\Novell\System Config\Network Provider\Graphical Login\NWLGE\Z Xcontext"

Valuename: "RunContext"

Wildcard Searching Allowed

Wildcards can be used within the username.

Input type: `Checkbox`

Keyname: "Network\Novell\System Config\Network Provider\Graphical Login\NWLGE\Z XContext"

Valuename: "AllowWild"

Search Timeout (sec)

Maximum amount of time to search the NDS for the user, increase the value if timeout errors occur.

Input type: `Numeric`

Keyname: "Network\Novell\System Config\Network Provider\Graphical Login\NWLGE\Z XContext\AllowWild"

Valuename: "SearchTimeout"

Tree and Catalog List

Enter the tree name as the valuename and the catalog as the value. This forces contextless logon to use a specific catalog for each tree in the list.

Input type: `Listbox`

Novell Client → Advanced Login

Disable Default Policy Support

This path on the authenticating server is searched for the policy file (*ntconfig.pol*).

Keyname: "Software\Novell\Workstation Manager\Policy Support"

Policy Path and Filename

Input type: `Edittext`

Valuename: "Check Default"

Novell Client → Advanced Login → Show on Login

Enable or disable features in the logon dialog box.

Keyname: "Software\Novell\Login"

Location List

The location list shows recent places where the user has logged in.

Valuename: "Location"

Advanced Button

The Advanced Button displays if this policy is checked.

Valuename: "Advanced"

Variable Button

The Variable Button displays if this policy is checked.

Valuename: "Variables"

Clear Connections

This checkbox displays if this policy is checked.

Valuename: "Clear Connections"

Novell Client → Default Capture → Output Setting

These policies set print options.

Keyname: "Network\Novell\System Config\Network Provider\Capture Flags"

Number of Copies

Number of Copies

Input type: `Numeric`

Valuename: "Number of Copies"

Form Feed

Valuename: "Form Feed"

Enable tabs

Valuename: "Enable Tabs"

Number of Spaces

Input type: `Numeric`

Valuename: "Number of Spaces"

Novell Client → Default Capture → Banner Settings

Enable Banner

A banner page prints out before the print job; it can be used to identify to whom the print job belongs.

Keyname: "Network\Novell\System Config\Network Provider\Capture Flags"

Valuename: "Enable Banner"

1st banner name

Input type: `Edittext`

Valuename: "1st Banner Name"

2nd banner name

Input type: `Edittext`

Valuename: "2nd Banner Name"

Novell Client → Default Capture → Other Settings

These policies set print options.

Keyname: "Network\Novell\System Config\Network Provider\Capture Flags"

Hold

Print jobs are put on hold.

Valuename: "Hold"

Notify

User is notified when print job is completed.

Valuename: "Notify"

Keep

The print job is kept in the print queue after printing.

Valuename: "Keep"

Auto endcap

Captured data is closed and sent to the printer after exiting the application.

Valuename: "AutoEndcap"

Seconds Before Timeout

Seconds Before Timeout

Number of seconds to wait after the final data is received before the print job is closed.

Input type: `Numeric`

Valuename: "Seconds before Timeout"

Novell Client → Advanced Settings → Connection

Auto Reconnect Level

Auto Reconnect Level determines the services that are restored after the loss of a network connection.

Keyname: "Network\Novell\System Config\Netware DOS Requester\Auto Reconnect Level"

Auto Reconnect Level

Input type: `Numeric`

Valuename: "0"

Auto Reconnect Timeout

Auto Reconnect Timeout is the time in minutes to drop AutoReconnect. Default: 10 minutes

Keyname: "Network\Novell\System Config\Netware DOS Requester\Auto Reconnect Timeout"

AutoReconnect Timeout

Input type: `Edittext`

Valuename: "0"

NetWare Protocol

Default=NDS BIND. NetWare Protocol allows you to list the order that the NetWare Name Services are accessed during authentication to the network.

Keyname: "Network\Novell\System Config\Netware DOS Requester\NetWare Protocol"

NetWare Protocol

Input type: `Dropdownlist`

Valuename: "0"

Resolve Name Using Primary Connection

Resolve name requests will be done over the primary connection only if set to on. If set to off, resolve name requests will be done over all connections.

Keyname: "Network\Novell\System Config\Netware DOS Requester\Resolve Name Using Primary"

Valuename: "0"

Novell Client → Advanced Settings → Environment, NETX compatibility

Cache NetWare Password

Specifies whether the NetWare Password from the first login is stored in memory and used to authenticate to additional NetWare resources.

Keyname: "Network\Novell\System Config\Network Provider\Cache NetWare Password"

Valuename: "0"

DOS Name

DOS Name is the operating system name used by the %OS parameter in login scripts.

Keyname: "NetWork\Novell\System Config\Netware Dos Requester\Dos Name"

DOS Name

Input type: `Edittext`

Valuename: "0"

End of Job

This causes an End of Job command to be sent to the fileserver, which releases all resources allocated on the file server to the current task.

Keyname: "Network\Novell\System Config\Netware DOS Requester\EOJ"

Valuename: "0"

Environment Pad

Keyname: "Network\Novell\System Config\Netware DOS Requester\Environment Pad"

Environment Pad

This policy adds a specified number of bytes to the DOS environment for DOS applications. Valid range of bytes is 17–512.

Input type: `Edittext`

Valuename: "0"

Force First Network Drive

Force First Network Drive specifies the network drive letter the *SYS:LOGIN* directory is mapped to after logging out. on returns you to the "First Network Drive." Off leaves you at the current drive.

Keyname: "Network\Novell\System Config\Netware DOS Requester\Force First Network Drive"

Valuename: "0"

Hold Files

Hold Files specifies whether files opened by a program using FCB_10 are held open until the program exits. "Checked" means they are. "Unchecked" means they can be closed by the program before it exits.

Keyname: "Network\Novell\System Config\Netware DOS Requester\Hold"

Valuename: "0"

Long Machine Type

Long Machine Type is the workstation type used by the *%MACHINE* parameter in login scripts.

Keyname: "Network\Novell\System Config\Netware DOS Requester\Long Machine Type"

Long Machine Type

Input type: `Edittext`

Valuename: "0"

Max Current Dir Length

Max Current Directory Length sets the length of the DOS prompt. Some applications do not function correctly if this value is set greater than 64.

Keyname: "Network\Novell\System Config\Netware DOS Requester\Max Cur Dir Length"

Max Current Dir Length

Input type: `Numeric`

Valuename: "0"

NWLanguage

NWLanguage determines the language that NetWare utilities will default to on the workstation.

Keyname: "Network\Novell\System Config\Language\NWLanguage"

NWLanguage

Input type: `Edittext`

Valuename: "(Default)"

Polled Broadcast Message Buffers

Polled Broadcast Message Buffers sets the number of broadcast messages saved on the client when Broadcast Message Mode is "polled."

Keyname: "Network\Novell\System Config\Netware DOS Requester\polled broadcast msg buffers"

Polled Broadcast Message Buffers

Input type: `Numeric`

Valuename: "0"

Remove Drive from Environment

Remove Drive from Environment determines if a search drive is removed from the path when a drive is deleted.

Keyname: "Network\Novell\System Config\Netware DOS Requester\Remove Drive From Environment"

Valuename: "0"

Search Dirs First

If Search Directores First is set to off, a DIR listing will display files first, then directories. If set to on, a DIR listing will display directories first, then files.

Keyname: "Network\Novell\System Config\Netware DOS Requester\Search Dir First"

Valuename: "0"

Search Mode

This policy sets the NetWare search mode for finding a file if it is not in the path of the local directory.

Keyname: "Network\Novell\System Config\Netware DOS Requester\Search Mode"

Search Mode

Input type: `Numeric`

Valuename: "0"

Set Station Time

If Set Station Time is set to on, the workstation"s time and date are synchronized with the NetWare server that the workstation attaches to initially.

Keyname: "Network\Novell\System Config\Netware DOS Requester\Set Station Time"

Valuename: "0"

Short Machine Type

Short Machine Type determines what overlay file is used when accessing older NetWare utilities.

Keyname: "Network\Novell\System Config\Netware DOS Requester\Short Machine Type"

Short Machine Type

Input type: `Edittext`

Valuename: "0"

Shrink Path to Dot

Allows network search drives in the DOS PATH set variable to either be truncated to a dot or be left with the full directory path.

Keyname: "Network\Novell\System Config\Netware DOS Requester\Shrink Path To Dot"

Valuename: "0"

Use Video BIOS

Use Video BIOS specifies whether the client uses BIOS or Direct Video Memory calls when a pop-up message is displayed. The BIOS method is Slower than Direct Video Memory calls.

Keyname: "Network\Novell\System Config\Nios\Use Video BIOS"

Valuename: "0"

Novell Client → Advanced Settings → File System

Lock Delay

The amount of time (in ticks) the client software waits before trying to get a lock. Use this if client workstations receive error messages when requesting a file from the server.

Keyname: "Network\Novell\System Config\Netware DOS Requester\Lock Delay"

Lock Delay

Valid range (Ticks): 1–65535.

Input type: `Edittext`

Valuename: "0"

Lock Retries

Lock Retries determines the number of retries to open or lock a file, after receiving a SHARE failure. Increase this value if you receive SHARE errors.

Keyname: "Network\Novell\System Config\Netware DOS Requester\Lock Retries"

Lock Retries

Input type: `Numeric`

Valuename: "0"

Read-Only Compatibility

Read-Only Compatibility determines whether a file marked read-only can be opened with a read/write access call. Some applications require this parameter to be on.

Keyname: "Network\Novell\System Config\Netware DOS Requester\READ ONLY COMPATIBILITY"

Valuename: "0"

Use Extended File Handles

If set to on, this will allow the client to open multiple files up to the server parameter MAXIMUM FILE LOCKS PER CONNECTION.

Keyname: "Network\Novell\System Config\Netware DOS Requester\Use Extended File Handles"

Valuename: "0"

Novell Client → Advanced Settings → Packet Management

Checksum

Checksum provides a higher level of data integrity by validating NCP packets.

Keyname: "Network\Novell\System Config\Netware DOS Requester\Checksum"

Checksum

Valid Range: 0–3

Input type: `Numeric`

Valuename: "0"

Large Internet Packets

When Large Internet Packets is on, it uses the maximum packet size negotiated between the NetWare server and the workstation, even across router and bridges.

Keyname: "Network\Novell\System Config\Netware DOS Requester\Large Internet Packets"

Valuename: "0"

Link Support Layer Max Buffer Size

Specifies the maximum supported packet size in bytes. It is used primarily for token ring networks.

Keyname: "Network\Novell\System Config\Link Support\Max Buffer Size"

Link Support Layer Max Buffer Size

Valid range: 638–24682

Input type: `Edittext`

Valuename: "0"

Packet Burst Buffers

Packet Burst Buffers specifies whether Packet Burst is used. Unchecking disables Packet Burst. Checking enables Packet Burst, which reduces overall network traffic and improves performance.

Keyname: "Network\Novell\System Config\Netware DOS Requester\PB Buffers"

Valuename: "0"

Packet Burst Read Window Size

Sets the maximum number of packets read per Read Burst. Normally this value should not be changed.

Keyname: "Network\Novell\System Config\Netware DOS Requester\PBURST Read Window Size"

Packet Burst Read Window Size

Valid Range: 3–255

Input type: `Numeric`

Valuename: "0"

Packet Burst Write Window Size

Sets the maximum number of packets per Write Burst. Normally this value should not be changed.

Keyname: "Network\Novell\System Config\Netware DOS Requester\PBURST Write Window Size"

Packet Burst Write Window Size

Valid Range: 3–255

Input type: `Numeric`

Valuename: "0"

Signature Level

Signature Level determines the level of enhanced security support. Increasing this value increases security but decreases performance.

Keyname: "Network\Novell\System Config\Netware DOS Requester\Signature Level"

Signature Level

Valid range: 0–3

Input type: `Numeric`

Valuename: "0"

Novell Client → Advanced Settings → Performance, Cache

Cache Writes

Caching file writes improves performance by saving files to workstation memory before saving them to the network.

Keyname: "Network\Novell\System Config\Netware DOS Requester\Cache Writes"

Valuename: "0"

Close Behind Ticks

The amount of time the client waits after a file is closed before flushing the file from the cache and writing it to disk. Increasing this value improves performance most when files are opened and closed frequently.

Keyname: "Network\Novell\System Config\Netware DOS Requester\Close Behind Ticks"

Close Behind Ticks

Valid range (Ticks): 0–65535

Input type: `Exittext`

Valuename: "0"

Delay Writes

Delay Writes keeps the file in cache for the amount of time specified by Close Behind Ticks after the application closes the file. This is used for applications that repeatedly close, and reopen files, such as overlay files.

Keyname: "Network\Novell\System Config\Netware DOS Requester\Delay Writes"

Valuename: "0"

File Cache Level

File Cache Level specifies the type of caching used at the client. The larger the value, the better the performance.

Keyname: "Network\Novell\System Config\Netware DOS Requester\File Cache Level"

File Cache Level

Valid Range: 0–3

Input type: `Numeric`

Valuename: "0"

File Write Through

File Write Through controls whether all files are opened in write-through mode.

Keyname: "Network\Novell\System Config\Netware DOS Requester\FILE WRITE THROUGH"

Valuename: "0"

Max Cache Size

Max Cache Size determines the largest size of the NetWare Cache. Larger values improve network file access performance but decreases the memory available for running applications or caching local drives.

Keyname: "Network\Novell\System Config\Netware DOS Requester\Max Cache Size"

Max Cache Size

Valid Range (kbytes) :0–49152

Input type: `Edittext`

Valuename: "0"

Name Cache Level

Name Cache Level specifies the type of name caching used by the client. 0 is disabled, 1 is enabled, and 2 is enabled with persistence. The larger the value, the better the performance.

Keyname: "Network\Novell\System Config\Netware DOS Requester\Name Cache Level"

Name Cache Level

Input type: `Numeric`

Valuename: "0"

Opportunistic Locking

Opportunistic Locking auto-detects opportunities to exclusively cache files. The On setting improves performance.

Keyname: "Network\Novell\System Config\Netware DOS Requester\Opportunistic Locking"

Valuename: "0"

True Commit

Set True Commit to on when processing critical data to guarantee data integrity. Setting to Off opts for performance over data integrity.

Keyname: "Network\Novell\System Config\Netware DOS Requester\True Commit"

Valuename: "0"

Novell Client → Advanced Settings → Printing

Network Printers

Network Printers sets the number of logical LPT ports the NetWare DOS requester can capture. This parameter allows you to capture and redirect LPT1 through LPT9.

Keyname: "Network\Novell\System Config\Netware DOS Requester\Network Printers"

Network Printers

Input type: `Numeric`

Valuename: "0"

Print Header

Print Header sets the size of the buffer (in bytes) that holds the information used to initialize the printer for each print job. Increase this value if you are using a complex print job, or printing to a PostScript printer.

Keyname: "Network\Novell\System Config\Netware DOS Requester\Print Header"

Print Header

Input type: `Numeric`

Valuename: "0"

Print Tail

Print Tail sets the size of the buffer (in bytes) that holds the information used to reset the printer after a print job.

Keyname: "Network\Novell\System Config\Netware DOS Requester\Print Tail"

Print Tail

Input type: `Numeric`

Valuename: "0"

Novell Client → Advanced Settings → Trouble Shooting

Alert Beep

Alert Beep specifies whether an audible beep should be sounded when a pop-up message is displayed.

Keyname: "Network\Novell\System Config\NIOS\Alert Beep"

Valuename: "0"

Handle Net Errors

Handle Net Errors determines the default method for handling critical network errors. On means INT 24 (i.e., other programs) handles network errors. Off returns NET_RECV_ERROR (i.e., the client handles the error).

Keyname: "Network\Novell\System Config\Netware DOS Requester\Handle Net Errors"

Valuename: "0"

Log File

Log File specifies the location of the LOG file used for client diagnostics (for example, *C:\Novell\Clent32\Log.txt*).

Keyname: "Network\Novell\System Config\NIOS\Log File"

Log File

Input type: `Edittext`

Valuename: "0"

Log File Size

Log File Size determines the maximum size of the LOG file used for client diagnostics.

Keyname: "Network\Novell\System Config\NIOS\Log File Size"

Log File

Valid range (bytes): 1–1048576

Input type: `Numeric`

Valuename: "0"

Message Timeout

Message Timeout defines the time in ticks before messages are cleared from the screen without user intervention. 0 means the user must clear the message manually. There are approximately 18 ticks per second.

Keyname: "Network\Novell\System Config\NetWare DOS Requester\Message Timeout"

Message Timeout

Valid range: 0–10000 ticks

Input type: `Numeric`

Valuename: "0"

Net Status Busy Timeout

Net Status Busy Timeout specifies the number of seconds to wait for a non-busy response from the server before the client displays an error message.

Keyname: "Network\Novell\System Config\Netware DOS Requester\Net Status Busy Timeout"

Net Status Busy Timeout

Valid Range (seconds): 1–600

Input type: `Numeric`

Valuename: "0"

Net Status Timeout

Net Status Timeout specifies the number of seconds to wait for a response from the network to an application"s request before the client displays an error message.

Keyname: "Network\Novell\System Config\Netware DOS Requester\Net Status Timeout"

Net Status Timeout

Valid Range (seconds): 1–600

Input type: `Numeric`

Valuename: "0"

Novell Client → Advanced Settings → WAN

LIP Start Size

Large Internet Packet Start Size determines the starting value for negotiating the large Internet packet size. Setting this value can shorten the initial negotiation time for packet size over slow links.

Keyname: "Network\Novell\System Config\Netware DOS Requester\LIP Start Size"

LIP Start Size

Valid range (bytes): 512–65535

Input type: `Edittext`

Valuename: "0"

Minimum Time to Net

On bridged WAN/satellite links with low time-to-net values, workstations may fail to make a connection under the following conditions: server is not running Packet Burst or Transfer rate is 2400 baud. Use 10000 on 2400 baud lines.

Keyname: "Network\Novell\System Config\Netware DOS Requester\Minimum Time To Net"

Minimum Time to Net

Valid range (milliseconds): 0–65535

Input type: `Edittext`

Valuename: "0"

NCP Max Timeout

NCP Max Timeout is the amount of time allowed to retry a network connection before an error message is displayed.

Keyname: "Network\Novell\System Config\Netware DOS Requester\NCP Max Timeout"

NCP Max Timeout

Valid range (seconds): 0–65535

Input type: `Edittext`

Valuename: "0"

Novell Client → Advanced Settings → Graphical Interface

Cancel Desktop Login

If set to Off, the user will have the opportunity to log in to the Windows 95/98 desktop and other network providers after canceling the Initial Client Login. If set to On, there will be no subsequent login opportunities.

Keyname: "Network\Novell\System Config\Network Provider\Initial Login"

Valuename: "Cancel Desktop Login"

Send Message

Enables/disables the send message function. This function is accessed from the context menu of the selected server in network neighborhood.

Keyname: "Network\Novell\System Config\Network Provider\Send Message"

Valuename: "Enable"

Show Edit Login Script Item

Enables/disables the Edit DS Login Script item on the User Administration menu. See the Show User Administration menu setting later in this chapter for further information on this menu.

Keyname: "Network\Novell\System Config\Network Provider\Menu Items"

Valuename: "Modify Login Script"

Show Novell System Tray Icon

Show the Novell (N) icon in the system tray on the taskbar.

Keyname: "Network\Novell\System Config\Network Provider\Menu Items"

Valuename: "Enable Systray Icon"

Show Scheduler System Tray Icon

Show the Scheduler icon in the system tray on the taskbar.

Keyname: "Network\Novell\System Config\Network Provider\Menu Items"

Valuename: "NoTrayIcon"

Show User Administration Menu

Enables/disables the menu item for User Administration. This menu item is displayed on the context menu of the selected server or tree in Network Neighborhood.

Keyname: "Network\Novell\System Config\Network Provider\Menu Items"

Valuename: "Enable User Info"

Network Client → Advanced Settings → SLP General

SLP Maximum Transmission Unit

This parameter specifies the maximum transmission unit (UDP packet size) for the link layer used. Erroneously setting this parameter either too large or too small will adversely affect the performance of SLP.

Keyname: "Network\Novell\System Config\SRVLOC\MTU"

SLP Maximum Transmission Unit

Valid Range (bytes): 576–4096

Input type: `Numeric`

Valuename: "0"

SLP Multicast Radius

This parameter is a number specifying the maximum number of subnets (number of routers plus 1) that SLP"s multicasting should traverse. A value of 1 confines multicasting to the local segments (no routers).

Keyname: "Network\Novell\System Config\SRVLOC\Multicast Radius"

SLP Multicast Radius

Valid range: 1–32

Input type: `Numeric`

Valuename: "0"

Use Broadcast for SLP Multicast

This parameter specifies that broadcasting should be used in all cases instead of IP multicasting.

Keyname: "Network\Novell\System Config\SRVLOC\Use Broadcast For Multicast"

Valuename: "0"

Use DHCP for SLP

This parameter specifies that Dynamic Host Configuration Protocol (DHCP) be used for obtaining SLP scope and Directory Agent configuration.

Keyname: "Network\Novell\System Config\SRVLOC\DHCP"

Valuename: "0"

Network Client → Advanced Settings → SLP Times

Give Up on Requests to SAS

Time in seconds to give up on requests to Service Agents.

Keyname: "Network\Novell\System Config\SRVLOC\TIME-8-QUIT-SA-Q"

Give Up on Requests to SAs

Valid Range (seconds): 1–60000

Input type: `Edittext`

Valuename: "0"

SLP Cache Replies

Time in minutes to cache replies by XID. This value is normally not changed.

Keyname: "Network\Novell\System Config\SRVLOC\TIME-0-CACHE-REPLIES"

SLP Cache Replies

Valid Range (minutes): 1–60

Input type: `Numeric`

Valuename: "0"

SLP Default Registration Lifetime

Time in seconds for the default registration lifetime of a service. Increasing the value increases network traffic to renew services more frequently.

Keyname: "Network\Novell\System Config\SRVLOC\TIME-1-REG-LIFETIME"

SLP Default Registration Lifetime

Valid Range (seconds): 60–60000

Input type: `Edittext`

Valuename: "0"

Wait Before Giving Up On DA

Time in seconds to wait before SLP gives up on requests to a Directory Agent.

Keyname: "Network\Novell\System Config\SRVLOC\TIME-6-QUIT-DA-WAIT"

Wait Before Giving Up On DA

Valid range (seconds): 1–60000

Input type: `Edittext`

Valuename: "0"

Wait Before Registering on Passive DA

Time in seconds to wait before registering services on passive Directory Agent discovery.

Keyname: "Network\Novell\System Config\SRVLOC\TIME-10-WAIT-REG-DA-PASSIVE"

Wait Before Registering on Passive DA

Valid Range (seconds): 1–60000

Input type: `Edittext`

Valuename: "0"

Novell.adm

Novell has distributed two versions of this template, one with the original Client 32 and the other with Client Version 3.1 (located in the install directory under *products\adm32\ibm_enu\policy95\nls\english*). The version specified here is Version 2.0 of the template included with Client Version 3.1. Note that this template has no user properties.

Computer Properties

Novell IPX 32-bit Protocol → IPX

IPX Retry Count

Sets the number of times the workstation should try to reach the destination. Increasing this value also increases the SPX retry count.

Keyname: "Network\Novell\System Config\Protocol IPX\IPX Retry Count"

IPX Retry Count

Valid range (seconds): 0–65535

Input type: `Edittext`

Valuename: "0"

Allow IPX access through interrupt 7AH

Allows DOS applications to use this interrupt to access IPX services.

Keyname: "Network\Novell\System Config\Protocol IPX\INT7A"

Valuename: "0"

Allow IPX access through interrupt 64H

Allows DOS applications to use this interrupt to access IPX services.

Keyname: "Network\Novell\System Config\Protocol IPX\INT64"

Valuename: "0"

IPX Diagnostics Enabled

Keyname: "Network\Novell\System Config\Protocol IPX\IPX Diagnostics"

Valuename: "0"

Pre-allocate VGNMA memory

Allocate conventional memory for VGNMA operations.

Keyname: "Network\Novell\System Config\Protocol IPX\PRE_ALLOCATE VGNMA MEMORY"

Valuename: "0"

Source Routing

For token ring environments.

Keyname: "Network\Novell\System Config\Protocol IPX\Source Routing"

Valuename: "0"

Novell IPX 32-bit Protocol → SPX

SPX Connections

Keyname: "Network\Novell\System Config\Protocol IPX\SPX Connections"

SPX Connections

Number of connections.

Input type: `Numeric`

Valuename: "0"

SPX Verify Timeout

Length of time SPX waits to send a packet to keep the session active.

Keyname: "Network\Novell\System Config\Protocol IPX\SPX Verify Timeout"

SPX Verify Timeout

Valid range (seconds): 1–65535

Input type: `Edittext`

Valuename: "0"

SPX Listen Timeout

Length of time SPX waits before requesting a packet to confirm that the connection is still valid.

Keyname: "Network\Novell\System Config\Protocol IPX\SPX Listen Timeout"

SPX Listen Timeout

Valid range (seconds): 1–65535

Input type: `Edittext`

Valuename: "0"

SPX Abort Timeout

Length of time to wait before terminating the session.

Keyname: "Network\Novell\System Config\Protocol IPX\SPX Abort Timeout"

SPX Abort Timeout

Valid range (seconds): 1–65535

Input type: `Edittext`

Valuename: "0"

Allow Connection Watchdogging

Keyname: "Network\Novell\System Config\Protocol IPX\SPX WatchDogs"

Valuename: "0"

Novell IPX 32-bit Protocol → IPX Advanced

Primary Logical Board

Primary board used by IPX.

Keyname: "Network\Novell\System Config\Protocol IPX\PRIMARY"

Primary Logical Board

Input type: `Dropdownlist`

Valuename: "0"

NetWare/IP → Parameters

Custom Configuration

Keyname: "Network\Novell\System Config\NWIP\Remote Config"

Valuename: "0"

NetWare/IP Domain Name

Input type: `Edittext`

Keyname: "Network\Novell\System Config\NWIP\NWIP DOMAIN NAME"

Valuename: "0"

Retries to DSS during startup

Retries to Domain SAP/RIP Server.

Input type: `Numeric`

Keyname: "Network\Novell\System Config\NWIP\AutoRetries"

Valuename: "0"

Number of seconds between retries

Input type: `Numeric`

Keyname: "Network\Novell\System Config\NWIP\AutoRetry Secs"

Valuename: "0"

Broadcast SAP nearest server queries to network

Input type: `Checkbox`

Keyname: "Network\Novell\System Config\NWIP\NSQ BROADCAST"

Valuename: "0"

NetWare /IP 1.1 compatibility

Found on NetWare 3.12 and 4.02 servers.

Input type: `Checkbox`

Keyname: "Network\Novell\System Config\NWIP\NWIP1_1 Compatibility"

Valuename: "0"

Verbose

Setting this policy may aid in troubleshooting.

Input type: `Checkbox`

Keyname: "Network\Novell\System Config\NWIP\Command Line"

Valuename: "0"

NetWare/IP → Servers

Nearest NetWare/IP Servers

Keyname: "Network\Novell\System Config\NWIP\Nearest NWIP Server"

Nearest NetWare IP Servers

Input type: `Listbox`

Preferred Domain SAP/RIP Servers

Keyname: "Network\Novell\System Config\NWIP\Preferred DSS"

Preferred Domain SAP/RIP Servers

Input type: `Listbox`

Novell SNMP Agent → SNMP

Enable Monitor Community

Makes the workstation a member of the read-only community, enabling it to do GET and GET NEXT operations for SNMP

Keyname: "Network\Novell\System Config\Desktop SNMP\enable monitor community"

Enable Monitor Community

Input type: `Dropdownlist`

Valuename: "0"

Monitor Community

Specifies the name of the group an SNMP management console must belong to in order to perform inventory queries on the workstation.

Keyname: "Network\Novell\System Config\Desktop SNMP\monitor community"

Monitor Community

Input type: `Edittext`

Valuename: "0"

Enable Control Community

Specifies whether a control community can access the workstation.

Keyname: "Network\Novell\System Config\Desktop SNMP\enable control community"

Enable Control Community

Input type: `Dropdownlist`

Valuename: "0"

Control Community

Name of the control community.

Keyname: "Network\Novell\System Config\Desktop SNMP\control community"

Control Community

Input type: `Edittext`

Valuename: "0"

System Name

Use the NetWare fileserver name or the IP hostname.

Keyname: "Network\Novell\System Config\Desktop SNMP\sysName"

System Name

Input type: `Edittext`

Valuename: "0"

System Location

Location description.

Keyname: "Network\Novell\System Config\Desktop SNMP\sysLocation"

System Location

Input type: `Edittext`

Valuename: "0"

System Contact

Human contact.

Keyname: "Network\Novell\System Config\Desktop SNMP\sysContact"

System Contact

Input type: `Edittext`

Valuename: "0"

Enable Authentication Traps

Sends an alert (trap) if an unauthorized person tries to use SNMP to access the computer.

Keyname: "Network\Novell\System Config\Desktop SNMP\snmpEnableAuthenTraps"

Valuename: "0"

Novell Host Resources MIB → Printers and Modems

Local Printer

Keyname: "Network\Novell\System Config\Host MIB\Printer"

Local Printers

Specifies information about local printers.

Input type: `Listbox`

Local Modems

Keyname: "Network\Novell\System Config\Host MIB\Modem"

Local Modems

Specifies information about local modems.

Input type: `Listbox`

Novell Host Resources MIB → Tape Drives

Local Tape Drives

Keyname: "Network\Novell\System Config\Host MIB\TapeDrive"

Local Tape Drives

Input type: `Listbox`

Novell Host Resources MIB → Software Search

Directory levels to search from root

Keyname: "Network\Novell\System Config\Host MIB\SWDirectorySearch-Depth"

Directory levels to search from root

Valid range: 0–4,294,967,295

Input type: `Edittext`

Valuename: "0"

Additional Search Paths

Keyname: "Network\Novell\System Config\Host MIB\SWDirectorySearch"

Additional Search Paths

Input type: `Listbox`

Novell Target Service Agent

The Target Service Agent is used to carry out tasks for SMS-compliant (Storage Management Service) backup engines like SBACKUP.

Username

Keyname: "Network\Novell\System Config\Netware TSA\UserName"

Username

Input type: `Edittext`

Valuename: "0"

Password

Keyname: "Network\Novell\System Config\Netware TSA\Password"

Password

Input type: `Edittext`

Valuename: "0"

Protocol

Keyname: "Network\Novell\System Config\Netware TSA\PrefProtocol"

Protocol

Input type: `Dropdownlist`

Valuename: "0"

Server Name

Keyname: "Network\Novell\System Config\Netware TSA\ServerName"

Server name

Input type: `Edittext`

Valuename: "0"

Auto Register on Reboot

Keyname: "Network\Novell\System Config\Netware TSA\AutoRegister"

Valuename: "0"

Show TSA Icon on Taskbar

Keyname: "Network\Novell\System Config\Netware TSA\TaskBarIcon"

Valuename: "0"

Include Drives

Drives A: through G: can be included

Keyname: "Network\Novell\System Config\Netware TSA\IncludeDrives"

Drive A:

Input type: `Checkbox`

Valuename: "Drive A"

Drive B:

Input type: `Checkbox`

Valuename: "Drive B"

Drive C:

Input type: `Checkbox`

Valuename: "Drive C"

Drive D:

Input type: `Checkbox`

Valuename: "Drive D"

Drive E:

Input type: `Checkbox`

Valuename: "Drive E"

Drive F:

Input type: `Checkbox`

Valuename: "Drive F"

Drive G:

Input type: `Checkbox`

Valuename: "Drive G"

Novell Workstation Manager

Enable Workstation Manager

Keyname: "Software\Novell\Workstation Manager"

Valuename: "Enabled"

NDS Refresh Rate

Valid Range (seconds): 1–60000

Input type: `Numeric`

Valuename: "NDS Refresh Rate"

File/Folder Shell Extensions

Keyname: "Network\Novell\System Config\Shell Extensions"

Show NetWare Rights property page

Valuename: "Rights"

Allow Users to add/remove/change Trustees

Valuename: "Trustees"

Allow Users to change Extended Properties

Valuename: "Properties"

Allow Users to change Compression

Overridden by "Allow users to change Extended Properties"

Valuename: "Compression"

Nwnt.adm

The template listed here is Version 1.5 included with Service Pack 1 of the Windows NT Novell Client Version 4.6. Note that this template has no user properties.

Computer Properties

Novell NetWare Client for Windows NT → Client

Preferred server

Preferred NetWare server used to authenticate the user. Setting this causes the client to automatically attempt to create a connection to the server.

Keyname: "System\CurrentControlSet\Services\NetWareWorkstation\Parameters"

Server name

Input type: `Edittext`

Valuename: "Preferred Server"

Preferred Tree

The directory tree the client connects to at logon.

Keyname: "System\CurrentControlSet\Services\NetWareWorkstation\Parameters"

Tree name

Input type: `Edittext`

Valuename: "Preferred Tree"

First Network Drive

The first available drive letter for network drives.

Keyname: "Software\Novell\Parameters"

First Network Drive

Input type: `Dropdownlist`

Valuename: "First Network Drive"

Novell NetWare Client for Windows NT → Client → Tree and Name Context List

Tree and Name Context List

This forces contextless logon to use a specific context for each tree in the list.

Keyname: "System\CurrentControlSet\Services\NetWareWorkstation\Parameters\Trees"

Tree and Name Context List

To add a tree/context pair, click on "Show" and then on "Add". Enter the tree name as the valuename and the context as the value.

Input type: `Listbox`

Novell NetWare Client for Windows NT → Default Login

Enable or disable the display of certain options in the logon dialog box.

Display Connection Page

Keyname: "Software\Novell\Graphical Login"

Valuename: "Connection Tab"

Login to tree

Input type: `Checkbox`

Valuename: "Tree Login"

Login to Server

Input type: `Checkbox`

Valuename: "Server Login"

Bindery connection

Input type: `Checkbox`

Valuename: “Bindery Connections”

Clear Current Connections

Input type: `Checkbox`

Valuename: “Clear Connections”

Display Script Page

Keyname: “Software\Novell\Graphical Login”

Valuename: “Script Tab”

Script

Input type: `Edittext`

Valuename: “Script”

Profile

Input type: `Edittext`

Valuename: “Profile”

Display Script Results Window

Input type: `Checkbox`

Valuename: “Display Results”

Close Script Results Automatically

Input type: `Checkbox`

Valuename: “Close Results”

Run login scripts

Input type: `Checkbox`

Valuename: “Login Script”

Display Variables Page

Keyname: “Software\Novell\Graphical Login”

Valuename: “Script Variable Tab”

%2 through %5

Four variable scripts can be displayed from %2 through %5.

Input type: `Edittext`

Keyname: “Software\Novell\Graphical Login\Variables\2” through “Software\Novell\Graphical Login\Variables\5”

Valuename: “”

Save Settings on Login Exit

Keyname: “Software\Novell\Graphical Login”

Valuename: “Save On Exit”

Novell NetWare Client for Windows NT → Contextless Login

This policy option is available only when connecting to NetWare 5 servers.

Enable

Contextless login allows the user to log on without specifying an NDS context.

Keyname: "Software\Novell\Graphical Login\NWLGE\Z XContext"

Valuename: "RunContext"

Wildcard Searching Allowed

Wildcards can be used within the username.

Input type: `Checkbox`

Valuename: "AllowWild"

Search Timeout (sec)

Maximum amounts of time to search the NDS for the user. Increase the value if timeout errors occur.

Input type: `Numeric`

Valuename: "SearchTimeout"

Novell NetWare Client for Windows NT → Advanced Login

Disable Default Policy Support

This path on the authenticating server is searched for the policy file (*ntconfig.pol*).

Keyname: "Software\Novell\NWGINA\Policy Support"

Policy Path and Filename

Input type: `Edittext`

Valuename: "Policy Path"

Welcome Screen Bitmap

Keyname: "Software\Novell\NWGINA\Welcome Screen"

Bitmap Filename in the local workstation NT directory

Input type: `Edittext`

Valuename: "Bitmap"

Welcome Screen Caption

Keyname: "Software\Novell\NWGINA\Welcome Screen"

Welcome Screen Caption

Input type: `Edittext`

Valuename: "Header Message"

Novell NetWare Client for Windows NT → Advanced Login → Show On Login

Keyname: "Software\Novell\Login"

Location List

The location list shows recent places where the user has logged in.

Valuename: "Location"

Advanced Button

The Advanced Button displays if this policy is checked.

Valuename: "Advanced"

Variables Button

The Variable Button displays if this policy is checked.

Valuename: "Variables"

Clear Connections

This checkbox displays if this policy is checked.

Valuename: "Clear Connections"

Workstation Only

This checkbox displays if this policy is checked.

Valuename: "Workstation Only"

Novell NetWare Client for Windows NT → Default Capture → Output Settings

These policies set print options.

Keyname: "Software\Novell\Network Provider\Capture Flags"

Number of copies

Number of copies

Input type: `Numeric`

Valuename: "Number of Copies"

Form Feed

Valuename: "Form Feed"

Enable tabs

Valuename: "Enable Tabs"

Number of spaces

Input type: `Numeric`

Valuename: "Number of Spaces"

Novell NetWare Client for Windows NT → Default Capture → Banner Settings

Enable banner

A banner page prints out before the print job, and can be used to identify the owner of the print job.

Keyname: "Software\Novell\Network Provider\Capture Flags"

Valuename: "Enable Banner"

1st banner name

Input type: `Edittext`

Valuename: "1st Banner Name"

2nd banner name

Input type: `Edittext`

Valuename: "2nd Banner Name"

Novell NetWare Client for Windows NT → Default Capture → Other Settings

These policies set additional print options.

Keyname: "Software\Novell\Network Provider\Capture Flags"

Hold

Print jobs are put on hold

Valuename: "Hold"

Keep

The print job is kept in the print queue after printing

Valuename: "Keep"

Notify

User is notified when print job is completed

Valuename: "Notify"

Novell NetWare Client for Windows NT → Advanced Settings → Environment, NETX Compatibility

DOS Name

DOS Name is the operating system name used by the *%OS* parameter.

Keyname: "System\CurrentControlSet\Services\NetWareWorkstation\Parameters"

DOS Name

Input type: `Edittext`

Valuename: "DOS Name"

Long Machine Type

Long Machine Type is the workstation type used by the *%MACHINE* parameter.

Keyname: "System\CurrentControlSet\Services\NetWareWorkstation\Parameters"

Long Machine Type

Input type: `Edittext`

Valuename: "Long Machine Type"

Receive Broadcast Message

The Receive Broadcast Message parameter sets the incoming messages a workstation can receive. If set to "All," the station will receive all messages; "Server Only" accepts server messages; and "None" restricts all incoming messages.

Keyname: "Software\Novell\Broadcast"

Receive broadcast Message

Input type: `Dropdownlist`

Valuename: "MODE"

Set Station Time

If set to On, the workstation"s time and date are synchronized with the server that it attaches to initially. The default is on.

Keyname: "Network\Novell\System Config\NWGINA\Login Screen"

Set Station Time

Input type: `Dropdownlist`

Valuename: "Synchronize Time"

Short Machine Type

Short Machine Type determines what overlay file is used when accessing older NetWare utilities.

Keyname: "System\CurrentControlSet\Services\NetWareWorkstation\Parameters"

Short Machine Type

Input type: `Edittext`

Valuename: "Short Machine Type"

Novell NetWare Client for Windows NT → Advanced Settings → Connection

Keyname: "System\CurrentControlSet\Services\NetWareWorkstation\Parameters"

Auto Reconnect

Set this parameter to On if you want to automatically reconnect when a network connection is unexpectedly lost. The default is on.

Auto Reconnect

Input type: `Dropdownlist`

Valuename: "Reconnect Level"

Replica Timeout

Replica Timeout

Timeout to the server containing the replica of system objects.

Input type: `Numeric`

Valuename: "ReplicaTimeout"

Novell NetWare Client for Windows NT → Advanced Settings → File System

DOS Long Name Support

Keyname: "System\CurrentControlSet\Services\NetWareWorkstation\Parameters"

DOS Long Name Support

Long filename support.

Input type: `Dropdownlist`

Valuename: "DosAppLongNameSupport"

Novell NetWare Client for Windows NT → Advanced Settings → Name Resolution

Limit SAP Broadcast Queries

This setting limits the use of SAP to locate servers when connections are present where the bindery can be queried. Setting to Off allows the use of SAP to locate servers if the bindery query fails.

Keyname: "Software\Novell\NetWareWorkstation\Policies\Network\IPX\Address Resolution Providers\LimitSAP"

Limit SAP Broadcast Queries

Input type: `Dropdownlist`

Valuename: "Level"

Name Resolution Timeout

This is the time in seconds the client will wait for the configured namespace providers to resolve the specified name to an address.

Keyname: "Software\\Novell\NetWareWorkstation\Policies\Network"

Name Resolution Timeout

Valid range: 1–180, default is 10

Input type: `Numeric`

Valuename: "Timeout in seconds"

Novell NetWare Client for Windows NT → Advanced Settings → Graphical Interface

Keyname: "Software\Novell\Network Provider\Menu Items"

Send Message

Keyname: "Software\Novell\Network Provider\Send Message"

Send Message

Right-clicking the taskbar icon can bring up the Send Message window.

Input type: `Dropdownlist`

Valuename: "Enable"

Show Edit Login Script Item

Show Edit Login Script Item

Input type: `Dropdownlist`

Valuename: "Modify Login Script"

Show Novell System Tray Icon

Show Novell System Tray Icon

Input type: `Dropdownlist`

Valuename: "Enable Systray Icon"

Show Scheduler System Tray Icon

Show Scheduler System Tray Icon

This incorrectly reads "Send Message".

Input type: `Dropdownlist`

Valuename: "Enable Scheduler Icon"

Show User Administration Menu

Show User Administration Menu

This incorrectly reads "Send Message".

Input type: `Dropdownlist`

Valuename: "Enable User Info"

Novell NetWare Client for Windows NT → Advanced Settings → SLP General

Keyname: "SYSTEM\CurrentControlSet\Services\SRVLOC\Parameters"

SLP Active Discovery

This parameter specifies that SLP is to dynamically discover services (use multicast or broadcast if a Discovery Agent is not available.

SLP Active Discovery

Input type: `Dropdownlist`

Valuename: "Active Discovery"

SLP Maximum Transmission Unit

This parameter specifies the maximum transmission unit (UDP packet size in bytes) for the link layer used. Setting this parameter to either too small or too large a value will adversely affect the performance of SLP.

SLP Maximum Transmission Unit

Input type: `Numeric`

Valuename: "MTU"

SLP Multicast Radius

This specifies the maximum number of subnets (number of routers plus 1) that SLPs multicasting should traverse. A value of 1 confines multicasting to the local segments (no routers).

SLP Multicast Radius

Valid Range: 1–32, default is 32

Input type: `Numeric`

Valuename: "Multicast Radius"

SLP Use Broadcast for Multicast

This specifies that broadcasting should be used instead of IP multicasting.

SLP Use Broadcast for Multicast

Input type: `Dropdownlist`

Valuename: "Use Broadcast For Multicas"

Use DHCP for SLP

This specifies that DHCP be used for obtaining SLP scope and Directory Agent configuration.

Use DHCP for SLP

Input type: `Dropdownlist`

Valuename: "DHCP"

Novell NetWare Client for Windows NT → Advanced Settings → SLP Times

Keyname: "SYSTEM\CurrentControlSet\Services\srvloc\Parameters"

Give Up On Requests to SAs

Time to give up on requests to Service Agents.

Give Up On Requests to SAs

Valid Range (seconds): 1–60000, default is 15

Input type: `Edittext`

Valuename: "TIME-8-QUIT-SA-Q"

Quit Idle Connects

Time for Directory Agents and Service Agents to close idle TCP connections.

Quit Idle Connects

Valid Range (minutes): 1–60000, default is 15

Input type: `Edittext`

Valuename: "TIME-12-QUIT-IDLE-CONNECTS"

SLP Cache Replies

Time to cache replies by XID. This value is not normally changed.

SLP Cache Replies

Valid Range (minutes): 1–60, default is 1

Input type: `Numeric`

Valuename: "TIME-0-CACHE-REPLIES"

SLP Default Registration Lifetime

Time for the default registration lifetime of a service. Increasing the value increases network traffic to renew services more frequently.

SLP Default Registration Lifetime

Valid Range (seconds): 60–60000, default is 10,800

Input type: `Edittext`

Valuename: "TIME-1-REG-LIFETIME"

Wait Before Giving Up On DA

Time to wait before giving up on requests to a Directory Agent.

Wait Before Giving Up On DA

Valid Range (seconds): 1–60000, default is 5

Input type: `Numeric`

Valuename: "TIME-6-QUIT-DA-WAIT"

Wait Before Registering On Passive DAs

Time to wait before registering services on passive Directory Agent discovery.

Wait Before Registering On Passive DAs

Valid Range (seconds): 1–60000, default is 2

Input type: `Edittext`

Valuename: "TIME-10-WAIT-REG-DA-PASSIVE"

Novell NetWare Client for Windows NT → Advanced Settings → Cache Performance

Opportunistic Locking

Opportunistic Locking auto-detects opportunities to exclusively cache files. Seting to On improves performance.

Keyname: "System\CurrentControlSet\Services\NetWareWorkstation\Parameters"

Opportunistic Locking

Input type: `Dropdownlist`

Valuename: "Opportunistic Locking"

Novell NetWare Client for Windows NT → Advanced Settings → Packet Management

Keyname: "System\CurrentControlSet\Services\NetWareWorkstation\Parameters"

Link Support Layer Max Buffer Size

Link Support Layer Buffer Size specifies the maximum supported packet size. Use this parameter to optimize performance for media (primarily token ring) that can use packets that are larger than the default size.

Link Support Layer Max Buffer Size

Input type: `Numeric`

Valuename: "Max Buffer Size"

Burst Mode

Burst Mode specifies whether Packet Burst is used. Off disables Packet Burst. On enables Packet Burst, which reduces overall network traffic and improves performance.

Burst Mode

Input type: `Dropdownlist`

Valuename: "Burst Mode"

Max Read Burst Size

Max Read Burst Size sets the maximum number of bytes per Read Burst. The read window size changes dynamically depending on network conditions.

Max Read Burst Size

Input type: `Numeric`

Valuename: "Max Read Burst Size"

Max Write Burst Size

Max Write Burst Size sets the maximum number of bytes per Write Burst. The write window size changes dynamically depending on network conditions.

Max Write Burst Size

Input type: `Numeric`

Valuename: "Max Write Burst Size"

Signature Level

Signature Level determines the level of enhanced security support. Increasing this value increases security, but decreases performance.

Signature Level

Input type: `Numeric`

Valuename: "Signature Level"

Novell NetWare Client For Windows NT → Advanced Settings → WAN

Keyname: "System\CurrentControlSet\Services\NetWareWorkstation\Parameters"

Large Internet Packets

When Large Internet Packets is on, it uses the maximum packet size negotiated between the NetWare server and the workstation, even across routers and bridges.

Large Internet Packets

Input type: `Dropdownlist`

Valuename: "Large Internet Packets"

Large Internet Packet Start Size

Large Internet Packet Start Size determines the starting value for negotiating the large Internet packet size. Setting this value can shorten the initial negotiation time for packet size over slow links.

Large Internet Packet Start Size

Input type: `Numeric`

Valuename: "LIP Start Size"

Minimum Time to Net

On bridged WAN/Satellite links with low time-to-net values, workstations may fail to make a connection under the following conditions: server is not running Packet Burst or Transfer rate is 2400 baud. Use 10000 on 2400 baud lines.

Minimum Time to Net

Input type: `Numeric`

Valuename: "Minimum Time To Net"

Novel NetWare/IP → Parameters

Custom Configuration

Keyname: "System\CurrentControlSet\Services\NetWareIP\Parameters"

Valuename: "Remote Config"

NetWare/IP Domain Name

Input type: `Edittext`

Valuename: "NWIP Domain Name"

Retries to DSS (Domain SAP/RIP Server) during startup

Input type: `Numeric`

Valuename: "Auto Retries"

Number of Seconds between retries

Input type: `Numeric`

Valuename: "AutoRetry Secs"

Broadcast SAP nearest server queries to network

Input type: `Checkbox`

Valuename: "NSQ Broadcast"

NetWare/IP 1.1 compatibility

Found on NetWare 3.12 and 4.02 servers.

Input type: `Checkbox`

Valuename: "NWIP1_1 Compatiblity"

Novell NetWare/IP → Servers

Nearest NetWare/IP Servers

Keyname: "System\CurrentControlSet\Services\NetWareIP\Parameters\Nearest NWIP Server"

Nearest NetWare/IP Servers

Input type: `Listbox`

Preferred Domain SAP/RIP Servers

Keyname: "System\CurrentControlSet\Services\NetWareIP\Parameters\Preferred DSS"

Preferred Domain SAP/RIP Servers

Input type: `Listbox`

Novell IPX Compatibility Adapter

Settings for native IP with IPX compatibility in NetWare 5.

Server Resolution Time Range

Keyname: "System\CurrentControlSet\Services\NWCMD\Parameters"

Server Resolution Time Range

Input type: `Numeric`

Valuename: "SlpTimeoutforRequester"

IPX Compatibility Scope

Keyname: "System\CurrentControlSet\Services\NWCMD\Parameters\Advertise_Scopes"

IPX Compatibility Scope

Input type: `Edittext`

Valuename: "0"

Workstation Manager

Workstation Manager

Workstation manager settings.

Keyname: "Software\Novell\Workstation Manager"

Valuename: "Enabled"

Tree

Input type: `Edittext`

Keyname: "Software\Novell\Workstation Manager\Identification"

Valuename: "Tree"

NDS Refresh Rate

Input type: `Numeric`

Keyname: "Software\Novell\Workstation Manager\Scheduler"

Valuename: "NDS Refresh Rate"

Enable Volatile User Caching

Allows volatile user account information to be retained for X number of days.

Input type: `Checkbox`

Keyname: "Software\Novell\Workstation Manager"

Valuename: "Volatile Cache Enable"

Days to Cache Volatile Users

Consider using non-volatile accounts if you need to set this value to a very high number.

Input type: `Numeric`

Keyname: "Software\Novell\Workstation Manager"

Valuename: "Volatile Cache Aging"

Zero Administration Kit Templates

These templates are from various Windows Zero Administration Kits (ZAK). Included in this section are the following templates:

Zak95.adm and *Zak98.adm*
: These templates contain a policy to set a custom shell for the Windows 95 and Windows 98 ZAK.

ZakWinNT.adm
: This template contains policies for the Windows NT4 ZAK. It has various policies including options to set custom folder locations, Internet Explorer security options, drive restrictions, and choose a program to load at startup.

Zak95.adm and Zak98.adm

These templates are included with the Windows 95 and Windows 98 Zero Administration Kits. They are combined here since the two templates are identical. Note that these templates have no computer properties.

User Properties

Zero-Administration Settings

Custom shell

Keyname: "Software\Microsoft\Windows\CurrentVersion\Policies\ZeroAdmin"

Shell name

A custom user interface, other than the default shell *explorer.exe*, may be set.

Input type: `Edittext`

Valuename: "Shell"

ZakwinNT.adm

This template is included with the Microsoft Zero Administration Kit for Windows NT4 server. Note that this template has no computer properties.

User Properties

ZAK Policies → Windows NT → User Profiles through System Policies

Keyname: "Software\Microsoft\Windows\CurrentVersion\Explorer\User Shell Folders"

AppData Folder

Enter Path to AppData folder

Input type: `Edittext`

Valuename: "AppData"

Favorites Folder

Enter Path to Favorites folder

Input type: `Edittext`

Valuename: "Favorites"

NetHood Folder

Enter Path to NetHood folder

Input type: `Edittext`

Valuename: "NetHood"

PrintHood Folder

Enter Path to PrintHood folder

Input type: `Edittext`

Valuename: "PrintHood"

Recent Folder

Enter Path to Recent folder

Input type: `Edittext`

Valuename: "Recent"

SendTo Folder

Enter Path to SendTo folder

Input type: `Edittext`

Valuename: "SendTo"

ZAK Policies → Windows NT → Internet Explorer Security

Configure the settings in IE defined under Active Content in the Security tab of the View → Options menu.

Keyname: "Software\Microsoft\Windows\CurrentVersion\Internet Settings"

Active Content

Allow downloading of ActiveX content

Input type: Checkbox

Valuename: "Code Download"

Enable ActiveX Controls and Plug-ins

Input type: Checkbox

Valuename: "Security_RunActiveXControls"

Run ActiveX Scripts

Input type: Checkbox

Valuename: "Security_RunScripts"

Enable Java Programs

Input type: Checkbox

Valuename: "Security_RunJavaApplets"

Active Content Security Level

Configures the safety-level settings in IE in the security tab in the View → Options menu.

Keyname: "Software\Microsoft\Internet Explorer\Security"

Select Security Level

If "No Security" is selected, Active Content will be downloaded without prompting the user.

Input type: Dropdownlist

Valuename: "Safety Warning Level"

Actionlist Keyname: "Software\Microsoft\Windows\CurrentVersion\Internet Settings"

Actionlist Valuename: "Trust Warning Level"

ZAK Policies → Windows NT → Drives → Restrictions

Show only selected drives

Keyname: "Software\Microsoft\Windows\CurrentVersion\Policies\Explorer"

Choose Drives that will be shown:

This policy conflicts with the Shell → Restrictions → Hide Drives policy defined in *common.adm*, *admin.adm* and *windows.adm*.

Input type: Dropdownlist

Valuename: "NoDrives"

ZAK Policies → Windows

Load

Keyname: "Software\Microsoft\Windows NT\CurrentVersion\Windows"

Enter Program to be run on Startup

Input type: `Edittext`

Valuename: "Load"

Internet Explorer Templates

These templates allow extensive customization of Internet Explorer 4 (IE4) and Internet Explorer 5 (IE5). Included in this section are the following templates:

Axaa.adm
: This template allows you to assign administrator-approved control, allowing only approved ActiveX controls and plug-ins to be executed by users.

Chat.adm
: This template contains policies for Microsoft Chat features and functions.

Conf.adm
: This template sets policies to control user and computer access privileges for NetMeeting.

Inetcorp.adm
: This template sets policies for Internet Explorer corporate settings.

Inetres.adm
: This template contains policies for restricting access to IE5 settings options.

Inetresm.adm
: This template contains policies for restricting access to IE4 settings options.

Inetset.adm
: This template sets policies for IE5 advanced settings.

Inetsetm.adm
: This template sets policies for IE4 advanced settings.

Ieak.adm
: This template sets policies for IE3.

Oe.adm
: This template sets a policy for the Microsoft Identity Manager, allowing multiple identities to be disabled. Multiple identities are identities created within a single user profile. It is used for Internet Explorer 5 applications such as Outlook Express, MSN Messenger Service and the Windows Address Book.

Oem.adm

This template sets policies for Outlook Express.

Subs.adm

This template sets restrictions on offline pages (IE4), allowing control over the amount of information downloaded. These settings are useful if server load is a concern.

Subsm.adm

This template sets similar policies to the *subs.adm* template, however, for IE5 rather than IE4.

Wmp.adm

This template contains policies to set and restrict the Windows Media Player and Radio toolbar.

Axaa.adm

This template is included with IEAK5, IEAK5.1 and Windows 98. See *http://www.microsoft.com/TechNet/IE/reskit/ie5/part1/ch07zone.asp* for more information. Note that this template has no computer properties.

User Properties

Administrator approved controls

Keyname: "Software\Policies\Microsoft\Windows\CurrentVersion\Internet Settings\AllowedControls"

Administrator Approved Controls

The user will be able to run only those Active-X controls and plug-ins that are checked.

PopupMenu Object

Input type: `Checkbox`

Valuename: "{7823A620-9DD9-11CF-A662-00AA00C066D2}"

Ikonic Menu Control

Input type: `Checkbox`

Valuename: "{F5131C24-E56D-11CF-B78A-444553540000}"

CarPoint Auto-Pricer Control

Input type: `Checkbox`

Valuename: "{DED22F57-FEE2-11D0-953B-00C04FD9152D}"

MSN Investor Chart Control

Input type: `Checkbox`

Valuename: "{9276B91A-E780-11D2-8A8D-00C04FA31D93}"

MSN Investor Ticker

Input type: `Checkbox`

Valuename: "{52ADE293-85E8-11D2-BB22-00104B0EA281}"

Microsoft Survey Control

Input type: `Checkbox`

Valuename: "{BD1F006E-174F-11D2-95C0-00C04F9A8CFA}"

Shockwave Flash

Input type: `Checkbox`

Valuename: "{D27CDB6E-AE6D-11CF-96B8-444553540000}"

NetShow File Transfer Control

Input type: `Checkbox`

Valuename: "{26F24A93-1DA2-11D0-A334-00AA004A5FC5}"

MCSI Menu Control

Input type: `Checkbox`

Valuename: "{275E2FE0-7486-11D0-89D6-00A0C90C9B67}"

MSNBC News Control

Input type: `Checkbox`

Valuename: "{2FF18E10-DE11-11D1-8161-00A0C90DD90C}"

DHTML Edit Control

Input type: `Checkbox`

Valuename: "{2D360201-FFF5-11D1-8D03-00A0C959BC0A}"

Microsoft Agent Control

Input type: `Checkbox`

Valuename: "{D45FD31B-5C6E-11D1-9EC1-00C04FD7081F}"

ActiveMovie Control

Input type: `Checkbox`

Valuename: "{05589FA1-C356-11CE-BF01-00AA0055595A}"

Windows Media Player

Input type: `Checkbox`

Valuename: "{22D6F312-B0F6-11D0-94AB-0080C74C7E95}"

Microsoft Scriptlet Component

Input type: `Checkbox`

Valuename: "{AE24FDAE-03C6-11D1-8B76-0080C744F389}"

Chat.adm

This template is included with IEAK5 as well as Windows 98. These templates are identical except for the first policy "Add to chat server list," which is not found in the Windows 98 version of this template. Although this template is included in IEAK5.1, it is an empty file. Note that this template has no computer properties.

User Properties

Microsoft Chat

Keyname: "Software\Microsoft\Microsoft Comic Chat"

Add to chat server list

Not found in the Windows 98 version of the template.

Additional server list

Input type: `Edittext`

Valuename: "PrepopulatedServers"

Change default chat server

Default chat server

Input type: `Edittext`

Valuename: "IRCServer"

Change default chat room

Default chat room

Input type: `Edittext`

Valuename: "IRCChannel"

Change default character

Default character

Input type: `Edittext`

Valuename: "Character"

Change default backdrop bitmap

Default backdrop

Input type: `Edittext`

Valuename: "Backdrop"

Change user"s profile for Microsoft Chat

User profile string

Input type: `Edittext`

Valuename: "Profile"

Turn on option to show only registered rooms in room list

Show only registered rooms in room list

Input type: `Checkbox`

Valuename: "ListRegistered"

Conf.adm

This template sets policies for Microsoft NetMeeting. The template for NetMeeting 2.x is included with IEAK5, the NetMeeting Resource Kit and Windows 98.

Conf.adm is also included with IEAK5.1, but since it sets policies for NetMeeting 3.x, it differs somewhat from the other version of this template. If a particular policy is present or absent from the *conf.adm* version found in IEAK5.1, this is noted in the policy comments section.

User Properties

NetMeeting Settings

Keyname: "Software\Microsoft\Conferencing\Policies"

Restrict the use of file transfer

Valuename: "RestrictFileTransfer"

Prevent the user from sending files

Prevents the user from sending files to other NetMeeting participants.

Input type: `Checkbox`

Valuename: "NoSendingFiles"

Prevent the user from receiving files.

Prevents the user from receiving files from other NetMeeting participants.

Input type: `Checkbox`

Valuename: "NoReceivingFiles"

Limit the maximum size of sent files (in k)

This policy is available only in the IEAK5.1 template.

Input type: `Numeric`

Valuename: "MaxFileSendSize"

Restrict the use of application sharing

This policy allows various restrictions on application sharing to be set.

Valuename: "RestrictAppSharing"

Disable all application sharing features

The option Share Application in the Tools menu is disabled, as is the Share Application button.

Input type: `Checkbox`

Valuename: "NoAppSharing"

Prevent users from sharing the clipboard

Clipboard contents cannot be shared. This policy is not found in the IEAK5.1 template.

Input type: `Checkbox`

Valuename: "NoSharedClip"

Prevent users from sharing anything

This policy is available only in the IEAK5.1 template.

Input type: `Checkbox`

Valuename: "NoSharing"

Prevent users from sharing the desktop

This policy is available only in the IEAK5.1 template.

Input type: `Checkbox`

Valuename: "NoSharingDesktop"

Prevent users from allowing others to control

This policy is available only in the IEAK5.1 template.

Input type: `Checkbox`

Valuename: "NoAllowControl"

Prevent users from sharing in true color

This policy is available only in the IEAK5.1 template.

Input type: `Checkbox`

Valuename: "NoTrueColorSharing"

Prevent users from sharing MS-DOS windows

The option "Prevent the user from sharing Explorer windows" must also be enabled for this restriction to be active.

Input type: `Checkbox`

Valuename: "NoSharingDosWindows"

Prevent users from sharing Explorer windows

Microsoft Explorer windows cannot be shared.

Input type: `Checkbox`

Valuename: "NoSharingExplorer"

Prevent users from collaborating

Collaboration is prevented during application sharing. This policy is not found in the IEAK5.1 template.

Input type: `Checkbox`

Valuename: "WorkAloneOnly"

Restrict the use of the options dialog

This policy allows specific tabs in the Options dialog box to be removed, preventing the user from making unwanted changes. The Options dialog box is found under the Tools menu.

Valuename: "OptionsDialogRestricted"

Disable the "General" options page

Input type: `Checkbox`

Valuename: "NoGeneralPage"

Disable the "My Information" options page

This policy is not found in the IEAK5.1 template.

Input type: `Checkbox`

Valuename: "NoMyInformationPage"

Disable the "Calling" options page

This policy is not found in the IEAK5.1 template.

Input type: `Checkbox`

Valuename: "NoSDDirPage"

Disable the "Advanced Calling" button

This policy is available only in the IEAK5.1 template.

Input type: `Checkbox`

Valuename: "NoAdvancedCalling"

Disable the "Security" options page

This policy is available only in the IEAK5.1 template.

Input type: `Checkbox`

Valuename: "NoSecurityPage"

Disable the "Audio" options page

Input type: `Checkbox`

Valuename: "NoAudioPage"

Disable the "Video" options page

Input type: `Checkbox`

Valuename: "NoVideoPage"

Disable the "Protocols" options page

This policy is not found in the IEAK5.1 template.

Input type: `Checkbox`

Valuename: "NoProtocolsPage"

Prevent the user from answering calls

Enabling this option prevents the user from being notified of incoming calls. This policy is not found in the IEAK5.1 template.

Prevent the user from answering calls

Input type: `Checkbox`

Valuename: "NoAnswering"

Prevent the user from using audio features

If this policy is enabled, you may want to disable the "Audio" options page.

Prevent the user from using audio features

Input type: `Checkbox`

Valuename: "NoAudio"

Prevent users from using Full Duplex audio

This policy is available only in the IEAK5.1 template.

Input type: `Checkbox`

Valuename: "NoFullDuplex"

Enable DirectSound

This policy is available only in the IEAK5.1 template.

Input type: `Checkbox`

Keyname: "Software\Microsoft\Conferencing\Audio control"

Valuename: "Direct Sound"

Prevent users from changing DirectSound usage

This policy is available only in the IEAK5.1 template.

Input type: `Checkbox`

Valuename: "NoChangeDirectSound"

Mute speaker by default

This policy is available only in the IEAK5.1 template.

Input type: `Checkbox`

Keyname: "Software\Microsoft\Conferencing\Audio Control"

Valuename: "SpeakerMute"

Mute microphone by default

This policy is available only in the IEAK5.1 template.

Input type: `Checkbox`

Keyname: "Software\Microsoft\Conferencing\Audio Control"

Valuename: "RecordMute"

Restrict the use of video

If this policy is enabled, you may want to disable the "Video" options page.

Valuename: "RestrictVideo"

Prevent the user from sending video

Input type: `Checkbox`

Valuename: "NoSendingVideo"

Prevent the user from receiving video

Input type: `Checkbox`

Valuename: "NoReceivingVideo"

Prevent the user from using directory services

The user is prevented from accessing server utilities, such as logging on/off or viewing directories.

Prevent users from using directory services

If you enable this policy, you may also want to disable the "Calling" options page, which prevents the user from changing directory features.

Input type: `Checkbox`

Valuename: "NoDirectoryServices"

Prevent users from adding new directory servers

This policy is available only in the IEAK5.1 template.

Input type: `Checkbox`

Valuename: "NoAddingDirectoryServers"

Prevent users from viewing the web directory

This policy is available only in the IEAK5.1 template.

Input type: `Checkbox`

Valuename: "NoWebDirectory"

Set the default Directory Server

This policy sets the default Internet Location Server (ILS) that the user logs onto when starting NetMeeting.

Directory Server

Input type: `Edittext`

Keyname: "Software\Microsoft\User Location Service\Client"

Valuename: "Server Name"

Set Exchange Server Property for NetMeeting Address

See Microsoft Exchange Server documentation for more information on these attributes. This policy is not found in the IEAK5.1 template.

Keyname: "Software\Microsoft\Conferencing\Policies"

Exchange Server Property

Input type: `Dropdownlist`

Valuename: "NetMeeting Address Property"

Preset User Information Category

This policy is not found in the IEAK5.1 template.

Keyname: "Software\Microsoft\Conferencing\Policies"

Note: only applicable for silent installs

Available categories are personal, business or adult.

Input type: `Dropdownlist`

Valuename: "RestrictedULS"

Set the NetMeeting home page

This is the web page that is accessed when the option Product News is chosen from the Help menu. This policy is available under computer properties in the IEAK5.1 template.

Keyname: "Software\Microsoft\Conferencing"

NetMeeting Home Page URL

Input type: `Edittext`

Valuename: "NetMeeting Home Page"

Set limit for audio/video throughput

Set this policy if you are concerned about excessive bandwidth use. This policy is not found in the IEAK5.1 template.

Keyname: "Software\Microsoft\Conferencing\QoS\Resources\1"

Average audio/video throughput limit (in bps):

Input type: `Edittext`

Valuename: "MaxUnits"

Set Security Options

This policy is available only in the IEAK5.1 template.

Set the security for calls

Input type: `Dropdownlist`

Valuename: "CallSecurity"

Set Calling Options

This policy is available only in the IEAK5.1 template.

Set the default calling mode

Input type: `Dropdownlist`

Keyname: "Software\Microsoft\Conferencing"

Valuename: "CallingMethod"

Prevent users from changing the calling mode

Input type: `Checkbox`

Valuename: "NoChangingCallMode"

Prevent users from automatically accepting incoming calls

Input type: `Checkbox`

Valuename: "NoAutoAcceptCalls"

Network Connection Speed

Input type: `Dropdownlist`

Keyname: "Software\Microsoft\Conferencing\Audio Control"

Valuename: "Typical Bandwidth"

Set Gatekeeper Options

This policy is only available in the IEAK5.1 template.

Keyname: "Software\Microsoft\Conferencing"

Default gatekeeper server

Input type: `Edittext`

Valuename: "Gatekeeper"

Set default gatekeeper addressing

Input type: `Dropdownlist`

Valuename: "GateKeeperAddressing"

Disable Chat

This policy is available only in the IEAK5.1 template.

Disable Chat

Input type: `Checkbox`

Valuename: "NoChat"

Disable NetMeeting 2.x Whiteboard

This policy is available only in the IEAK5.1 template.

Disable NetMeeting 2.x Whiteboard

Input type: `Checkbox`

Valuename: "NoOldWhiteBoard"

Disable Whiteboard

This policy is available only in the IEAK5.1 template.

Disable Whiteboard

Input type: `Checkbox`

Valuename: "NoNewWhiteBoard"

Configure Intranet support options

This policy is available only in the IEAK5.1 template.

NetMeeting Intranet Support Web URL

Input type: `Edittext`

Valuename: "IntranetSupportURL"

Show the Intranet Support page the first time NetMeeting starts

Input type: `Checkbox`

Valuename: "ShowFirstTimeURL"

Disable Manual Codec Configuration

This policy is available only in the IEAK5.1 template.

Disable Manual Codec Configuration

Input type: `Checkbox`

Valuename: "NoAdvancedAudio"

Computer Properties

Net Meeting Protocols

Specify the NetMeeting home page

This computer policy is available only in the IEAK5.1 template. However, the same policy exists in the user properties for other template versions.

URL

Input type: `Edittext`

Keyname: "Software\Microsoft\Conferencing"

Valuename: "NetMeeting Home Page"

NetMeeting Protocols

This policy is not found in the IEAK5.1 template.

Disable TCP/IP

Input type: `Checkbox`

Keyname: "Software\Microsoft\Conferencing\Transports\TCPIP"

Valuename: "Disabled"

Disable null modem

Input type: `Checkbox`

Keyname: "Software\Microsoft\Conferencing\Transports\DIRCB"

Valuename: "Disabled"

Restrict the use of audio

This policy is available only in the IEAK5.1 template.

Create an audio log file

Input type: `Checkbox`

Keyname: "Software\Microsoft\Conferencing\debug"

Valuename: "retaillog"

Specify limit for audio/video throughout

This policy is available only in the IEAK5.1 template.

Average audio/video throughput limit (in k):

Input type: `Numeric`

Keyname: "Software\Microsoft\Conferencing"

Valuename: "MaximumBandwidth"

Restrict the use of Remote Desktop Sharing

This policy is available only in the IEAK5.1 template.

Disable Remote Desktop Sharing on all platforms

Input type: `Checkbox`

Keyname: "Software\Microsoft\Conferencing"

Valuename: "NoRDS"

Disable Remote Desktop Sharing on Windows 9x

Input type: `Checkbox`

Keyname: "Software\Microsoft\Conferencing"

Valuename: "NoRDSWin9x"

Ieak.adm

This template is included with the Windows NT4 ZAK, and the original Internet Explorer Administration Kit (for IE3). It is compatible with both Windows NT4 and Windows 9x workstations.

User Properties

Set the value for your proxy servers

Should the proxy be enabled?

Sets values for your proxies separated by semicolons.

Keyname: "Software\Microsoft\Windows\CurrentVersion\Internet Settings"

Valuename: "ProxyEnable"

Format: <URL>:<Port number>

Input type: `Edittext`

Valuename: "ProxyServer"

For which values should the proxy be overridden?

Input type: `Edittext`

Valuename: "ProxyOverride"

Online support for Internet Explorer

Set the URL for the online support materials

Keyname: "Software\Microsoft\Internet Explorer\Help_Menu_URLs"

Enter the URL for the online support materials

Input type: `Edittext`

Valuename: "Online_Support"

Definition of Home and Search pages

Change the Start or Search pages?

Keyname: "Software\Microsoft\Internet Explorer\Main"

Enter the URL for the home page

Input type: `Edittext`

Valuename: "Start Page"

Enter the URL for the search page

Input type: `Edittext`

Valuename: "Search Page"

Internet Explorer user interface restrictions

Keyname: "Software\Microsoft\Internet Explorer\RestrictUI"

Disable controls for temporary Internet files

Valuename: "Cache"

Disable all checkboxes at the bottom of the Advanced tab
Valuename: “Other”

Disable all controls in the Cryptography Protocols dialog box.
Valuename: “Crypto”

Disable all controls in the Warnings group box
Valuename: “Warnings”

Disable all controls in the Mail and News group box
Valuename: “MailNews”

Disable all controls in the Viewers group box
Valuename: “FileTypes”

Disable the checkbox for controlling default browser
Valuename: “Default”

Disable all controls in the Dialing group box
Valuename: “Dialing”

Disable all controls in the Proxy Server group box
Valuename: “Proxy”

Disable all controls in the Customize group box
Valuename: “Places”

Disable all controls in the History group box
Valuename: “History”

Disable all controls in the Properties dialog box (launched from the Fonts Settings dialog box)
Valuename: “Fonts”

Disable Set Default and checkbox controls in the Font Settings Dialog Box
Valuename: “Internationl”

Disable all controls in the Multimedia group box
Valuename: “Multimedia”

Disable all controls in the Toolbar group box
Valuename: “Toolbar”

Disable all controls in the Colors group box
Valuename: “Colors”

Disable all controls in the Links group box
Valuename: “Links”

Disable all controls in the Ratings group box
Valuename: “Ratings”

Disable all controls in the Active controls group box
Valuename: "ActiveX"

Disable just the Allow Downloading Of Active Content Checkbox
Input type: `Checkbox`

Valuename: "ActiveDownload"

Disable only the Enable ActiveX Controls_Plugins checkbox
Input type: `Checkbox`

Valuename: "ActiveControls"

Disable only the Run ActiveX Scripts checkbox
Input type: `Checkbox`

Valuename: "ActiveScript"

Disable only the Enable Java Programs checkbox
Input type: `Checkbox`

Valuename: "ActiveJava"

Disable all controls in the Safety Level dialog box
Input type: `Checkbox`

Valuename: "ActiveSafety"

Disable all controls in the Certificates group box
Valuename: "Certif"

Disable only the Personal button in the Certificates group box
Input type: `Checkbox`

Valuename: "CertifPers"

Disable only the Site button in the Certificates group box
Input type: `Checkbox`

Valuename: "CertifSite"

Disable only the Publishers button in the Certificates group box
Input type: `Checkbox`

Valuename: "CertifPub"

Computer Properties

Customize the text in the title bar

Set text on the Internet Explorer titlebar
Keyname: "Software\Microsoft\Internet Explorer\Main"

Enter the text to be displayed on the title bar
Input type: `Edittext`

Valuename: "Window Title"

Inetcorp.adm

This policy template is included with IEAK5 and IEAK5.1. The two versions differ somewhat, as indicated in the appropriate policy comments section.

User Properties

Dial-Up Settings

Dial-up Settings

In IEAK5.1 this policy was instead included in the *inetres.adm* template.

Keyname: "Software\Microsoft\Windows\CurrentVersion\Internet Settings"

Use Automatic Discovery for Dial-Up connections

Input type: `Checkbox`

Valuename: "DialupAutodetect"

Language Settings

Language Settings

This will be effective only if the appropriate language pack has been installed. In IEAK5.1 this policy was instead included in the *inetres.adm* template.

Keyname: "Software\Microsoft\Internet Explorer\International"

Default language for menus and dialogs

Input type: `Dropdownlist`

Valuename: "ResourceLocale"

Temporary Internet Files (User)

Temporary Internet Files (User)

Keyname: "Software\Microsoft\Windows\CurrentVersion\Internet Settings"

Check for newer versions of stored pages

Input type: `Dropdownlist`

Valuename: "SyncMode5"

Temporary Internet Files (User)

Keyname: "Software\Microsoft\Windows\CurrentVersion\Internet Settings\5.0\Cache\Content"

Set amount of disk space to use (in kilobytes)

Input type: `Numeric`

Valuename: "CacheLimit"

Auto-Proxy Caching

In IEAK5.1 this policy was instead included in the *inetres.adm* template.

Keyname: "Software\Microsoft\Windows\CurrentVersion\Internet Settings"

Disable caching of Auto-Proxy scripts

Input type: `Checkbox`

Valuename: "EnableAutoProxyResultCache"

Computer Properties

Temporary Internet Files (Machine)

Temporary Internet Files (Machine)

Keyname: "Software\Microsoft\Windows\CurrentVersion\Internet Settings\5.0\Cache\Content"

Set amount of disk space to use (in kilobytes)

Input type: `Numeric`

Valuename: "CacheLimit"

User Profiles

Keyname: "Software\Microsoft\Windows\CurrentVersion\Internet Settings\Cache"

Disable Roaming Cache

Input type: `Checkbox`

Valuename: "UserProfiles"

Actionlist Keyname: "Software\Microsoft\Windows\CurrentVersion\Internet Settings\5.0\Cache\Content"

Actionlist Valuename: "PerUserItem"

User Proxy Settings

In IEAK5.1, this policy was instead included in the *inetres.adm* template.

Keyname: "Software\Microsoft\Windows\CurrentVersion\Internet Settings"

Make proxy settings per-machine (rather than per-user)

Input type: `Checkbox`

Valuename: "ProxySettingsPerUser"

Code Download

Code Download

When IE navigates to a page that requires an ActiveX control or Java code not previously installed on the workstation, selected URLs are searched for the required items. A custom URL can be specified containing code common to an organization. For additional details, see the Internet Component Download documentation in the Internet Client SDK.

Keyname: "Software\Microsoft\Windows\CurrentVersion\Internet Settings"

Path

An example download path is: *CODEBASE;<http://activex.microsoft.com/objects/ocget.dll>*

Input type: `Edittext`

Valuename: "CodeBaseSearchPath"

Related Sites and Errors

Related Sites

This policy is not included in the IEAK5.1 template.

Keyname: "Software\Microsoft\Internet Explorer\Extensions\{c95fe080-8f5d-11d2-a20b-00aa003c157a}"

Disable the Show Related Links menu item and browser toolbar button

Comment

Input type: `Checkbox`

Valuename: "clsid"

Suppress the following errors

This user policy was instead included as a computer policy in the IEAK5.1 *inetres.adm* template. This same key and its values can be placed in HKCU to suppress these HTTP errors on a per-user rather than a workstation basis.

Keyname: "Software\Microsoft\Internet Explorer\Main\ErrorThresholds"

400

Bad Request

Input type: `Checkbox`

Valuename: "400"

403

Forbidden

Input type: `Checkbox`

Valuename: "403"

404

Not Found

Input type: Checkbox

Valuename: "404"

405

Method Not Allowed

Input type: Checkbox

Valuename: "405"

406

Not Acceptable

Input type: Checkbox

Valuename: "406"

408

Request Time-out

Input type: Checkbox

Valuename: "408"

409

Conflict

Input type: Checkbox

Valuename: "409"

410

Gone

Input type: Checkbox

Valuename: "410"

500

Internal Server Error

Input type: Checkbox

Valuename: "500"

501

Not Implemented

Input type: Checkbox

Valuename: "501"

505

HTTP version not supported

Input type: `Checkbox`

Valuename: "505"

Office File Types

Select the file types that should not browse in the same window

These user policies were instead included as computer policies in the IEAK5.1 *inetres.adm* template.

Excel Sheet 8

Input type: `Checkbox`

Keyname: "Software\Classes\Excel.Sheet.8"

Valuename: "BrowserFlags"

PowerPoint Show 8

Input type: `Checkbox`

Keyname: "Software\Classes\PowerPoint.Show.8"

Valuename: "BrowserFlags"

Excel Chart 8

Input type: `Checkbox`

Keyname: "Software\Classes\Excel.Chart.8"

Valuename: "BrowserFlags"

Word Document 8

Input type: `Checkbox`

Keyname: "Software\Classes\Word.Document.8"

Valuename: "BrowserFlags"

Inetres.adm

This template is included with the Windows 98 ZAK, IEAK5 and IEAK5.1. The versions differ somewhat, as indicated in the policy comments section.

User Properties

Internet Property Pages

These pages are found under the Tools → Options menu. Check these policies to prevent the user from making changes to the IE setup.

Internet Property Pages

Keyname: "Software\Policies\Microsoft\Internet Explorer\Control Panel"

Disable viewing the General Page

Input type: `Checkbox`

Valuename: "GeneralTab"

Disable viewing the Security Page

Input type: `Checkbox`

Valuename: "SecurityTab"

Disable viewing the Content Page

Input type: `Checkbox`

Valuename: "ContentTab"

Disable viewing the Connections Page

Input type: `Checkbox`

Valuename: "ConnectionsTab"

Disable viewing the Programs Page

Input type: `Checkbox`

Valuename: "ProgramsTab"

Disable viewing the Advanced Page

Input type: `Checkbox`

Valuename: "AdvancedTab"

Disable changing any settings on the Advanced Page

Input type: `Checkbox`

Valuename: "Advanced"

General Page

Keyname: "Software\Policies\Microsoft\Internet Explorer\Control Panel"

Disable changing home page settings

Input type: `Checkbox`

Valuename: "HomePage"

Disable changing Temporary Internet files settings

Input type: `Checkbox`

Valuename: "Cache"

Disable changing history settings

Input type: `Checkbox`

Valuename: "History"

Disable changing color settings

Input type: `Checkbox`

Valuename: "Colors"

Disable changing link color settings

Input type: Checkbox

Valuename: "Links"

Disable changing font settings

Input type: Checkbox

Valuename: "Fonts"

Disable changing language settings

Input type: Checkbox

Valuename: "Languages"

Disable changing accessibility settings

Input type: Checkbox

Valuename: "Accessibility"

Connections Page

Keyname: "Software\Policies\Microsoft\Internet Explorer\Control Panel"

Disable Internet Connection Wizard

Input type: Checkbox

Valuename: "Connwiz Admin Lock"

Disable changing connection settings

Input type: Checkbox

Valuename: "Connection Settings"

Disable changing proxy settings

Input type: Checkbox

Valuename: "Proxy"

Disable changing Automatic Configuration settings

Input type: Checkbox

Valuename: "Autoconfig"

Content Page

Keyname: "Software\Policies\Microsoft\Internet Explorer\Control Panel"

Disable changing ratings settings

Input type: Checkbox

Valuename: "Ratings"

Disable changing certificate settings

Input type: `Checkbox`

Valuename: "Certificates"

Disable changing Profile Assistant settings

Input type: `Checkbox`

Valuename: "Profiles"

Disable AutoComplete for forms and saving of submitted strings

Input type: `Checkbox`

Valuename: "FormSuggest"

Do not allow users to save passwords in AutoComplete for forms

Input type: `Checkbox`

Valuename: "FormSuggest Passwords"

Programs Page

Keyname: "Software\Policies\Microsoft\Internet Explorer\Control Panel"

Disable changing Messaging settings

Input type: `Checkbox`

Valuename: "Messaging"

Disable changing Calendar and Contact settings

Input type: `Checkbox`

Valuename: "CalendarContact"

Disable the Reset Web Settings feature

Input type: `Checkbox`

Valuename: "ResetWebSettings"

Disable Changing checking if Internet Explorer is the default browser

Input type: `Checkbox`

Valuename: "Check_If_Default"

Browser Menus

Keyname: "Software\Policies\Microsoft\Internet Explorer\Restrictions"

File Menu

Disable Save As . . . menu option

Save and Save As are disabled.

Input type: `Checkbox`

Valuename: "NoBrowserSaveAs"

Disable new menu option

In addition, Ctrl-N is disabled.

Input type: `Checkbox`

Valuename: "NoFileNew"

Disable Open menu option

In addition, Ctrl-O and Ctrl-L are disabled.

Input type: `Checkbox`

Valuename: "NoFileOpen"

Disable Save As Web Page Complete format

Input type: `Checkbox`

Keyname: "Software\Policies\Microsoft\Internet Explorer\Infodelivery\Restrictions"

Valuename: "NoBrowserSaveWebComplete"

Disable closing of the browser

This policy is useful if you use IE as an alternate shell program. In addition, Alt-F4 is disabled.

Input type: `Checkbox`

Valuename: "NoBrowserClose"

View Menu

Disable Source menu option

Input type: `Checkbox`

Valuename: "NoViewSource"

Disable Fullscreen menu option

In addition, F11 is disabled.

Input type: `Checkbox`

Valuename: "NoTheaterMode"

Favorite Menus

Hide Favorites Menu

Adding or organizing favorites is disabled.

Input type: `Checkbox`

Valuename: "NoFavorites"

Tools Menu

Disable Internet Options...menu option

The changing of browser settings is disabled.

Input type: `Checkbox`

Valuename: "NoBrowserOptions"

Help menu

Keyname: "Software\Policies\Microsoft\Internet Explorer"

Remove "Tip of the Day" menu option

Input type: **Checkbox**

Valuename: "remove tip of the day"

Remove "For Netscape Users" menu option

Input type: **Checkbox**

Valuename: "remove netscape help"

Remove "Tour" menu option

Input type: **Checkbox**

Valuename: "remove tutorial"

Remove "Send Feedback" menu option

Input type: **Checkbox**

Valuename: "remove feedback"

Context Menu [right click]

Disable Context Menu

The right click context menu is disabled

Input type: **Checkbox**

Valuename: "NoBrowserContextMenu"

Disable Open in New Window menu option

Input type: **Checkbox**

Valuename: "NoOpeninNewWnd"

File Download Dialog

Disable Save this program to disk option

This policy prevents the user from being able to choose a download directory by not displaying the Save As dialog box.

Input type: **Checkbox**

Valuename: "NoSelectDownloadDir"

Toolbars

Toolbar Restrictions

Keyname: "Software\Microsoft\Windows\CurrentVersion\Policies\Explorer"

Disable customizing browser toolbar buttons

Input type: **Checkbox**

Valuename: "NoToolbarCustomize"

Disable customizing browser toolbars

Input type: `Checkbox`

Valuename: "NoBandCustomize"

Default Toolbar Buttons

These policies are only included here in the IEAK5.1 template. In other versions they are included in the *inetset.adm* template.

Keyname: "Software\Microsoft\Windows\CurrentVersion\Policies\Explorer"

Show small icons

Input type: `Checkbox`

Keyname: "Software\Microsoft\Windows\CurrentVersion\Explorer\SmallIcons"

Valuename: "SmallIcons"

Back button

Button can be turned off or on.

Input type: `Dropdownlist`

Valuename: "Btn_Back"

Actionlist Valuename: "SpecifyDefaultButtons"

Forward button

Button can be turned off or on.

Input type: `Dropdownlist`

Valuename: "Btn_Forward"

Actionlist Valuename: "SpecifyDefaultButtons"

Stop button

Button can be turned off or on.

Input type: `Dropdownlist`

Valuename: "Btn_Stop"

Actionlist Valuename: "SpecifyDefaultButtons"

Refresh button

Button can be turned off or on.

Input type: `Dropdownlist`

Valuename: "Btn_Refresh"

Actionlist Valuename: "SpecifyDefaultButtons"

Home button

Button can be turned off or on.

Input type: `Dropdownlist`

Valuename: "Btn_Home"

Actionlist Valuename: "SpecifyDefaultButtons"

Search button

Button can be turned off or on.

Input type: `Dropdownlist`

Valuename: "Btn_Search"

Actionlist Valuename: "SpecifyDefaultButtons"

History button

Button can be turned off or on.

Input type: `Dropdownlist`

Valuename: "Btn_History"

Actionlist Valuename: "SpecifyDefaultButtons"

Favorites button

Button can be turned off or on.

Input type: `Dropdownlist`

Valuename: "Btn_Favorites"

Actionlist Valuename: "SpecifyDefaultButtons"

Folders button

Button can be turned off or on.

Input type: `Dropdownlist`

Valuename: "Btn_Folders"

Actionlist Valuename: "SpecifyDefaultButtons"

Fullscreen button

Button can be turned off or on.

Input type: `Dropdownlist`

Valuename: "Btn_Fullscreen"

Actionlist Valuename: "SpecifyDefaultButtons"

Tools button

Button can be turned off or on.

Input type: `Dropdownlist`

Valuename: "Btn_Tools"

Actionlist Valuename: "SpecifyDefaultButtons"

Mail button

Button can be turned off or on.

Input type: `Dropdownlist`

Valuename: "Btn_MailNews"

Actionlist Valuename: "SpecifyDefaultButtons"

Font size button

Button can be turned off or on.

Input type: `Dropdownlist`

Valuename: "Btn_Size"

Actionlist Valuename: "SpecifyDefaultButtons"

Print button

Button can be turned off or on.

Input type: `Dropdownlist`

Valuename: "Btn_Print"

Actionlist Valuename: "SpecifyDefaultButtons"

Edit button

Button can be turned off or on.

Input type: `Dropdownlist`

Valuename: "Btn_Edit"

Actionlist Valuename: "SpecifyDefaultButtons"

Discussions button

Button can be turned off or on.

Input type: `Dropdownlist`

Valuename: "Btn_Discussions"

Actionlist Valuename: "SpecifyDefaultButtons"

Cut button

Button can be turned off or on.

Input type: `Dropdownlist`

Valuename: "Btn_Cut"

Actionlist Valuename: "SpecifyDefaultButtons"

Copy button

Button can be turned off or on.

Input type: `Dropdownlist`

Valuename: "Btn_Copy"

Actionlist Valuename: "SpecifyDefaultButtons"

Paste button

Button can be turned off or on.

Input type: `Dropdownlist`

Valuename: "Btn_Paste"

Actionlist Valuename: "SpecifyDefaultButtons"

Encoding button

Button can be turned off or on.

Input type: `Dropdownlist`

Valuename: "Btn_Encoding"

Actionlist Valuename: "SpecifyDefaultButtons"

Favorites and Search

Favorites Import/Export

Keyname: "Software\Policies\Microsoft\Internet Explorer"

Disable importing and exporting of favorites

Input type: `Checkbox`

Valuename: "DisableImportExportFavorites"

Search

Keyname: "Software\Policies\Microsoft\Internet Explorer\Infodelivery\Restrictions"

Disable Search Customization

Input type: `Checkbox`

Valuename: "NoSearchCustomization"

Disable Find Files via F3 within the browser

Input type: `Checkbox`

Keyname: "Software\Policies\Microsoft\Internet Explorer\Restrictions"

Valuename: "NoFindFiles"

Persistence

Persistence is the ability of Web information to be saved on the client during current and future Internet sessions, consequently increasing performance.

Keyname: "Software\Policies\Microsoft\Internet Explorer\Persistence"

File Size Limits for Local Machine Zone

Per Domain[in kilobytes]

Input type: `Numeric`

Keyname: "Software\Policies\Microsoft\Internet Explorer\Persistence\0"

Valuename: "DomainLimit"

Per Document [in kilobytes]

Input type: `Numeric`

Keyname: "Software\Policies\Microsoft\Internet Explorer\Persistence\0"

Valuename: "DocumentLimit"

File Size Limits for Intranet Zone

Per Domain [in kilobytes]

Input type: `Numeric`

Keyname: "Software\Policies\Microsoft\Internet Explorer\Persistence\1"

Valuename: "DomainLimit"

Per Document [in kilobytes]

Input type: `Numeric`

Keyname: "Software\Policies\Microsoft\Internet Explorer\Persistence\1"

Valuename: "DocumentLimit"

File Size Limits for Trusted Sites Zone

Per Domain [in kilobytes]

Input type: `Numeric`

Keyname: "Software\Policies\Microsoft\Internet Explorer\Persistence\2"

Valuename: "DomainLimit"

Per Document [in kilobytes]

Input type: `Numeric`

Keyname: "Software\Policies\Microsoft\Internet Explorer\Persistence\2"

Valuename: "DocumentLimit"

File Size Limits for Internet Zone

Per Domain [in kilobytes]

Input type: `Numeric`

Keyname: "Software\Policies\Microsoft\Internet Explorer\Persistence\3"

Valuename: "DomainLimit"

Per Document [in kilobytes]

Input type: `Numeric`

Keyname: "Software\Policies\Microsoft\Internet Explorer\Persistence\3"

Valuename: "DocumentLimit"

File Size Limits for Restricted Sites Zone

Per Domain [in kilobytes]

Input type: `Numeric`

Keyname: "Software\Policies\Microsoft\Internet Explorer\Persistence\4"

Valuename: "DomainLimit"

Per document [in kilobytes]

Input type: `Numeric`

Keyname: "Software\Policies\Microsoft\Internet Explorer\Persistence\4"

Valuename: "DocumentLimit"

Dial-Up Settings

This policy is only included here in the IEAK5.1 template. In other versions it is included in the *inetcorp.adm* template.

Use Automatic Discovery for Dial-Up connections

Input type: `Checkbox`

Keyname: "Software\Microsoft\Windows\CurrentVersion\Internet Settings"

Valuename: "DialupAutodetect"

Language Settings

This policy is only included here in the IEAK5.1 template. In other versions it is included in the *inetcorp.adm* template.

Default language for menus and dialogs

Input type: `Dropdownlist`

Keyname: "Software\Microsoft\Internet Explorer\International"

Valuename: "ResourceLocale"

Temporary Internet Files (User)

Auto-Proxy Caching

This policy is only included here in the IEAK5.1 template. In other versions it is included in the *inetcorp.adm* template.

Disable caching of Auto-Proxy scripts

Input type: `Checkbox`

Keyname: "Software\Microsoft\Windows\CurrentVersion\Internet Settings"

Valuename: "EnableAutoProxyResultCache"

Advanced Settings

Browsing

This policy is only included here in the IEAK5.1 template. In other versions it is included in the *inetset.adm* template.

Launch browser in full screen mode

Input type: `Checkbox`

Keyname: "Software\Microsoft\Internet Explorer\Main"

Valuename: "FullScreen"

Computer Properties

Security Page

This page is found under the Tools → Options menu. Check these policies to prevent the user from making changes to the setup.

Keyname: "Software\Policies\Microsoft\Windows\CurrentVersion\Internet Settings"

Security Page

Use only *machine settings for security zones*

Input type: `Checkbox`

Valuename: "Security_HKLM_only"

Do not allow users to change policies for any security zone

Input type: `Checkbox`

Valuename: "Security_options_edit"

Do not allow users to add/delete sites from a security zone

Input type: `Checkbox`

Valuename: "Security_zones_map_edit"

Trusted Publishers

This policy is not included with the IEAK5.1 template.

Keyname: "Software\Policies\Microsoft\Internet Explorer\Infodelivery\Restrictions"

Only allow controls from Trusted Publishers

Input type: `Checkbox`

Valuename: "TrustedPublisherLockdown"

Software Updates

Keyname: "Software\Policies\Microsoft\Internet Explorer\Infodelivery\Restrictions"

Automatic Install

Disable Automatic Install of Internet Explorer components

Input type: Checkbox

Valuename: "NoJITSetup"

Periodic Update Check

Disable Periodic Check for Internet Explorer software updates and bug fixes

Input type: Checkbox

Valuename: "NoUpdateCheck"

Microsoft Logo5 Software Update Channel Notifications

Keyname: "Software\Microsoft\Windows\CurrentVersion\Policies\Explorer"

Disable software update shell notifications on program launch

Input type: Checkbox

Valuename: "NoMSAppLogo5ChannelNotify"

Startup Restrictions

Startup Restrictions

Keyname: "Software\Policies\Microsoft\Internet Explorer\Infodelivery\Restrictions"

Disable showing the splash screen

Input type: Checkbox

Valuename: "NoSplash"

Maintenance Mode Settings

Maintenance Mode Settings

This policy is not included with the IEAK5.1 template.

Keyname: "Software\Policies\Microsoft\Internet Explorer\Main"

Disable adding Internet Explorer Components via Add/Remove Programs

Input type: Checkbox

Valuename: "Add Component Option"

Disable uninstalling Internet Explorer 5 and Internet tools

Input type: Checkbox

Valuename: "Uninstall Option"

Disable the Internet Explorer 5 Repair utility

Input type: `Checkbox`

Valuename: "Repair IE Option"

Toolbars

Toolbar Restrictions

This policy is included with only the IEAK5.1 template as a computer policy. In other versions it is only a user policy.

Keyname: "Software\Microsoft\Windows\CurrentVersion\Policies\Explorer"

Disable customizing browser toolbar buttons

Input type: `Checkbox`

Valuename: "NoToolbarCustomize"

Disable customizing browser toolbars

Input type: `Checkbox`

Valuename: "NoBandCustomize"

Temporary Internet Files (Machine)

User Proxy Settings

This policy is only included here in the IEAK5.1 template. In other versions, it is included in the *inetcorp.adm* template.

Make proxy settings per-machine (rather than per-user)

Input type: `Checkbox`

Keyname: "Software\Microsoft\Windows\CurrentVersion\Internet Settings"

Valuename: "ProxySettingsPerUser"

Related Sites and Errors

Suppress the following errors

This policy is included with only the IEAK5.1 template as a computer policy. In other versions, it is only a user policy.

Keyname: "Software\Microsoft\Internet Explorer\Main\ErrorThresholds"

400

Bad Request

Input type: `Checkbox`

Valuename: "400"

403

Forbidden

Input type: `Checkbox`

Valuename: "403"

404

Not Found

Input type: `Checkbox`

Valuename: "404"

405

Method Not Allowed

Input type: `Checkbox`

Valuename: "405"

406

Not Acceptable

Input type: `Checkbox`

Valuename: "406"

408

Request Time-out

Input type: `Checkbox`

Valuename: "408"

409

Conflict

Input type: `Checkbox`

Valuename: "409"

410

Gone

Input type: `Checkbox`

Valuename: "410"

500

Internal Server Error

Input type: `Checkbox`

Valuename: "500"

501

Not Implemented

Input type: `Checkbox`

Valuename: "501"

505

HTTP version not supported

Input type: `Checkbox`

Valuename: "505"

Office File Types

Select the file types that should not browse in the same window

This policy is only included here with the IEAK5.1 template. In other versions it is included in the *inetcorp.adm* template.

Excel Sheet 8

Input type: `Checkbox`

Keyname: "Software\Classes\Excel.Sheet.8"

Valuename: "BrowserFlags"

PowerPoint Show 8

Input type: `Checkbox`

Keyname: "Software\Classes\PowerPoint.Show.8"

Valuename: "BrowserFlags"

Excel Chart 8

Input type: `Checkbox`

Keyname: "Software\Classes\Excel.Chart.8"

Valuename: "BrowserFlags"

Word Document 8

Input type: `Checkbox`

Keyname: "Software\Classes\Word.Document.8"

Valuename: "BrowserFlags"

Inetresm.adm

This template is included with the Windows 98 CD-ROM and is optimized for IE4.

User Properties

General Page

General Page

Keyname: "Software\Policies\Microsoft\Internet Explorer\Control Panel"

Disable changing home page settings

Input type: `Checkbox`

Valuename: "HomePage"

Disable changing cache settings

Input type: `Checkbox`

Valuename: "Cache"

Disable changing history settings

Input type: `Checkbox`

Valuename: "History"

Disable changing color settings

Input type: `Checkbox`

Valuename: "Colors"

Disable changing link color settings

Input type: `Checkbox`

Valuename: "Links"

Disable changing font settings

Input type: `Checkbox`

Valuename: "Fonts"

Disable changing language settings

Input type: `Checkbox`

Valuename: "Languages"

Disable changing accessibility settings

Input type: `Checkbox`

Valuename: "Accessibility"

Content Page

Keyname: "Software\Policies\Microsoft\Internet Explorer\Control Panel"

Disable changing ratings settings

Input type: `Checkbox`

Valuename: "Ratings"

Disable changing certificate settings

Input type: `Checkbox`

Valuename: "Certificates"

Disable changing Profile Assistant settings

Input type: `Checkbox`

Valuename: "Profiles"

Disable changing Microsoft Wallet settings

Input type: `Checkbox`

Valuename: "Wallet"

Connections Page

Keyname: "Software\Policies\Microsoft\Internet Explorer\Control Panel"

Disable Internet Connection Wizard

Input type: `Checkbox`

Valuename: "Connection Wizard"

Disable changing connection settings

Input type: `Checkbox`

Valuename: "Connection Settings"

Disable changing proxy settings

Input type: `Checkbox`

Valuename: "Proxy"

Disable changing Automatic Configuration settings

Input type: `Checkbox`

Valuename: "Autoconfig"

Programs Page

Keyname: "Software\Policies\Microsoft\Internet Explorer\Control Panel"

Disable changing Messaging settings

Input type: `Checkbox`

Valuename: "Messaging"

Disable changing Calendar and Contact settings

Input type: `Checkbox`

Valuename: "CalendarContact"

Disable Changing checking if Internet Explorer is the default browser

Input type: `Checkbox`

Valuename: "Check_If_Default"

Advanced

Keyname: "Software\Policies\Microsoft\Internet Explorer\Control Panel"

Disable changing settings on Advanced Tab

Input type: `Checkbox`

Valuename: "Advanced"

Channels Settings

Keyname: "Software\Policies\Microsoft\Internet Explorer\Infodelivery\Restrictions"

Disables Channel UI (user interface)

Input type: `Checkbox`

Valuename: "NoChannelUI"

Disables adding and subscribing to channels

Input type: `Checkbox`

Valuename: "NoAddingChannels"

Disables editing channel properties and channel subscriptions

Input type: `Checkbox`

Valuename: "NoEditingChannels"

Disables removing channels and subscriptions to channels

Input type: `Checkbox`

Valuename: "NoRemovingChannels"

Disables adding site subscriptions

Input type: `Checkbox`

Valuename: "NoAddingSubscriptions"

Disables editing site subscriptions

Input type: `Checkbox`

Valuename: "NoEditingSubscriptions"

Disables removing site subscriptions

Input type: `Checkbox`

Valuename: "NoRemovingSubscriptions"

Disables channel logging

Input type: `Checkbox`

Valuename: "NoChannelLogging"

Disables Update Now and Update All for channels and subscriptions

Input type: `Checkbox`

Valuename: "NoManualUpdates"

Disables all scheduled channel and site subscriptions

Input type: `Checkbox`

Valuename: "NoScheduledUpdates"

Disables unattended dialing by subscriptions

Input type: **Checkbox**

Valuename: "NoUnattendedDialing"

Disables password caching for channel and site subscriptions

Input type: **Checkbox**

Valuename: "NoSubscriptionPasswords"

Disables downloading of channel subscription content-change notification will still work

Input type: **Checkbox**

Valuename: "NoChannelContent"

Disables downloading of site subscription content-change notification will still work

Input type: **Checkbox**

Valuename: "NoSubscriptionContent"

Disables editing and creating of schedule groups

Input type: **Checkbox**

Valuename: "NoEditingScheduleGroups"

Computer Properties

Security Page

Keyname: "Software\Policies\Microsoft\Windows\CurrentVersion\Internet Settings"

Security Page

Use only *machine settings for security zones*

Input type: **Checkbox**

Valuename: "Security_HKLM_only"

Do not allow users to change policies for any security zone

Input type: **Checkbox**

Valuename: "Security_options_edit"

Do not allow users to add/delete sites from a security zone

Input type: **Checkbox**

Valuename: "Security_zones_map_edit"

Code Download

Keyname: "Software\Microsoft\Windows\CurrentVersion\Internet Settings"

Path

Input type: `Edittext`

Valuename: “CodeBaseSearchPath”

Inetset.adm

This policy template is included with IEAK5 and IEAK5.1. The two versions differ somewhat, as indicated in the appropriate policy comments section.

User Properties

AutoComplete

Keyname: “Software\Microsoft\Internet Explorer\Main”

AutoComplete Settings

Fills in web addresses, usernames and passwords automatically

Use inline AutoComplete for Web addresses

Input type: `Checkbox`

Keyname: “Software\Microsoft\Windows\CurrentVersion\Explorer\AutoComplete”

Valuename: “Append Completion”

Use inline AutoComplete in Windows Explorer

Input type: `Checkbox`

Keyname: “Software\Microsoft\Windows\CurrentVersion\Explorer\AutoComplete”

Valuename: “Use AutoComplete”

Use AutoComplete for Web addresses

Input type: `Checkbox`

Keyname: “Software\Microsoft\Windows\CurrentVersion\Explorer\AutoComplete”

Valuename: “AutoSuggest”

Use AutoComplete for forms

Input type: `Checkbox`

Valuename: “Use FormSuggest”

Use AutoComplete for usernames and passwords on forms

Input type: `Checkbox`

Valuename: “FormSuggest Passwords”

Prompt to save passwords

Input type: `Checkbox`

Valuename: "FormSuggest PW Ask"

Toolbars

Default Toolbar Buttons

Most buttons can be set to appear in the toolbar (checked) or not (unchecked). In IEAK5.1, this policy was instead included in the *inetres.adm* template.

Keyname: "Software\Microsoft\Windows\CurrentVersion\Policies\Explorer"

Show small icons

Input type: `Checkbox`

Keyname: "Software\Microsoft\Windows\CurrentVersion\Explorer\SmallIcons"

Valuename: "SmallIcons"

Back button

Input type: `Dropdownlist`

Valuename: "Btn_Back"

Actionlist Valuename: "SpecifyDefaultButtons"

Forward button

Input type: `Dropdownlist`

Valuename: "Btn_Forward"

Actionlist Valuename: "SpecifyDefaultButtons"

Stop button

Input type: `Dropdownlist`

Valuename: "Btn_Stop"

Actionlist Valuename: "SpecifyDefaultButtons"

Refresh button

Input type: `Dropdownlist`

Valuename: "Btn_Refresh"

Actionlist Valuename: "SpecifyDefaultButtons"

Home button

Input type: `Dropdownlist`

Valuename: "Btn_Home"

Actionlist Valuename: "SpecifyDefaultButtons"

Search button

Input type: `Dropdownlist`

Valuename: "Btn_Search"

Actionlist Valuename: "SpecifyDefaultButtons"

History button

Input type: `Dropdownlist`

Valuename: "Btn_History"

Actionlist Valuename: "SpecifyDefaultButtons"

Favorites button

Input type: `Dropdownlist`

Valuename: "Btn_Favorites"

Actionlist Valuename: "SpecifyDefaultButtons"

Folders button

Input type: `Dropdownlist`

Valuename: "Btn_Folders"

Actionlist Valuename: "SpecifyDefaultButtons"

Fullscreen button

Input type: `Dropdownlist`

Valuename: "Btn_Fullscreen"

Actionlist Valuename: "SpecifyDefaultButtons"

Tools button

Input type: `Dropdownlist`

Valuename: "Btn_Tools"

Actionlist Valuename: "SpecifyDefaultButtons"

Mail button

Input type: `Dropdownlist`

Valuename: "Btn_MailNews"

Actionlist Valuename: "SpecifyDefaultButtons"

Font size button

Input type: `Dropdownlist`

Valuename: "Btn_Size"

Actionlist Valuename: "SpecifyDefaultButtons"

Print button

Input type: `Dropdownlist`

Valuename: "Btn_Print"

Actionlist Valuename: "SpecifyDefaultButtons"

Edit button

Input type: `Dropdownlist`

Valuename: "Btn_Edit"

Actionlist Valuename: "SpecifyDefaultButtons"

Discussions button

Input type: `Dropdownlist`

Valuename: "Btn_Discussions"

Actionlist Valuename: "SpecifyDefaultButtons"

Cut button

Input type: `Dropdownlist`

Valuename: "Btn_Cut"

Actionlist Valuename: "SpecifyDefaultButtons"

Copy button

Input type: `Dropdownlist`

Valuename: "Btn_Copy"

Actionlist Valuename: "SpecifyDefaultButtons"

Paste button

Input type: `Dropdownlist`

Valuename: "Btn_Paste"

Actionlist Valuename: "SpecifyDefaultButtons"

Encoding button

Input type: `Dropdownlist`

Valuename: "Btn_Encoding"

Actionlist Valuename: "SpecifyDefaultButtons"

Display Settings

The display settings will override any set within the web page itself.

Keyname: "Software\Microsoft\Internet Explorer\Settings"

Text Size

Default Size

Input type: `Dropdownlist`

Keyname: "Software\Microsoft\Internet Explorer\International\Scripts"

Valuename: "Default_IEFontSize"

General Colors

Background color

Input type: `Edittext`

Valuename: "Background Color"

Text color

Input type: `Edittext`

Valuename: "Text Color"

Use Window colors

Uses Windows default colors.

Input type: `Checkbox`

Keyname: "Software\Microsoft\Internet Explorer\Main"

Valuename: "Use_DlgBox_Colors"

Link colors

Link color

Input type: `Edittext`

Valuename: "Anchor Color"

Visited link color

Input type: `Edittext`

Valuename: "Anchor Color Visited"

Use hover color

Input type: `Checkbox`

Valuename: "Use Anchor Hover Color"

Hover color

Input type: `Edittext`

Valuename: "Anchor Color Hover"

Advanced settings

Keyname: "Software\Microsoft\Internet Explorer\Main"

Connection

Enable Autodialing

Auto-dial whenever a TCP/IP Winsock call is made (e.g., when Outlook is opened).

Input type: `Checkbox`

Keyname: "Software\Microsoft\Windows\CurrentVersion\Internet Settings"

Valuename: "EnableAutodial"

Browsing

Disable script debugging

Debugging is used by web developers to test scripts on their web pages

Input type: `Checkbox`

Valuename: "Disable Script Debugger"

Launch browser in full screen mode

In IEAK5.1 this policy was instead included in the *inetres.adm* template.

Input type: `Checkbox`

Valuename: "FullScreen"

Show friendly URLs

The status bar will display the short name of the web page instead of the full URL.

Input type: `Checkbox`

Keyname: "Software\Microsoft\Internet Explorer"

Valuename: "Show_FullURL"

Use smooth scrolling

Input type: `Checkbox`

Valuename: "SmoothScroll"

Enable page transitions

One web page fades into another.

Input type: `Checkbox`

Valuename: "Page_Transitions"

Browse in a new process

A separate version of IE will launch every time IE is opened. This policy is not included in any IEAK5.1 templates.

Input type: `Checkbox`

Keyname: "Software\Microsoft\Windows\CurrentVersion\Explorer\BrowseNewProcess"

Valuename: "BrowseNewProcess"

Enable page hit counting

Input type: `Checkbox`

Keyname: "Software\Microsoft\Windows\CurrentVersion\Webcheck"

Valuename: "NoChannelLogging"

Automatically check for Internet Explorer updates

Input type: `Checkbox`

Keyname: "Software\Microsoft\Internet Explorer\Main"

Valuename: "NoUpdateCheck"

Underline links

Input type: `Dropdownlist`

Valuename: "Anchor Underline"

Use Web Based FTP

This supports only viewing and downloading of FTP files.

Input type: `Checkbox`

Keyname: "Software\Microsoft\Ftp"

Valuename: "Use Web Based FTP"

Show Go button in Address bar

Input type: `Checkbox`

Valuename: "ShowGoButton"

Show friendly http error messages

Input type: `Checkbox`

Valuename: "Friendly http errors"

Display a notification about every script error

Input type: `Checkbox`

Valuename: "Error Dlg Displayed On Every Error"

Multimedia

Show pictures

Input type: `Checkbox`

Valuename: "Display Inline Images"

Play animations

Input type: `Checkbox`

Valuename: "Play_Animations"

Play videos

Input type: `Checkbox`

Valuename: "Display Inline Videos"

Play Sounds

Input type: `Checkbox`

Valuename: "Play_Background_Sounds"

Smart image dithering

Input type: Checkbox

Keyname: "Software\Microsoft\Internet Explorer"

Valuename: "SmartDithering"

Show image download placeholders

Input type: Checkbox

Valuename: "Show image placeholders"

Security

Enable Profile Assistant

The user is prompted for which information to share when web pages request PA information.

Input type: Checkbox

Keyname: "Software\Microsoft\Internet Explorer\Security\P3Global"

Valuename: "Enabled"

Delete saved pages when browser closed

Pages are deleted from the temporary Internet folder.

Input type: Checkbox

Keyname: "Software\Microsoft\Windows\CurrentVersion\Internet Settings\Cache"

Valuename: "Persistent"

Do not save encrypted pages to disk

Secured information is removed from the temporary Internet folder.

Input type: Checkbox

Keyname: "Software\Microsoft\Windows\CurrentVersion\Internet Settings"

Valuename: "DisableCachingOfSSLPages"

Warn if forms submit is being redirected

Input type: Checkbox

Keyname: "Software\Microsoft\Windows\CurrentVersion\Internet Settings"

Valuename: "WarnOnPostRedirect"

Warn if changing between secure and not secure mode

Input type: Checkbox

Keyname: "Software\Microsoft\Windows\CurrentVersion\Internet Settings"

Valuename: "WarnonZoneCrossing"

Java VM

Keyname: "Software\Microsoft\Java VM"

Java logging enabled

Creates a log of all Java activity, useful for troubleshooting.

Input type: `Checkbox`

Valuename: "EnableLogging"

Java JIT compiler enabled

Java applets are created internally using MS Virtual Machine.

Input type: `Checkbox`

Valuename: "EnableJIT"

Printing

Print background colors and images

Input type: `Checkbox`

Valuename: "Print_Background"

Searching

Search Provider Keyword (type INTRANET if you have an internal Autosearch server):

Input type: `Edittext`

Keyname: "Software\Microsoft\Internet Explorer\SearchURL"

Valuename: "Provider"

When searching from the address bar

Searching from the address bar can be disabled.

Input type: `Dropdownlist`

Valuename: "AutoSearch"

HTTP1.1 settings

Use HTTP1.1

Clear this option if you are having problems connecting to older web sites.

Input type: `Checkbox`

Keyname: "Software\Microsoft\Windows\CurrentVersion\Internet Settings"

Valuename: "EnableHttp1_1"

Use HTTP1.1 through proxy connections

Clear this option if you are having problems connecting to older web sites.

Input type: `Checkbox`

Keyname: "Software\Microsoft\Windows\CurrentVersion\Internet Settings"

Valuename: "ProxyHttp1.1"

Signup Settings

This policy exists only in the IEAK5.1 version of the template.

Disable Automatic Signup

Input type: `Checkbox`

Keyname: "Software\Microsoft\IEAK"

Valuename: "NoAutomaticSignup"

Internet Connection Wizard Settings

This policy exists only in the IEAK5.1 version of the template.

Do not run Internet Connection Wizard

Input type: `Checkbox`

Keyname: "Software\Microsoft\Internet Connection Wizard"

Valuename: "Completed"

URL Encoding

URL Encoding

Keyname: "Software\Microsoft\Windows\CurrentVersion\Internet Settings"

Always send URLs as UTF-8 (requires restart)

A standard that defines characters so they are readable in any language.

Input type: `Checkbox`

Valuename: "UrlEncoding"

Computer Properties

Component Updates

Keyname: "Software\Microsoft\Internet Explorer\Main"

Periodic check for updates to Internet Explorer and Internet tools

URL to be displayed for updates

Input type: `Edittext`

Valuename: "Update_Check_Page"

Update check interval (in days)

Input type: `Numeric`

Valuename: "Update_Check_Interval"

Help Menu → About Internet Explorer

Keyname: "Software\Microsoft\Windows\CurrentVersion"

Cipher Strength Update Information URL:

URL defined for this hyperlink (in the About IE window) containing update information on the browser encryption strength.

Input type: `Edittext`

Valuename: "IEAKUpdateUrl"

Inetsetm.adm

This template is included with the Windows 98 CD-ROM and optimized for IE4.

User Properties

Colors

The display settings will override any set within the web page itself

Keyname: "Software\Microsoft\Internet Explorer\Settings"

General Colors

Background color

Input type: `Edittext`

Valuename: "Background Color"

Text color

Input type: `Edittext`

Valuename: "Text Color"

Use Window colors

Use Windows default colors.

Input type: `Checkbox`

Keyname: "Software\Microsoft\Internet Explorer\Main"

Valuename: "Use_DlgBox_Colors"

Link colors

Link color

Input type: `Edittext`

Valuename: "Anchor Color"

Visited link color

Input type: `Edittext`

Valuename: "Anchor Color Visited"

Use hover color

Input type: `Checkbox`

Valuename: "Use Anchor Hover Color"

Hover color

Input type: `Edittext`

Valuename: "Anchor Color Hover"

Fonts

Keyname: "Software\Microsoft\Internet Explorer\International\1252"

Western Proportional Font

Input type: `Edittext`

Valuename: "IEPropFontName"

Western Fixed Font

Input type: `Edittext`

Valuename: "IEPropFontDef"

Advanced settings

Keyname: "Software\Microsoft\Internet Explorer\Main"

Browsing

Disable script debugging

Debugging is used by web developers to test scripts on their web pages.

Input type: `Checkbox`

Valuename: "Disable Script Debugger"

Launch channels in full screen mode

Input type: `Checkbox`

Keyname: "Software\Microsoft\Internet Explorer\Channels"

Valuename: "FullScreen"

Launch browser in full screen mode

Input type: `Checkbox`

Valuename: "FullScreen"

Use autocomplete

Input type: `Checkbox`

Keyname: "Software\Microsoft\Windows\CurrentVersion\Explorer\AutoComplete"

Valuename: "Use AutoComplete"

Show friendly URLs

The status bar will display the short name of the web page instead of the full URL.

Input type: `Checkbox`

Keyname: "Software\Microsoft\Internet Explorer"

Valuename: "Show_FullURL"

Enable smooth scrolling

Input type: `Checkbox`

Valuename: "SmoothScroll"

Enable page transitions

One web page will fade into another.

Input type: `Checkbox`

Valuename: "Page_Transitions"

Browse in a new process

A separate version of IE will launch every time IE is opened.

Input type: `Checkbox`

Keyname: "Software\Microsoft\Windows\CurrentVersion\Explorer\BrowseNewProcess"

Valuename: "BrowseNewProcess"

Enable page hit counting

Input type: `Checkbox`

Keyname: "Software\Microsoft\Windows\CurrentVersion\Webcheck"

Valuename: "NoChannelLogging"

Enable scheduled subscription updates

Input type: `Checkbox`

Keyname: "Software\Microsoft\Windows\CurrentVersion\Webcheck"

Valuename: "NoScheduledUpdates"

Underline links

Input type: `Dropdownlist`

Valuename: "Anchor Underline"

Multimedia

Show pictures

Input type: `Checkbox`

Valuename: "Display Inline Images"

Play animations

Input type: `Checkbox`

Valuename: "Play_Animations"

Play videos

Input type: `Checkbox`

Valuename: "Display Inline Videos"

Play Sounds

Input type: `Checkbox`

Valuename: "Play_Background_Sounds"

Smart image dithering

Input type: `Checkbox`

Keyname: "Software\Microsoft\Internet Explorer"

Valuename: "SmartDithering"

Security

Keyname: "Software\Microsoft\Windows\CurrentVersion\Internet Settings"

Enable Profile Assistant

The user is prompted for which information to share when web pages request PA information.

Input type: `Checkbox`

Keyname: "Software\Microsoft\Internet Explorer\Security\P3Global"

Valuename: "Enabled"

Delete saved pages when browser closed

Pages are deleted from the temporary Internet folder.

Input type: `Checkbox`

Keyname: "Software\Microsoft\Windows\CurrentVersion\Internet Settings\Cache"

Valuename: "Persistent"

Do not save encrypted pages to disk

Secured information is removed from the temporary Internet folder.

Input type: `Checkbox`

Valuename: "DisableCachingOfSSLPages"

Warn if forms submit is being redirected

Input type: `Checkbox`

Valuename: "WarnOnPostRedirect"

Warn if changing between secure and insecure mode

Input type: `Checkbox`

Valuename: "WarnonZoneCrossing"

Cookies

Input type: `Dropdownlist`

Valuename: "AllowCookies"

Java VM

Keyname: "Software\Microsoft\Java VM"

Java JIT compiler enabled

Java applets are created internally using MS Virtual Machine.

Input type: `Checkbox`

Valuename: "EnableJIT"

Java logging enabled

Creates a log of all Java activity, useful for troubleshooting.

Input type: `Checkbox`

Valuename: "EnableLogging"

Printing

Print background colors and images

Input type: `Checkbox`

Valuename: "Print_Background"

Searching

Autoscan common root domains

Input type: `Checkbox`

Valuename: "SearchForExtensions"

Search when URL fails

Input type: `Dropdownlist`

Valuename: "Do404Search"

Toolbars

Show font button

Input type: `Checkbox`

Keyname: "Software\Microsoft\Internet Explorer\Toolbar"

Valuename: "ShowFonts"

Small icons

Input type: `Checkbox`

Keyname: "Software\Microsoft\Windows\CurrentVersion\Explorer\SmallIcons"

Valuename: "SmallIcons"

HTTP1.1 settings

Use HTTP1.1

Clear this option if you are having problems connecting to older web sites.

Input type: `Checkbox`

Keyname: "Software\Microsoft\Windows\CurrentVersion\Internet Settings"

Valuename: "EnableHttp1_1"

Use HTTP1.1 through proxy connections

Clear this option if you are having problems connecting to older web sites.

Input type: `Checkbox`

Keyname: "Software\Microsoft\Windows\CurrentVersion\Internet Settings"

Valuename: "ProxyHttp1.1"

Computer Properties

Languages

Languages

Keyname: "Software\Microsoft\Internet Explorer\International"

Choose the default language preference(s)

Input type: `Edittext`

Valuename: "AcceptLanguage"

Modem settings

Modem Settings

Keyname: "Software\Microsoft\Windows\CurrentVersion\Internet Settings"

Connection Type

Input type: `Dropdownlist`

Valuename: "EnableAutoDial"

Number of times to attempt connection

Input type: `Numeric`

Valuename: "RedialAttempts"

Number of seconds to wait between attempts

Input type: `Numeric`

Valuename: "RedialWai"

Minutes to wait before disconnecting

Input type: `Numeric`

Valuename: "DisconnectIdleTime"

Enable Autodialing

Input type: `Checkbox`

Valuename: "EnableAutodial"

Connect without user intervention

Input type: `Checkbox`

Valuename: "EnableUnattended"

Disconnect if idle after specified number of minutes

Input type: `Checkbox`

Valuename: "EnableAutoDisconnect"

Perform system security check before dialing

Input type: `Checkbox`

Valuename: "EnableSecurityCheck"

Programs

Programs

Program to use for Calendar

Input type: `Edittext`

Keyname: "Software\Clients\Calendar"

Valuename: "(Default)"

Program to use for Contacts

Input type: `Edittext`

Keyname: "Software\Clients\Contacts"

Valuename: "(Default)"

Program to use for Internet call

Input type: `Edittext`

Keyname: "Software\Clients\Internet Call"

Valuename: "(Default)"

Oe.adm

This template is included with IEAK5 and IEAK5.1, and allows the use of multiple identities to be disabled. Note that this template has no user properties.

Computer Properties

Identity Manager

Restrict Identities

Prevent users from configuring or using Identities

All existing identities (except the original identity) will be disabled.

Input type: `Checkbox`

Keyname: "Software\Policies\Microsoft\Windows\CurrentVersion\Identities"

Valuename: "Locked Down"

Oem.adm

This template is included with the Windows 98 CD-ROM. Note that this template has no computer properties.

User Properties

General Settings

Mail and news security zones

Keyname: "Software\Microsoft\Outlook Express"

Put mail and news in the Restricted Sites zone (instead of the Internet zone)

Input type: `Checkbox`

Valuename: "Security Zone"

HTML mail and news composition settings

Mail: Make plain text message composition the default for mail messages (instead of HTML mail)

Input type: `Checkbox`

Keyname: "Software\Microsoft\Outlook Express\Mail"

Valuename: "Message Send HTML"

News: Make HTML message composition the default for news posts (instead of plain text)

Input type: Checkbox

Keyname: "Software\Microsoft\Outlook Express\News"

Valuename: "Message Send HTML"

View Customization

Keyname: "Software\Microsoft\Outlook Express"

Folder and Message Navigational Elements

Turn on Outlook Bar

Input type: Checkbox

Valuename: "OutBar"

Turn off Folder List

Disable the tree view of folders

Input type: Checkbox

Valuename: "Tree"

Turn on Folder Bar

Enable the horizontal line that displays the selected folder"s name.

Input type: Checkbox

Valuename: "FolderBar"

Turn off the Tip of the Day

Input type: Checkbox

Valuename: "Tip of the Day"

Subs.adm and Subsm.adm

The *subs.adm* template listed here is included with IEAK5 and IEAK5.1, while the *subsm.adm* template is included with the Windows 98 CD-ROM. The *subsm.adm* template options, with one exception (Maximum Channel Size), are contained within the *subs.adm* template. Other versions of the *subs.adm* template are included with IEAK Versions 1 and 4, but these versions had problems with text strings extending past the width of the properties windows. See MS Knowledge-base article 187552. Note that these templates have no computer properties.

User Properties

Offline Pages

Keyname: "Software\Policies\Microsoft\Internet Explorer\Infodelivery\Restrictions"

Offline Pages

Disable adding channels

Input type: Checkbox

Valuename: "NoAddingChannels"

Disable removing channels

Input type: Checkbox

Valuename: "NoRemovingChannels"

Disable adding schedules for offline pages

Input type: Checkbox

Valuename: "NoAddingSubscriptions"

Disable editing schedules for offline pages

Input type: Checkbox

Valuename: "NoEditingSubscriptions"

Disable removing schedules for offline page

Input type: Checkbox

Valuename: "NoRemovingSubscriptions"

Disable offline page hit logging

Input type: Checkbox

Valuename: "NoChannelLogging"

Disable all scheduled offline pages

Input type: Checkbox

Valuename: "NoScheduledUpdates"

Disable password caching for offline pages

Input type: Checkbox

Valuename: "NoSubscriptionPasswords"

Disable channel user interface (UI) completely

Input type: Checkbox

Valuename: "NoChannelUI"

Disable downloading of site subscription content

Input type: Checkbox

Valuename: "NoSubscriptionContent"

Disable editing and creating of schedule groups

Input type: `Checkbox`

Valuename: "NoEditingScheduleGroups"

Maximum size of subscriptions in kilobytes (0 disables restriction):

Input type: `Numeric`

Valuename: "MaxSubscriptionSize"

Maximum KB of channel subscription (0 disables restriction)

Available only in *subsm.adm*.

Input type: `Numeric`

Valuename: "MaxChannelSize"

Maximum number of offline pages

Input type: `Numeric`

Valuename: "MaxSubscriptionCount"

Minimum number of minutes between scheduled updates

Input type: `Numeric`

Valuename: "MinUpdateInterval"

Time to begin preventing scheduled updates

Input type: `Numeric`

Valuename: "UpdateExcludeBegin"

Time to end preventing scheduled updates

Input type: `Numeric`

Valuename: "UpdateExcludeEnd"

Maximum offline page crawl depth

Note that a high setting could make the amount of information being downloaded exponentially large.

Input type: `Dropdownlist`

Valuename: "MaxWebcrawlLevels"

Wmp.adm

The template version indicated here is included with IEAK5. A similar template is included with IEAK5.1, which includes the same policies except for those under the category Customize Network Settings.

User Properties

Customizations

Customize the Windows Media Player

Keyname: "Software\Policies\Microsoft\WindowsMediaPlayer"

Prevent automatic codec download

Input type: `Checkbox`

Valuename: "NoCodecDownload "

Title bar of the Windows Media Player

Input type: `Edittext`

Valuename: "TitleBar"

Button name on Windows Media Player navigation bar

Input type: `Edittext`

Valuename: "ShowCaseButton "

URL for button on Windows Media Player navigation bar

Input type: `Edittext`

Valuename: "ShowCaseURL"

Customize Network Settings

These policies are not included in the IEAK5.1 templates.

Keyname: "Software\Microsoft\NetShow\Player\General"

Default number of milliseconds to buffer data

Input type: `Numeric`

Valuename: "Buffering_Time"

Enable HTTP protocol

Input type: `Checkbox`

Valuename: "EnableHTTP"

Enable Multicast

Input type: `Checkbox`

Valuename: "EnableMulticast"

Enable TCP protocol

Input type: `Checkbox`

Valuename: "EnableTCP"

Enable UDP protocol

Input type: `Checkbox`

Valuename: "EnableUDP"

Use Proxy

Input type: `Checkbox`

Keyname: "Software\Microsoft\NetShow\Player\Local"

Valuename: "ProxyEnabled"

Use custom proxy settings (do not detect)

Input type: `Checkbox`

Keyname: "Software\Microsoft\NetShow\Player\Local"

Valuename: "EnableAutoProxy"

Proxy Hostname

Input type: `Edittext`

Keyname: "Software\Microsoft\NetShow\Player\Local"

Valuename: "ProxyHost"

Proxy host port

Input type: `Numeric`

Keyname: "Software\Microsoft\NetShow\Player\Local"

Valuename: "ProxyPort"

Computer Properties

Favorites

Windows Media Player Favorites

Keyname: "Software\Policies\Microsoft\WindowsMediaPlayer"

Do not install the default Windows Media Player Favorites in Media Folder

Input type: `Checkbox`

Valuename: "NoMediaFavorites"

Radio toolbar settings

Keyname: "Software\Policies\Microsoft\WindowsMediaPlayer"

Disable Radio toolbar (may require a reboot)

Input type: `Checkbox`

Valuename: "NoRadioBar"

Actionlist Keyname: "Software\Microsoft\Windows\CurrentVersion\RunOnce"

Actionlist Valuename: "Register OCX"

Disable menu for finding new Radio Stations
Input type: `Checkbox`

Valuename: "NoFindNewStations"

URL for finding new Radio Stations
Input type: `Edittext`

Valuename: "DefaultURLFindNewStations"

Office 97 Templates

These templates allow extensive customization of the Office 97 suite of applications. Included in this section are the following templates:

Access97.adm
This template contains policies for Access 97, part of the Office 97 suite.

Off97nt4.adm, Off97w95.adm, Off97w98.adm
These templates include policies for Microsoft Excel 97, PowerPoint 97 and Word 97. Many of these policies correspond to settings found in the Options dialog box of the Tools menu. As well, the templates include settings common to all Office programs, plus a few settings for Internet Explorer 3.0 and Microsoft Bookshelf.

Outlk97.adm
This template contains policies for Outlook 97, part of the Office 97 suite.

Query97.adm
This template contains policies for Microsoft Query 97 and ODBC 3.0.

Access97.adm

This template is included with the Office 97 Resource Kit, the Windows 95 ZAK and the Windows NT ZAK. The policy categories are arranged according to the Access 97 menu options. For example, Access97 → Tools_Options → View refers to the View tab in the Options dialog box of the Tools menu. Note that this template has no computer properties.

Office 97 Templates

User Properties

Access97 → Tools_Options → View

Keyname: "Software\Microsoft\Office\8.0\Access\Settings"

Status Bar
Show Status Bar

Valuename: "Show Status Bar"

Startup Dialog

Show Startup Dialog Box

Valuename: "Show Startup Dialog Box"

Hidden Objects

Show Hidden Objects

Valuename: "Show Hidden Objects"

System Objects

Show System Objects

Valuename: "Show System Objects"

Macro Names Column

Show Names Column in Macro Design

Valuename: "Show Macro Names Column"

Macro Conditions Column

Show Conditions Column in Macro Design

Valuename: "Show Conditions Column"

Access 97 → Tools_Options → General

Keyname: "Software\Microsoft\Office\8.0\Access\Settings"

Sort Order

New Database Sort Order

Specifies the default language alphabetical sort order for new databases.

Input type: `Dropdownlist`

Valuename: "New Database Sort Order"

Sound

To set the "Feedback with Sound" policy, see the Office category.

There is no Key or Valuename: associated with this, it"s an inactive policy for information purposes only.

Hyperlink Colors

Already viewed

Input type: `Dropdownlist`

Valuename: "Hyperlink Followed Fore Color"

Not yet viewed

Input type: `Dropdownlist`

Valuename: "Hyperlink Unfollowed Fore Color"

Hyperlink Underline

Underlines hyperlinks.

Valuename: "Underline Hyperlinks"

Hyperlink Address

Shows hyperlink addresses in status bar

Valuename: "Show Hyperlink Addresses in Status Bar"

Print Margins

Left Margin

Input type: `Dropdownlist`

Valuename: "Left Margin"

Right Margin

Input type: `Dropdownlist`

Valuename: "Right Margin"

Top Margin

Input type: `Dropdownlist`

Valuename: "Top Margin"

Bottom Margin

Input type: `Dropdownlist`

Valuename: "Bottom Margin"

Access 97 → Tools_Options → Edit/Find

Keyname: "Software\Microsoft\Office\8.0\Access\Settings"

Find/Replace

Default Find/Replace Behavior

Input type: `Dropdownlist`

Valuename: "Default Find/Replace Behavior"

Record Changes

Confirm record changes.

Valuename: "Confirm Record Changes"

Document Deletions

Confirm document deletions.

Valuename: "Confirm Document Deletions"

Action Queries

Confirm action queries.

Valuename: "Confirm Action Queries"

Access 97 → Tools_Options → Datasheet

Keyname: "Software\Microsoft\Office\8.0\Access\Settings"

Default Colors

Font

Input type: `Dropdownlist`

Valuename: "Default Font Color"

Background

Input type: `Dropdownlist`

Valuename: "Default Background Color"

Gridlines

Input type: `Dropdownlist`

Valuename: "Default Gridlines Color"

Default Font

Name

Input type: `Combobox`

Valuename: "Default Font Name"

Weight

Input type: `Dropdownlist`

Valuename: "Default Font Weight"

Size

Input type: `Numeric`

Valuename: "Default Font Size"

Underline

Input type: `Checkbox`

Valuename: "Default Font Underline"

Italic

Input type: `Checkbox`

Valuename: "Default Font Italic"

Horizontal Gridlines

Horizontal gridlines showing by default.

Valuename: "Default Gridlines Horizontal"

Vertical Gridlines

Vertical Gridlines showing by default.

Valuename: "Default Gridlines Vertical"

Column Width

Default column Width

Input type: `Dropdownlist`

Valuename: "Default Column Width"

Cell Effect

Default Cell Effect

Input type: `Dropdownlist`

Valuename: "Default Cell Effect"

Animations

Shows animations.

Valuename: "Show Animations"

Access 97 → Tools_Options → Tables/Queries

Keyname: "Software\Microsoft\Office\8.0\Access\Settings"

Field Sizes

Default Text Field Size

Input type: `Numeric`

Valuename: "Default Text Field Size"

Default Number Field Size

Input type: `Dropdownlist`

Valuename: "Default Number Field Size"

Field Type

Default Field Type

Input type: `Dropdownlist`

Valuename: "Default Field Type"

AutoIndex

AutoIndex on Import/Create

Input type: `Edittext`

Valuename: "AutoIndex on Import/Create"

Show Table Names

Valuename: "Show Table Names"

Output All Fields

Valuename: "Output All Fields"

Enable AutoJoin

Valuename: "Enable AutoJoin"

Run Permissions

Run Permissions

Input type: `Dropdownlist`

Valuename: "Run Permissions"

Access 97 → Tools_Options → Forms/Reports

Keyname: "Software\Microsoft\Office\8.0\Access\Settings"

Selection Behavior

Selection Behavior

Input type: `Dropdownlist`

Valuename: "Selection Behavior"

Form Template

Form Template

Input type: `Edittext`

Valuename: "Form Template"

Report Template

Report Template

Input type: `Edittext`

Valuename: "Report Template"

Event Procedures

Always use Event Procedures.

Valuename: "Always Use Event Procedures"

Access 97 → Tools_Options → Keyboard

Keyname: "Software\Microsoft\Office\8.0\Access\Settings"

Move After Enter

Move After Enter

Input type: `Dropdownlist`

Valuename: "Move After Enter"

Arrow Key Behavior

Arrow Key Behavior

Input type: `Dropdownlist`

Valuename: "Arrow Key Behavior"

Behavior Entering Field

Behavior Entering Field

Input type: `Dropdownlist`

Valuename: "Behavior Entering Field"

Cursor Stop

Cursor Stops at First/Last Field.

Valuename: "Cursor Stops at First/Last Field"

Access 97 → Tools_Options → Module

Keyname: "Software\Microsoft\VBA\MSAccess"

Font

Name

Input type: `Combobox`

Valuename: "FontFace"

Size

Input type: `Numeric`

Valuename: "FontHeight"

Coding Options

Auto Indent

Input type: `Checkbox`

Valuename: "AutoIndent"

Auto Syntax Check

Input type: `Checkbox`

Valuename: "SyntaxChecking"

Break On All Errors

Input type: `Checkbox`

Valuename: "BreakOnAllErrors"

Require Variable Declaration

Input type: `Checkbox`

Valuename: "RequireDeclaration"

Compile On Demand

Input type: `Checkbox`

Valuename: "CompileOnDemand"

Auto Statement Builder

Input type: `Checkbox`

Valuename: "AutoStatement"

Auto Quick Info

Input type: `Checkbox`

Valuename: "AutoQuickTips"

Auto Value Tips

Input type: `Checkbox`

Valuename: "AutoValueTips"

Tab Width

Input type: `Numeric`

Valuename: "TabWidth"

Access 97 → Tools_Options → Module → Window Options

Keyname: "Software\Microsoft\VBA\MSAccess"

Full Module View

Valuename: "FullModuleView"

Procedure Separator

Valuename: "EndProcLine"

Drag-and-Drop Text Editing

Valuename: "DragDropInEditor"

Debug Window On Top

Keyname: "Software\Microsoft\Office\8.0\Access\Settings"

Valuename: "Debug Window on Top"

Margin Indicator Bar

Valuename: "IndicatorBar"

Access 97 → Tools_Options → Advanced

Keyname: "Software\Microsoft\Office\8.0\Access\Settings"

Default Record Locking

Default Record Locking

Input type: `Dropdownlist`

Valuename: "Default Record Locking"

Ignore DDE Requests

Valuename: "Ignore DDE Requests"

Enable DDE Refresh

Valuename: "Enable DDE Refresh"

OLE/DDE Timeout

OLE/DDE Timeout (sec)

Input type: `Numeric`

Valuename: "OLE/DDE Timeout (sec)"

Update Retries

Number of Update Retries

Input type: `Numeric`

Valuename: "Number of Update Retries"

ODBC Refresh

ODBC Refresh Interval (sec)

Input type: `Numeric`

Valuename: "ODBC Refresh Interval (sec)"

Refresh Interval

Refresh Interval (sec)

Input type: `Numeric`

Valuename: "Refresh Interval (sec)"

Update Retry

Update Retry Interval (msec)

Input type: `Numeric`

Valuename: "Update Retry Interval (msec)"

Default Open Mode

Default Open Mode for Databases

Input type: `Dropdownlist`

Valuename: "Default Open Mode for Databases"

Access 97 → Internet → Help_Microsoft on the Web

Keyname: "Software\Microsoft\Office\8.0\Access\WebHelp"

Customize submenu

To enter your own commands to be displayed for this Help option, use the format "DisplayName, URL or UNC". For more details, refer to the ORK. There are eight command options.

Command1 (to 8)

Input type: `Edittext`

Valuename: "Command1" through "Command8"

Reset submenu to original defaults

Resets the Microsoft on the Web submenu to original values.

Actionlist Valuename: "Command1" through "Command8"

Disable submenu

Disables the Microsoft on the Web submenu.

Actionlist Valuename: "Command1" through "Command8"

Off97w95.adm, Off97nt4.adm and Off97w98.adm

These templates are included with the Office 97 resource kit, the Windows 95 and 98 ZAK and the Windows NT ZAK. The *off97w95.adm* and *off97w98.adm* templates are identical; however, the *off97nt4.adm* template differs from the Windows 9x templates in two ways:

- The Valuename for Chart Gallery is "Gallery Path" in the Windows 9x templates, but "GalleryPath" in the Windows NT4 template.
- The Windows NT4 template allows the pathname of the Personal Folder to include environment variables (such as *%USERNAME%*).

The policy categories are arranged according to the application menu options. For example, Office97 → Assistant → Options tab refers to the Options tab of the Office Assistant menu.

User Properties

Office 97 → Common

Policies for options shared by all of the Office 97 applications.

Personal Folder

Use the *off97w95.adm* template for Windows 95 and *off97nt4.adm* template for Windows NT 4.0. To enable per app default file locations, see the ORK

Keyname: "Software\Microsoft\Windows\CurrentVersion\Explorer\User Shell Folders"

Path to Personal folder used by all apps

Only the Windows NT4 version of this template allows environment variables to be used in the folder path name.

Input type: `Edittext`

Valuename: "Personal"

Actionlist Keynames: "Software\Microsoft\Office\8.0\Excel\Microsoft Excel", "Software\Microsoft\Office\8.0\Access\Settings", "Software\Microsoft\Office\8.0\PowerPoint\Recent Folder List\Default", "Software\Microsoft\Office\8.0\Binder", "Software\Microsoft\Office\8.0\Word\Options"

Actionlist Valuenames: "DefaultPath", "Default Database Directory", "", "DefaultDirectory", "DOC-PATH"

User Templates

Keyname: "Software\Microsoft\Office\8.0\Common\FileNew\LocalTemplates"

Path to User Templates folder

Input type: `Edittext`

Valuename: ""

Workgroup Templates

Keyname: "Software\Microsoft\Office\8.0\Common\FileNew\SharedTemplates"

Path to Workgroup Template folder

Input type: `Edittext`

Valuename: ""

Sound

Provides feedback with sound.

Keyname: "Software\Microsoft\Office\8.0\Common\General"

Valuename: "Sound"

Chart Gallery

The path to a custom chart gallery for applications other than Excel (gallery filename is *Grusrgal.gra*; the filename for the Excel custom chart gallery is *Xlusrgal.gra*).

Keyname: "Software\Microsoft\Office\8.0\Graph\Microsoft Graph"

Chart gallery path

Input type: `Edittext`

Valuename (Win95 only): "Gallery Path"

Valuename (NT4 only): "GalleryPath"

Office 97 → Assistant

Keyname: "Software\Microsoft\Office\8.0\Common\Assistant"

Default State

Default State

Input type: `Dropdownlist`

Valuename: "AsstState"

Choose File

Uses Assistant Source Path policy in Default Computer to set location of additional *.*act* files.

Filename of assistant (.act)*

Input type: `Combobox`

Valuename: "AsstFile"

Position

Distance from left of screen

Input type: `Numeric`

Valuename: "AsstLeft"

Distance from top of screen

Input type: `Numeric`

Valuename: "AsstTop"

Office97 → Assistant → Options Tab

Respond to F1 Keyname:

Valuename: "AsstAssistWithHelp"

Help with wizards

Valuename: "AsstAssistWithWizards"

Display Alerts

Valuename: "AsstAssistWithAlerts"

Search for both product and programming help

Valuename: "AsstSearchInProgram"

Move when in the way

Valuename: "AsstMoveWhenInTheWay"

Guess help topics

Valuename: "AsstGuessHelp"

Make sounds

Valuename: "AsstSounds"

Using features more effectively

Valuename: "AsstFeatureTips"

Using the mouse more effectively

Valuename: "AsstMousetips"

Keyboard shortcuts

Valuename: "AsstKeyboardShortcutTips"

Only show high priority tips

Valuename: "AsstOnlyHighPriorityTips"

Show the Tip of the Day at startup

Valuename: "AsstShowTipOfDay"

Office 97 → Internet → FTP Sites

Keyname: "Software\Microsoft\Office\8.0\Common\WebHelp"

Delete FTP sites

Clear first 10 ftp sites before any new sites are added.

Keyname: "Software\Microsoft\Office\8.0\Common\Internet\FTP Sites"

Valuename: "name"

Actionlist Keynames: "Software\Microsoft\Office\8.0\Common\Internet\FTP Sites\site_0" through "Software\Microsoft\Office\8.0\Common\Internet\FTP Sites\site_9"

Actionlist Valuename: "Site Name"

Add FTP Sites

These FTP sites will appear in the menu under File → Open → Look in. Site name must include *ftp://prefix* (room for 10 sites).

Keyname: "Software\Microsoft\Office\8.0\Common\Internet\FTP Sites"

Site (10 available)

Input type: `Edittext`

Keynames: "Software\Microsoft\Office\8.0\Common\Internet\FTP Sites\site_x00" through "Software\Microsoft\Office\8.0\Common\Internet\FTP Sites\site_x09"

Valuename: "Site Name"

Office 97 → Internet → Web Search

Keyname: "Software\Microsoft\Office\8.0\Common\Internet\WebSearch"

Internet Lookup Options

For each parameter, enter the list of values with the following syntax: (<server1 value>);(<server2 value>);(<serverN value>).

Server Friendly Name

Input type: `Edittext`

Valuename: "FriendlyName"

Server Base URL or UNC

Input type: `Edittext`

Valuename: "BaseURL"

Index Path

Input type: `Edittext`

Valuename: "IndexPath"

Template Path

Input type: `Edittext`

Valuename: "TemplatePath"

GIF Path

Input type: `Edittext`

Valuename: "GIFPath"

Properties

Input type: `Edittext`

Valuename: "Properties"

Protocol

Input type: `Edittext`

Valuename: "Protocol"

Sort By

Input type: `Edittext`

Valuename: "SortBy"

Office 97 → Internet → Help_ Microsoft on the Web

Customize submenu

To enter your own commands to be displayed for this Help option, use the format "DisplayName,URL or UNC". For more details, refer to the ORK.

CommandX

Command1 through Command8 are available.

Input type: `Edittext`

Valuename: "Command1" through "Command8"

Reset submenu to original defaults

Resets the Microsoft on the Web submenu to original values.

Actionlist Valuenames: "Command1" through "Command8"

Disable submenu

Disables the Microsoft on the Web submenu.

Actionlist Valuenames: "Command1" through "Command8"

Office 97 → Tools_Customize

Options

Keyname: "Software\Microsoft\Office\8.0\Common\Toolbars"

Menu Animation

Input type: `Dropdownlist`

Valuename: "Animation"

Large Icons

Input type: `Checkbox`

Valuename: "BtnSize"

Show ToolTips

Input type: `Checkbox`

Valuename: "Tooltips"

Always show shortcut Keynames

Input type: `Checkbox`

Valuename: "ShowKbdShortcuts"

Office Wizards

Assistant helps with toolbar customize wizard.

Keyname: "Software\Microsoft\Office\8.0\Common\Assistant"

Valuename: "AsstOfficeWizards"

Office 97 → Binder Options

Single Print Job

Print binder as single job.

Keyname: "Software\Microsoft\Office\8.0\Binder"

Valuename: "NoSinglePrintJob"

Office 97 → Visual Basic Editor → Help_Microsoft on the Web

Keyname: "Software\Microsoft\Office\8.0\VBE\WebHelp"

Customize submenu

To enter your own commands to be displayed for this Help option, use the format "DisplayName,URL or UNC". For more details, refer to the ORK.

CommandX

Command1 through Command8 are available.

Input type: `Edittext`

Valuename: "Command1" through "Command8"

Reset submenu to original defaults

Resets the Microsoft on the Web submenu to original values.

Actionlist Valuenames: "Command1" through "Command8"

Disable submenu

Disables the Microsoft on the Web submenu.

Actionlist Valuenames: "Command1" through "Command8"

Excel 97 → Tools_Options → Edit

Keyname: "Software\Microsoft\Office\8.0\Excel\Microsoft Excel"

Move Enter Direction

Move selection after Enter

Input type: `Dropdownlist`

Valuename: "MoveEnterDir"

Fixed Decimal

Automatically fix 2 decimal places.

Valuename: "AutoDec"

Excel 97 → Tools_Options → General

Keyname: "Software\Microsoft\Office\8.0\Excel\Microsoft Excel"

Recently Used File List

Number of entries on recently used file list

Input type: `Numeric`

Valuename: "DefFileMRU"

Default Sheets

Sheets in new workbook

Input type: `Numeric`

Valuename: "DefSheets"

Font

Name, Size

Input type: `Combobox`

Valuename: "Font"

Alternate Startup Folder

Alternate startup file location

Input type: `Edittext`

Valuename: "AltStartup"

Excel 97 → Tools_Options → Transition

Keyname: "Software\Microsoft\Office\8.0\Excel\Microsoft Excel"

Default Save

Keyname: "Software\Microsoft\Office\8.0\Excel\Default Save"

Save Excel files as:

Input type: `Dropdownlist`

Valuename: "Default Format"

Menu Keyname

Enter ASCII value for keyname of choice (e.g., "/"=47)

Excel menu or Help Keyname:

Input type: `Edittext`

Valuename: "MenuKey"

Excel 97 → Tools_Options → BitFields

Use these policies with caution! This registry value holds flag bits for up to 16 setting. See the Office 97 Resource Kit for a list of the flags. See Options6 for how to enable Macro virus protection.

Keyname: "Software\Microsoft\Office\8.0\Excel\Microsoft Excel"

Options value

Options Value

Input type: `Edittext`

Valuename: "Options"

Options3 value

Options3 Value

Input type: `Edittext`

Valuename: "Options3"

Options5 value

Options5 value

Input type: `Edittext`

Valuename: "Options5"

Options6 value

Options6 value

Entering a value of 8 in the edit box will enable macro virus protection according to MS KB article Q169811.

Input type: `Edittext`

Valuename: "Options6"

Options 95 value

Options95 value

Input type: `Edittext`

Valuename: "Options95"

Excel 97 → Microsoft Map

Keyname: "Software\Microsoft\Office\8.0\Microsoft Map\Preferences"

Map Matching

Map Matching

Input type: `Dropdownlist`

Valuename: "SearchThorough"

Time Limit (secs)

Input type: `Numeric`

Valuename: "SearchTimeLimit"

Sizing Units

Feature Sizing Units

Input type: `Dropdownlist`

Valuename: "SizingUnits"

Compact Legends

Compact legends by default.

Valuename: "LegendsCompact"

Auto Correct

Automatically correct spelling errors in place names.

Valuename: "AutoCorrect"

Excel 97 → Internet → Help, Microsoft on the Web

Keyname: "Software\Microsoft\Office\8.0\Excel\WebHelp"

Customize submenu

To enter your own commands to be displayed for this Help option, use the format "DisplayName,URL or UNC". For more details, refer to the ORK.

CommandX

Command1 through Command8 are available.

Input type: `Edittext`

Valuename: "Command1" through "Command8"

Reset submenu to original defaults

Resets the Microsoft on the Web submenu to original values.

Actionlist Valuenames: "Command1" through "Command8"

Disable submenu

Disables the Microsoft on the Web submenu.

Actionlist Valuenames: "Command1" through "Command8"

Excel 97 → Internet → Converters

Keyname: "Software\Microsoft\Office\8.0\Excel\WebHelp"

Future File Format Converters

To provide an Intranet site for future file format converters (such as future versions of Office), enter a URL or UNC path, e.g., *http://mycorp/support.html.*

URL for Converter

Input type: `Edittext`

Valuename: "Converters"

Excel 97 → Miscellaneous

Keyname: "Software\Microsoft\Office\8.0\Excel\Microsoft Excel"

Personal Toolbars

Path to roving custom toolbar include trailing "\" after folder name (i.e., server\share\folder\)

The custom toolbar is called *username8.xlb.*

Input type: `Edittext`

Valuename: "CmdBarFile"

Run Query

Path to saved queries folder

Input type: `Edittext`

Valuename: "SavedQueriesFolder"

Chart Gallery

Path to custom chart gallery, for Excel only (gallery filename is *Xlusrgal.gra*).

Chart gallery path

Input type: `Edittext`

Valuename (Win95 only): "Gallery Path"

Valuename (NT4 only): "GalleryPath"

Powerpoint 97 → Tools_Options → View

Keyname: "Software\Microsoft\Office\8.0\PowerPoint\Options"

Startup dialog

Valuename: "StartupDialog"

New slide dialog

Valuename: "NewSlideDialog"

Status bar

Valuename: "ShowStatusBar"

Vertical ruler

Valuename: "VerticalRuler"

Popup menu on right mouse click
Valuename: "SSRightMouse"

Show popup menu button
Valuename: "SSMenuButton"

End with blank slide
Valuename: "SSEndOnBlankSlide"

Powerpoint 97 → Tools_Options → General

Keyname: "Software\Microsoft\Office\8.0\PowerPoint\Options"

Recently Used File List
Enable recently used file list
Input type: `Checkbox`

Valuename: "MRUListActive"

Size of recently used file list
Input type: `Numeric`

Valuename: "SizeOfMRUList"

Macro Virus Protection
Enables macro virus protection.

Valuename: "MacroVirusProtection"

Link Sounds File Size
Link sounds with file size greater than (Kb):
Input type: `Numeric`

Valuename: "Link sound size"

PowerPoint 97 → Tools_Options → Edit

Keyname: "Software\Microsoft\Office\8.0\PowerPoint\Options"

Replace straight quotes with smart quotes
Valuename: "SmartQuotes"

Automatic word selection
Valuename: "WordSelection"

Use smart cut and paste
Valuename: "SmartCutPaste"

Drag-and-Drop text editing
Valuename: "DragAndDrop"

Inserting
New charts take on PowerPoint font.

Valuename: "PPTColorsForNewGraphs"

Undo

Maximum number of undos

Input type: `Numeric`

Valuename: "Number of Undos"

PowerPoint 97 → Tools_Options → Print

Background Printing

Enables background printing.

Keyname: "Software\Microsoft\Office\8.0\PowerPoint\Options"

Valuename: "BackgroundPrint"

PowerPoint 97 → Tools_Options → Save

Keyname: "Software\Microsoft\Office\8.0\PowerPoint\Options"

Allow fast saves

Valuename: "Fast saves"

Prompt for file properties

Opens the properties dialog box when you save a file for the first time.

Valuename: "PromptForFileProperties"

Full text search information

Valuename: "SaveFullTextSearchInfo"

AutoRecovery

Save AutoRecovery info

Input type: `Checkbox`

Valuename: "SaveAutoRecoveryInfo"

AutoRecovery save frequency {min}

Input type: `Numeric`

Valuename: "FrequencyToSaveAutoRecoveryInfo"

Default Save

Keyname: "Software\Microsoft\Office\8.0\PowerPoint\Default Save"

Save PowerPoint files as:

Input type: `Dropdownlist`

Valuename: "Default Format"

PowerPoint 97 → Tools_Options → Spelling

Keyname: "Software\Microsoft\Office\8.0\PowerPoint\Options"

Background spelling
Valuename: "Background spell checking"

Hide spelling errors
Valuename: "Do not underline errors"

Suggest Always
Valuename: "Suggest Always"

Ignore words in UPPERCASE
Valuename: "Ignore UPPERCASE words"

Ignore words with numbers
Valuename: "Ignore words with numbers"

PowerPoint 97 → Tools_Options → Advanced

Keyname: "Software\Microsoft\Office\8.0\PowerPoint\Options"

Picture

Render 24-bit bitmaps at highest quality

Input type: `Checkbox`

Valuename: "Always render high quality 24-bit images"

Export pictures

Input type: `Dropdownlist`

Valuename: "Produce 8-bit metafiles"

PowerPoint 97 → Internet → Help_Microsoft on the Web

Keyname: "Software\Microsoft\Office\8.0\PowerPoint\WebHelp"

Customize submenu
To enter your own commands to be displayed for this Help option, use the format "DisplayName,URL or UNC". For more details, refer to the ORK.

CommandX
Command1 through Command8 are available.

Input type: `Edittext`

Valuename: "Command1" through "Command8"

Reset submenu to original defaults
Resets the Microsoft on the Web submenu to original values.

Actionlist Valuenames: "Command1" through "Command8"

Disable submenu
Disables the Microsoft on the Web submenu.

Actionlist Valuenames: "Command1" through "Command8"

PowerPoint 97 → Internet → Converters

Future File Format Converters

To provide an Intranet site for future file format converters, enter a URL or UNC path, e.g., *http://mycorp/support.html.*

Keyname: "Software\Microsoft\Office\8.0\PowerPoint\WebHelp"

URL for Converter

Input type: `Edittext`

Valuename: "Converters"

PowerPoint 97 → Miscellaneous

Personal Toolbars

Keyname: "Software\Microsoft\Office\8.0\PowerPoint\Command Bars"

Path to roving custom toolbar

The custom toolbar is called *username8.xlb.*

Input type: `Edittext`

Valuename: "CmdBarFile"

Multimedia Directory

Keyname: "Software\Microsoft\Office\8.0\PowerPoint\Recent Folder List\MultimediaDir"

Multimedia Directory

Input type: `Edittext`

Valuename: ""

Template Directory

Keyname: "Software\Microsoft\Office\8.0\PowerPoint\Recent Folder List\TemplateDir"

Template Directory

Input type: `Edittext`

Valuename: ""

Picture Directory

Keyname: "Software\Microsoft\Office\8.0\PowerPoint\Recent Folder List\PictureDir"

Picture Directory

Input type: `Edittext`

Valuename: ""

No Edit Time

Do not display valid edit time in document statistics, time is displayed as 0 minutes.

Keyname: "Software\Microsoft\Office\8.0\PowerPoint\Options"

Valuename: "NoEditTime"

Word 97 → Tools_Options → General

Keyname: "Software\Microsoft\Office\8.0\Word\Options"

Help for WordPerfect users

Help for WordPerfect users

Input type: `Dropdownlist`

Valuename: "WPHelp"

Macro Virus Protection

Enable macro virus protection

Valuename: "EnableMacroVirusProtection"

Word 97 → Tools_Options → Edit

Picture Editor

Keyname: "Software\Microsoft\Office\8.0\Word\Options"

Picture Editor:

Input type: `Dropdownlist`

Valuename: "PICEDITCLASS"

Word 97 → Tools_Options → Print

Background Print

Allows background printing.

Keyname: "Software\Microsoft\Office\8.0\Word\Options"

Valuename: "BackgroundPrint"

Word 97 → Tools_Options → Save

Keyname: "Software\Microsoft\Office\8.0\Word\Default Save"

Default Save

Save Word files as

Input type: `Dropdownlist`

Valuename: "Default Format"

Background Save

Allows background saves.

Keyname: "Software\Microsoft\Office\8.0\Word\Options"

Valuename: "BackgroundSave"

Word 97 → Tools_Options → Spelling & Grammar

Keyname: "Software\Microsoft\Office\8.0\Word\Options"

Background Spelling

Check spelling as you type.

Valuename: "AutoSpell"

Background Grammar

Check grammar as you type.

Valuename: "AutoGrammar"

Word 97 → Tools_Options → File Locations

Keyname: "Software\Microsoft\Office\8.0\Word\Options"

Clipart Pictures

Path to Clipart Pictures folder

Input type: `Edittext`

Valuename: "PICTURE-PATH"

AutoRecover Files

Path to AutoRecover Files folder

Input type: `Edittext`

Valuename: "AUTOSAVE-PATH"

Tools

Path to folder containing dictionaries, filters and text converters

Input type: `Edittext`

Valuename: "TOOLS-PATH"

Startup

Path to Startup folder

Input type: `Edittext`

Valuename: "STARTUP-PATH"

Word 97 → Tools_AutoCorrect → AutoFormat

Plain Text WordMail Documents

Always AutoFormat plain text WordMail documents.

Keyname: "Software\Microsoft\Office\8.0\Word\Options"

Valuename: "PlainTextAutoFormat"

Word 97 → Internet → Help_Microsoft on the Web

Keyname: "Software\Microsoft\Office\8.0\Word\WebHelp"

Customize submenu

To enter your own commands to be displayed for this Help option, use the format "DisplayName,URL or UNC". For more details, refer to the ORK.

CommandX

Command1 through Command8 are available.

Input type: `Edittext`

Valuename: "Command1" through "Command8"

Reset submenu to original defaults

Resets the Microsoft on the Web submenu to original values.

Actionlist Valuenames: "Command1" through "Command8"

Disable submenu

Disables the Microsoft on the Web submenu.

Actionlist Valuenames: "Command1" through "Command8"

Word 97 → Internet → Converters

Future File Format Converters

To provide an Intranet site for future file format converters, enter a URL or UNC path, e.g., *http://mycorp/support.html.*

Keyname: "Software\Microsoft\Office\8.0\Word\WebHelp"

URL for Converter

Input type: `Edittext`

Valuename: "Converters"

Word 97 → Web Page Authoring

Keyname: "Software\Microsoft\Office\8.0\Word\HTML"

Bullet Path

Bullet Path

Input type: `Edittext`

Valuename: "Bullet-Path"

Dialog Bullet Path

Dialog Bullet Path

Input type: `Edittext`

Valuename: "Dlg-Bullet-Path"

Horizontal Line Path

Horizontal Line Path

Input type: `Edittext`

Valuename: "HorizontalLine-Path"

Dialog Horizontal Line Path

Dialog Horizontal Line Path

Input type: `Edittext`

Valuename: "Dlg-HorizontalLine-Path"

Local Content

Local Content

Input type: `Edittext`

Valuename: "LocalContent"

Workgroup Content

Workgroup Content

Input type: `Edittext`

Valuename: "WorkgroupContent"

Local Page Styles

Local Page Styles

Input type: `Edittext`

Valuename: "LocalPageStyles"

Workgroup Page Styles

Workgroup Page Styles

Input type: `Edittext`

Valuename: "WorkgroupPageStyles"

Clipart URL

Clipart URL

Input type: `Edittext`

Valuename: "Clipart-URL"

Template URL

Template URL

Input type: `Edittext`

Valuename: "Template-URL"

AutoUpDate

AutoUpDate

Input type: `Edittext`

Valuename: "AutoUpDate"

AutoUpDate Address

AutoUpDate Address

Input type: `Edittext`

Valuename: "AutoUpDateAddress"

Word 97 → Miscellaneous

Keyname: "Software\Microsoft\Office\8.0\Word\Options"

Date Format

Default date Format

Input type: `Combobox`

Valuename: "DATEFORMAT"

Time Format

Default Time Format

Input type: `Combobox`

Valuename: "TIMEFORMAT"

No Edit Time

Do not display edit time in document statistics.

Valuename: "NoEditTime"

Windows

Internet Settings

Note that these policies are also available in the *ieak.adm* template.

Keyname: "Software\Microsoft\Windows\CurrentVersion\Internet Settings"

Proxy Server

Input type: `Edittext`

Valuename: "ProxyServer"

Proxy Override

Input type: `Edittext`

Valuename: "ProxyOverride"

Proxy Enable

Input type: `Checkbox`

Valuename: "ProxyEnable"

Internet Explorer 3.0

Options_Navigation

Change the URL of the home or search page

Keyname: "Software\Microsoft\Internet Explorer\Main"

Start Page

Input type: `Edittext`

Valuename: "Start Page"

Search Page

Input type: `Edittext`

Valuename: "Search Page"

Bookshelf

Location of Bookshelf Content

Keyname: "Software\Microsoft\Microsoft Reference\Bookshelf\96L\Options"

Location of Bookshelf Content

Input type: `Edittext`

Valuename: "Drive"

Remove Tools_Look Up Reference menu from Excel

By default, Look Up is disabled for Run from Network Server installs. Use this policy to remove the item from the menu.

Keyname: "Software\Microsoft\Office\8.0\Excel\Init Commands"

Valuename: "bshxl1"

Computer Properties

Office 97

Default Save

Note: If the Assistant is not installed, there is no prompt before a file is saved in the default format. See the "Default Save" policy under Default User to specify save formats for each of the apps.

Keyname: "Software\Microsoft\Office\8.0\Common\Default Save"

Prompt Text

Input type: `Edittext`

Valuename: "Prompt Text"

Disable Password Caching

Password cache files (*.pwl*) for share-level resources or applications are no longer generated. Since it is possible to uncover a user"s password by cracking the password files, checking this policy increases security.

Keyname: "Software\Microsoft\Office\8.0\Common\Security"

Valuename: "DisablePwdCaching"

Uninstall

Note that this will work only if the installation is completely local. Shared components on the network or CD will not be updated.

Keyname: "Software\Microsoft\Windows\CurrentVersion\Uninstall\Office8.0"

Command to point Add/Remove to new network install location

Input type: `Edittext`

Valuename: "UninstallString"

Office 97 → Assistant

Keyname: "Software\Microsoft\Office\8.0\Common\Assistant"

Installed Path

Location of actor (.act) and preview (.acp) files

Input type: `Edittext`

Valuename: "AsstPath"

Source Path

Location where additional actor (.act) files can be found

Input type: `Edittext`

Valuename: "AsstSourcePath"

Excel 97 → Microsoft Map

Keyname: "Software\Microsoft\Shared Tools\Map\Directories"

Map Data

Directory where map data is stored

Input type: `Edittext`

Valuename: "MapData"

Search Paths

Enter the paths as one string with semicolons separating each entry.

Directories where shared map data is stored

Input type: `Edittext`

Valuename: "SearchPaths"

Excel 97 → Converters

Excel 9.0 Import Converter

When Office 9.0 is released, we will make available a converter that allows Excel 8.0 to read Excel 9.0 files. Until then, don"t set this policy.

Keyname: "Software\Microsoft\Office\8.0\Excel\Microsoft Excel"

Path for Excel 9.0 import converter

Input type: `Edittext`

Valuename: "FileFilterPath"

PowerPoint 97 → Converters

PowerPoint 9.0 Import Converter

When Office 9.0 is released, we will make available a converter that allows PowerPoint 8.0 to read PowerPoint 9.0 files. Until then, don"t set this policy.

Keyname: "Software\Microsoft\Office\8.0\PowerPoint\Translators\Import\PP9X32"

Path for PowerPoint 9.0 import converter

Input type: `Edittext`

Valuename: "Path"

Word 97 → Spelling Advanced

Default AutoCorrect File

The default AutoCorrect file is *mso97.acl*. Use this policy to set an alternate filename.

Keyname: "Software\Microsoft\Shared Tools\AutoCorrect\8.0"

Path to default AutoCorrect file for new users

Input type: `Edittext`

Valuename: "Path"

Custom Dictionaries

Keyname: "Software\Microsoft\Shared Tools\Proofing Tools\Custom Dictionaries"

Paths to additional dictionaries by number. Value Name=2–10 Value=Dictionary Path

Input type: `Listbox`

Word 97 → Spelling Advanced → New Dictionary Locations

(Use these policies if Microsoft provides updated dictionaries between releases.)

Spelling English (United States)

Keyname: "Software\Microsoft\Shared Tools\Proofing Tools\Spelling\1033\Normal"

Path to MSSP2_EN.LEX

Input type: **Edittext**

Valuename: "Dictionary"

Spelling English (British)

Keyname: "Software\Microsoft\Shared Tools\Proofing Tools\Spelling\2057\Normal"

Path to MSSP2_EN.LEX

Input type: **Edittext**

Valuename: "Dictionary"

Spelling English (Australia)

Keyname: "Software\Microsoft\Shared Tools\Proofing Tools\Spelling\3081\Normal"

Path to MSSP2_EN.LEX

Input type: **Edittext**

Valuename: "Dictionary"

Thesaurus English (United States)

Keyname: "Software\Microsoft\Shared Tools\Proofing Tools\Thesaurus\1033\Normal"

Path to MSTH_AM.LEX

Input type: **Edittext**

Valuename: "Dictionary"

Thesaurus English (British)

Keyname: "Software\Microsoft\Shared Tools\Proofing Tools\Thesaurus\2057\Normal"

Path to MSTH_AM.LEX

Input type: **Edittext**

Valuename: "Dictionary"

Hyphenation English (United States)

Keyname: "Software\Microsoft\Shared Tools\Proofing Tools\Hyphenation\1033\Normal"

Path to HY_EN.LEX

Input type: **Edittext**

Valuename: "Dictionary"

Hyphenation English (British)

Keyname: "Software\Microsoft\Shared Tools\Proofing Tools\Hyphenation\2057\Normal"

Path to HY_EN.LEX

Input type: `Edittext`

Valuename: "Dictionary"

Grammar English (United States)

Keyname: "Software\Microsoft\Shared Tools\Proofing Tools\Grammar\1033\Normal"

Path to MSGR_EN.LEX

Input type: `Edittext`

Valuename: "Dictionary"

Word 97 → Converters

Word 9.0 Import Converter

When Office 9.0 is released, we will make available a converter that allows Word 8.0 to read Word 9.0 files. Until then, don"t set this policy.

Keyname: "Software\Microsoft\Shared Tools\Text Converters\Import\MSWord9"

Path for Word 9.0 import converter

Input type: `Edittext`

Valuename: "Path"

Name of converter

Input type: `Edittext`

Valuename: "Name"

Clip Art Gallery 3.0

Path to *.cag* database containing regular ClipArt (*.wmf* files), multimedia (*.avi* and *.wav* files), or photos (*.bmp*, *.jpg*, *.gif*, etc.).

Concurrent Database #1 through Database #3

This policy allows you to divide your clipart into a maximum of three different files.

Keynames: "Software\Microsoft\ClipArt Gallery\3.0\ConcurrentDatabases\Policy Database 1" through "Software\Microsoft\ClipArt Gallery\3.0\ConcurrentDatabases\Policy Database3"

Path

Input type: `Edittext`

Valuename: "CAG"

Windows

Network Install Tab

Keyname: "Software\Microsoft\Windows\CurrentVersion"

Location of INI file with list of network install locations

Input type: `Edittext`

Valuename: "AppInstallPath"

Outlk97.adm

This template is included with the Office 97 Resource Kit, the Windows 98 ZAK, and the Windows NT ZAK. The policy categories are arranged according to the application menu options.

User Properties

Microsoft Outlook 97 → Tools | Options → General

Keyname: "Software\Microsoft\Office\8.0\Outlook\Options\General"

Warn Before Deleting

Warn before permanently deleting items.

Valuename: "WarnDelete"

Synchronize Folders

When online, synchronize all folders upon exiting.

Valuename: "SyncAtClose"

Microsoft Outlook 97 → Tools | Options → E-Mail

Keyname: "Software\Microsoft\Office\8.0\Outlook\Options\General"

Process delivery, read, and recall receipts on arrival

Valuename: "AutoProcRcpts"

Process requests and responses on arrival

Valuename: "AutoProcReq"

Delete receipts and blank meeting responses after processing

Valuename: "AutoDelRcpts"

WordMail

Keyname: "Software\Microsoft\Office\8.0\Outlook"

Use WordMail as an email editor

Input type: `Dropdownlist`

Valuename: "DefaultWordMail"

Actionlist Keyname: "Software\Microsoft\Office\8.0\Word\Options\OutlookEditor"

Actionlist Valuename: ""

WordMail Template

Keyname: "Software\Microsoft\Office\8.0\Word\Stationery"

Path and filename of WordMail template

Input type: `Edittext`

Valuename: "Default Template"

Microsoft Outlook 97 → Tools | Options → Calendar

Keyname: "Software\Policies\Microsoft\Office\9.0\Outlook\Options\Calendar"

Work week

Work week

Length of work week.

Input type: `Dropdownlist`

Valuename: "Workday"

First day of the week

First day of the week

Choose the first day of the week.

Input type: `Dropdownlist`

Valuename: "FirstDOW"

First week of year

First week of the year

Choose the first week of the year.

Input type: `Dropdownlist`

Valuename: "FirstWOY"

Working hours

Start time

Input type: `Dropdownlist`

Valuename: "CalDefStart"

End time

Input type: `Dropdownlist`

Valuename: "CalDefEnd"

Appointment defaults

Duration (min)

Input type: `Numeric`

Valuename: "DefDuration"

Reminder (min)

Input type: `Numeric`

Valuename: "RemindDefault"

Show Week Numbers

Show Week Numbers.

Valuename: "WeekNum"

Use Schedule

Checking or clearing this setting will have no effect, since this policy is a machine setting and so must be set using the Default Computer properties.

Microsoft Outlook 97 → Tools | Options → Task/Notes

Keyname: "Software\Microsoft\Office\8.0\Outlook\Options\Tasks"

Reminder Time

Reminder time

Input type: `Dropdownlist`

Valuename: "TaskRemindTime"

Set Reminders

Set reminders on tasks with due dates.

Valuename: "TaskAutoRemind"

Track Tasks

Keep updated copies of assigned tasks on my task list.

Valuename: "AddToUpdList"

Send Status Reports

Send status reports when assigned tasks are completed.

Valuename: "AddToSOCList"

Task color options

Overdue tasks

Input type: `Dropdownlist`

Valuename: "OverdueColor"

Completed tasks

Input type: `Dropdownlist`

Valuename: "CompleteColor"

Work Settings

Hours per day

Input type: `Dropdownlist`

Valuename: "UnitsPerDay"

Hours per week

Input type: `Dropdownlist`

Valuename: "UnitsPerWeek"

Note Defaults

Keyname: "Software\Microsoft\Office\8.0\Outlook\Options\Note"

Color

Input type: `Dropdownlist`

Valuename: "NoteColor"

Size

Input type: `Dropdownlist`

Valuename: "NoteSize"

Show time and date

Input type: `Checkbox`

Valuename: "NoteDatestamp"

Microsoft Outlook 97 → Tools | Options → Journal

Journaling tracks activity for specific items in a timeline format.

Automatically record these items

E-mail Message

Input type: `Checkbox`

Keyname: "Software\Microsoft\Shared Tools\Outlook\Journaling\E-mail Message"

Valuename: "Enabled"

Fax

Input type: `Checkbox`

Keyname: "Software\Microsoft\Shared Tools\Outlook\Journaling\Fax"

Valuename: "Enabled"

Meeting cancellation

Input type: `Checkbox`

Keyname: "Software\Microsoft\Shared Tools\Outlook\Journaling\Meeting Cancellation"

Valuename: "Enabled"

Meeting request

Input type: Checkbox

Keyname: "Software\Microsoft\Shared Tools\Outlook\Journaling\Meeting Request"

Valuename: "Enabled"

Meeting response

Input type: Checkbox

Keyname: "Software\Microsoft\Shared Tools\Outlook\Journaling\Meeting Response"

Valuename: "Enabled"

Task request

Input type: Checkbox

Keyname: "Software\Microsoft\Shared Tools\Outlook\Journaling\Task Request"

Valuename: "Enabled"

Task response

Input type: Checkbox

Keyname: "Software\Microsoft\Shared Tools\Outlook\Journaling\Task Response"

Valuename: "Enabled"

Also record these files

Microsoft Access

Input type: Checkbox

Keyname: "Software\Microsoft\Shared Tools\Outlook\Journaling\Microsoft Access"

Valuename: "Enabled"

Microsoft Office Binder

Input type: Checkbox

Keyname: "Software\Microsoft\Shared Tools\Outlook\Journaling\Microsoft Binder"

Valuename: "Enabled"

Microsoft Excel

Input type: Checkbox

Keyname: "Software\Microsoft\Shared Tools\Outlook\Journaling\Microsoft Excel"

Valuename: "Enabled"

Microsoft PowerPoint

Input type: `Checkbox`

Keyname: "Software\Microsoft\Shared Tools\Outlook\Journaling\Microsoft PowerPoint"

Valuename: "Enabled"

Microsoft Word

Input type: `Checkbox`

Keyname: "Software\Microsoft\Shared Tools\Outlook\Journaling\Microsoft Word"

Valuename: "Enabled"

Journal Entry Options

Keyname: "Software\Microsoft\Office\8.0\Outlook\Options\Journal"

Double-clicking a journal entry

Input type: `Dropdownlist`

Valuename: "Journal Open Assoc Item"

Microsoft Outlook 97 → Tools | Options → Reminders

Reminder Options

Keyname: "Software\Microsoft\Office\8.0\Outlook\Options\Reminders"

Display the reminder

Input type: `Checkbox`

Valuename: "Type"

Play the reminder sound

Input type: `Checkbox`

Valuename: "PlaySound"

Sound filename

Input type: `Edittext`

Keyname: "AppEvents\Schemes\Apps\Office97\Office97-Reminder\.current"

Valuename: ""

Microsoft Outlook 97 → Tools | Options → Spelling

Keyname: "Software\Microsoft\Office\8.0\Outlook\Options\Spelling"

Suggest Replacements

Always suggests replacements for misspelled words.

Valuename: "SpellAlwaysSuggest"

Check Spelling

Always checks spelling before sending.

Valuename: "Check"

Ignore Uppercase

Ignores words in UPPERCASE

Valuename: "SpellIgnoreUpper"

Ignore Numbers

Ignores words with numbers.

Valuename: "SpellIgnoreNumbers"

Ignore Original

Ignores original message text in reply or forward.

Valuename: "SpellIgnoreProtect"

Microsoft Outlook 97 → Internet → Help_Microsoft on the Web

Keyname: "Software\Microsoft\Office\8.0\Outlook\WebHelp"

Customize submenu

To enter your own commands to be displayed for this Help option, use the format "DisplayName,URL or UNC". For more details, refer to the ORK.

CommandX

Command1 through Command 8 are available.

Input type: `Edittext`

Valuename: "Command1" through "Command8"

Reset submenu to original defaults

Resets the Microsoft on the Web submenu to original values.

Actionlist Valuenames: "Command1" through "Command8"

Disable submenu

Disables the Microsoft on the Web submenu.

Actionlist Valuenames: "Command1" through "Command8"

Microsoft Outlook 97 → Internet → Converters

Future File Format Converters

To provide an Intranet site for future file format converters (such as future versions of Office), enter a URL or UNC path, e.g., *http://mycorp/support.html.*

Keyname: "Software\Microsoft\Office\8.0\Outlook\WebHelp"

URL for Converter

Input type: `Edittext`

Valuename: "Converters"

Microsoft Outlook 97 → Miscellaneous

Disable Forms Designer

Disable Outlook forms designer

Keyname: "Software\Microsoft\Office\8.0\Outlook"

Valuename: "NoOutlookFormsDesigner"

Computer Properties

Outlook 97

Use Schedule+

Uses Microsoft Schedule 7.0 as primary calendar. Setting this policy (checked or blank) grays out the option and prevents users from changing their calendars.

Keyname: "Software\Microsoft\Office\8.0\Outlook\SchedPlusOption"

Valuename: "UseSchedPlus"

Actionlist Valuename: "UserCanChange"

Rpc_Binding_Order

Enters the binding order with commas between each item.

Example: ncalrpc,ncacn_ip_tcp,ncacn_spx,ncacn_np

Keyname: "Software\Microsoft\Exchange\Exchange Provider"

Rpc_Binding_Order

Input type: `Edittext`

Valuename: "Rpc_Binding_Order"

Query97.adm

This template is included with the Office 97 resource kit, the Windows 98 ZAK and the Windows NT ZAK. The policy categories for Microsoft Query are arranged according to the Query 97 menu options. Note that this template has no computer properties.

User Properties

Query 97 → File_New

Data Source Folders

Keyname: "Software\Microsoft\Office\8.0\Query\DataSourceFolders"

Enter paths to data sources

This policy can be used to make a list of folders to be displayed in the Choose Data Source dialog box (under New in the File menu).

Input type: `Listbox`

Use Wizard

Create and edit queries using the Query Wizard.

Keyname: "Software\Microsoft\Office\8.0\Query\Wizard"

Valuename: "UseWizard"

Query 97 → Edit_Options

Keyname: "Software\Microsoft\Office\8.0\Query\Microsoft Query"

Disable Options

This policy disables (grays out) the Edit_options menu item.

Valuename: "DisableOptions"

Connection Timeout

Cancel the connection if not connected within . . . seconds

Sets the ODBC query time limit before a time-out error occurs, a value of 0 means there is no timeout limit.

Input type: `Numeric`

Valuename: "ODBCTimeout"

Limit Records

Limit the number of records returned to . . . records

Sets the ODBC query record limit, a setting of 0 means there is no record limit.

Input type: `Numeric`

Valuename: "Records"

Auto Disconnect

Keep connections open until MS Query is closed.

Valuename: "AutoDisconnect"

Disable Edit

Disable ability to edit query records.

Valuename: "AllowEdit"

Query 97 → Table Options

Keyname: "Software\Microsoft\Office\8.0\Query\Table Options"

Show Tables

Valuename: "Tables"

Show Views

Valuename: "Views"

Show System Tables

Valuename: "SysTables"

Show Synonyms

Valuename: "Synonyms"

Query 97 → Records

Automatic Query

When this policy is checked each time a field is added to a query the query is updated. Set this option to cleared if you have large queries that take a long time to run.

Keyname: "Software\Microsoft\Office\8.0\Query\Microsoft Query"

Valuename: "Auto Query"

ODBC 3.0

Default DSN Folder

Keyname: "Software\ODBC\ODBC.INI\ODBC File DSN"

Folder where ODBC 3.0 File DSNs are created

A DSN is an ODBC data source name file containing a database name, the ODBC used to access the database, and other connection information and settings.

Input type: `Edittext`

Valuename: "DefaultDSNDir"

Office 2000 Templates

These templates contain customization and restrmuiction policies for Microsoft Office 2000. Since Office 97 did not recognize the data type REG_EXPAND_SZ, those policies could not use environmental variables. However, because Office 2000 can recognize this data type, environmental variables can be used in some of these policies (indicated in the comment section of the policies themselves). Note that Windows 9x does not create environment variables automatically, and so they must be created and defined within network logon scripts.

This section includes the following templates:

Access9.adm
: This template contains policies for Microsoft Access 2000, part of the Office 2000 suite.

Clipgal5.adm
: This template contains policies for Clip Gallery, part of the Office 2000 suite. The Clip Gallery indexes clip art plus other multimedia files such as sound and video clips.

Excel9.adm
: This template contains policies for Excel 2000, part of the Office 2000 suite.

Frontpg4.adm
: This template contains policies for FrontPage 2000, part of the Office 2000 suite.

Instlr1.adm
: This template contains policies for the Windows installer. The Windows installer allows an administrator to automate the installation of Microsoft Office 2000.

Office9.adm
: This template contains policies common to all Office 2000 applications.

Outlk9.adm
: This template contains policies for Outlook 2000, part of the Office 2000 suite.

Ppoint9.adm
: This template contains policies for PowerPoint 2000, part of the Office 2000 suite.

Pub9.adm
: This template contains policies for Publisher, part of the Office 2000 suite.

Word9.adm
: This template contains policies for Word 2000, part of the Office 2000 suite.

Access9.adm

This template is included with the Office Resource Kit 2000 (ORK2000). Note that this template has no computer properties.

User Properties

Microsoft Access 2000 → Tools | Options... → Web Options → General

Keyname: "Software\Policies\Microsoft\Office\9.0\Access\Internet"

Hyperlink color

Hyperlink color

Input type: `Dropdownlist`

Valuename: "HyperlinkColor"

Followed hyperlink color

Followed hyperlink color

Input type: `Dropdownlist`

Valuename: "FollowedHyperlinkColor"

Underline hyperlinks

Check to enforce settings on; uncheck to enforce setting Off

Input type: `Checkbox`

Valuename: "DoNotUnderlineHyperlinks"

Microsoft Access 2000 → Tools | Macro → Security

Keyname: "Software\Policies\Microsoft\Office\9.0\Access\Security"

Security Level

Input type: `Dropdownlist`

Valuename: "Level"

Trust all installed add-ins and templates

Check to enforce setting on; uncheck to enforce setting off

If checked, even documents with unsigned macros will be trusted.

Input type: `Checkbox`

Valuename: "DontTrustInstalledFiles"

Microsoft Access 2000 → Customize error message

List of error messages to customize

Enter error ID for Valuename and custom button text for Value.

Keyname: "Software\Policies\Microsoft\Office\9.0\Access\CustomizableAlerts"

List of error messages to customize

The valuename is the numeric value for the error message, and the value is the text that will appear on the button.

Input type: `Listbox`

Actionlist Valuename: "PolicyOn"

Microsoft Access 2000 → Disable items in user interface → Predefined

To make menu options completely unavailable, disable the toolbar button and menu command as well as the shortcut key. Even if both a menu command and its corresponding shortcut key are disabled, the command is still available through Visual Basic Assistant (VBA) so that macros using the command can be created.

Disable command bar buttons and menu items

Keyname: "Software\Policies\Microsoft\Office\9.0\Access\DisabledCmdBarItemsCheckBoxes"

Actionlistoff Valuename: "FileOpenSearchTheWeb"

File → Open... → Tools → Find...

Input type: Checkbox

Valuename: "FileOpenToolsFind"

File → Send to → Mail Recipient

Input type: Checkbox

Valuename: "FileSendToMailRecipient"

Insert → Hyperlink

Input type: Checkbox

Valuename: "InsertHyperlink"

Tools → Online Collaboration

Input type: Checkbox

Valuename: "ToolsCollaboration"

Tools → Security...

Input type: Checkbox

Valuename: "ToolsSecurity"

Tools → Security → set database Password

Input type: Checkbox

Valuename: "ToolsSecuritySetPwd"

Tools → Security Database Security

Input type: Checkbox

Valuename: "ToolsSecurityDBSec"

Tools → Security → User and Group Permissions...

Input type: Checkbox

Valuename: "ToolsSecurityPerms"

Tools → Security → User and Group Accounts

Input type: `Checkbox`

Valuename: "ToolsSecurityAccts"

Tools → Security → User-Level Security Wizard

Input type: `Checkbox`

Valuename: "ToolsSecuritySecWiz"

Tools → Security → Encrypt | Decrypt Database

Input type: `Checkbox`

Valuename: "ToolsSecurityEncrypt"

Tools → Macro

Input type: `Checkbox`

Valuename: "ToolsMacro"

Tools → Macro → Visual Basic Editor

Input type: `Checkbox`

Valuename: "ToolsMacroVBE"

Tools → Macro → Run Macro

Input type: `Checkbox`

Valuename: "ToolsMacroRunMacro"

Tools → Macro → Convert Macros to Visual Basic

Input type: `Checkbox`

Valuename: "ToolsMacroConvertMacros"

Tools → Macro → Create Menu from Macro

Input type: `Checkbox`

Valuename: "ToolsMacroCreateMenu"

Tools → Macro → Create Toolbar from Macro

Input type: `Checkbox`

Valuename: "ToolsMacroCreateToolbar"

Tools → Macro → Create Shortcut Menu from Macro

Input type: `Checkbox`

Valuename: "ToolsMacroCreateShortcutMenu"

Tools → Add-Ins...

Input type: `Checkbox`

Valuename: "ToolsAddins"

Tools → Customize

Input type: Checkbox

Valuename: "ToolsCustomize"

Tools → Options...

Input type: Checkbox

Valuename: "ToolsOptions"

Help → Office on the Web

Input type: Checkbox

Valuename: "HelpOfficeWeb"

Help → Detect and Repair...

Input type: Checkbox

Valuename: "HelpRepair"

Web → Refresh Current Page

Input type: Checkbox

Valuename: "WebRefreshCurrentPage"

Web → Start Page

Input type: Checkbox

Valuename: "WebStartPage"

Web → Search the Web

Input type: Checkbox

Valuename: "WebSearchTheWeb"

Actionlist Valuename: "FileOpenSearchTheWeb"

Web → Favorites

Input type: Checkbox

Valuename: "WebFavorites"

Web → Go

Input type: Checkbox

Valuename: "WebGo"

Web → Address

Input type: Checkbox

Valuename: "WebAddress"

Disable shortcut keys

Keyname: "Software\Policies\Microsoft\Office\9.0\Access\DisabledShortcut-KeysCheckBoxes"

Ctrl+F (Find...)

Input type: `Checkbox`

Valuename: "Find"

Ctrl+K (Insert → Hyperlink...)

Input type: `Checkbox`

Valuename: "InsertHyperlink"

Alt+F11 (Tools → Macro → Visual Basic Editor)

Input type: `Checkbox`

Valuename: "ToolsMacroVBE"

Microsoft Access 2000 → Disable Items in user interface → Custom

Disable command bar buttons and menu items

Keyname: "Software\Policies\Microsoft\Office\9.0\Access\DisabledCmdBar-ItemsList"

Enter a command bar ID to disable

Look up control IDs for buttons and menu items using VBA.

Input type: `Listbox`

Disable shortcut keys

Keyname: "Software\Policies\Microsoft\Office\9.0\Access\DisabledShortcut-KeysList"

Enter a Key and modifier to disable

To disable a custom shortcut key, look up the virtual key code corresponding to the shortcut key. Enter it in the format "key,modifier". For example Alt-K would be entered as 75,16.

Input type: `Listbox`

Microsoft Access 2000 → Miscellaneous

Do not prompt to convert older databases

Keyname: "Software\Policies\Microsoft\Office\9.0\Access\Settings"

Check to force setting on: uncheck to force setting off

Input type: `Checkbox`

Valuename: "NoConvertDialog"

Custom Answer Wizard database path

Keyname: "Software\Policies\Microsoft\Office\9.0\Access\Answer Wizard"

Custom Answer Wizard database path

Customized help can be created using the Answer Wizard Builder. Environmental variables can be used to define the path.

Input type: `Edittext`

Valuename: "AdminDatabase"

Clipgal5.adm

This template is included with the Office Resource Kit 2000 (ORK2000).

User Properties

Microsoft Clip Gallery 5.0

Disable Clips Online access from Clip Gallery

Check to force setting on; uncheck to force setting off.

Disable access to the Clip Gallery Live web site.

Input type: `Checkbox`

Keyname: "Software\Policies\Microsoft\Office\9.0\ClipGallery"

Valuename: "DisableClipsOnline"

Excel9.adm

This template is included with the Office Resource Kit 2000 (ORK2000).

User Properties

Microsoft Excel 2000 → Tools | Options → View

Keyname: "Software\Policies\Microsoft\Office\9.0\Excel\Options\BinaryOptions"

Show Formula bar in Normal View

Check to enforce setting on; uncheck to enforce setting off

Input type: `Checkbox`

Valuename: "fFmlaF_1_1"

Show Status bar in Normal View

Check to enforce setting on; uncheck to enforce setting off

Input type: `Checkbox`

Valuename: "fStatusBar_2_1"

Show Formula bar in Full View

Check to enforce setting on; uncheck to enforce setting off

Input type: `Checkbox`

Valuename: "fFmlaFull_68_1"

Show Status bar in Full View

Check to enforce setting on; uncheck to enforce setting off

Input type: `Checkbox`

Valuename: "fStatusFull_67_1"

Windows in Taskbar

Check to enforce setting on; uncheck to enforce setting off

Input type: `Checkbox`

Keyname: "Software\Policies\Microsoft\Office\9.0\Excel\Options"

Valuename: "ShowWindowsInTaskbar"

Comments

Comments

Comment and indicator, or indicator only.

Input type: `Dropdownlist`

Valuename: "vmdNoteDisp_38_2"

Actionlist Valuename: "fNoteOffv5_35_1"

Microsoft Excel2000 → Tools | Options → Edit

Keyname: "Software\Policies\Microsoft\Office\9.0\Excel\Options\BinaryOptions"

Edit directly in cell

Check to enforce setting on; uncheck to enforce setting off

Input type: `Checkbox`

Valuename: "fNoInCell_66_1"

Allow cell drag and drop

Check to enforce setting on; uncheck to enforce setting off

Input type: `Checkbox`

Valuename: "fDisableDman_36_1"

Alert before overwriting cells

Check to enforce setting on; uncheck to enforce setting off

Input type: `Checkbox`

Valuename: "fNoDragWarning_76_1"

Move selection after Enter

Check to enforce setting on; uncheck to enforce setting off

Input type: `Checkbox`

Valuename: "fEnterMove_75_1"

Move selection after Enter direction

Move selection after Enter direction

Input type: `Dropdownlist`

Keyname: "Software\Policies\Microsoft\Office\9.0\Excel\Options"

Valuename: "MoveEnterDir"

Fixed decimal to 2 places

Check to enforce setting on; uncheck to enforce setting off

Input type: `Checkbox`

Keyname: "Software\Policies\Microsoft\Office\9.0\Excel\Options"

Valuename: "AutoDec"

Cut, copy, and sort objects with cells

Check to enforce setting on; uncheck to enforce setting off

Input type: `Checkbox`

Valuename: "fObjWCellMove_71_1"

Ask to update automatic links

Check to enforce setting on; uncheck to enforce setting off

Input type: `Checkbox`

Valuename: "fUpdateExt_78_1"

Provide feedback with Animation

Check to enforce setting on; uncheck to enforce setting off

Input type: `Checkbox`

Valuename: "fAnimationsOK_129_1"

Enable AutoComplete for cell values

Check to enforce setting on; uncheck to enforce setting off

Input type: `Checkbox`

Valuename: "fAutoComplete_128_1"

Extend list formats and formulas

Check to enforce setting on; uncheck to enforce setting off

Input type: `Checkbox`

Keyname: "Software\Policies\Microsoft\Office\9.0\Excel\Options"

Valuename: "ExtendList"

Enable automatic percent entry

Check to enforce setting on; uncheck to enforce setting off

Input type: `Checkbox`

Valuename: "fDisableAutoPercent_99_1"

Microsoft Excel 2000 → Tools|Options → General

Keyname: "Software\Policies\Microsoft\Office\9.0\Excel\Options\BinaryOptions"

R1C1 reference style

Check to enforce setting on: uncheck to enforce setting off

Row and column (R1C1) reference style

Input type: `Checkbox`

Valuename: "fRefA1_4_1"

Ignore other applications

Check to enforce setting on; uncheck to enforce setting off

Input type: `Checkbox`

Valuename: "fDdeEnabled_6_1"

Recently used file list

Entries on recently used file list

Input type: `Numeric`

Keyname: "Software\Policies\Microsoft\Office\9.0\Excel\Options"

Valuename: "DefFileMRU"

Actionlist Valuename: "fNoMRU_70_1"

Prompt for workbook properties

Check to enforce setting on; uncheck to enforce setting off

Input type: `Checkbox`

Valuename: "fPromptSumInfo_65_1"

Zoom on roll with IntelliMouse

Check to enforce setting on; uncheck to enforce setting off

Input type: `Checkbox`

Valuename: "fRollZoom_98_1"

Default Sheets

Sheets in new workbook

Input type: `Numeric`

Keyname: "Software\Policies\Microsoft\Office\9.0\Excel\Options"

Valuename: "DefSheets"

Font

Name, Size

Input type: `Combobox`

Keyname: "Software\Policies\Microsoft\Office\9.0\Excel\Options"

Valuename: "Font"

Default file location

Default file location

Environmental variables can be used in this policy.

Input type: `Edittext`

Keyname: "Software\Policies\Microsoft\Office\9.0\Excel\Options"

Valuename: "DefaultPath"

Alternate startup file location

Alternate startup file location

Environmental variables can be used in this policy

Input type: `Edittext`

Keyname: "Software\Policies\Microsoft\Office\9.0\Excel\Options"

Valuename: "AltStartup"

Microsoft Excel 2000 → Tools|Options... → Web Options → General

Keyname: "Software\Policies\Microsoft\Office\9.0\Excel\Internet"

Save any additional data necessary to maintain formulas

Check to enforce setting on; uncheck to enforce setting off

Input type: `Checkbox`

Valuename: " DoNotSaveHiddenData "

Load pictures from Web pages not created in Excel

Check to enforce setting on; uncheck to enforce setting off

Input type: `Checkbox`

Valuename: "DoNotLoadPictures"

Microsoft Excel 2000 → Tools|Options... → Transition

Save Excel files as

Keyname: "Software\Policies\Microsoft\Office\9.0\Excel\Options"

Save Excel files as

Input type: `Dropdownlist`

Valuename: "DefaultFormat"

Microsoft Excel menu or Help key

Enter ASCII value for key of choice (e.g., "/"=47)

Keyname: "Software\Policies\Microsoft\Office\9.0\Excel\Options"

Help Key

Input type: `Edittext`

Valuename: "MenuKey"

Microsoft Excel menus or Lotus 1-2-3 Help

Input type: `Dropdownlist`

Keyname: "Software\Policies\Microsoft\Office\9.0\Excel\Options\BinaryOptions"

Valuename: "fLotusHelp_34_1"

Transition navigation keys

Keyname: "Software\Policies\Microsoft\Office\9.0\Excel\Options\BinaryOptions"

Check to enforce setting on; uncheck to enforce setting off

Uses an alternate command set to move through the worksheets.

Input type: `Checkbox`

Valuename: "fISI_33_1"

Microsoft Excel 2000 → Tools | Options... → Chart

Keyname: "Software\Policies\Microsoft\Office\9.0\Excel\Options\BinaryOptions"

Show names

Check to enforce setting on; uncheck to enforce setting off

Input type: `Checkbox`

Valuename: "fShowChartNames_96_1"

Show values

Check to enforce setting on; uncheck to enforce setting off

Input type: `Checkbox`

Valuename: "fShowChartTipValues_97_1"

Microsoft Excel 2000 → Tools | Options... → Right-to-Left

Keyname: "Software\Policies\Microsoft\Office\9.0\Excel\Options"

Default direction

Default direction

Input type: `Dropdownlist`

Valuename: "DefaultSheetR2L"

Cursor movement

Cursor movement

Input type: `Dropdownlist`

Valuename: "CursorVisual"

Show control characters

Check to enforce setting on; uncheck to enforce setting off

Input type: `Checkbox`

Valuename: "ControlCharacters"

Microsoft Excel 2000 → Tools|Macro → Record New Macro..

Store macro in Personal Macro Workbook by default

Keyname: "Software\Policies\Microsoft\Office\9.0\Excel\Options\Binary-Options"

Check to enforce setting on; uncheck to enforce setting off

Input type: `Checkbox`

Valuename: "fGlobalSheet_37_1"

Microsoft Excel 2000 → Tools|Macro → Security

Keyname: "Software\Policies\Microsoft\Office\9.0\Excel\Security"

Security Level

Security Level

Input type: `Dropdownlist`

Valuename: "Level"

Trust all installed add-ins and templates

Check to enforce setting on; uncheck to enforce setting off

If checked, even documents with unsigned macros will be trusted.

Input type: `Checkbox`

Valuename: "DontTrustInstalledFiles "

Microsoft Excel 2000 → Customize error messages

List of error messages to customize

Enters error ID for Valuename and custom button text for Value.

Keyname: "Software\Policies\Microsoft\Office\9.0\Excel\CustomizableAlerts"

Actionlist Valuename: "PolicyOn"

List of error messages to customize

The Valuename is the numeric value for the error message, and the Value is the text that will appear on the button.

Input type: `Listbox`

Microsoft Excel 2000 → Disable items in user interface → Predefined

To make menu options completely unavailable, disable the toolbar button and menu command as well as the shortcut key. Even if both a menu command and its corresponding shortcut key are disabled, the command is still available through Visual Basic Assistant (VBA) so that macros using the command can be created.

Disable command bar buttons and menu items

Keyname: "Software\Policies\Microsoft\Office\9.0\Excel\DisabledCmd-BarItemsCheckBoxes"

Actionlistoff Valuenames: "FilePublishAsWebPage", "WebOptions", "General-Options", "FileOpenSearchTheWeb"

File | Open... | Tools | Find..

Input type: `Checkbox`

Valuename: "FileOpenToolsFind"

File | Save as Web Page...

Input type: `Checkbox`

Valuename: "FileSaveAsWebPage"

Actionlist Valuename: "FilePublishAsWebPage"

File | Web Page Preview

Input type: `Checkbox`

Valuename: "FileWebPagePreview"

File | Send to | Mail Recipient

Input type: `Checkbox`

Valuename: "FileSendToMailRecipient"

Insert | Hyperlink

Input type: `Checkbox`

Valuename: "InsertHyperlink"

Tools | Protection

Input type: `Checkbox`

Valuename: "ToolsProtect"

Tools | Protection | Protect Sheet

Input type: `Checkbox`

Valuename: "ToolsProtectSheet"

Tools | Protection | Protect Workbook

Input type: `Checkbox`

Valuename: "ToolsProtectWorkbook"

Tools | Protection | Protect and Share Workbook

Input type: Checkbox

Valuename: "ToolsProtectShare"

Tools | Online Collaboration

Input type: Checkbox

Valuename: "ToolsCollaboration"

Tools | Macro

Input type: Checkbox

Valuename: "ToolsMacro"

Tools | Macro | Macros...

Input type: Checkbox

Valuename: "ToolsMacroMacros"

Tools | Macro | Record New Macro

Input type: Checkbox

Valuename: "ToolsMacroRecord"

Tools | Macro | Security

Input type: Checkbox

Valuename: "ToolsMacroSecurity"

Tools | Macro | Visual Basic Editor

Input type: Checkbox

Valuename: "ToolsMacroVBE"

Tools | Macro | Microsoft Script Editor

Input type: Checkbox

Valuename: "ToolsMacroWeb"

Tools | Add-Ins...

Input type: Checkbox

Valuename: "ToolsAddins"

Tools | Customize

Input type: Checkbox

Valuename: "ToolsCustomize"

Tools | Options...

Input type: Checkbox

Valuename: "ToolsOptions"

Actionlist Valuenames: "WebOptions", "GeneralOptions"

Help | Office on the Web

Input type: Checkbox

Valuename: "HelpOfficeWeb"

Help | Detect and Repair...

Input type: Checkbox

Valuename: "HelpRepair"

Web | Refresh Current Page

Input type: Checkbox

Valuename: "WebRefreshCurrentPage"

Web | Start Page

Input type: Checkbox

Valuename: "WebStartPage"

Web | Search the Web

Input type: Checkbox

Valuename: "WebSearchTheWeb"

Actionlist Valuename: "FileOpenSearchTheWeb"

Web | Favorites

Input type: Checkbox

Valuename: "WebFavorites"

Web | Go

Input type: Checkbox

Valuename: "WebGo"

Web | Address

Input type: Checkbox

Valuename: "WebAddress"

Disable shortcut keys

Keyname: "Software\Policies\Microsoft\Office\9.0\Excel\DisabledShortcutKeysCheckBoxes"

Ctrl+F (Find)

Input type: Checkbox

Valuename: "Find"

Ctrl+K (Insert | Hyperlink)

Input type: Checkbox

Valuename: "InsertHyperlink"

Alt+F8 (Tools | Macro | Macros)

Input type: `Checkbox`

Valuename: "ToolsMacroMacros"

Alt+F11 (Tools |Macro | Visual Basic Editor)

Input type: `Checkbox`

Valuename: "ToolsMacroVBE"

Alt+Shift+F11 (Tools |Macro |Microsoft Script Editor)

Input type: `Checkbox`

Valuename: "ToolsMacroWeb"

Microsoft Excel 2000 → Disable items in user interface → Custom

Disable command bar buttons and menu items

Keyname: "Software\Policies\Microsoft\Office\9.0\Excel\DisabledCmd-BarItemsList"

Enter a command bar ID to disable

Look up control IDs for buttons and menu items using VBA.

Input type: `Listbox`

Disable shortcut keys

Keyname: "Software\Policies\Microsoft\Office\9.0\Excel\DisabledShortcut-KeysList"

Enter a key and modifier to disable

To disable a custom shortcut key, look up the virtual key code corresponding to the shortcut key. Enter it in the format "key,modifier". For example, Alt-K would be entered as 75,16.

Input type: `Listbox`

Microsoft Excel 2000 → Miscellaneous

Keyname: "Software\Policies\Microsoft\Office\9.0\Excel\Options"

Chart gallery path

Chart gallery path

Environmental variables can be used in this policy.

Input type: `Edittext`

Valuename: "GalleryPath"

Custom Answer Wizard database path

Keyname: "Software\Policies\Microsoft\Office\9.0\Excel\Answer Wizard"

Custom Answer Wizard database path

Customized help can be created using the Answer Wizard Builder. Environmental variables can be used to define the path.

Input type: `Edittext`

Valuename: "AdminDatabase"

Enable four-digit year display

Check to enforce setting on; uncheck to enforce setting off

Input type: `Checkbox`

Valuename: "EnableFourDigitYearDisplay"

Frontpg4.adm

This template is included with the Office Resource Kit 2000 (ORK2000). Note that this template has no computer properties.

User Properties

Microsoft Front Page 2000 → Disable items in user interface → Predefined

Disable command bar buttons and menu items

Keyname: "Software\Policies\Microsoft\Office\9.0\FrontPage\DisabledCmdBarItemsCheckBoxes"

File | Open... | Tools |Find...

Input type: `Checkbox`

Valuename: "FileOpenToolsFind"

View | Toobars | Customize...

Input type: `Checkbox`

Valuename: "ViewToolbarsCustomize"

Format | Style

Input type: `Checkbox`

Valuename: "FormatStyle"

Format |Style Sheet Links...

Input type: `Checkbox`

Valuename: "FormatStyleSheetLinks"

Format |Position

Input type: `Checkbox`

Valuename: "FormatPosition"

Insert | Advanced | ActiveXControl ...
Input type: Checkbox

Valuename: "InsertAdvActiveXControl"

Insert | Component | Office Spreadsheet
Input type: Checkbox

Valuename: "InsertCompWebCalc"

Insert | Component | Office PivotTable
Input type: Checkbox

Valuename: "InsertCompPivotList"

Insert | Component | Office Chart
Input type: Checkbox

Valuename: "InsertCompWebChart"

Insert | Advanced | Java Applet...
Input type: Checkbox

Valuename: "InsertAdvJavaApplet"

Insert | Component | Banner Ad Manager...
Input type: Checkbox

Valuename: "InsertCompBannerAdManager"

Insert | Component | Hover Button
Input type: Checkbox

Valuename: "InsertCompHoverButton"

Insert | Component | Hit Counter...
Input type: Checkbox

Valuename: "InsertCompHitCounter"

Insert | Component | Search Form...
Input type: Checkbox

Valuename: "InsertCompSearchForm"

Insert | Component | Confirmation Field...
Input type: Checkbox

Valuename: "InsertCompConfirmationField"

Insert | Component | Marquee...
Input type: Checkbox

Valuename: "InsertCompMarquee"

Insert | Picture | Video...
Input type: Checkbox

Valuename: "InsertPictureVideo"

Insert | Advanced | Design-Time Control

Input type: Checkbox

Valuename: "InsertAdvDTC"

Insert | Advanced | Plugin

Input type: Checkbox...

Valuename: "InsertAdvPlugIn"

Insert | Advanced | Show Design-Time Controls

Input type: Checkbox

Valuename: "InsertAdvShowDTC"

Insert | Database | Results...

Input type: Checkbox

Valuename: "InsertDBResults"

Insert | Database | Column Value...

Input type: Checkbox

Valuename: "InsertDBColValue"

Format | Dynamic HTML Effects

Input type: Checkbox

Valuename: "FormatDHTMLEffects"

Format | Page Transition...

Input type: Checkbox

Valuename: "FormatPageTransitions"

Format | Theme

Input type: Checkbox

Valuename: "FormatTheme"

Format | Shared Borders...

Input type: Checkbox

Valuename: "FormatSharedBorders"

Tools | Security | Permissions...

Input type: Checkbox

Valuename: "ToolsSecurityPermissions"

Tools | Security | Change Password...

Input type: Checkbox

Valuename: "ToolsSecurityChangePassword"

Tools | Add-ins...
Input type: Checkbox

Valuename: "ToolsAddIns"

Tools | Customize
Input type: Checkbox

Valuename: "ToolsCustomize"

Tools | Web Settings...
Input type: Checkbox

Valuename: "ToolsWebSettings"

Tools | Macro | Macros...
Input type: Checkbox

Valuename: "ToolsMacroMacros"

Tools | Macro | Visual Basic Editor
Input type: Checkbox

Valuename: "ToolsMacroVBE"

Tools | Macro | Microsoft Script Editor
Input type: Checkbox

Valuename: "ToolsMacroMSE"

Tools | Options
Input type: Checkbox

Valuename: "ToolsOptions"

Help | Office on the Web
Input type: Checkbox

Valuename: "HelpOfficeWeb"

Help | Detect and Repair
Input type: Checkbox

Valuename: "HelpRepair"

Microsoft FrontPage2000 → Disable items in user interface → Custom

Disable command bar buttons and menu items
Keyname: "Software\Policies\Microsoft\Office\9.0\FrontPage\DisabledCmd-BarItemsList"

Enter a command bar ID to disable
Input type: Listbox

Instlr1.adm

This template is included with the Office Resource Kit 2000 (ORK2000).

User Properties

Windows Installer

Keyname: "Software\Policies\Microsoft\Windows\Installer"

Always install with elevated privileges

Check to enforce setting on; uncheck to enforce setting off

This policy allows the software package to have administrator privileges when installing into system areas.

Input type: `Checkbox`

Valuename: "AlwaysInstallElevated"

Search order

Search order

Order in which to search the three types of sources: n=network, m=media (CD), u=URL. Leave letter(s) out to remove that type of source from the search. A few valid examples: nmu, n, nu, mn.

Input type: `Edittext`

Valuename: "SearchOrder"

Leave transform at package source

Check to enforce setting on; uncheck to enforce setting off

This policy sets the location of transforms to the root of the source of the installation package.

Input type: `Checkbox`

Valuename: "TransformsAtSource"

Disable rollback

Check to enforce setting on; uncheck to enforce setting off

If enabled, the installer does not store rollback files (files deleted during installation). Use of this policy is not recommended, since it will prevent the workstation from being restored to its original state if an installation is unsuccessful.

Input type: `Checkbox`

Valuename: "DisableRollback"

Computer Properties

Windows Installer

Keyname: "Software\Policies\Microsoft\Windows\Installer"

Always install with elevated privileges

Check to enforce setting on; uncheck to enforce setting off

This policy allows the software package to have administrator privileges when installing into system areas.

Input type: `Checkbox`

Valuename: "AlwaysInstallElevated"

Disable Windows Installer

Disable Windows Installer

This policy allows the installer to be completely disabled, disabled only for non-managed applications, or always enabled.

Input type: `Dropdownlist`

Valuename: "DisableMSI"

Disable browse dialog box for new source

Check to enforce setting on; uncheck to enforce setting off

This policy prevents users from browsing to locate installer sources.

Input type: `Checkbox`

Valuename: "DisableBrowse"

Disable patching

Check to enforce setting on; uncheck to enforce setting off

A patch will update an application from one version to another. An administrator may want to disable patching in certain environments.

Input type: `Checkbox`

Valuename: "DisablePatch"

Allow user control over installs

Check to enforce setting on; uncheck to enforce setting off

The user is allowed control over installation settings.

Input type: `Checkbox`

Valuename: "EnableUserControl"

Disable IE security prompt for Window Installer scripts

Check to enforce setting on; uncheck to enforce setting off

This policy will allow a web page to install applications without a user"s knowledge.

Input type: Checkbox

Valuename: "SafeForScripting"

Office9.adm

This template is included with the Office Resource Kit 2000 (ORK2000). Note that this template has no computer properties.

User Properties

Microsoft Office 2000 → Tools | Customize | Options

Keyname: "Software\Policies\Microsoft\Office\9.0\Common\Toolbars"

Menus show recently used commands first

Check to enforce setting on; uncheck to enforce setting off

Input type: Checkbox

Valuename: "AdaptiveMenus"

Show full menus after a short delay

Check to enforce setting on; uncheck to enforce setting off

Input type: Checkbox

Valuename: "AutoExpandMenus"

Large Icons

Check to enforce setting on; uncheck to enforce setting off

Input type: Checkbox

Valuename: "BtnSize"

List font names in their font

Check to enforce setting on; uncheck to enforce setting off

Input type: Checkbox

Valuename: "FontView"

Show Screen Tips on toolbars

Check to enforce setting on; uncheck to enforce setting off

Input type: Checkbox

Valuename: "Tooltips"

Show shortcut keys in Screen Tips

Check to enforce setting on; uncheck to enforce setting off

Input type: Checkbox

Valuename: "ShowKbdShortcuts"

Menu animations

Menu animations

Input type: `Dropdownlist`

Valuename: "Animation"

Microsoft Office 2000 → Tools | AutoCorrect (Excel, PowerPoint and Access)

Keyname: "Software\Policies\Microsoft\Office\9.0\Common\AutoCorrect"

Correct TWo INitial CApitals

Check to enforce setting on; uncheck to enforce setting off

Input type: `Checkbox`

Valuename: "CorrectTwoInitialCapitals"

Capitalize first letter of sentence

Check to enforce setting on; uncheck to enforce setting off

Input type: `Checkbox`

Valuename: "CapitalizeSentence"

Capitalize names of days

Check to enforce setting on; uncheck to enforce setting off

Input type: `Checkbox`

Valuename: "CapitalizeNamesOfDays"

Correct accidental us of cAPS LOCK key

Check to enforce setting on; uncheck to enforce setting off

Input type: `Checkbox`

Valuename: "ToggleCapsLock"

Replace text as you type

Check to enforce setting on; uncheck to enforce setting off

Input type: `Checkbox`

Valuename: "ReplaceText"

Microsoft Office 2000 → Tools | Options | General | Web Options... → General

Rely on CSS for font formatting

Cascading style sheets are not supported by some older browsers.

Keyname: "Software\Policies\Microsoft\Office\9.0\Common\Internet"

Check to enforce CSS on, uncheck to enforce CSS off

Input type: `Checkbox`

Valuename: "DoNotRelyOnCSS"

Use the CSS setting for Word as an E-mail editor

Input type: `Checkbox`

Valuename: "UseRelyOnCSSForMail"

Microsoft Office 2000 → Tools | Options | General | Web Options... → Files

Keyname: "Software\Policies\Microsoft\Office\9.0\Common\Internet"

Organize supporting files in a folder

Check to enforce setting on; uncheck to enforce setting off

This will be forced on if "Use long filenames" is forced off

Input type: `Checkbox`

Valuename: "DoNotOrganizeInFolder"

Use long filenames whenever possible

Check to enforce setting on; uncheck to enforce setting off

Input type: `Checkbox`

Valuename: "DoNotUseLongFileNames"

Update links on save

Check to enforce setting on; uncheck to enforce setting off

Input type: `Checkbox`

Valuename: "DoNotUpdateLinksOnSave"

Check if Office is the default editor for Web pages created in Office

Check to enforce setting on; uncheck to enforce setting off

Input type: `Checkbox`

Valuename: "DoNotCheckIfOfficeIsHTMLEditor"

Download Office Web Components

Download Office Web Components from

Input type: `Checkbox`

Valuename: "DownloadComponents"

Location

Environmental variables can be used in this policy.

Input type: `Edittext`

Valuename: "LocationOfComponents"

Microsoft Office 2000 → Tools | Option | General | Web Options → Pictures

Keyname: "Software\Policies\Microsoft\Office\9.0\Common\Internet"

Rely on VML for displaying graphics in browsers

Check to enforce setting on; uncheck to enforce setting off

Image files are created from drawing objects when a document is saved as a web page.

Input type: `Checkbox`

Valuename: "RelyOnVML"

Allow PNG as an output format

Check to enforce setting on; uncheck to enforce setting off

Portable Network Graphics is allowed as a format.

Input type: `Checkbox`

Valuename: "AllowPNG"

Target Monitor

Screen size

Input type: `Dropdownlist`

Valuename: "ScreenSize"

Pixels per inch

Input type: `Dropdownlist`

Valuename: "PixelsPerInch"

Microsoft Office 2000 → Tools | Options | General | Web Options → Encoding

Default or specific encoding

Keyname: "Software\Policies\Microsoft\Office\9.0\Common\Internet"

Always save Web pages in the default encoding

Input type: `Checkbox`

Valuename: "AlwaysSaveInDefaultEncoding"

Save this document as

Input type: `Dropdownlist`

Valuename: "Encoding"

Microsoft Office 2000 → Help | Office on the Web

Office on the Web URL

Keyname: "Software\Policies\Microsoft\Office\9.0\Common\Internet"

Office on the Web URL

Input type: `Edittext`

Valuename: "OfficeOnTheWeb"

Microsoft Office 2000 → Shared paths

Keyname: "Software\Policies\Microsoft\Office\9.0\Common\General"

User templates path

User templates path

Environmental variables can be used in this policy.

Input type: `Edittext`

Valuename: "UserTemplates"

Shared templates path

Shared templates path

Environmental variables can be used in this policy.

Input type: `Edittext`

Valuename: "SharedTemplates"

Shared themes path

Shared themes path

Environmental variables can be used in this policy.

Input type: `Edittext`

Valuename: "WorkgroupThemes"

Web queries path

Web queries path

Environmental variables can be used in this policy.

Input type: `Edittext`

Valuename: "UserQueriesFolder"

Microsoft Office 2000 → Assistant → General

Choose Assistant File

Keyname: "Software\Policies\Microsoft\Office\Common\Assistant"

Choose Assistant file

Input type: `Combobox`

Valuename: "AsstFile"

Tip timeout

Keyname: "Software\Policies\Microsoft\Office\9.0\Common\Assistant"

Time tip bulb remains on (sec)

Input type: `Numeric`

Valuename: "AsstTipTimeout"

Microsoft Office 2000 → Assistant → Options Tab

Keyname: "Software\Policies\Microsoft\Office\9.0\Common\Assistant"

Use the Office Assistant

Keyname: "Software\Policies\Microsoft\Office\Common\Assistant"

Check to enforce setting on; uncheck to enforce setting off

Input type: `Checkbox`

Valuename: "AsstState"

Respond to F1 key

Check to enforce setting on; uncheck to enforce setting off

Input type: `Checkbox`

Valuename: "AsstAssistWithHelp"

Help with wizards

Check to enforce setting on; uncheck to enforce setting off

Input type: `Checkbox`

Valuename: "AsstAssistWithWizards"

Display alerts

Check to enforce setting on; uncheck to enforce setting off

Input type: `Checkbox`

Valuename: "AsstAssistWithAlerts"

Search for both product and programming help

Check to enforce setting on; uncheck to enforce setting off

Input type: `Checkbox`

Valuename: "AsstSearchInProgram"

Move when in the way

Check to enforce setting on; uncheck to enforce setting off

Input type: `Checkbox`

Valuename: "AsstMoveWhenInTheWay"

Guess Help topics

Check to enforce setting on; uncheck to enforce setting off

Input type: `Checkbox`

Valuename: "AsstGuessHelp"

Make sounds

Check to enforce setting on; uncheck to enforce setting off

Input type: `Checkbox`

Valuename: "AsstSounds"

Using features more effectively

Check to enforce setting on; uncheck to enforce setting off

Input type: `Checkbox`

Valuename: "AsstFeatureTips"

Using the mouse more effectively

Check to enforce setting on; uncheck to enforce setting off

Input type: `Checkbox`

Valuename: "AsstMousetips"

Keyboard shortcuts

Check to enforce setting on; uncheck to enforce setting off

Input type: `Checkbox`

Valuename: "AsstKeyboardShortcutTips"

Only show high priority tips

Check to enforce setting on; uncheck to enforce setting off

Input type: `Checkbox`

Valuename: "AsstOnlyHighPriorityTips"

Show the Tip of the Day at startup

Check to enforce setting on; uncheck to enforce setting off

Input type: `Checkbox`

Valuename: "AsstShowTipOfDay"

Microsoft Office 2000 → Assistant → Help on the Web

Keyname: "Software\Policies\Microsoft\Office\9.0\Common\Internet"

Feedback button label

Feedback button label

Replace the button label on the Assistant balloon that starts with "None of the above..."

Input type: `Edittext`

Valuename: "AWFeedbackBalloonLabel"

Feedback dialog text

Feedback Dialog Text

Replace the feedback dialog text that starts with "Click the Send and go to the web button below..."

Input type: `Edittext`

Valuename: "AWFeedbackDialogText"

Feedback URL

Feedback URL

Redirect feedback to a different URL.

Input type: `Edittext`

Valuename: "AWFeedbackURL"

Microsoft Office 2000 → Language settings → User Interface

Keyname: "Software\Policies\Microsoft\Office\9.0\Common\LanguageResources"

Display menus and dialog boxes in (language)

Display menus and dialog boxes in (language)

Select language.

Input type: `Dropdownlist`

Valuename: "UILanguage"

Display help in

Display help in

Select language

Input type: `Dropdownlist`

Valuename: "HelpLanguage"

Microsoft Office 2000 → Language settings → Enabled Languages

Keyname: "Software\Policies\Microsoft\Office\9.0\Common\LanguageResources"

Preferred Asian or right-to-left language

Preferred Asian or right-to-left language

Input type: `Dropdownlist`

Valuename: "ExeMode"

Installed version of Microsoft Office

Installed version of Microsoft Office

Input type: `Dropdownlist`

Valuename: "InstallFlavor"

Microsoft Office 2000 → Language settings → Enabled Languages → Show controls and enable editing for

Afrikaans, Albanian, Arabic, Armenian, Assamese, Azeri (Cyrillic), Azeri (Latin), Basque, Belarusian, Bengali, Catalan, Chinese (Simplified), Chinese (Traditional), Croatian, Czech, Danish, Dutch, English (Australian), English (Canadian), English (U.K.), English (U.S.), Estonian, Faeroese, Farsi, Finnish, French, French (Canadian), Frisian, Georgian, German, German (Austrian), German (Swiss), Greek,

Gujarati, Hebrew, Hungarian, Icelandic, Indonesian, Italian, Japanese, Kannada, Kashmiri, Kazakh, Konkani, Korean, Latvian, Lithuanian (Classic), Macedonian, Malay, Malayalam, Manipuri, Marathi, Nepali, Norwegian (Bokmal), Norwegian (Nynorsk), Oriya, Polish, Portuguese, Portuguese (Brazilian), Punjabi, Romanian, Russian, Sanskrit, Serbian (Cyrillic), Serbian (Latin), Sindi, Slovak, Slovenian, Spanish, Swahili, Swedish, Tamil, Tatar, Telugu, Thai, Turkish, Ukranian, Usbek (Cyrillic), Uzbek (Latin), Vietnamese

These language options are available as separate checkboxes, but are shown together here for the sake of brevity.

Keyname: "Software\Policies\Microsoft\Office\9.0\Common\LanguageResources"

Check to enforce setting on; uncheck to enforce setting off

The Valuenames below refer respectively to the languages mentioned above.

Input type: `Checkbox`

Valuenames: "1078", "1052", "1025", "1067", "1101", "2092", "1068", "1069", "1059", "1093", "1026", "1027", "2052", "1028", "1050", "1029", "1030", "1043", "3081", "4105", "2057", "1033", "1061", "1080", "1065", "1035", "1036" , "3084", "1122", "1079", "1031", "3079", "2055", "1032", "1095", "1037", "1081", "1038", "1039", "1057", "1040", "1041", "1099", "1120", "1087", "1111", "1042", "1062", "1063", "2087", "1071", "1086", "1100", "1112", "1102", "1121", "1044", "2068", "1096", "1045", "2070" "1046", "1094", "1048", "1049", "1103", "3098", "2074", "1113", "1051", "1060", 3082", "1089", "1053", "1097", "1092", "1098", "1054", "1055", "1058", "1056", "2115", "1091", "1066"

Microsoft Office 2000 → Language settings → Other

Keyname: "Software\Policies\Microsoft\Office\9.0\Common\LanguageResources"

Do not adjust defaults to user"s locale

Check to enforce setting on; uncheck to enforce setting off

Input type: `Checkbox`

Valuename: "Pure"

Disallow Taiwan calendar

Check to enforce setting on; uncheck to enforce setting off

Input type: `Checkbox`

Valuename: "ShowDates"

Microsoft Office 2000 → Customizable error messages

Keyname: "Software\Policies\Microsoft\Office\9.0\Common\General"

Base URL

Base URL

Enter the URL followed by a question mark (?). Or, to include custom parameters, enter the URL, a question mark, your query string, and then an ampersand (&).

Input type: `Edittext`

Valuename: "CustomizableAlertBaseURL"

Default button text

Default button text

Input type: `Edittext`

Valuename: "CustomizableAlertDefaultButtonText"

List of error messages to customize

The valuename is the numeric value for the error message, and the value is the text that will appear on the button.

Keyname: "Software\Policies\Microsoft\Office\9.0\Common\CustomizableAlerts"

List of error messages to customize

Input type: `Listbox`

Default save prompt text

Default save prompt text

Input type: `Edittext`

Valuename: "SavePromptText"

Microsoft Office 2000 → Disable items in user interface

Tooltip for disabled toolbar buttons and menu items

Keyname: "Software\Policies\Microsoft\Office\9.0\Common\Toolbars"

Tooltip for disabled toolbar buttons and menu items

Input type: `Edittext`

Valuename: "AttemptDisabledActionMessage"

Microsoft Office 2000 → Graph settings

Graph gallery path

Keyname: "Software\Policies\Microsoft\Office\9.0\Graph\Options"

Graph gallery path

Environmental variables can be used in this policy.

Input type: `Edittext`

Valuename: "GalleryPath"

List of error messages to customize
Keyname: "Software\Policies\Microsoft\Office\9.0\Graph\CustomizableAlerts"

Actionlist Valuename: "PolicyOn"

List of error messages to customize
The Valuename is the numeric value for the error message, and the value is the text that will appear on the button.

Input type: `Listbox`

Custom Answer Wizard database path
Keyname: "Software\Policies\Microsoft\Office\9.0\Graph\Answer Wizard"

Custom Answer Wizard database path
Customized help can be created using the Answer Wizard Builder. Environmental variables can be used to define the path.

Input type: `Edittext`

Valuename: "AdminDatabase"

Microsoft Office 2000 → Miscellaneous

Keyname: "Software\Policies\Microsoft\Office\9.0\Common\General"

Provide feedback with sound
Check to enforce setting on; uncheck to enforce setting off
Input type: `Checkbox`

Valuename: "Sound"

User system font instead of Tahoma
Check to enforce setting on; uncheck to enforce setting off
Input type: `Checkbox`

Valuename: "UseOfficeUIFont"

Do not track document editing time
Check to enforce setting on; uncheck to enforce setting off
Input type: `Checkbox`

Valuename: "NoTrack"

Disable Clipboard Toolbar triggers
Check to enforce setting on; uncheck to enforce setting off
Input type: `Checkbox`

Valuename: "AcbControl"

Do not replace tabs with spaces in HTML
Keyname: "Software\Policies\Microsoft\Office\9.0\Common\Internet"

Check to enforce setting on; uncheck to enforce setting off

Input type: `Checkbox`

Valuename: "ExportRealTabs"

Do not upload media files

Keyname: "Software\Policies\Microsoft\Office\9.0\Common\Internet"

Check to enforce setting on; uncheck to enforce setting off

Input type: `Checkbox`

Valuename: "DoNotUploadMedia"

Outlk9.adm

This template is included with the Office Resource Kit 2000 (ORK2000).

User Properties

Microsoft Outlook 2000 → Tools | Options → Preferences → E-mail options

Message handling

Keyname: "Software\Policies\Microsoft\Office\9.0\Outlook\Preferences"

After moving or deleting an open item

Choose action from `Dropdownlist`.

Input type: `Dropdownlist`

Valuename: "AfterMove"

Close original message when reply or forward

Input type: `Checkbox`

Valuename: "CloseOrig"

Save copies of messages in Sent Items folder

Input type: `Checkbox`

Valuename: "SaveSent"

Display a notification message when new mail arrives

Input type: `Checkbox`

Valuename: "Notification"

On replies and forwards

Keyname: "Software\Policies\Microsoft\Office\9.0\Outlook\Preferences"

When replying to a message

Choose action from `Dropdownlist`.

Input type: `Dropdownlist`

Valuename: "ReplyStyle"

When forwarding a message

Choose action from `Dropdownlist`.

Input type: `Dropdownlist`

Valuename: "ForwardStyle"

Prefix each line with

Input type: `Edittext`

Valuename: "PrefixText"

Allow user"s comments to be marked

Input type: `Checkbox`

Valuename: "Annotation"

Mark user"s comments with

Input type: `Edittext`

Valuename: "AnnotationText"

Microsoft Outlook 2000 → Tools | Option → Preferences → E-mail Options → Advanced E-mail Options

Save Messages

Keyname: "Software\Policies\Microsoft\Office\9.0\Outlook\Options\General"

Save unsent items in the folder

Input type: `Dropdownlist`

Valuename: "SAVE_LOC"

Autosave unsent messages every xx minutes (0=No autoSave):

Input type: `Numeric`

Valuename: "SAVE_MIN"

More save Messages

Keyname: "Software\Policies\Microsoft\Office\9.0\Outlook\Preferences"

In folders other than the Inbox, save replies with original message

Input type: `Checkbox`

Valuename: "SaveReplies"

Save forwarded messages

Input type: `Checkbox`

Valuename: "SaveFW"

When new items arrive

Keyname: "Software\Policies\Microsoft\Office\9.0\Outlook\Preferences"

Play a sound

Input type: `Checkbox`

Valuename: "PlaySound"

Briefly change the mouse cursor

Input type: `Checkbox`

Valuename: "ChangePointer"

When sending a message

Keyname: "Software\Policies\Microsoft\Office\9.0\Outlook\Preferences"

Set importance

Input type: `Dropdownlist`

Valuename: "Importance"

Set sensitivity

Input type: `Dropdownlist`

Valuename: "Sensitivity"

Allow commas as address separators

Input type: `Checkbox`

Valuename: "AllowCommasInRecip"

Automatic name checking

Input type: `Checkbox`

Valuename: "AutoNameCheck"

Delete meeting request from Inbox when responding

Input type: `Checkbox`

Valuename: "DeleteWhenRespond"

Microsoft Outlook 2000 → Tools | Options → Preferences → E-mail options → Tracking Options

Options

Process request and responses on arrival

Input type: `Checkbox`

Keyname: "Software\Policies\Microsoft\Office\9.0\Outlook\Options\General"

Valuename: "AutoProcReq"

Process receipts on arrival

Input type: `Checkbox`

Keyname: "Software\Policies\Microsoft\Office\9.0\Outlook\Options\General"

Valuename: "AutoProcRcpts"

After processing, move receipts

Input type: `Checkbox`

Keyname: "Software\Policies\Microsoft\Office\9.0\Outlook\Preferences"

Valuename: "MoveReceipts"

Delete blank voting and meeting responses after processing

Input type: `Checkbox`

Keyname: "Software\Policies\Microsoft\Office\9.0\Outlook\Options\General"

Valuename: "AutoDelRcpts"

Request a read receipt for all messages a user sends

Input type: `Checkbox`

Keyname: "Software\Policies\Microsoft\Office\9.0\Outlook\Preferences"

Valuename: "ReadReceipt"

Request deliver rcpt for all msgs a user sends (Exchange only)

Input type: `Checkbox`

Keyname: "Software\Policies\Microsoft\Office\9.0\Outlook\Preferences"

Valuename: "DeliveryReceipt"

When Outlook is asked to respond to a read receipt request

Input type: `Dropdownlist`

Keyname: "Software\Policies\Microsoft\Office\9.0\Outlook\Options\Mail"

Valuename: "Receipt Response"

Microsoft Outlook 2000 → Tools | Options → Preferences → E-mail options → Calendar options

Keyname: "Software\Policies\Microsoft\Office\9.0\Outlook\Options\Calendar"

Reminders on Calendar items

Keyname: "Software\Policies\Microsoft\Office\9.0\Outlook\Preferences"

Calendar items have reminders

Input type: `Checkbox`

Valuename: "ApptReminders"

Calendar item defaults

Default length of Calendar items (minutes)

Input type: `Numeric`

Valuename: "DefDuration"

Default length of Calendar item reminders (minutes)

Input type: `Numeric`

Valuename: "RemindDefault"

Work week

Length of work week

Input type: `Dropdownlist`

Valuename: "Workday"

First day of the week

Choose the first day of the week

Input type: `Dropdownlist`

Valuename: "FirstDOW"

First week of year

Choose the first week of the year

Input type: `Dropdownlist`

Valuename: "FirstWOY"

Working hours

Start time

Input type: `Dropdownlist`

Valuename: "CalDefStart"

End time

Input type: `Dropdownlist`

Valuename: "CalDefEnd"

Calendar week numbers

Display week numbers in Calendar

Input type: `Checkbox`

Valuename: "WeekNum"

Meeting Requests using iCalendar

Send meeting requests using iCalendar by default

iCalendar is supported by many different management programs, allowing users to schedule meetings across an organization or the Internet.

Input type: `Checkbox`

Valuename: "SendMtgAsICAL"

Microsoft Outlook 2000 → Tools | Options → Preferences → Calendar Options → Free/Busy options

Options

Keyname: "Software\Policies\Microsoft\Office\9.0\Outlook\Preferences"

Months of Free/Busy information published

Input type: `Numeric`

Valuename: "FBPublishRange"

Free/Busy updated on the server every xxx seconds

Input type: `Numeric`

Valuename: "FBUpdateSecs"

Internet Free/Busy Options

Keyname: "Software\Policies\Microsoft\Office\9.0\Outlook\Options\Calendar\"Internet Free/Busy""

Publish free/busy information

Input type: `Checkbox`

Valuename: "Publish to Internet"

Publish at this URL:

Input type: `Edittext`

Valuename: "Write URL"

Search at this URL:

Input type: `Edittext`

Valuename: "Read URL"

Microsoft Outlook 2000 → Tools | Options → Preferences → Task Options

Keyname: "Software\Policies\Microsoft\Office\9.0\Outlook\Options\Tasks"

Color options

Overdue color

Input type: `Dropdownlist`

Valuename: "OverdueColor"

Complete color

Input type: `Dropdownlist`

Valuename: "CompleteColor"

Task reminder options

Set default reminder time

Input type: `Dropdownlist`

Valuename: "TaskRemindTime"

Microsoft Outlook 2000 → Tools | Options → Preferences → Contact options

Select the default setting for how to file new contacts

Keyname: "Software\Policies\Microsoft\Office\9.0\Outlook\Contact"

Default Full Name order

Input type: `Dropdownlist`

Valuename: "NameParserStyle"

Default File As order

Input type: `Dropdownlist`

Valuename: "FileAsOrder"

Microsoft Outlook 2000 → Tools | Option → Preferences → Journal options

Journaling tracks activity for specific items in a timeline format.

Level of journaling

Keyname: "Software\Policies\Microsoft\Office\9.0\Outlook\Options\Journal"

Select level of journaling

Input type: `Dropdownlist`

Valuename: "EnableJournal"

Disable journaling of these Outlook items

E-mail Message

Input type: `Checkbox`

Keyname: "Software\Microsoft\Shared Tools\Outlook\Journaling\E-mail Message"

Valuename: "AutoJournaled"

Meeting cancellation

Input type: `Checkbox`

Keyname: "Software\Microsoft\Shared Tools\Outlook\Journaling\Meeting Cancellation"

Valuename: "AutoJournaled"

Meeting request

Input type: `Checkbox`

Keyname: "Software\Microsoft\Shared Tools\Outlook\Journaling\Meeting Request"

Valuename: "AutoJournaled"

Meeting response

Input type: `Checkbox`

Keyname: "Software\Microsoft\Shared Tools\Outlook\Journaling\Meeting Response"

Valuename: "AutoJournaled"

Task request

Input type: `Checkbox`

Keyname: "Software\Microsoft\Shared Tools\Outlook\Journaling\Task Request"

Valuename: "AutoJournaled"

Task response

Input type: `Checkbox`

Keyname: "Software\Microsoft\Shared Tools\Outlook\Journaling\Task Response"

Valuename: "AutoJournaled"

Automatically journal these items

E-mail Message

Input type: `Checkbox`

Keyname: "Software\Microsoft\Shared Tools\Outlook\Journaling\E-mail Message"

Valuename: "Enabled"

Meeting cancellation

Input type: `Checkbox`

Keyname: "Software\Microsoft\Shared Tools\Outlook\Journaling\Meeting Cancellation"

Valuename: "Enabled"

Meeting request

Input type: `Checkbox`

Keyname: "Software\Microsoft\Shared Tools\Outlook\Journaling\Meeting Request"

Valuename: "Enabled"

Meeting response

Input type: `Checkbox`

Keyname: "Software\Microsoft\Shared Tools\Outlook\Journaling\Meeting Response"

Valuename: "Enabled"

Task request

Input type: `Checkbox`

Keyname: "Software\Microsoft\Shared Tools\Outlook\Journaling\Task Request"

Valuename: "Enabled"

Task response

Input type: `Checkbox`

Keyname: "Software\Microsoft\Shared Tools\Outlook\Journaling\Task Response"

Valuename: "Enabled"

Automatically journal files from these applications

Microsoft Access

Input type: `Checkbox`

Keyname: "Software\Microsoft\Shared Tools\Outlook\Journaling\Microsoft Access"

Valuename: "Enabled"

Microsoft Excel

Input type: `Checkbox`

Keyname: "Software\Microsoft\Shared Tools\Outlook\Journaling\Microsoft Excel"

Valuename: "Enabled"

Microsoft PowerPoint

Input type: `Checkbox`

Keyname: "Software\Microsoft\Shared Tools\Outlook\Journaling\Microsoft PowerPoint"

Valuename: "Enabled"

Microsoft Word

Input type: `Checkbox`

Keyname: "Software\Microsoft\Shared Tools\Outlook\Journaling\Microsoft Word"

Valuename: "Enabled"

Journal entry options

Keyname: "Software\Policies\Microsoft\Office\9.0\Outlook\Options\Journal"

Double-clicking a journal entry

Input type: `Dropdownlist`

Valuename: "Journal Open Assoc Item"

Microsoft Outlook 2000 → Tools | Option → Preferences → Notes options

Notes appearance

Keyname: "Software\Policies\Microsoft\Office\9.0\Outlook\Options\Note"

Color

Input type: `Dropdownlist`

Valuename: "NoteColor"

Size

Input type: `Dropdownlist`

Valuename: "NoteSize"

Microsoft Outlook 2000 → Tools | Options → Mail Services (Corporate or Workgroup configuration)

Synchronize

Keyname: "Software\Policies\Microsoft\Office\9.0\Outlook\Options\General"

When online, synchronize all folders upon exiting

Input type: `Checkbox`

Valuename: "SyncAtClose"

When online, automatically synchronize all offline folders

Input type: `Checkbox`

Valuename: "AutoSyncOn"

Online synchronization interval (minutes)

Input type: `Numeric`

Valuename: "AutoSyncInt"

When offline, automatically synchronize

Input type: `Checkbox`

Valuename: "AutoSyncOffline"

Offline synchronization interval (minutes)

Input type: `Numeric`

Valuename: "AutoSyncIntOffline"

Profile Prompt

Keyname: "Software\Policies\Microsoft\Exchange\Client\Options"

Prompt for a profile to be used

Input type: `Checkbox`

Valuename: "PickLogonProfile"

Microsoft Outlook 2000 → Tools | Options → Mail Delivery (Internet Only Configuration)

Keyname: "Software\Policies\Microsoft\Office\9.0\Outlook\Options\Mail"

Mail account options

Send messages immediately

Input type: `Checkbox`

Valuename: "Send Mail Immediately"

Automatically check for new messages

Input type: `Checkbox`

Valuename: "Poll For Mail"

Interval to check for new messages (minutes)

Input type: `Numeric`

Valuename: "Poll For Mail Interval"

Dial-up options

Warn before switching dial-up connection

Input type: `Checkbox`

Valuename: "Warn on Dialup"

Hang up when finished sending, receiving, or updating

Input type: `Checkbox`

Valuename: "Hangup after Spool"

Automatically dial when checking for new messages

Input type: `Checkbox`

Valuename: "Poll on DUN"

Don"t download large messages

Input type: `Checkbox`

Valuename: "Skip Large Messages"

Message Size Limit (KB)

Input type: `Numeric`

Valuename: "Message Size Limit"

Microsoft Outlook 2000 → Tools | Option → Mail Format

Keyname: "Software\Policies\Microsoft\Office\9.0\Outlook\Options\Mail"

Message format/editor (Corporate or Workgroup Configuration)

Use the following Format/Editor for messages when Outlook is in Corporate or Workgroup configuration

Input type: `Dropdownlist`

Valuename: "ExchangeEditor"

Message format/editor (Internet Only Configuration)

Use the following Format/Editor for messages, when Outlook is in Internet Only configuration

Input type: `Dropdownlist`

Valuename: "InternetEditor"

Send pictures from the Internet

When using HTML format, send pictures from Internet

Input type: `Checkbox`

Valuename: "Send Pictures With Document"

Stationery Fonts

"Software\Policies\Microsoft\Office\9.0\Outlook\Options\Stationery"

Stationery font options

Input type: `Dropdownlist`

Valuename: "Font Override"

Microsoft Outlook 2000 → Tools | Options → Mail Format → Message format settings (Internet Only Configuration)

HTML message format settings

Keyname: "Software\Policies\Microsoft\Office\9.0\Outlook\Options\Mail"

Encode text using

Input type: `Dropdownlist`

Valuename: "Message HTML Encoding Format"

Allow 8-bit characters in headers

Input type: `Checkbox`

Valuename: "Message HTML Allow 8bit in Header"

Automatically wrap at <x> characters when sending

Input type: `Numeric`

Valuename: "Message HTML Character Line Wrap"

Text message format settings

Keyname: "Software\Policies\Microsoft\Office\9.0\Outlook\Options\Mail"

Select MIME/UUENCODE format

Input type: `Dropdownlist`

Valuename: "Message Plain Format MIME"

Encode text using

Input type: `Dropdownlist`

Valuename: "Message Plain Encoding Format"

Allow 8-bit characters in headers

Input type: `Checkbox`

Valuename: "Message Plain Allow 8bit in Header"

Automatically wrap at <x> characters when sending

Input type: `Numeric`

Valuename: "Message Plain Character Line Wrap"

Microsoft Outlook 2000 → Tools | Options → Mail Format → International Options

English message headers and flags

Keyname: "Software\Policies\Microsoft\Office\9.0\Outlook\Preferences"

Use English for message headers on replies or forwards

Input type: `Checkbox`

Valuename: "ENMessageHeaders"

Use English for message flags

Input type: `Checkbox`

Valuename: "ENMessageFlags"

Encoding for incoming and outgoing messages

Keyname: "Software\Policies\Microsoft\Office\9.0\Outlook\Options\MSHTML\International"

Use this encoding for outgoing messages

Input type: `Dropdownlist`

Valuename: "Default_CodePageOut"

Use this encoding for unmarked received messages

Input type: `Dropdownlist`

Valuename: "Default_CodePageIn"

Microsoft Outlook 2000 → Tools | Options → Mail Format → Signature

Don"t add signature

Keyname: "Software\Policies\Microsoft\Office\9.0\Outlook\Preferences"

Don"t add signature when replying or forwarding

Input type: `Checkbox`

Valuename: "AddSigToReplyNote"

Microsoft Outlook 2000 → Tools | Options → Spelling

General

Keyname: "Software\Policies\Microsoft\Office\9.0\Outlook\Options\Spelling"

Always suggest replacement for misspelled words

Input type: `Checkbox`

Valuename: "SpellAlwaysSuggest"

Always check spelling before sending

Input type: `Checkbox`

Valuename: "Check

Ignore words in UPPERCASE

Input type: `Checkbox`

Valuename: "SpellIgnoreUpper"

Ignore words with numbers

Input type: `Checkbox`

Valuename: "SpellIgnoreNumbers"

Ignore original message text in reply or forward

Input type: `Checkbox`

Valuename: "SpellIgnoreProtect"

Microsoft Outlook 2000 → Tools | Option → Security

Keyname: "Software\Microsoft\Office\9.0\Outlook\Security"

Required Certificate Authority

X.509 issue DN that restricts choice of certifying authorities

Enter certificate authority name (for example, Verisign, Inc.).

Input type: `Edittext`

Valuename: "RequiredCA"

Minimum encryption setting

Minimum key size (bits)

Input type: `Numeric`

Valuename: "MinEncKey"

S/MIME interoperability with external clients

Behavior for handling S/MIME messages

Input type: `Dropdownlist`

Valuename: "ExternalSMime"

Outlook Rich Text in S/MIME messages

Always send Outlook Rich Text formatting in S/MIME messages

Input type: `Checkbox`

Valuename: "ForceTNEF"

Microsoft Outlook 2000 → Tools | Options → Other

Keyname: "Software\Policies\Microsoft\Office\9.0\Outlook\Preferences"

Empty Deleted Items Folder

Empty the Deleted Items folder upon exiting

Input type: `Checkbox`

Valuename: "EmptyTrash"

AutoArchive

Turn on AutoArchive

Input type: `Checkbox`

Valuename: "DoAging

Number of days between AutoArchiving

Input type: `Numeric`

Valuename: "EveryDays"

Prompt before AutoArchiving

Input type: `Checkbox`

Valuename: "PromptForAging"

Delete expired items when AutoArchiving (email folders only)

Input type: `Checkbox`

Valuename: "DeleteExpired"

Preview Pane

Mark messages as read in preview window

Input type: `Checkbox`

Valuename: "PreviewMarkMessage"

Wait xxx seconds before marking items as read

Input type: `Numeric`

Valuename: "PreviewWaitSeconds"

Mark item as read when selection changes

Input type: `Checkbox`

Valuename: "PreviewDontMarkUntilChange"

Single key reading using spacebar

Input type: `Checkbox`

Keyname: "Software\Policies\Microsoft\Office\9.0\Outlook\Options\General"

Valuename: "SingleKeyReading"

Microsoft Outlook 2000 → Tools | Options → Other → Advanced

General

Keyname: "Software\Policies\Microsoft\Office\9.0\Outlook\Preferences"

When selecting text, automatically select entire word

Input type: `Checkbox`

Valuename: "WordSelect"

More Options

Keyname: "Software\Policies\Microsoft\Office\9.0\Outlook\Options\General"

Warn before permanently deleting items

Input type: `Checkbox`

Valuename: "WarnDelete"

Appearance options—Notes

Keyname: "Software\Policies\Microsoft\Office\9.0\Outlook\Options\Note"

When viewing Notes, show time and date

Input type: `Checkbox`

Valuename: "NoteDateStamp"

Appearance options—Tasks

Keyname: "Software\Policies\Microsoft\Office\9.0\Outlook\Options\Tasks"

Task working hours per day (in minutes)

Input type: `Numeric`

Valuename: "UnitsPerDay"

Task working hours per week (in minutes)

Input type: `Numeric`

Valuename: "UnitsPerWeek"

Microsoft Outlook 2000 → Tools | Options → Other → Advanced → Reminder Options

Reminders

Keyname: "Software\Policies\Microsoft\Office\9.0\Outlook\Options\Reminders"

Display the reminder

Input type: `Checkbox`

Valuename: "Type"

Play reminder sound

Input type: Checkbox

Valuename: "PlaySound"

More reminders

Keyname: "AppEvents\Schemes\Apps\Office97\Office97-Reminder\.Current"

Path and .wav file to play for reminder

Input type: Edittext

Valuename: ""

Microsoft Outlook 2000 → Tools | Options → Other → Advanced → Advanced Tasks

Advanced Tasks

Keyname: "Software\Policies\Microsoft\Office\9.0\Outlook\Options\Tasks"

Set reminders on tasks with due dates

Input type: Checkbox

Valuename: "TaskAutoRemind"

Keep updated copies of assigned tasks on user"s task list

Input type: Checkbox

Valuename: "AddToUpdList"

Send status reports when assigned tasks are completed

Input type: Checkbox

Valuename: "AddToSOCList"

Microsoft Outlook 2000 → Tools | Options → Other → Right-to-Left

Layout options

Keyname: "Software\Policies\Microsoft\Office\9.0\Outlook\Options\Calendar"

Set layout direction

Input type: Dropdownlist

Valuename: "Calendar Direction"

Set global text direction

Input type: Dropdownlist

Valuename: "Text Direction"

Set primary language

Input type: Dropdownlist

Valuename: "ME Date Type"

Use secondary calendar

Input type: `Checkbox`

Valuename: "Show BothCal"

Set secondary calendar language

Input type: `Dropdownlist`

Valuename: "Support Hijri"

Microsoft Outlook 2000 → Customize error message

List of error messages to customize

Keyname: "Software\Policies\Microsoft\Office\9.0\Outlook\CustomizableAlerts"

List of error messages to customize

The valuename is the numeric value for the error message, and the value is the text that will appear on the button.

Input type: `Listbox`

Microsoft Outlook 2000 → Disable items in user interface → Predefined

To make menu options completely unavailable, disable the toolbar button and menu command as well as the shortcut key. Even if both a menu command and its corresponding shortcut key are disabled, the command is still available through Visual Basic Assistant (VBA) so that macros using the command can be created.

Disable command bar buttons and menu items

Keyname: "Software\Policies\Microsoft\Office\9.0\Outlook\DisabledCmdBarItemsCheckBoxes"

All folders and items: Tools | Customize

Input type: `Checkbox`

Valuename: "ToolsCustomize"

All folders and items: Help | Office on the Web

Input type: `Checkbox`

Valuename: "HelpOfficeWeb"

All folders and items: Help | Detect and Repair

Input type: `Checkbox`

Valuename: "HelpRepair"

All folders: Favorite menu

Input type: `Checkbox`

Valuename: "WebFavorites"

All folders: Go menu

Input type: **Checkbox**

Valuename: "WebGo"

All folders: File | Open in default browser

Input type: **Checkbox**

Valuename: "OpenDefaultBrowser"

All folders: File | New | Outlook Bar shortcut to Web page

Input type: **Checkbox**

Valuename: "OutlookBarWebShortcut"

All folders: Go | Internet Call

Input type: **Checkbox**

Valuename: "GoInternetCall"

Inbox: Tools | Services

Input type: **Checkbox**

Valuename: "ToolsServices"

Mail item: View | Bcc Field

Input type: **Checkbox**

Valuename: "ViewBccField"

Actionlist Keyname: "Software\Policies\Microsoft\Office\9.0\Outlook\Preferences"

Actionlist Valuename: "ShowBcc"

Mail item: View | From Field

Input type: **Checkbox**

Valuename: "ViewFromField"

Actionlist Keyname: "Software\Policies\Microsoft\Office\9.0\Outlook\Preferences"

Actionlist Valuename: "ShowFrom"

Contact item: Actions | Display Map of Address

Input type: **Checkbox**

Valuename: "ActionDisplayMap"

Web toolbar: Refresh Current Page

Input type: **Checkbox**

Valuename: "WebRefreshCurrentPage"

Web toolbar: Start Page

Input type: `Checkbox`

Valuename: "WebStartPage"

Web toolbar: Search the Web

Input type: `Checkbox`

Valuename: "WebSearchTheWeb"

Actionlist Valuename: "FileOpenSearchTheWeb"

Web toolbar: Address

Input type: `Checkbox`

Valuename: "WebAddress"

Disable shortcut keys

Keyname: "Software\Policies\Microsoft\Office\9.0\Outlook\DisabledShortcut-KeysCheckBoxes"

Ctrl+Enter (Send in a Mail item}

Input type: `Checkbox`

Valuename: "CtrlEnter"

Microsoft Outlook 2000 → Disable items in user interface → Custom

Disable command bar buttons and menu items

Keyname: "Software\Policies\Microsoft\Office\9.0\Outlook\DisabledCmd-BarItemsList"

Enter a command bar ID to disable

Look up control IDs for buttons and menu items using VBA.

Input type: `Listbox`

Disable shortcut keys

Keyname: "Software\Policies\Microsoft\Office\9.0\Outlook\DisabledShortcut-KeysList"

Enter a key and modifier to disable

To disable a custom shortcut key, look up the virtual key code corresponding to the shortcut key. Enter it in the format "key,modifier". For example, Alt-K would be entered as 75,16.

Input type: `Listbox`

Microsoft Outlook 2000 → Miscellaneous

Resource scheduling

Keyname: "Software\Policies\Microsoft\Office\9.0\Outlook\Options\Calen-dar"

Enable direct booking of resources

Input type: `Checkbox`

Valuename: "EnableDirectBooking"

Default recurrence length (days):

Input type: `Numeric`

Valuename: "RecurrencesDefault"

NetMeeting

Keyname: "Software\Policies\Microsoft\Office\9.0\Outlook"

Disable all NetMeeting options and online meetings in Outlook

Input type: `Checkbox`

Valuename: "DisableOnlineMeetings"

Categories

Keyname: "Software\Policies\Microsoft\Office\9.0\Outlook\Categories"

Contents of Master Category list

Input type: `Edittext`

Valuename: "MasterList"

Date format for importing cc.Mail (DB8only)

Keyname: "Software\Policies\Microsoft\Office\9.0\Outlook"

If importing cc.Mail (DB8 only), set the appropriate date format:

Input type: `Dropdownlist`

Valuename: "ccm_date_tmpl"

Junk email filtering

Keyname: "Software\Policies\Microsoft\Office\9.0\Outlook\JunkEmail"

Junk email filtering is available

Input type: `Checkbox`

Valuename: "Disable"

Auto-repair of MAPI32.DLL

Keyname: "Software\Microsoft\Office\9.0\Outlook"

Choose a FIXPAMI.EXE option

Outlook requires the correct version of *mapi32.dll* be installed for it to function properly. Sometimes, other programs install a version that is incompatible with Outlook. Rather than run the *fixmapi.exe* utility manually. Outlook can run it automatically any time it detects a problem

Input type: `Dropdownlist`

Valuename: "FixMapi"

Net Folders

Keyname: "Software\Policies\Microsoft\Office\9.0\Outlook\NetFolder"

Net Folders is available

Input type: `Checkbox`

Valuename: "Enable"

Microsoft Outlook 2000 → Miscellaneous → Exchange settings

Exchange view information

Keyname: "Software\Microsoft\Office\9.0\Outlook"

Publish Exchange views in Public Folders

Input type: `Checkbox`

Valuename: "ExchVwPub"

Publish Exchange views in Personal (non-public) Folders

Input type: `Checkbox`

Valuename: "ExchVwPsnl"

Folder size display

Keyname: "Software\Microsoft\Office\9.0\Outlook"

Display "Folder Size" button in folder properties dialog

Input type: `Checkbox`

Valuename: "ChkFldrSize"

OST Creation

Keyname: "Software\Microsoft\Office\9.0\Outlook\OST"

Type of OST that is created

The off-line folder file (OST)

Input type: `Dropdownlist`

Valuename: "NoOST"

Personal distribution lists (Exchange only)

Keyname: "Software\Microsoft\Office\9.0\Outlook\Options\Mail"

Always validate personal DLs when sending mail

Input type: `Checkbox`

Valuename: "ExpandPDLUsingCache"

Microsoft Outlook 2000 → Miscellaneous → Outlook Today settings

Outlook Today availability

Keyname: "Software\Policies\Microsoft\Office\9.0\Outlook\Today"

Outlook Today is available

Input type: `Checkbox`

Valuename: "Disable"

URL for custom Outlook Today

Keyname: "Software\Policies\Microsoft\Office\9.0\Outlook\Today"

Enter the URL of Outlook Today"s web page

Input type: `Edittext`

Valuename: "Url"

Folders in the Messages section of Outlook Today

Keyname: "Software\Microsoft\Office\9.0\Outlook\Today\Folders"

Folder 1 through Folder 10

The folders listed below will appear in the messages section of Outlook Today. To add a folder, type the name of the folder in any of the fields below. For example, "inbox\friendsmail".

Input type: `Edittext`

Valuename: "0" through "9"

Microsoft Outlook 2000 → Miscellaneous → Folder Home Pages for Outlook special folders

Disable Folder Home Pages

Keyname: "Software\Policies\Microsoft\Office\9.0\Outlook\Webview"

Disable Folder home Pages for all folders

Input type: `Checkbox`

Valuename: "Disable"

Folder Home Page Security

Keyname: "Software\Policies\Microsoft\Office\9.0\Outlook\Webview"

Disable script access to Outlook object model

Input type: `Checkbox`

Valuename: "DisableScripting"

Inbox Folder Home Page

Keyname: "Software\Policies\Microsoft\Office\9.0\Outlook\Webview\Inbox"

Show associated web page

Input type: `Checkbox`

Valuename: "Show"

URL address of associated web page

Input type: `Edittext`

Valuename: "Url"

Turn off Internet Explorer security checks for this web page

Input type: `Checkbox`

Valuename: "Security"

Calendar Folder Home Page

Keyname: "Software\Policies\Microsoft\Office\9.0\Outlook\Webview\Calendar"

Show associated web page

Input type: `Checkbox`

Valuename: "Show"

URL address of associated web page

Input type: `Edittext`

Valuename: "Url"

Turn off Internet Explorer security checks for this web page

Input type: `Checkbox`

Valuename: "Security"

Contacts Folder Home Page

Keyname: "Software\Policies\Microsoft\Office\9.0\Outlook\Webview\Contacts"

Show associated web page

Input type: `Checkbox`

Valuename: "Show"

URL address of associated web page

Input type: `Edittext`

Valuename: "Url"

Turn off Internet Explorer security checks for this web page

Input type: `Checkbox`

Valuename: "Security"

Deleted Items Folder Home Page

Keyname: "Software\Policies\Microsoft\Office\9.0\Outlook\Webview\"Deleted Items""

Show associated web page

Input type: `Checkbox`

Valuename: "Show"

URL address of associated web page

Input type: `Edittext`

Valuename: "Url"

Turn off Internal Explorer security checks for this web page

Input type: `Checkbox`

Valuename: "Security"

Drafts Folder Home Page

Keyname: "Software\Policies\Microsoft\Office\9.0\Outlook\Webview\Drafts"

Show associated web page

Input type: `Checkbox`

Valuename: "Show"

URL address of associated web page

Input type: `Edittext`

Valuename: "Url"

Turn off Internet Explorer security checks for this web page

Input type: `Checkbox`

Valuename: "Security"

Journal Folder Home Page

Keyname: "Software\Policies\Microsoft\Office\9.0\Outlook\Webview\Journal"

Show associated web page

Input type: `Checkbox`

Valuename: "Show"

URL address of associated web page

Input type: `Edittext`

Valuename: "Url"

Turn off Internet Explorer security checks for this web page

Input type: `Checkbox`

Valuename: "Security"

Notes Folder Home Page

Keyname: "Software\Policies\Microsoft\Office\9.0\Outlook\Webview\Notes"

Show associated web page

Input type: `Checkbox`

Valuename: "Show"

URL address of associated web page

Input type: `Edittext`

Valuename: "Url"

Turn off Internet Explorer security checks for this web page

Input type: `Checkbox`

Valuename: "Security"

Outbox Folder Home Page

Keyname: "Software\Policies\Microsoft\Office\9.0\Outlook\Webview\Outbox"

Show associated web page

Input type: `Checkbox`

Valuename: "Show"

URL address of associated web page

Input type: `Edittext`

Valuename: "Url"

Turn off Internet Explorer security checks for this web page

Input type: `Checkbox`

Valuename: "Security"

Sent Items Folder Home Page

Keyname: "Software\Policies\Microsoft\Office\9.0\Outlook\Webview\"Sent Mail""

Show associated web page

Input type: `Checkbox`

Valuename: "Show"

URL address of associated web page

Input type: `Edittext`

Valuename: "Url"

Turn off Internet Explorer security checks for this web page

Input type: `Checkbox`

Valuename: "Security"

Tasks Folder Home Page

Keyname: "Software\Policies\Microsoft\Office\9.0\Outlook\Webview\Tasks"

Show associated web page

Input type: `Checkbox`

Valuename: "Show"

URL address of associated web page

Input type: `Edittext`

Valuename: "Url"

Turn off Internet Explorer security checks for this web page

Input type: `Checkbox`

Valuename: "Security"

Computer Properties

Microsoft Outlook 2000

Outlook mail configuration

Keyname: "Software\Policies\Microsoft\Office\9.0\Outlook\Setup"

Disable Reconfigure Mail Support button

Input type: `Checkbox`

Valuename: "MailSupport"

Using Schedule+ as Outlook Calendar

Keyname: "Software\Microsoft\Office\9.0\Outlook\SchedPlusOption"

Use Microsoft Schedule+ 7.x as primary calendar application

Input type: `Checkbox`

Valuename: "UseSchedPlus"

Prevent users from Changing primary calendar application

Keyname: "Software\Microsoft\Office\9.0\Outlook\SchedPlusOption"

User cannot change primary calendars app

Setting this policy prevents users from changing their primary calendars between Schedule+ and Outlook.

Input type; `Checkbox`

Valuename: "UserCanChange"

S/MIME password settings

Keyname: "Software\Microsoft\Cryptography\Defaults\Provider\Microsoft Exchange Cryptographic Provider v1.0"

Default S/MIME password time (minutes)

Input type: `Numeric`

Valuename: "DefPwdTime"

Maximum S/MIME password time (minutes)

Input type: `Numeric`

Valuename: "MaxPwdTime"

PPoint9.adm

This template is included with the Office Resource Kit 2000 (ORK2000). Note that this template has no computer properties.

User Properties

Microsoft PowerPoint 2000 → Tools | Options → View

Keyname: "Software\Policies\Microsoft\Office\9.0\PowerPoint\Options"

Startup dialog

Check to enforce setting on; uncheck to enforce setting off

Input type: Checkbox

Valuename: "StartupDialog"

New slide dialog

Check to enforce setting on; uncheck to enforce setting off

Input type: Checkbox

Valuename: "NewSlideDialog"

Status bar

Check to enforce setting on; uncheck to enforce setting off

Input type: Checkbox

Valuename: "ShowStatusBar"

Vertical ruler

Check to enforce setting on; uncheck to enforce setting off

Input type: Checkbox

Valuename: "VerticalRuler"

Windows in taskbar

Check to enforce setting on; uncheck to enforce setting off

Input type: Checkbox

Valuename: "ShowWindowsInTaskbar"

Popup menu on right mouse click

Check to enforce setting on; uncheck to enforce setting off

Input type: Checkbox

Valuename: "SSRightMouse"

Show popup menu button

Check to enforce setting on; uncheck to enforce setting off

Input type: Checkbox

Valuename: "SSMenuButton"

End with black slide

Check to enforce setting on; uncheck to enforce setting off

Input type: `Checkbox`

Valuename: "SSEndOnBlankSlide"

Microsoft PowerPoint 2000 → Tools | Options → General

Keyname: "Software\Policies\Microsoft\Office\9.0\PowerPoint\Options"

Recently used file list

Enable recently used file list

Input type: `Checkbox`

Valuename: "MRUListActive"

Size of recently used file list

Input type: `Numeric`

Valuename: "SizeOfMRUList"

Link Sounds File Size

Link sounds with file size greater than (Kb):

Input type: `Numeric`

Valuename: "Link sound size"

Microsoft PowerPoint 2000 → Tools | Options → Web Options... → General

Keyname: "Software\Policies\Microsoft\Office\9.0\PowerPoint\Internet"

Slide Navigation

Add slide navigation controls

Input type: `Checkbox`

Valuename: "HideNavigation"

Colors:

Input type: `Dropdownlist`

Valuename: "FrameColors"

Show slide animation while browsing

Check to enforce setting on; uncheck to enforce setting off

Input type: `Checkbox`

Valuename: "ShowSlideAnimation"

Resize graphics to fit browser window

Check to enforce setting on; uncheck to enforce setting off

Input type: `Checkbox`

Valuename: "DoNotResizeGraphics"

Microsoft PowerPoint 2000 → Tools | Options → Edit

Keyname: "Software\Policies\Microsoft\Office\9.0\PowerPoint\Options"

Replace straight quotes with smart quotes

Check to enforce setting on; uncheck to enforce setting off

Input type: `Checkbox`

Valuename: "SmartQuotes"

When selecting, automatically select entire word

Check to enforce setting on; uncheck to enforce setting off

Input type: `Checkbox`

Valuename: "WordSelection"

Use smart cut and paste

Check to enforce setting on; uncheck to enforce setting off

Input type: `Checkbox`

Valuename: "SmartCutPaste"

Drag–and-drop text editing

Check to enforce setting on; uncheck to enforce setting off

Input type: `Checkbox`

Valuename: "DragAndDrop"

Auto-fit text to text placeholder

Check to enforce setting on; uncheck to enforce setting off

Input type: `Checkbox`

Valuename: "AutoFitText"

AutoFormat as you type

Check to enforce setting on; uncheck to enforce setting off

Input type: `Checkbox`

Valuename: "AutoFormatAsYouType"

New charts take on PowerPoint font

Check to enforce setting on; uncheck to enforce setting off

Input type: `Checkbox`

Valuename: "PPTColorsForNewGraphs"

Maximum number of undos

Maximum number of undos

Input type: `Numeric`

Valuename: "Number of Undos"

Microsoft PowerPoint 2000 → Tools | Options → Print

Keyname: "Software\Policies\Microsoft\Office\9.0\PowerPoint\Options"

Background printing

Check to enforce setting on: uncheck to enforce setting off

Input type: `Checkbox`

Valuename: "BackgroundPrint"

Print True Type fonts as graphics

Check to enforce setting on; uncheck to enforce setting off

Input type: `Checkbox`

Valuename: "Send TrueType fonts as bitmaps"

Print inserted objects at printer resolution

Check to enforce setting on; uncheck to enforce setting off

Input type: `Checkbox`

Valuename: "Send printer information to OLE servers"

Microsoft PowerPoint 2000 → Tools | Options → Save

Keyname: "Software\Policies\Microsoft\Office\9.0\PowerPoint\Options"

Allow fast saves

Check to enforce setting on; uncheck to enforce setting off

Input type: `Checkbox`

Valuename: "Fast saves"

Prompt for file properties

Check to enforce setting on; uncheck to enforce setting off

Input type: `Checkbox`

Valuename: "PromptForFileProperties"

Save AutoRecover info

Enable save AutoRecover info

Active presentations will be saved at a regular interval.

Input type: `Checkbox`

Valuename: "SaveAutoRecoveryInfo"

AutoRecover save frequency (minutes)

Input type: `Numeric`

Valuename: "FrequencyToSaveAutoRecoveryInfo"

Convert charts when saving as previous version

Check to enforce setting on; uncheck to enforce setting off

Input type: `Checkbox`

Valuename: "ConvertCharts"

Save PowerPoint files as

Save PowerPoint files as

Input type: `Dropdownlist`

Valuename: "DefaultFormat"

Default file location

Keyname: "Software\Policies\Microsoft\Office\9.0\PowerPoint\RecentFolder-List"

Default file location

Environmental variables can be used in this policy.

Input type: `Edittext`

Valuename: "Default"

Microsoft PowerPoint 2000 → Tools | Options → Spelling and Style

Keyname: "Software\Policies\Microsoft\Office\9.0\PowerPoint\Options"

Check spelling as you type

Check to enforce setting on; uncheck to enforce setting off

Input type: `Checkbox`

Valuename: "Background spell checking"

Always suggest corrections

Check to enforce setting on; uncheck to enforce setting off

Input type: `Checkbox`

Valuename: "AlwaysSuggest"

Ignore words in UPPERCASE

Check to enforce setting on; uncheck to enforce setting off

Input type: `Checkbox`

Valuename: "Ignore UPPERCASE words"

Ignore words with numbers

Check to enforce setting on: uncheck to enforce setting off

Input type: `Checkbox`

Valuename: "Ignore words with numbers"

Check style

Keyname: "Software\Policies\Microsoft\Office\9.0\PowerPoint\Style Checker"

Check to enforce setting on; uncheck to enforce setting off

Input type: `Checkbox`

Valuename: "TextOffPlaceholder"

Microsoft PowerPoint 2000 → Tools | Options → Spelling and Style → Style Options → Case and End Punctuation

Keyname: "Software\Policies\Microsoft\Office\9.0\PowerPoint\Style Checker"

Check slide title case

Check slide title case

Input type: `Checkbox`

Valuename: "CheckTitleStyle"

Slide title case

Input type: `Dropdownlist`

Valuename: "TitleCase"

Check body text case

Check body text case

Input type: `Checkbox`

Valuename: "CheckBodyStyle"

Body text case

Input type: `Dropdownlist`

Valuename: "BodyCase"

Check slide title punctuation

Check slide title punctuation

Input type: `Checkbox`

Valuename: "CheckTitlePeriods"

Slide title punctuation

Input type: `Dropdownlist`

Valuename: "TitlePeriods"

Check body punctuation

Check body punctuation

Input type: `Checkbox`

Valuename: "CheckBodyPeriods"

Body punctuation

Input type: `Dropdownlist`

Valuename: "BodyPeriods"

Slide title end punctuation other than period

Slide title end punctuation other than period

Input type: `Edittext`

Valuename: "TitleAddlPuncChr"

Body text end punctuation other than period

Body text end punctuation other than period

Input type: `Edittext`

Valuename: "BodyAddlPuncChr"

Microsoft PowerPoint 2000 → Tools | Options → Spelling and Style → Style Options → Visual Clarity

Keyname: "Software\Policies\Microsoft\Office\9.0\PowerPoint\Style Checker"

Check number of fonts

Check number of fonts

Input type: `Checkbox`

Valuename: "CheckMaxFontNum"

Number of fonts should not exceed

Input type: `Numeric`

Valuename: "MaxFontNum"

Check title text size

Check title text size

Input type: `Checkbox`

Valuename: "CheckTitleMinFontSize"

Title text should be at least

Input type: `Dropdownlist`

Valuename: "TitleMinFontSize"

Check box text size

Check box text size

Input type: `Checkbox`

Valuename: "CheckBodyMinFontSize"

Body text should be at least

Input type: `Dropdownlist`

Valuename: "BodyMinFontSize"

Check number of bullets

Check number of bullets

Input type: `Checkbox`

Valuename: "CheckBulletsMaxBullets"

Number of bullets should not exceed

Input type: `Numeric`

Valuename: "BodyMaxBullets"

Check number of lines per title

Check number of lines per title

Input type: `Checkbox`

Valuename: "CheckTitleMaxLines"

Number of lines per title should not exceed

Input type: `Numeric`

Valuename: "TitleMaxLines"

Check number of lines per bullet

Check number of lines per bullet

Input type: `Checkbox`

Valuename: "CheckBulletsMaxLines"

Number of lines per bullet should not exceed

Input type: `Numeric`

Valuename: "BulletsMaxLines"

Microsoft PowerPoint 2000 → Tools | Options → Asian

Keyname: "Software\Policies\Microsoft\Office\9.0\PowerPoint\Options"

True inline conversion for Japanese IME

Check to enforce setting on; uncheck to enforce setting off

Input type: `Checkbox`

Valuename: "True Inline Conversion"

Convert font-associated text

Convert font-associated text

Input type: `Checkbox`

Valuename: "Convert Font-Associated Text"

For

Input type: `Dropdownlist`

Valuename: "Language to Convert Font-Associated Text"

Allow Font subsetting

Check to enforce setting on; uncheck to enforce setting off

Input type: `Checkbox`

Valuename: "Embed only a subset of a Far East font"

Microsoft PowerPoint 2000 → Tools | Macro → Security

Keyname: "Software\Policies\Microsoft\Office\9.0\PowerPoint\Security"

Security Level

Security Level

Input type: `Dropdownlist`

Valuename: "Level"

Trust all installed add-ins and templates

Check to enforce setting on, uncheck to enforce setting off

If checked, even documents with unsigned macros will be trusted.

Input type: `Checkbox`

Valuename: "DontTrustInstalledFiles"

Microsoft PowerPoint 2000 → Slide Show | Online Broadcast | Setup and schedule... → Broadcast Settings

Keyname: "Software\Policies\Microsoft\Office\9.0\PowerPoint\Broadcast"

Send audio

Check to enforce setting on; uncheck to enforce setting off

Input type: `Checkbox`

Valuename: "EnableAudio"

Send video

Check to enforce setting on; uncheck to enforce setting off

Input type: `Checkbox`

Valuename: "EnableVideo"

Camera/microphone is connected to another computer

Camera/microphone is connected to another computer

Input type: `Edittext`

Valuename: "REXComputerName"

Recording

Record the broadcast

Input type: `Checkbox`

Valuename: "Archive"

Save it in the following location

Input type: `Edittext`

Valuename: "ArchiveLoc"

Microsoft PowerPoint 2000 → Slide Show | Online Broadcast | Setup and Schedule... → Broadcast Settings → Other Broadcast Settings

Keyname: "Software\Policies\Microsoft\Office\9.0\PowerPoint\Broadcast"

Chat server URL

Chat server URL

Input type: `Edittext`

Valuename: "ChatURL"

Chat file CAB

Chat file CAB

Input type: `Edittext`

Valuename: "ChatFile"

Override default chat client

Check to enforce setting on; uncheck to enforce setting off

Input type: `Checkbox`

Valuename: "ChatFileExists"

Media Player ActiveX download

Media Player ActiveX download

Input type: `Edittext`

Valuename: "NsCore"

Transfer Control ActiveX download

Transfer Control ActiveX download

Input type: `Edittext`

Valuename: "NsFile"

Media Player non-ActiveX download

Media Player non-ActiveX download

Input type: `Edittext`

Valuename: "NsPlay"

Event URL

Event URL

Input type: `Edittext`

Valuename: "BrowserLoc"

Mail to

Mail to

Input type: `Edittext`

Valuename: "MailTo"

Help page URL

Help page URL

Input type: `Edittext`

Valuename: "HelpURL"

Video/audio test page URL

Video-audio test page URL

Input type: `Edittext`

Valuename: "TestVideoURL"

Microsoft PowerPoint 2000 → Slide Show | Online Broadcast | Setup and Schedule... → Server Options

Shared file location

Keyname: "Software\Policies\Microsoft\Office\9.0\PowerPoint\Broadcast"

Shared file location

Input type: `Edittext`

Valuename: "FileServerLoc"

Local NetShow server on this LAN

Keyname: "Software\Policies\Microsoft\Office\9.0\PowerPoint\Broadcast\NetShow"

Local NetShow server on this LAN

Input type: `Edittext`

Valuename: "ServerName"

The server will access presentation files from

Keyname: "Software\Policies\Microsoft\Office\9.0\PowerPoint\Broadcast\NetShow"

The server will access presentation files from

Input type: `Edittext`

Valuename: "NetShowFileLoc"

Microsoft PowerPoint 2000 → Slide Show | Online Broadcast | Setup and Schedule... → Server Options → Other NetShow Settings

Keyname: "Software\Policies\Microsoft\Office\9.0\PowerPoint\Broadcast\NetShow"

Connect Timeout

Connect Timeout

Input type: `Numeric`

Valuename: "ConnectTimeout"

FECRedundancyRatio

FECRedundancyRatio

Input type: `Numeric`

Valuename: "FECRedundancyRatio"

Netshow Server high bandwidth

Netshow Server high bandwidth

Input type: `Numeric`

Valuename: "FileTransferHiBandwidth"

Netshow Server low bandwidth

Netshow Server low bandwidth

Input type: `Numeric`

Valuename: "FileTransferLowBandwidth"

Multicast TTL

Multicast TTL

Input type: `Numeric`

Valuename: "MulticastTTL"

Unicast rollover

Check to enforce setting on; uncheck to enforce setting off

Input type: `Checkbox`

Valuename: "UnicastRollover"

Location of audio ASD file

Keyname: "Software\Policies\Microsoft\Office\9.0\PowerPoint\Broadcast\NetShow\Options"

Location of audio ASD file

Input type: `Edittext`

Valuename: "AudioAsd"

Location of video ASD file

Keyname: "Software\Policies\Microsoft\Office\9.0\PowerPoint\Broadcast\NetShow\Options"

Location of video ASD file

Input type: `Edittext`

Valuename: "VideoAsd"

Contact address

Keyname: "Software\Policies\Microsoft\Office\9.0\PowerPoint\Broadcast\NetShow\Options"

Contact address

Input type: `Edittext`

Valuename: "ContactAddress"

Contact phone number

Keyname: "Software\Policies\Microsoft\Office\9.0\PowerPoint\Broadcast\NetShow\Options"

Contact phone number

Input type: `Edittext`

Valuename: "ContactPhone"

Copyright

Keyname: "Software\Policies\Microsoft\Office\9.0\PowerPoint\Broadcast\NetShow\Options"

Copyright

Input type: `Edittext`

Valuename: "Copyright"

Multicast address

Keyname: "Software\Policies\Microsoft\Office\9.0\PowerPoint\Broadcast\NetShow\Options"

Multicast address

Input type: `Edittext`

Valuename: "MulticastAddress"

Read/write admin URL

Keyname: "Software\Policies\Microsoft\Office\9.0\PowerPoint\Broadcast\NetShow\Options"

Read/write admin URL

Input type: `Edittext`

Valuename: "ReadWriteAdminURL"

Read only admin URL

Keyname: "Software\Policies\Microsoft\Office\9.0\PowerPoint\Broadcast\NetShow\Options"

Read only admin URL

Input type: `Edittext`

Valuename: "ReadonlyAdminURL"

Drop dead time

Keyname: "Software\Policies\Microsoft\Office\9.0\PowerPoint\Broadcast\NetShow\Options"

Drop dead time

Input type: `Numeric`

Valuename: "DropDeadTime"

Microsoft PowerPoint 2000 → Customizable error messages

List of error messages to customize

Keyname: "Software\Policies\Microsoft\Office\9.0\PowerPoint\CustomizableAlerts"

Actionlist Valuename: "PolicyOn"

List of error messages to customize

The valuename is the numeric value for the error message, and the value is the text that will appear on the button.

Input type: `Listbox`

Microsoft PowerPoint 2000 → Disable items in user interface → Predefined

To make menu options completely unavailable, disable the toolbar button and menu command as well as the shortcut key. Even if both a menu command and its corresponding shortcut key are disabled, the command is still available through Visual Basic Assistant (VBA) so that macros using the command can be created.

Disable command bar buttons and menu items

Keyname: "Software\Policies\Microsoft\Office\9.0\PowerPoint\DisabledCmdBarItemsCheckBoxes"

Actionlist Valuenames: "WebOptions", "FilePublishAsWebPage", "FileOpenSearchTheWeb"

File | Open... | Tools | Find

Input type: `Checkbox`

Valuename: "FileOpenToolsFind"

File | Save as Web Page...

Input type: `Checkbox`

Valuename: "FileSaveAsWebPage"

Actionlist Valuename: "FilePublishAsWebPage"

File | Web Page Preview

Input type: `Checkbox`

Valuename: "FileWebPagePreview"

File | Send To | Mail Recipient

Input type: `Checkbox`

Valuename: "FileSendToMailRecipient"

Insert | Hyperlink

Input type: `Checkbox`

Valuename: "InsertHyperlink"

Tools | Online Collaboration

Input type: Checkbox

Valuename: "ToolsCollaboration"

Tools | Macro

Input type: Checkbox

Valuename: "ToolsMacro"

Tools | Macro | Macros...

Input type: Checkbox

Valuename: "ToolsMacroMacros"

Tools | Macro | Record New Macro...

Input type: Checkbox

Valuename: "ToolsMacroRecord"

Tools | Macro | Security...

Input type: Checkbox

Valuename: "ToolsMacroSecurity"

Tools | Macro | Visual Basic Editor

Input type: Checkbox

Valuename: "ToolsMacroVBE"

Tools | Macro | Microsoft Script Editor

Input type: Checkbox

Valuename: "ToolsMacroWeb"

Tools | Add-Ins...

Input type: Checkbox

Valuename: "ToolsAddins"

Tools | Customize

Input type: Checkbox

Valuename: "ToolsCustomize"

Tools | Options...

Input type: Checkbox

Valuename: "ToolsOptions"

Actionlist Valuename: "WebOptions"

Help | Office on the Web

Input type: Checkbox

Valuename: "HelpOfficeWeb"

Help | Detect and Repair...

Input type: **Checkbox**

Valuename: "HelpRepair"

Web | Refresh Current Page

Input type: **Checkbox**

Valuename: "WebRefreshCurrentPage"

Web | Start page

Input type: **Checkbox**

Valuename: "WebStartPage"

Web | Search the Web

Input type: **Checkbox**

Valuename: "WebSearchTheWeb"

Actionlist Valuename: "FileOpenSearchTheWeb"

Web | Favorites

Input type: **Checkbox**

Valuename: "WebFavorites"

Web | Go

Input type: **Checkbox**

Valuename: "WebGo"

Web | Address

Input type: **Checkbox**

Valuename: "WebAddress"

Disable shortcut keys

Keyname: "Software\Policies\Microsoft\Office\9.0\PowerPoint\DisabledShortcutKeysCheckBoxes"

Ctrl+F (Find...)

Input type: **Checkbox**

Valuename: "Find"

Ctrl+K (Insert | Hyperlink...)

Input type: **Checkbox**

Valuename: "InsertHyperlink"

Alt+F8 (Tools | Macro | Macros...)

Input type: **Checkbox**

Valuename: "ToolsMacroMacros"

Alt+F11 (Tools | Macro | Visual Basic Editor)
Input type: `Checkbox`

Valuename: "ToolsMacroVBE"

Alt+Shift+F11 (Tools | Macro | Microsoft Script Editor)
Input type: `Checkbox`

Valuename: "ToolsMacroWeb"

Microsoft PowerPoint 2000 → Disable items in user interface → Custom

Disable command bar buttons and menu items
Keyname: "Software\Policies\Microsoft\Office\9.0\PowerPoint\DisabledCmdBarItemsList"

Enter a command bar ID to disable
Look up control IDs for buttons and menu items using VBA.

Input type: `Listbox`

Disable shortcut keys
Keyname: "Software\Policies\Microsoft\Office\9.0\PowerPoint\DisabledShortcutKeysList"

Enter a key and modifier to disable
To disable a custom shortcut key, look up the virtual key code corresponding to the shortcut key. Enter it in the format "key,modifier". For example, Alt-K would be entered as 75,16.

Input type: `Listbox`

Microsoft PowerPoint 2000 → Miscellaneous

Custom Answer Wizard database path
Keyname: "Software\Policies\Microsoft\Office\9.0\PowerPoint\Answer Wizard"

Custom Answer Wizard database path
Customized help can be created using the Answer Wizard Builder. Environmental variables can be used to define the path.

Input type: `Edittext`

Valuename: "AdminDatabase"

Pub9.adm

This template is included with the Office Resource Kit 2000 (ORK2000). Note that this template has no computer properties.

User Properties

Microsoft Publisher 2000 → Default File Locations

Keyname: "Software\Policies\Microsoft\Office\9.0\Publisher"

Publication location

Publication location

Input type: `Edittext`

Valuename: "Doc_Path"

Picture location

Picture location

Input type: `Edittext`

Valuename: "Picture_Path"

Microsoft Publisher 2000 → Tools | Options → General

Keyname: "Software\Policies\Microsoft\Office\9.0\Publisher\Preferences"

Preview fonts in font list

Check to enforce setting on; uncheck to enforce setting off

Input type: `Checkbox`

Valuename: "PreviewFonts"

Use Catalog at startup

Check to enforce setting on; uncheck to enforce setting off

This policy can be used to disable the choice of how to create a publication that appears when Publisher is started.

Input type: `Checkbox`

Valuename: "UseStartupDlg"

Show rectangle for text in web graphic region

Check to enforce setting on; uncheck to enforce setting off

Input type: `Checkbox`

Valuename: "ShowOverlapGroups"

Microsoft Publisher 2000 → Tools | Options → Edit

Keyname: "Software\Policies\Microsoft\Office\9.0\Publisher\Preferences"

Drag-and-drop text editing

Check to enforce setting on; uncheck to enforce setting off

Input type: `Checkbox`

Valuename: "TextDragNDrop"

When selecting, automatically select entire word

Check to enforce setting on; uncheck to enforce setting off

Input type: Checkbox

Valuename: "AutoWordSel"

When formatting, automatically format entire word

Check to enforce setting on; uncheck to enforce setting off

Input type: Checkbox

Valuename: "AutoWordFormat"

Automatically hyphenate in new text frames

Check to enforce setting on; uncheck to enforce setting off

Input type: Checkbox

Valuename: "DefAutoHyph"

Use single click object creation

Check to enforce setting on; uncheck to enforce setting off

Input type: Checkbox

Valuename: "SingleClickCreate"

Microsoft Publisher 2000 → Tools | Options → User Assistance

Keyname: "Software\Policies\Microsoft\Office\9.0\Publisher\Preferences"

Preview Web site with Preview Troubleshooter

Check to enforce setting on; uncheck to enforce setting off

Input type: Checkbox

Valuename: "UseWebTroubleShooter"

Use Quick Publication wizard for blank publications

Check to enforce setting on; uncheck to enforce setting off

Input type: Checkbox

Valuename: "UseQuickPub"

Step through wizard questions

Check to not step through the wizard questions

Input type: Checkbox

Valuename: "NoSeqWizards"

Update personal information when saving

Check to enforce setting on; uncheck to enforce setting off

Input type: Checkbox

Valuename: "SavePersonalInfo"

Show tippages

Check to enforce setting on; uncheck to enforce setting off

Tippages are the tips and comments that appear in a balloon the first time a new function is used.

Input type: `Checkbox`

Valuename: "EnableFirstTimeHelp"

Remind to save publication

Check to enforce setting on; uncheck to enforce setting off

Automatic reminder to save the file

Input type: `Checkbox`

Valuename: "AutoSaveOn"

Minutes between save reminders

Minutes between save reminders

Input type: `Dropdownlist`

Valuename: "AutosaveMinutes"

Use helpful mouse pointers

Check to enforce setting on; uncheck to enforce setting off

Input type: `Checkbox`

Valuename: "UseCoolCursor"

Microsoft Publisher 2000 → Tools | Options → Print

Automatically display Print Troubleshooter

Keyname: "Software\Policies\Microsoft\Office\9.0\Publisher\Preferences"

Check to enforce setting on; uncheck to enforce setting off

Input type: `Checkbox`

Valuename: "UsePrintTroubleShooter"

Microsoft Publisher 2000 → Spelling

Keyname: "Software\Policies\Microsoft\Office\9.0\Publisher\Spelling"

Check spelling as you type

Check to enforce setting on; uncheck to enforce setting off

Input type: `Checkbox`

Valuename: "Background Spell Checking"

Ignore words in UPPERCASE

Check to enforce setting on; uncheck to enforce setting off

Input type: `Checkbox`

Valuename: "Ignore UpperCase"

Show repeated words

Check to enforce setting on; uncheck to enforce setting off

Highlight duplicated words (e.g., that that)

Input type: Checkbox

Valuename: "Show Repeated Words"

Word9.adm

This template is included with the Office Resource Kit 2000 (ORK2000). Note that this template has no computer properties.

User Properties

Microsoft Word 2000 → Tools | Options → View → Show

Keyname: "Software\Policies\Microsoft\Office\9.0\Word\Options\vpref"

Highlight

Check to enforce setting on; uncheck to enforce setting off

Input type: Checkbox

Valuename: "fShowHighlight_533_1"

Bookmarks

Check to enforce setting on; uncheck to enforce setting off

Input type: Checkbox

Valuename: "grpfvisi_146_1"

Status Bar

Check to enforce setting on; uncheck to enforce setting off

Input type: Checkbox

Valuename: "fStatusBar_83_1"

Actionlist Valuename: "fStatLine_3_1"

Screen Tips

Check to enforce setting on; uncheck to enforce setting off

Input type: Checkbox

Valuename: "grpfvisi_159_1"

Animated text

Check to enforce setting on; uncheck to enforce setting off

Input type: Checkbox

Valuename: "fShowTextSfx_71_1"

Horizontal scroll bar

Check to enforce setting on; uncheck to enforce setting off

Input type: `Checkbox`

Valuename: "fHorzScrollBar_100_1"

Vertical scroll bar

Check to enforce setting on; uncheck to enforce setting off

Input type: `Checkbox`

Valuename: "fVertScrollBar_101_1"

Picture placeholders

Check to enforce setting on; uncheck to enforce setting off

Input type: `Checkbox`

Valuename: "grpfvisi_134_1"

Field codes

Check to enforce setting on; uncheck to enforce setting off

Input type: `Checkbox`

Valuename: "grpfvisi_141_2"

Field shading

Field shading

Input type: `Dropdownlist`

Valuename: "grpfvisi_147_2"

Left scroll bar

Check to enforce setting on; uncheck to enforce setting off

This policy also sets right ruler (Print View only).

Input type: `Checkbox`

Valuename: "fBidiControls_1180_1"

Microsoft Word 2000 → Tools | Options → View → Formatting marks

Keyname: "Software\Policies\Microsoft\Office\9.0\Word\Options\vpref"

Tab characters

Check to enforce setting on; uncheck to enforce setting off

Input type: `Checkbox`

Valuename: "grpfvisi_128_1"

Spaces

Check to enforce setting on; uncheck to enforce setting off

Input type: `Checkbox`

Valuename: "grpfvisi_129_1"

Paragraph marks

Check to enforce setting on; uncheck to enforce setting off

Input type: `Checkbox`

Valuename: "grpfvisi_130_1"

Hidden text

Check to enforce setting on; uncheck to enforce setting off

Input type: `Checkbox`

Valuename: "grpfvisi_135_1"

Optional hyphens

Check to enforce setting on; uncheck to enforce setting off

Input type: `Checkbox`

Valuename: "grpfvisi_132_1"

Optional breaks

Check to enforce setting on; uncheck to enforce setting off

Input type: `Checkbox`

Valuename: "grpfvisi_151_1"

All

Check to enforce setting on; uncheck to enforce setting off

Input type: `Checkbox`

Valuename: "grpfvisi_133_1"

Microsoft Word 2000 → Tools | Options → View → Print and Web Layout options

Keyname: "Software\Policies\Microsoft\Office\9.0\Word\Options\vpref"

Drawings

Check to enforce setting on; uncheck to enforce setting off

Input type: `Checkbox`

Valuename: "grpfvisi_149_1"

Object anchors

Check to enforce setting on; uncheck to enforce setting off

Input type: `Checkbox`

Valuename: "grpfvisi_140_1"

Text boundaries

Check to enforce setting on; uncheck to enforce setting off

Input type: `Checkbox`

Valuename: "grpfvisi_144_1"

Vertical ruler (Print view only)

Check to enforce setting on; uncheck to enforce setting off

Input type: `Checkbox`

Valuename: "fVertRuler_103_1"

Microsoft Word 2000 → Tools | Options → View → Outline and Normal options

Keyname: "Software\Policies\Microsoft\Office\9.0\Word\Options\vpref"

Wrap to window

Check to enforce setting on; uncheck to enforce setting off

Input type: `Checkbox`

Valuename: "fWrapToWnd_106_1"

Draft font

Check to enforce setting on; uncheck to enforce setting off

Input type: `Checkbox`

Valuename: "fDraftFont_104_1"

Style area width

Style area width

Input type: `Dropdownlist`

Valuename: "xwSelBar_112_8"

Microsoft Word 2000 → Tools | Options → General

Keyname: "Software\Policies\Microsoft\Office\9.0\Word\Options\vpref"

Blue background, white text

Check to enforce setting on; uncheck to enforce setting off

Input type: `Checkbox`

Valuename: "fBlue_73_1"

Provide feedback with animation

Check to enforce setting on; uncheck to enforce setting off

Input type: `Checkbox`

Valuename: "fAnimateScreenMove_42_1"

Confirm conversion at Open

Check to enforce setting on; uncheck to enforce setting off

Input type: `Checkbox`

Valuename: "fConfirmCvrtr_17_1"

Update automatic links at Open

Check to enforce setting on; uncheck to enforce setting off

Input type: `Checkbox`

Valuename: "fNoCalcLinksOnOpen_90_1"

Mail as attachment

Check to enforce setting on; uncheck to enforce setting off

Input type: `Checkbox`

Valuename: "fMailAsAttachment_72_1"

Recently used file list

Number of entries

Input type: `Numeric`

Valuename: "cFilesMRU_32_4"

Help for WordPerfect users

Check to enforce setting on; uncheck to enforce setting off

Input type: `Checkbox`

Valuename: "fWPCommandKeys_18_1"

Navigation keys for WordPerfect users

Check to enforce setting on; uncheck to enforce setting off

Input type: `Checkbox`

Valuename: "fWPNavigationKeys_20_1"

Asian fonts also apply to Latin text

Check to enforce setting on; uncheck to enforce setting off

Input type: `Checkbox`

Valuename: "fSeparateFont_105_1"

Measurement units

Select units

Input type: `Dropdownlist`

Valuename: "ut_64_4"

Show pixels for HTML features

Check to enforce setting on; uncheck to enforce setting off

Input type: `Checkbox`

Valuename: "fUsePixelsInDialogs_95_1"

Use character units

Check to enforce setting on; uncheck to enforce setting off

Input type: `Checkbox`

Valuename: "fUseCharUnit_1537_1"

English Word 6.0/95 documents

English Word 6.0/95 documents

Input type: `Dropdownlist`

Valuename: "fAsianText_110_2"

Microsoft Word 2000 → Tools | Options → Web Options... → General

Disable features not supported by browser

Keyname: "Software\Policies\Microsoft\Office\9.0\Word\Options\vpref"

Disable features not supported by browser

Input type: `Dropdownlist`

Valuename: "verCompat_649_7"

Microsoft Word 2000 → Tools | Options → Web Options... → Files

Keyname: "Software\Policies\Microsoft\Office\9.0\Common\Internet"

Check if Word is the default editor for all other Web pages

Check to enforce setting on; uncheck to enforce setting off

Input type: `Checkbox`

Valuename: "DoNotCheckIfWordIsDefaultHTMLEditor"

Microsoft Word 2000 → Tools | Options → Edit

Keyname: "Software\Policies\Microsoft\Office\9.0\Word\Options\vpref"

Typing replaces selection

Check to enforce setting on; uncheck to enforce setting off

Input type: `Checkbox`

Valuename: "fAutoDelete_6_1"

Drag-and-drop text editing

Check to enforce setting on; uncheck to enforce setting off

Input type: `Checkbox`

Valuename: "fDragNDrop_0_1"

Use the INS key for paste

Check to enforce setting on; uncheck to enforce setting off

Input type: `Checkbox`

Valuename: "fInsForPaste_7_1"

Tabs and backspace set left indent

Keyname: "Software\Policies\Microsoft\Office\9.0\Word\Options\Assist"

Check to enforce setting on; uncheck to enforce setting off

Input type: `Checkbox`

Valuename: "fTabIndent_128_1"

Use smart cut and paste

Check to enforce setting on; uncheck to enforce setting off

Input type: `Checkbox`

Valuename: "fSmartCutPaste_19_1"

Allow accented uppercase in French

Check to enforce setting on; uncheck to enforce setting off

Input type: `Checkbox`

Valuename: "fAccentOnUpper_84_1"

When selecting, automatically select entire word

Check to enforce setting on; uncheck to enforce setting off

Input type: `Checkbox`

Valuename: "fAutoWordSel_68_1"

Picture editor

Keyname: "Software\Policies\Microsoft\Office\9.0\Word\Options"

Picture editor

Input type: `Dropdownlist`

Valuename: "PICEDITCLASS"

Enable click and type

Check to enforce setting on; uncheck to enforce setting off

Input type: `Checkbox`

Valuename: "fClickType_108_1"

IME Control Active

Check to enforce setting on; uncheck to enforce setting off

Global Input Method Editor (IME), allows users to type using Asian languages.

Input type: `Checkbox`

Valuename: "fIMEClose_96_1"

IME TruelnLine

Check to enforce setting on; uncheck to enforce setting off

Global Input Method Editor (IME), allows users to type using Asian languages.

Input type: `Checkbox`

Valuename: "fTrueInLine_1088_1"

Microsoft Word 2000 → Tools | Options → Print → Printing Options

Keyname: "Software\Policies\Microsoft\Office\9.0\Word\Options\vprsu"

Draft output

Check to enforce setting on; uncheck to enforce setting off

Input type: `Checkbox`

Valuename: "DraftOutput_2_1"

Update fields

Check to enforce setting on; uncheck to enforce setting off

Input type: Checkbox

Valuename: "UpdateFields_5_1"

Update links

Check to enforce setting on; uncheck to enforce setting off

Input type: Checkbox

Valuename: "UpdateLinks_13_1"

Allow A4/Letter paper resizing

Keyname: "Software\Policies\Microsoft\Office\9.0\Word\Options\vpref"

Check to enforce setting on; uncheck to enforce setting off

Input type: Checkbox

Valuename: "fMapStdSizes_15_1"

Background Printing

Keyname: "Software\Policies\Microsoft\Office\9.0\Word\Options"

Check to enforce setting on; uncheck to enforce setting off

Input type: Checkbox

Valuename: "BackgroundPrint"

Reverse print order

Check to enforce setting on; uncheck to enforce setting off

Input type: Checkbox

Valuename: "ReversePrint_6_1"

Microsoft Word 2000 → Tools | Options → Print → Include with document

Keyname: "Software\Policies\Microsoft\Office\9.0\Word\Options\vprsu"

Document Properties

Check to enforce setting on; uncheck to enforce setting off

Input type: Checkbox

Valuename: "DocProps_1_1"

Field codes

Check to enforce setting on; uncheck to enforce setting off

Input type: Checkbox

Valuename: "FieldCodes_4_1"

Comments

Check to enforce setting on; uncheck to enforce setting off

Input type: Checkbox

Valuename: "Comments_3_1"

Hidden text

Check to enforce setting on; uncheck to enforce setting off

Input type: Checkbox

Valuename: "HiddenText_0_1"

Drawing objects

Check to enforce setting on; uncheck to enforce setting off

Input type: Checkbox

Valuename: "DrawnObjects_14_1"

Microsoft Word 2000 → Tools | Options → Print → Options for Duplex Printing

Keyname: "Software\Policies\Microsoft\Office\9.0\Word\Options\vprsu"

Front of sheet

Check to enforce setting on; uncheck to enforce setting off

Input type: Checkbox

Valuename: "fPrOrder1_21_1"

Back of sheet

Check to enforce setting on; uncheck to enforce setting off

Input type: Checkbox

Valuename: "fPrOrder2_22_1"

Microsoft Word 2000 → Tools | Options → Save

Keyname: "Software\Policies\Microsoft\Office\9.0\Word\Options\vpref"

Always create backup copy

Check to enforce setting on; uncheck to enforce setting off

Do not enforce on "Always create backup copy" if you want to "Allow fast saves." The two cannot occur together, and enabling this option will disable fast saves.

Input type: Checkbox

Valuename: "fAlwaysBackupDuringSave_8_1"

Allow fast saves

Check to enforce setting on; uncheck to enforce setting off

Note that fast saves cannot occur over a network. You cannot force on "Allow fast saves" if you have already forced on "Always create backup copy."

Input type: Checkbox

Valuename: "fAllowFastSaves_9_1"

Prompt for document properties

Check to enforce setting on; uncheck to enforce setting off

Input type: `Checkbox`

Valuename: "fPromptSI_4_1"

Prompt to save Normal template

Check to enforce setting on; uncheck to enforce setting off

Uncheck this option if you do not want to receive the prompt to save changes to the global template (*normal.dot*).

Input type: `Checkbox`

Valuename: "fPmtSaveGlobalDot_107_1"

Allow background saves

Keyname: "Software\Policies\Microsoft\Office\9.0\Word\Options"

Check to enforce setting on; uncheck to enforce setting off

This option was disabled by default in earlier versions of Word.

Input type: `Checkbox`

Valuename: "BackgroundSave"

Save AutoRecover info

Save AutoRecover info every (min)

Input type: `Numeric`

Valuename: "AutoRecover_192_8"

Add Bi-Directional Marks when saving Text files

Check to enforce setting on; uncheck to enforce setting off

Text files are saved with bi-directional control characters; this preserves the directionality of characters when using right-to-left languages.

Input type: `Checkbox`

Valuename: "fAddCtrlSave_1181_1"

Save Word files as

Keyname: "Software\Policies\Microsoft\Office\9.0\Word\Options"

Save Word files as

Input type: `Dropdownlist`

Valuename: "DefaultFormat"

Disable features not supported by Word 97

Check to enforce setting on; uncheck to enforce setting off

By disabling incompatible features, the document is optimized for viewing in Word 97.

Input type: `Checkbox`

Valuename: "Word97Compat_120_1"

Microsoft Word 2000 → Tools | Options → Spelling and Grammar

Keyname: "Software\Policies\Microsoft\Office\9.0\Word\Options\vpref"

Check spelling as you type

Check to enforce setting on; uncheck to enforce setting off

Input type: `Checkbox`

Valuename: "fSplBkg_99_1"

Always suggest corrections

Check to enforce setting on; uncheck to enforce setting off

Input type: `Checkbox`

Valuename: "fSplAutoSugg_24_1"

Suggest from main dictionary only

Check to enforce setting on; uncheck to enforce setting off

Input type: `Checkbox`

Valuename: "fSplSuggFrUserDict_28_1"

Ignore words in UPPERCASE

Check to enforce setting on; uncheck to enforce setting off

Input type: `Checkbox`

Valuename: "fSplIgnoreCaps_25_1"

Ignore words with numbers

Check to enforce setting on; uncheck to enforce setting off

Input type: `Checkbox`

Valuename: "fSplIgnoreDigits_27_1"

Ignore Internet and file addresses

Check to enforce setting on; uncheck to enforce setting off

Input type: `Checkbox`

Valuename: "fFilenamesEmailAliases_536_1"

Use German post reform rules

Keyname: "Software\Policies\Microsoft\Shared Tools\Proofing Tools\Spelling"

Check to enforce setting on; uncheck to enforce setting off

This option is relevant only for German language documents.

Input type: `Checkbox`

Valuename: "GermanPostReform"

Combine aux verb/adj.

Check to enforce setting on; uncheck to enforce setting off

This option is relevant only for Korean language documents.

Input type: `Checkbox`

Valuename: "fSplAuxFind_560_1"

Use auto-change list

Check to enforce setting on; uncheck to enforce setting off

Input type: `Checkbox`

Valuename: "fSplMisSearch_561_1"

Process compound nouns

Check to enforce setting on; uncheck to enforce setting off

This option is relevant only for Korean language documents.

Input type: `Checkbox`

Valuename: "fSplCompoundNoun_1540_1"

Hebrew

Keyname: "Software\Policies\Microsoft\Office\9.0\Word\Options"

Hebrew

This option is relevant only for Hebrew language documents.

Input type: `Dropdownlist`

Valuename: "BiDi Spelling"

Arabic modes

Arabic modes

This option is relevant only for Arabic language documents.

Input type: `Dropdownlist`

Valuename: "wSpell_1192_8"

Check grammar as you type

Check to enforce setting on; uncheck to enforce setting off

Input type: `Checkbox`

Valuename: "fGramBkg_535_1"

Check grammar with spelling

Check to enforce setting on; uncheck to enforce setting off

Input type: `Checkbox`

Valuename: "fRunGrammar_596_1"

Show readability statistics

Check to enforce setting on; uncheck to enforce setting off

Input type: `Checkbox`

Valuename: "fShowStats_16_1"

Writing style

Writing style

Input type: `Dropdownlist`

Valuename: "fgosWritingStyle_50_4"

Microsoft Word 2000 → Tools | Options → File Locations

Keyname: "Software\Policies\Microsoft\Office\9.0\Word\Options"

Document

Documents

Environmental variables can be used in this policy.

Input type: `Edittext`

Valuename: "DOC-PATH"

Clipart pictures

Clipart pictures

Environmental variables can be used in this policy.

Input type: `Edittext`

Valuename: "PICTURE-PATH"

AutoRecover files

AutoRecover files

Environmental variables can be used in this policy.

Input type: `Edittext`

Valuename: "AUTOSAVE-PATH"

Tools

Tools

Environmental variables can be used in this policy.

Input type: `Edittext`

Valuename: "TOOLS-PATH"

Startup

Startup

Environmental variables can be used in this policy.

Input type: `Edittext`

Valuename: "STARTUP-PATH"

Microsoft Word 2000 → Tools | Options → Hangul Hanja Conversion

These options are relevant only for Japanese language documents.

Keyname: "Software\Policies\Microsoft\Office\9.0\Word\Options\vpref"

Fast conversion

Check to enforce setting on; uncheck to enforce setting off

Input type: `Checkbox`

Valuename: "fFastConvert_563_1"

Display recently used items

Check to enforce setting on; uncheck to enforce setting off

Input type: `Checkbox`

Valuename: "fHHCEnableMRU_564_1"

Ignore Hangul ending

Check to enforce setting on; uncheck to enforce setting off

Input type: `Checkbox`

Valuename: "fHHCEndingCheck_565_1"

Multiple words conversion

Multiple words conversion

Input type: `Dropdownlist`

Valuename: "fHangulToHanja_566_1"

Microsoft Word 2000 → Tools | Options → Right-to-left

This option is relevant only for documents using a right-to-left language such as Hebrew.

Keyname: "Software\Policies\Microsoft\Office\9.0\Word\Options\vpref"

Document view

Document view

Input type: `Dropdownlist`

Valuename: "fDocViewDir_1186_1"

Add control Characters in Cut and Copy

Check to enforce setting on; uncheck to enforce setting off

Input type: `Checkbox`

Valuename: "fAddCtrlCopy_1182_1"

Add double quotes for Hebrew alphabet numbering

Check to enforce setting on; uncheck to enforce setting off

Input type: `Checkbox`

Valuename: "fHebDoubleQuote_1199_1"

Numeral

Numeral

Input type: `Dropdownlist`

Valuename: "fNumForm_1168_2"

Movement

Movement

Input type: `Dropdownlist`

Valuename: "fMoveOr_1175_1"

Visual selection

Visual selection

Input type: `Dropdownlist`

Valuename: "fSelectOr_1176_1"

Control characters

Check to enforce setting on; uncheck to enforce setting off

Input type: `Checkbox`

Valuename: "grpfvisi_152_1"

Diacritics

Check to enforce setting on; uncheck to enforce setting off

Input type: `Checkbox`

Valuename: "fShowDiac_1177_1"

Different color for diacritics

Check to enforce setting on; uncheck to enforce setting off

Input type: `Checkbox`

Valuename: "fUseColorDiac_1178_1"

Month names

Month names

Input type: `Dropdownlist`

Valuename: "fAraDate_1172_2"

Microsoft Word 2000 → Tools | AutoCorrect... → AutoCorrect

Keyname: "Software\Policies\Microsoft\Office\9.0\Word\Options\Assist"

Correct Two Initial Capitals

Check to enforce setting on; uncheck to enforce setting off

Input type: `Checkbox`

Valuename: "fTwoInitialCaps_24_1"

Capitalize first letter of sentence

Check to enforce setting on; uncheck to enforce setting off

Input type: `Checkbox`

Valuename: "fInitialCap_32_1"

Capitalize names of days

Check to enforce setting on; uncheck to enforce setting off

Input type: Checkbox

Valuename: "fCapDayNames_48_1"

Correct accidental use of cAPS LOCK key

Check to enforce setting on; uncheck to enforce setting off

Input type: Checkbox

Valuename: "fCapsLock_40_1"

Replace text as you type

Check to enforce setting on; uncheck to enforce setting off

Input type: Checkbox

Valuename: "fCorrectTyping_16_1"

Microsoft Word 2000 → Tools | AutoCorrect... → AutoFormat as you type → Apply as you type

Keyname: "Software\Policies\Microsoft\Office\9.0\Word\Options\Assist"

Headings

Check to enforce setting on; uncheck to enforce setting off

Input type: Checkbox

Valuename: "fHeading_232_1"

Borders

Check to enforce setting on; uncheck to enforce setting off

Input type: Checkbox

Valuename: "fBotBord_280_1"

Tables

Check to enforce setting on; uncheck to enforce setting off

Input type: Checkbox

Valuename: "fTable_344_1"

Dates

Check to enforce setting on; uncheck to enforce setting off

Input type: Checkbox

Valuename: "fDate_328_1"

Automatic bulleted lists

Check to enforce setting on; uncheck to enforce setting off

Input type: Checkbox

Valuename: "fBulletList_248_1"

Automatic numbered lists

Check to enforce setting on; uncheck to enforce setting off

Input type: `Checkbox`

Valuename: "fNumberedList_264_1"

First line indent

Check to enforce setting on; uncheck to enforce setting off

Input type: `Checkbox`

Valuename: "fFirstIndent_296_1"

Closings

Check to enforce setting on; uncheck to enforce setting off

Input type: `Checkbox`

Valuename: "fClosing_312_1"

Microsoft Word 2000 → Tools | AutoCorrect... → AutoFormat as you type → Replace as you type

Keyname: "Software\Policies\Microsoft\Office\9.0\Word\Options\Assist"

Straight quotes with smart quotes

Check to enforce setting on; uncheck to enforce setting off

Input type: `Checkbox`

Valuename: "fSmartQuote_8_1"

Ordinals (1st) with superscript

Check to enforce setting on; uncheck to enforce setting off

Input type: `Checkbox`

Valuename: "fNumSupScript_104_1"

Fractions (1/2) with fraction character

Check to enforce setting on; uncheck to enforce setting off

Input type: `Checkbox`

Valuename: "fFraction_96_1"

Symbol characters (--) with symbols

Check to enforce setting on; uncheck to enforce setting off

Input type: `Checkbox`

Valuename: "fEmDash_112_1"

**Bold* and _italic_ with real formatting*

Check to enforce setting on; uncheck to enforce setting off

Input type: `Checkbox`

Valuename: "fBoldItalic_120_1"

Internet and network paths with hyperlinks

Check to enforce setting on; uncheck to enforce setting off

Input type: **Checkbox**

Valuename: "fHyperlink_200_1"

Match parentheses

Check to enforce setting on; uncheck to enforce setting off

Input type: **Checkbox**

Valuename: "fAutoPair_144_1"

Autospace

Check to enforce setting on; uncheck to enforce setting off

Input type: **Checkbox**

Valuename: "fSbDbSpace_152_1"

Dash-like characters

Check to enforce setting on; uncheck to enforce setting off

Input type: **Checkbox**

Valuename: "fDbDashes_136_1"

Microsoft Word 2000 → Tools | AutoCorrect... AutoFormat at you type → Automatically as you type

Keyname: "Software\Policies\Microsoft\Office\9.0\Word\Options\Assist"

Format beginning of list item like the one before it

Check to enforce setting on; uncheck to enforce setting off

Input type: **Checkbox**

Valuename: "fLeadInEmph_176_1"

Define styles based on your formatting

Check to enforce setting on; uncheck to enforce setting off

Input type: **Checkbox**

Valuename: "fAutoStyleDef_184_1"

Microsoft Word 2000 → Tools | Macro → Security...

Keyname: "Software\Policies\Microsoft\Office\9.0\Word\Security"

Security level

Security Level

Set the security level to Medium if you want to receive a prompt to enable or disable macros. Setting this policy too high will cause a "macros in this project are disabled" error message.

Input type: `Edittext`

Valuename: "Level"

Trust all installed add-ins and templates

Check to enforce setting on; uncheck to enforce setting off

If checked, even documents with unsigned macros will be trusted.

Input type: `Checkbox`

Valuename: "DontTrustInstalledFiles"

Microsoft Word 2000 → Tools | Language → Set Language

Detect language automatically

Keyname: "Software\Policies\Microsoft\Office\9.0\Word\Options\vpref"

Check to enforce setting on; uncheck to enforce setting off

Input type: `Checkbox`

Valuename: "fLangAutoDetect_1552_1"

Microsoft Word 2000 → Tools | Language → Chinese Translation

This option is relevant only for Chinese language documents.

Keyname: "Software\Policies\Microsoft\Shared Tools\Proofing Tools\TCSC Translator"

Translation Direction

Translation Direction

Input type: `Dropdownlist`

Valuename: "TranslationTarget"

Use Taiwan, Hong Kong and Macao character variants

Check to enforce setting on; uncheck to enforce setting off

Input type: `Checkbox`

Valuename: "UseVariants"

Translate common terms

Check to enforce setting on; uncheck to enforce setting off

Input type: `Checkbox`

Valuename: "TranslateCommonTerms"

Microsoft Word 2000 → Customizable error messages

List of error messages to customize

Keyname: "Software\Policies\Microsoft\Office\9.0\Word\CustomizableAlerts"

List of error messages to customize

The valuename is the numeric value for the error message, and the value is the text that will appear on the button.

Input type: `Listbox`

Actionlist Valuename: "PolicyOn"

Microsoft Word 2000 → Disable items in user interface → Predefined

To make menu options completely unavailable, disable the toolbar button and menu command as well as the shortcut key. Even if both a menu command and its corresponding shortcut key are disabled, the command is still available through Visual Basic Assistant (VBA) so that macros using the command can be created.

Disable command bar buttons and menu items

Keyname: "Software\Policies\Microsoft\Office\9.0\Word\DisabledCmdBarItemsCheckBoxes"

Actionlist Valuenames: "WebOptions", "GeneralOptions", "FileOpenSearchTheWeb"

File | Open... | Tools | Find...

Input type: `Checkbox`

Valuename: "FileOpenToolsFind"

File | Save as Web Page...

Input type: `Checkbox`

Valuename: "FileSaveAsWebPage"

File | Web Page Preview

Input type: `Checkbox`

Valuename: "FileWebPagePreview"

File | Send to | Mail Recipient

Input type: `Checkbox`

Valuename: "FileSendToMailRecipient"

Insert | Hyperlink

Input type: `Checkbox`

Valuename: "InsertHyperlink"

Tools | Protect Document...

Input type: `Checkbox`

Valuename: "WToolsProtectDoc"

Tools | Online Collaboration

Input type: `Checkbox`

Valuename: "ToolsCollaboration"

Tools | Macro

Input type: Checkbox

Valuename: "ToolsMacro"

Tools | Macro | Macros...

Input type: Checkbox

Valuename: "ToolsMacroMacros"

Tools | Macro | Record New Macro...

Input type: Checkbox

Valuename: "ToolsMacroRecord"

Tools | Macro | Security...

Input type: Checkbox

Valuename: "ToolsMacroSecurity"

Tools Macro | Visual Basic Editor

Input type: Checkbox

Valuename: "ToolsMacroVBE"

Tools | Macro Microsoft Script Editor

Input type: Checkbox

Valuename: "ToolsMacroWeb"

Tools | Templates and Add-ins...

Input type: Checkbox

Valuename: "ToolsTemplateAddins"

Tools | Customize...

Input type: Checkbox

Valuename: "ToolsCustomize"

Tools | Options...

Input type: Checkbox

Valuename: "ToolsOptions"

Actionlist Valuenames: "WebOptions", "GeneralOptions"

Help | Office on the Web

Input type: Checkbox

Valuename: "HelpOfficeWeb"

Help | Detect and Repair...

Input type: Checkbox

Valuename: "HelpRepair"

Web | Refresh Current Page

Input type: Checkbox

Valuename: "WebRefreshCurrentPage"

Web | Start Page

Input type: Checkbox

Valuename: "WebStartPage"

Web | Search the Web

Input type: Checkbox

Valuename: "WebSearchTheWeb"

Actionlist Valuename: "FileOpenSearchTheWeb"

Web | Favorites

Input type: Checkbox

Valuename: "WebFavorites"

Web | Go

Input type: Checkbox

Valuename: "WebGo"

Web | Address

Input type: Checkbox

Valuename: "WebAddress"

Disable shortcut keys

Keyname: "Software\Policies\Microsoft\Office\9.0\Word\DisabledShortcut-KeysCheckBoxes"

Ctrl+F (Find...)

Input type: Checkbox

Valuename: "Find"

Ctrl+K (Insert | Hyperlink...)

Input type: Checkbox

Valuename: "InsertHyperlink"

Alt+F8 (Tools | Macro | Macros...)

Input type: Checkbox

Valuename: "ToolsMacroMacros"

Alt+F11 (Tools | Macro | Visual Basic Editor)

Input type: Checkbox

Valuename: "ToolsMacroVBE"

Alt+Shift+F11 (Tools | Macro | Microsoft Script Editor)

Input type: `Checkbox`

Valuename: "ToolsMacroWeb"

Microsoft Word 2000 → Disable items in user interface → Custom

Disable command bar buttons and menu items

Keyname: "Software\Policies\Microsoft\Office\9.0\Word\DisabledCmdBarItemsList"

Enter a command bar ID to disable

Looks up control IDs for buttons and menu items using Visual Basic Assistant.

Input type: `Listbox`

Disable shortcut keys

Keyname: "Software\Policies\Microsoft\Office\9.0\Word\DisabledShortcutKeysList"

Enter a key and modifier to disable

To disable a custom shortcut key, look up the virtual key code corresponding to the shortcut key. Enter it in the format "key,modifier". For example, Alt-K would be entered as 75,16.

Input type: `Listbox`

Microsoft Word 2000 → Miscellaneous

Keyname: "Software\Policies\Microsoft\Office\9.0\Word\Options"

Volume preference

Volume preference

Input type: `Dropdownlist`

Valuename: "VolumePref"

Custom Answer Wizard database path

Keyname: "Software\Policies\Microsoft\Office\9.0\Word\Answer Wizard"

Custom Answer Wizard database path

Customized help can be created using the Answer Wizard Builder. Environmental variables can be used to define the path.

Input type: `Edittext`

Valuename: "AdminDatabase"

Alternate revision bar position in printed document

Check to enforce setting on; uncheck to enforce setting off

Input type: Checkbox

Valuename: "AlternateRevBars"

Disable MRU list in font dropdown list

Check to enforce setting on; uncheck to enforce setting off

Most recently used fonts will not appear in font list

Input type: Checkbox

Valuename: "NoFontMRUList"

Miscellaneous Templates

The following three miscellaneous templates listed on the Microsoft Knowledgebase included in this section are:

Cpanel.adm
: This template can be used to prevent specific Control Panel applets from being displayed in Windows 9x or Windows NT4 workstations.

Date.adm
: This template sets the short date style, which can also be set using the Regional Settings Control Panel applet.

Scrsave.adm
: This template allows a specific screensaver to be set on a per-user basis.

All three templates are compatible with both Windows NT4 and Windows 9x workstations.

Cpanel.adm

The original text used to create this template can be found in the Microsoft Knowledgebase article Q207750. Other applets can be easily added to this template using the same format (see Chapter 8). Note that this template has no computer properties.

User Properties

Control Panel Icons

Keyname: "Control Panel\Don't Load"

Deny Access to Accessibility Properties
Valuename: "Access.cpl"

Deny Access to Add/Remove Programs Properties
Valuename: "appwiz.cpl"

Deny Access to Console Properties
Valuename: "console.cpl"

Deny Access to Compaq Insight Agents
Valuename: "cpqmgmt.cpl"

Deny Access to PC Card Properties
Valuename: "devapps.cpl"

Deny Access to Internet Properties
Valuename: "inetcpl.cpl"

Deny Access to Regional Settings Properties
Valuename: "intl.cpl"

Deny Access to Joystick Properties
Valuename: "Joy.cpl"

Deny Access to Licensing Properties
Valuename: "liccpa.cpl"

Deny Access to Mouse, Fonts, Board, Printer Properties
Valuename: "main.cpl"

Deny Access to Monitoring Agent Properties
Valuename: "bhctrl.cpl"

Deny Access to Multimedia Properties
Valuename: "mmsys.cpl"

Deny Access to Modem Properties
Valuename: "modem.cpl"

Deny Access to Network Properties
Valuename: "ncpa.cpl"

Deny Access to ODBC Properties
Valuename: "odbccp32.cpl"

Deny Access to Port Properties
Valuename: "Ports.cpl"

Deny Access to Server Properties
Valuename: "srvmgr.cpl"

Deny Access to System Properties
Valuename: "sysdm.cpl"

Deny Access to Telephony Properties
Valuename: "telephon.cpl"

Deny Access to Date/Time Properties
Valuename: "timedate.cpl"

Deny Access to UPS Properties
Valuename: "UPS.cpl"

Date.adm

The original text used to create this template can be found in the Microsoft Knowledgebase article Q216661. Note that this template has no comptuer properties.

User Properties

Date

Short Date Format
Please enter the date mask. For example: MM/dd/yyyy
Input type: `Edittext`
Keyname: "Control Panel\International"
Valuename: "sShortDate"

Scrsave.adm

Although the screen saver password can be enabled using this template, it cannot be specified. The original text used to create this template can be found in the Microsoft Knowledgebase article Q195655. Note that this template has no computer properties.

User Properties

Screen Saver Policies

Screen Saver
Enter the location of the Screen Saver
Input type: `Edittext`
Keyname: "Control Panel\Desktop"
Valuename: "SCRNSAVE.EXE"

Enable Screen Saver

Keyname: "Control Panel\Desktop"

Valuename: "ScreenSaveActive"

Enable Screen saver password

Keyname: "Control Panel\Desktop"

Valuename: "ScreenSaverIsSecure"

Sample Acceptable-Use Policy

System policies can only provide a certain level of security (see Chapter 5, *It's Not Perfect*). Beyond this, each individual user must take responsibility for his or her own activities on the network. In the case of schools, parents must also take responsibility for the activities of their children. To ensure that all users understand the expectations of network use, I recommend that you implement an acceptable-use policy for your organization.

Acceptable-Use Policy and Agreement

The following sample policy is geared towards a school, however it could easily be customized to any situation.

Network Mission

The network, and through the network the Internet, offers an abundance of educational material as well as opportunities for collaboration and the exchange of ideas and information. Successful operation requires that all users view the network as a shared resource, and work together to maintain its integrity by behaving in a responsible, conscientious manner.

Definition of User

A *user* is defined as any person who has been assigned a valid network logon by the network administrator. Such logons (or accounts) should be used only by the owner of the account in a legal and ethical fashion.

The Acceptable-Use Policy

This policy describes the types of network applications that are contrary to our network mission and which are therefore prohibited. These are guidelines only and are not meant to be an exhaustive list of prohibited activities.

Responsibility of Users for Their Account Security

Users are responsible for the use of their individual account and should take all reasonable precautions to prevent others from being able to use their account. Under no conditions should a user provide his or her password to another person. Users will immediately notify the network administrator if they have identified a possible security problem relating to misappropriated passwords.

Illegal or Destructive Activities

Users may not use the network for any purpose that violates the law or threatens the integrity of the network or individual workstations. For example:

- Users will not attempt to gain unauthorized access to the network, or go beyond their authorized access. This includes attempting to log on through another person's account or access another person's files, attempting to obtain passwords, or attempting to remove any existing network security functions. Users will not actively search for security problems, because this will be construed as an illegal attempt to gain access.
- Users must not intentionally develop or use programs to harass other users or to attempt to violate the security or alter software components of any other network, service or system. Examples of such activities include hacking, cracking into, monitoring or using systems without authorization, scanning ports, conducting denial-of-service attacks and distributing viruses or other harmful software.
- Users must not attempt to damage hardware, software or data belonging to the school or other users. This includes adding, altering or deleting files or programs on local or network hard drives and removing or damaging equipment such as mice, motherboards, speakers or printers.
- Further examples of unacceptable use include, but are not limited to: fraudulent use of credit card numbers to purchase online merchandise, distributing licensed software or installing software such as games in violation of software license agreements (piracy).

Inappropriate Material

Users will not use the network to access or distribute material that is obscene, pornographic, indecent or hateful, that advocates illegal acts or that advocates violence or discrimination toward other people. This includes but is not restricted to distribution through email, newsgroups or web pages. Exceptions may be made if the purpose of such access is to conduct research and if access is approved by both the teacher and the parent. If a user inadvertently accesses such information, they should immediately disclose the inadvertent access to their teacher or the network administrator.

Respect for Other Users

Restrictions against inappropriate language or images apply to personal email, newsgroup postings and material posted on web pages. Users will not use obscene, profane, vulgar, inflammatory, threatening or disrespectful language. Users will not post false or defamatory information about a person or organization. Users will not post information that, if acted upon, could cause damage to individuals or property.

Users will not harass another person. Harassment is acting in a manner that distresses or annoys another person. This includes, but is not limited to, distribution of unsolicited advertising, chain letters, email spamming (sending an annoying or unnecessary message to a large number of people). If a user is told by a person to stop sending them messages, the user must stop. Users will not post personal contact information about other people, including address, telephone, home address, work address, etc. Users will not forward a message that was sent to them privately without permission of the person who sent them the message. Users must not send mail that does not accurately identify the sender, the sender's return email address, and the email address of origin.

Resource Limits

Users will not download large files that are not absolutely necessary. If necessary, users will download the file at a time when the network is not being heavily used and immediately remove the file from the network workstation to their personal computer. Users have a right to temporary use of disk storage space and are responsible for keeping their disk usage below the maximum size allocated. Extremely large files, if left on the network for an extended period, may be removed at the discretion of the network administrator.

Users will check their email frequently, delete unwanted messages promptly, and stay within their email quota. Users will subscribe only to discussion group mail lists that advance and are relevant to their education or professional/career development. Users will unsubscribe to discussion groups before any vacation, break, or other extended absence from school.

Theft of Intellectual Property

Users must respect the legal protection provided by copyright law and license agreements related to content, text, music, computer software and any other protected materials. Users will not plagiarize works that they find on the Internet. Plagiarism is taking the ideas or writings of others and presenting them as if they were original to the user. Users will respect the rights of copyright owners. Copyright infringement occurs when an individual inappropriately reproduces a work that is protected by a copyright. If a work contains language that specifies acceptable use of that work, the user should follow the expressed requirements. If the user is unsure whether or not they can use a work, they should request permission from the copyright owner.

Web Sites

Web pages may include student pictures and first name only unless their legal guardian requests in writing that this information not be posted. Web pages may include pictures and the full name of staff members unless it is requested in writing that this information not be posted. If a personal or class web page is created, a notice must be included to inform the public that the opinions expressed on the page are those of the creator of the web page, not the school. A statement on the web page must acknowledge the authorship of the page.

Personal Safety of Students

Students will not post personal contact information about themselves or other people. This includes information such as email address, telephone number, home address, or work address. School address and email address may be used when it is necessary to receive information. Students will not agree to meet with someone they have met online without their parents' approval and participation. Students will promptly disclose to their teacher or other school employees any message they receive that is inappropriate or makes them feel uncomfortable.

Violation of This Policy

In the event there is an allegation that a student has violated the Acceptable-Use Policy and Agreement, the student will be provided with a written notice of the alleged violation and an opportunity to present an explanation before an administrator. Disciplinary actions will be tailored to meet specific concerns related to the violation and to assist the student in gaining the self-discipline necessary to behave appropriately on a computer network.

The school may at its sole discretion determine whether a use of the network is a violation of this policy. Violations of this policy may result in a demand for immediate removal of offending material, blocked access, suspension or termination of the users account, or other action appropriate to the violation. The school reserves the right to act without notice when necessary, as determined by the administration. The school may involve, and will cooperate with, law enforcement officials if criminal activity is suspected. Violators may also be subject to civil or criminal liability under applicable law.

Agreement

I have read and agree to follow the rules contained in this policy. I understand that if I violate the rules, my account can be terminated, and I may face other disciplinary measures. I hereby release the school, its personnel and any institutions with which it is affiliated from any and all claims and damages of any nature arising from the use of, or inability to use, the system, including but not limited to claims that may arise from the unauthorized use of the system to purchase products or services.

Student

Student Signature ______________________________ Date____________
Student Name (print) ______________________________ Grade____________
School ____

Legal Guardian

I will instruct my child regarding any restrictions against accessing material that are set forth in the Acceptable-Use Policy. I will emphasize the importance of following the rules for personal safety and give permission to issue an account for my child and certify that the information contained in this form is correct.

Legal Guardian Signature ______________________________ Date____________
Legal Guardian Name (print) ______________________________________
Home Address ______________________________ Phone____________

Employee

Signature ______________________________ Date____________
Name (print) ______________________________________
Position ______________________________________
School or Department ______________________________________

B

Third-Party Security Programs

There are numerous gaps in the security provided by the System Policy Editor (SPE) to Windows 9x workstations. Chapter 5, *It's Not Perfect*, reviews many of these gaps, but depending on your user's level of knowledge and degree of malice, you may find the only answer to these weaknesses is a third-party security program. In this case, the best solution is often a combination of the SPE for customization and standardization of application settings and a third-party security program for added file-level and boot protection.

There are scores of security programs available, however, this appendix includes only a few of those that were considered some of the better choices by administrators who emailed me with their suggestions. This list is not intended to be a review of each program or a recommendation of one over the other but simply information on some of the features available from different software vendors. Since security programs are frequently updated, review the indicated web site for new information on any given program.

Security Programs

For a security program to be listed here, it had to be more than a simplified interface for system policies. The application had to provide a minimum of file-level security, as well as allowing most of the same restrictions available through the SPE. Thus, you can assume that each program noted allows the most common SPE restrictions such as hiding Control Panel applets, removing the ability to run the Registry Editor, restricting access to an MS-DOS shell, and so on. The information on each program was gathered only from the vendor's web site and so may not include all available features.

Folder Guard by Winability

Web site: *http://www.winability.com/home*

Listed price is $49.95/workstation. Multiuser licenses are available by contacting the vendor. The program can be used on a networked or standalone workstation.

Features

The vendor states that the program is compatible with the use of system policies.

Individual users can be set up.

File and folder access permissions can be set to read-only, no access or full access.

Specific applications (such as backup programs) can be given write permission to otherwise read-only drives or folders.

User activities and access violations can be tracked to a log file.

Filters can be purchased that allow finer control over folder access, including write access but no execute access to floppy drives. A freeware abridged version called Folder Guard Jr. for Windows is available. This version allows folders to be hidden or access restricted via a password. Folder Guard Jr. is free because it displays commercial messages in a separate window while Windows is running.

Fortres101 by Fortres Grand Corp

Web site: *http://www.fortres.com*

Listed educational prices range from $49/workstation to $395/building. Listed corporate prices range from $49/workstation to $1495/building. The program can be used on a networked or standalone workstation.

Features

Groups or individual users can be set up.

Can disable Windows hotkeys such as Ctrl-Alt-Del, Alt-Tab, Ctrl-Esc and the Windows key can be disabled.

File and folder access permissions can be set to read-only, no access or full access.

Passwords can be set, but only for desktop icons not for program files.

Provides a certain degree of Internet filtering through an internal proxy that can block inappropriate Internet sites.

An add-on program, called CentralControl that allows central network management of security settings is available.

Foolproof by SmartStuff Software

Web site: *http://www.smartstuff.com*

Prices were not listed, but are available by phoning a sales representative at (800) 671-3999. The program can be used on a networked or standalone workstation.

Features

Groups or individual users can be set up.

Provides boot protection so that a user booting with a floppy disk cannot access the local drive.

File and folder access permissions can be set to read-only, no access, or full access.

File saving can be directed to specific folders or media such as floppy disks.

Allows central network management of security settings.

Full Armor Zero Administration by Full Armor

Web site: *http://www.fullarmor.com*

Prices are available by contacting the vendor at (800) 653-1783. The program can be used on a networked or standalone workstation (Windows 9x, NT or 2000).

Features

The vendor states that the program is compatible with the use of system policies.

Individual groups or users can be set up.

File and folder access permissions can be set.

File savings can be directed to specific folders.

CD-ROM protection allows for the authorized use of specified CD volume labels only.

Printing can be restricted to specific printers.

Includes an undo feature that allows system recovery configuration (registry, applications or files) to be recovered.

Allows central network management of security settings.

Full Control by Bardon Data Systems

Web site: *http://www.bardon.com*

Listed price is $59.95/workstation. Educational and multiuser licenses are available by contacting the vendor. The program can be used on a networked or standalone workstation.

Features

Individual users can be set up.

The entire keyboard can be disabled during the boot process.

Windows hotkeys such as Ctrl-Alt-Del, Alt-Tab, Ctrl-Esc, and the Windows key can be disabled through the use of password-only access.

File and folder access permissions can be set to read-only, no access or full access even in safe mode.

The CD-ROM drive can be software locked to prevent CDs from being removed.

File saving can be directed to specific folders.

Printing can be restricted to specific printers and maximum number of pages/copies.

Time limits can be set for individual program use.

User activities and access violations can be tracked to a log file.

A "rollback" feature allows changes to system files to be undone, even from a command prompt.

A remote administration feature allows control across the network to update the workstation, alter the registry, run applications, log off, shut down or reboot the workstation.

Includes network-based license metering, allowing only a certain number of copies of a program to be run at any one time.

On Guard by Power On Software

Web site: *http://www.poweronsw.com*

Listed price is $69.95/workstation. Multiuser licenses are available by contacting the vendor. The program can be used on a networked or standalone workstation.

Features

Group or individual users can be set up.

File and folder access permissions can be set to read-only, no access or full access.

Delete, rename, copy and move permissions can be restricted.

File saving can be directed to specific folders or media such as floppy disks.

User activities and access violations can be tracked to a log file.

Security settings can be saved to the network and downloaded to other workstations.

PcLockout'97 by PC-Plus Systems

Web site: *http://www.pcplus.com.au/~pcplus/pclock.html*

Educational site licenses are available for about $3.50 ($5 AUD)/workstation. The program can be used on a networked or standalone workstation.

The vendor states that the program is compatible with the use of system policies.

Individual users can be set up.

Provides boot protection so that a user booting with a floppy disk cannot access the local drive.

The entire keyboard can be disabled during the boot process.

Windows hotkeys such as Ctrl-Alt-Del, Alt-Tab, Ctrl-Esc, and the Windows key can be disabled.

File and folder access permissions can be set to read-only, no access, or full access on the local hard drives. Floppy disks can be set to read-only for the entire disk.

Using a password, an administrator can log in on the fly to make changes.

Access to peripherals (serial and parallel ports) can be restricted on a password basis.

The workstation can be set to automatically boot into a restricted mode with no password input, while still allowing a four-second window for the administrator to press a hotkey and enter a password to gain unrestricted access.

Security settings can be saved to the network and downloaded to other workstations.

S to Infinity (formerly Cerberus) by UniPress Software

Web site: *http://www.unipress.com/stoi/stoi.html*

Multiuser licenses are available, with prices ranging from $114/workstation for 20 users to $20/workstation for 5,000–10,000 users. The program can be used on a networked or standalone Windows (3.x, 9x or NT) workstation.

Features

The vendor states that the program is compatible with the use of system policies.

Individual users can be set up, including multiple administrators.

Windows hotkeys such as Ctrl-Alt-Del, Alt-Tab, Ctrl-Esc, and the Windows key can be disabled.

File and folder access permissions can be set to read-only, no access or full access. The program additionally supports file encryption.

Specific applications (such as backup programs) can be given write permission to otherwise read-only drives or folders.

Access permissions can be set for individual registry keys.

The program allows central network management of security settings.

An optional backup location for the security settings can be defined.

StopLight 95 Pro by Safetynet

Web site: *http://www.safe.net*

Listed price is $149/workstation. A light version is available for $49.99/workstation. The program can be used on a networked or standalone workstation.

Features

Individual users (up to 255/computer) can be set up.

Provides boot protection so that a user booting with a floppy disk cannot access the local drive.

File and folder access permissions include read, write, create, delete and execute.

A version that allows central network administration, called StopLight Lan, is also available.

WinSelect Policy by Hyper Technologies Inc.

Web site: *http://www.hypertec.com*

Multiuser licenses are available, with prices ranging from $25/workstation for 1-5 workstations to $10/workstation for 200+ workstations. This version is for standalone workstations only, although a networked version is available and can be obtained by contacting the vendor.

Features

Individual users can be set up.

Windows hotkeys such as Ctrl-Alt-Del, Alt-Tab, Ctrl-Esc and the Windows key can be disabled.

File and folder access permissions can be set to read-only, no access or full access.

Delete, rename and create permissions can be restricted.

Printing can be restricted to specific printers and maximum number of pages/copies.

Hypertec also has a program called Deep Freeze, which will restore all Windows settings back to a specific configuration when the computer is rebooted. Educational prices are available.

Test Before You Buy

Before deciding on any one package, first install a trial copy of the application on a typical workstation (make sure you back up your registry before you do this). Then evaluate the program for ease of use, degree of protection of local files and folders and whether you can easily circumvent the security. Chapter 5 has a checklist of typical methods to bypass a security program; try each method to see if you can successfully disable the security.

Finally, test the workstation for software conflicts. Use each application fully including printing and saving files. Use your Web browser and any multimedia or programming applications. You may find that some security settings are too restrictive or that applications crash due to file access errors imposed by the security program.

Index

M

N

S

T

V

W

X

Z

About the Author

Stacey Anderson-Redick has been working in the computer industry for the past 12 years as a network administrator and technician. She currently holds the position of network administrator/technician for a private school. Prior to that, Stacey worked as a network administrator/technician for a medical genetics department, while also co-investigating birth defects research.

Stacey has her own web page devoted to the System Policy Editor: *http://www.cadvision.com/redicks/security.htm*. Her site has gotten over 50,000 hits since its inception in 1998.

Colophon

Our look is the result of reader comments, our own experimentation, and feedback from distribution channels. Distinctive covers complement our distinctive approach to technical topics, breathing personality and life into potentially dry subjects.

The animal on the cover of *Windows System Policy Editor* is a Crested Caracara. Caracaras are long-legged raptors that inhabit open country, forest, or savanna. Populations occur in Florida, northern Baja California, southwestern Arizona, Texas, Cuba, and Mexico, for which it is the national bird. The Crested Caracara has been called the "four-point-bird," because it shows white in all fours points in flight—head, tail, and wingtips. There is a black terminal band on the tail, and it has a black shaggy crest on a white head and neck. The crest makes the Crested Caracara look like a bald eagle with a bad toupee. The body is black, but many birds have a dark brown tint to them.

They are insectivorious or omnivorious, but mostly feed on carrion. Their diet also includes living prey, such as small turtles, frogs, lizards, and snakes. Caracaras are generally sluggish, spending most of their time perching or walking about on the ground, although they can run quite swiftly.

Maureen Demspey was the copyeditor and production editor for *Windows System Policy Editor*. Emily Quill and Colleen Gorman provided quality control. Brenda Miller wrote the index.

Ellie Volckhausen designed the cover of this book, based on a series design by Edie Freedman. The cover image is a 19th-century engraving from the Dover Pictorial Archive. Emma Colby produced the cover layout with QuarkXPress 3.32 using Adobe's ITC Garamond font.

Alicia Cech and David Futato designed the interior layout based on a series design by Nancy Priest. Mike Sierra implemented the design in FrameMaker 5.5.6. The text and heading fonts are ITC Garamond Light and Garamond Book. The illustrations that appear in the book were produced by Robert Romano and Rhon Porter using Macromedia FreeHand 8 and Adobe Photoshop 5. This colophon was written by Maureen Dempsey.

Whenever possible, our books use RepKover™, a durable and flexible lay-flat binding. If the page count exceeds RepKover's limit, perfect binding is used.

More Titles from O'Reilly

Windows NT System Administration

DNS on Windows NT

By Paul Albitz, Matt Larson & Cricket Liu
1st Edition October 1998
348 pages, ISBN 1-56592-511-4

DNS on Windows NT is a special edition of the classic *DNS and BIND*, which Microsoft recommends to Windows NT users and administrators. This book discusses one of the Internet's fundamental building blocks: the distributed host information database that's responsible for translating names into addresses, routing mail to its proper destination, and many other services.

Windows NT TCP/IP Network Administration

By Craig Hunt & Robert Bruce Thompson
1st Edition October 1998
504 pages, ISBN 1-56592-377-4

Windows NT TCP/IP Network Administration is a complete guide to setting up and running a TCP/IP network on Windows NT. It starts with the fundamentals – the protocols, routing, and setup. Beyond that, it covers all the important networking services provided as part of Windows NT, including IIS, RRAS, DNS, WINS, and DHCP. This book is the NT administrator's indispensable guide.

Microsoft Exchange Server in a Nutshell

By Mitch Tulloch
1st Edition April 1999
404 pages, ISBN 1-56592-601-3

This resource guides experienced sysadmins through implementing and configuring Microsoft Exchange Server 5.5, whether they're setting up a single Exchange server or a multisite rollout with connectivity to foreign mail systems. The heart of the book is an alphabetical reference for the Exchange directory objects, the GUI tools, and the command-line tools.

Managing Microsoft Exchange Server

By Paul Robichaux
1st Edition July 1999
718 pages, ISBN 1-56592-545-9

Targeted at medium-sized installations and up, this book addresses the difficult problems these users face: Internet integration, storage management, cost of ownership, system security, and performance management. Going beyond the basics, it provides hands-on advice about what you need to know after you have your first site up-and-running and are facing issues of growth, optimization, or recovery planning.

Essential Windows NT System Administration

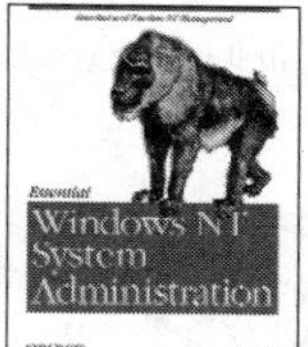

By AEleen Frisch
1st Edition January 1998
486 pages, ISBN 1-56592-274-3

This book combines practical experience with technical expertise to help you manage Windows NT systems as productively as possible. It covers the standard utilities offered with the Windows NT operating system and from the Resource Kit, as well as important commercial and free third-party tools. By the author of O'Reilly's bestselling book, *Essential System Administration.*

How to stay in touch with O'Reilly

1. Visit Our Award-Winning Web Site

http://www.oreilly.com/

★"Top 100 Sites on the Web" —*PC Magazine*
★"Top 5% Web sites" —*Point Communications*
★"3-Star site" —*The McKinley Group*

Our web site contains a library of comprehensive product information (including book excerpts and tables of contents), downloadable software, background articles, interviews with technology leaders, links to relevant sites, book cover art, and more. File us in your Bookmarks or Hotlist!

2. Join Our Email Mailing Lists

New Product Releases

To receive automatic email with brief descriptions of all new O'Reilly products as they are released, send email to:
listproc@online.oreilly.com
Put the following information in the first line of your message (*not* in the Subject field):
subscribe oreilly-news

O'Reilly Events

If you'd also like us to send information about trade show events, special promotions, and other O'Reilly events, send email to:
listproc@online.oreilly.com
Put the following information in the first line of your message (*not* in the Subject field):
subscribe oreilly-events

3. Get Examples from Our Books via FTP

There are two ways to access an archive of example files from our books:

Regular FTP

- ftp to:
  ftp.oreilly.com
  (login: anonymous
  password: your email address)
- Point your web browser to:
  ftp://ftp.oreilly.com/

FTPMAIL

- Send an email message to:
  ftpmail@online.oreilly.com
  (Write "help" in the message body)

4. Contact Us via Email

order@oreilly.com
To place a book or software order online. Good for North American and international customers.

subscriptions@oreilly.com
To place an order for any of our newsletters or periodicals.

books@oreilly.com
General questions about any of our books.

software@oreilly.com
For general questions and product information about our software. Check out O'Reilly Software Online at **http://software.oreilly.com/** for software and technical support information. Registered O'Reilly software users send your questions to: **website-support@oreilly.com**

cs@oreilly.com
For answers to problems regarding your order or our products.

booktech@oreilly.com
For book content technical questions or corrections.

proposals@oreilly.com
To submit new book or software proposals to our editors and product managers.

international@oreilly.com
For information about our international distributors or translation queries. For a list of our distributors outside of North America check out:
http://www.oreilly.com/www/order/country.html

5. Work with Us

Check out our website for current employment opportunites:
www.jobs@oreilly.com
Click on "Work with Us"

O'Reilly & Associates, Inc.
101 Morris Street, Sebastopol, CA 95472 USA
TEL 707-829-0515 or 800-998-9938
(6am to 5pm PST)
FAX 707-829-0104

International Distributors

UK, Europe, Middle East and Africa (except France, Germany, Austria, Switzerland, Luxembourg, Liechtenstein, and Eastern Europe)

INQUIRIES
O'Reilly UK Limited
4 Castle Street
Farnham
Surrey, GU9 7HS
United Kingdom
Telephone: 44-1252-711776
Fax: 44-1252-734211
Email: information@oreilly.co.uk

ORDERS
Wiley Distribution Services Ltd.
1 Oldlands Way
Bognor Regis
West Sussex PO22 9SA
United Kingdom
Telephone: 44-1243-779777
Fax: 44-1243-820250
Email: cs-books@wiley.co.uk

France

INQUIRIES
Éditions O'Reilly
18 rue Séguier
75006 Paris, France
Tel: 33-1-40-51-52-30
Fax: 33-1-40-51-52-31
Email: france@editions-oreilly.fr

ORDERS
GEODIF
61, Bd Saint-Germain
75240 Paris Cedex 05, France
Tel: 33-1-44-41-46-16 (French books)
Tel: 33-1-44-41-11-87 (English books)
Fax: 33-1-44-41-11-44
Email: distribution@eyrolles.com

Germany, Switzerland, Austria, Eastern Europe, Luxembourg, and Liechtenstein

INQUIRIES & ORDERS
O'Reilly Verlag
Balthasarstr. 81
D-50670 Köln
Germany
Telephone: 49-221-973160-91
Fax: 49-221-973160-8
Email: anfragen@oreilly.de (inquiries)
Email: order@oreilly.de (orders)

Canada (French language books)

Les Éditions Flammarion ltée
375, Avenue Laurier Ouest
Montréal (Québec) H2V 2K3
Tel: 00-1-514-277-8807
Fax: 00-1-514-278-2085
Email: info@flammarion.qc.ca

Hong Kong

City Discount Subscription Service, Ltd.
Unit D, 3rd Floor, Yan's Tower
27 Wong Chuk Hang Road
Aberdeen, Hong Kong
Tel: 852-2580-3539
Fax: 852-2580-6463
Email: citydis@ppn.com.hk

Korea

Hanbit Media, Inc.
Chungmu Bldg. 201
Yonnam-dong 568-33
Mapo-gu
Seoul, Korea
Tel: 822-325-0397
Fax: 822-325-9697
Email: hant93@chollian.dacom.co.kr

Philippines

Global Publishing
G/F Benavides Garden
1186 Benavides Street
Manila, Philippines
Tel: 632-254-8949/637-252-2582
Fax: 632-734-5060/632-252-2733
Email: globalp@pacific.net.ph

Taiwan

O'Reilly Taiwan
No. 3, Lane 131
Hang-Chow South Road
Section 1, Taipei, Taiwan
Tel: 886-2-23968990
Fax: 886-2-23968916
Email: taiwan@oreilly.com

China

O'Reilly Beijing
Room 2410
160, FuXingMenNeiDaJie
XiCheng District
Beijing, China PR 100031
Tel: 86-10-66412305
Fax: 86-10-86631007
Email: beijing@oreilly.com

India

Computer Bookshop (India) Pvt. Ltd.
190 Dr. D.N. Road, Fort
Bombay 400 001 India
Tel: 91-22-207-0989
Fax: 91-22-262-3551
Email: cbsbom@giasbm01.vsnl.net.in

Japan

O'Reilly Japan, Inc.
Yotsuya Y's Building
7 Banch 6, Honshio-cho
Shinjuku-ku
Tokyo 160-0003 Japan
Tel: 81-3-3356-5227
Fax: 81-3-3356-5261
Email: japan@oreilly.com

All Other Asian Countries

O'Reilly & Associates, Inc.
101 Morris Street
Sebastopol, CA 95472 USA
Tel: 707-829-0515
Fax: 707-829-0104
Email: order@oreilly.com

Australia

Woodslane Pty., Ltd.
7/5 Vuko Place
Warriewood NSW 2102
Australia
Tel: 61-2-9970-5111
Fax: 61-2-9970-5002
Email: info@woodslane.com.au

New Zealand

Woodslane New Zealand, Ltd.
21 Cooks Street (P.O. Box 575)
Waganui, New Zealand
Tel: 64-6-347-6543
Fax: 64-6-345-4840
Email: info@woodslane.com.au

Latin America

McGraw-Hill Interamericana
Editores, S.A. de C.V.
Cedro No. 512
Col. Atlampa
06450, Mexico, D.F.
Tel: 52-5-547-6777
Fax: 52-5-547-3336
Email: mcgraw-hill@infosel.net.mx